FROM BACH TO STRAVINSKY

FROM BACH
TO
STRAVINSKY

THE HISTORY OF MUSIC
BY
ITS FOREMOST CRITICS

Edited by David Ewen

W · W · NORTON & COMPANY, INC.

NEW YORK · PUBLISHERS

DESIGNED BY ROBERT S. JOSEPHY
PRINTED IN THE UNITED STATES OF AMERICA
FOR THE PUBLISHERS BY THE VAIL-BALLOU PRESS

IT IS the art of music which most completely realizes this artistic ideal, this perfect identification of form and matter. In its ideal, consummate moments, the end is not distinct from the means, the form from the matter, the subject from the expression; they inhere in and completely saturate each other; and to it, therefore, to the condition of its perfect moments, all the arts may be supposed to constantly tend and aspire. Music, then, and not poetry, as is so often supposed, is the true type or measure of perfect art. Therefore, although each art has its uncommunicable element, its untranslatable order of impressions, its unique mode of reaching the "imaginative reason," yet the arts may be represented as continually struggling after the law or principle of music, to a condition which music alone completely realizes; and one of the chief functions of aesthetic criticism, dealing with the products of art, new or old, is to estimate the degree in which each of those products approaches, in this sense, to the musical law.

WALTER PATER

TABLE OF CONTENTS

INTRODUCTION

THIS book is designed to present the history of music from the eighteenth century to the present day, with the emphasis on the composers themselves, their works, their lives, their personalities. Unlike other
histories of music, its concern is only secondarily with the development
of composition in form, fabric, and technique: its primary aim is to introduce the reader to an understanding of each great composer, through
the critic best suited, by temperament and scholarship, to a broad interpretation and appreciation of his individual genius.

The editor has made no attempt to produce an anthology of music
criticism. Much of the distinguished critical writing of the past loses its
force for the reader to-day, because the issues with which it was contro-
versially concerned are no longer alive; criticism of eighteenth- and
nineteenth-century composers by their contemporaries bristles with partisanship and with predictions which have not been fulfilled. It has therefore seemed wisest to confine the selections dealing with these composers
to articles written during the last thirty years, in which enthusiasms and
reservations are less personal and consequently more valuable.

Inevitably the basis of selection will be questioned; the editor should
therefore explain that his chief purpose has been to include every composer, within the period covered, who is universally recognized to be of
the first importance. It was not possible without greatly expanding the
limits of the book to represent in individual chapters composers of smaller
genius, such as Gluck and Fauré; or composers of specific national importance, such as Dvořak, Smetana, Grieg, Sibelius. Instead, it has
seemed advisable to group these in a number of introductory and transi-
tional chapters (I, II, VIII, XIV, XVIII, and XX), covering as far as
possible the important schools of composition. This applies also to the
composers of the romantic movement: Weber, Mendelssohn, Liszt,
Berlioz.

Likewise, it is impossible for a book of this kind to come strictly up to
date. In every country the history of music continues to be made, but
criticism has not yet nominated the giants of the future. Bearing in mind

that the purpose of the book is to contribute to the reader's understanding of the accepted great men of music, it has seemed wiser to include none of the younger contemporary generation, since material on this subject, however interesting from another point of view, must necessarily be to some extent controversial; and therefore to include no living composers younger than Schönberg and Stravinsky.

It would be inconsistent with all these purposes to present material of a technical nature or containing too much musicological detail. This has rendered more difficult the task of selection, but the editor believes that the chapters here gathered together will better serve the object he had in mind and make easier reading for any one with a general interest in the history of music.

Thanks are due to Mr. Douglas Moore, Associate Professor of Music at Columbia University, for his supervision of biographical data and lists of compositions.

ACKNOWLEDGMENTS

FOR permission to reprint the various chapters in the present work, acknowledgments are made as follows:

The Periods of Musical History by Daniel Gregory Mason. From the author's *Beethoven and His Forerunners,* by permission of The Macmillan Company.

The Beginnings of Opera by Carl Engel. By arrangement with the author; hitherto unpublished.

Bach by C. Sanford Terry. From the author's *Bach: An Historical Approach,* by permission of the Oxford University Press.

Handel by Romain Rolland. From the author's *Handel,* by permission of the author and of Henry Holt and Co.

Haydn by W. Oliver Strunk. By arrangement with the author; hitherto unpublished.

Mozart by W. J. Turner. From *The Heritage of Music,* by permission of the Oxford University Press.

Beethoven by C. Hubert H. Parry. From the author's *Studies of Great Composers,* by permission of George Routledge and Sons, Ltd.

The Romantic Movement by Paul Bekker. From the author's *The Story of Music,* by permission of W. W. Norton & Co., Inc.

Schubert by C. Hubert H. Parry. From the author's *Studies of Great Composers,* by permission of George Routledge and Sons, Ltd.

Chopin by J. Cuthbert Hadden. From the author's *Chopin,* by permission of E. P. Dutton and Co.

Schumann by W. H. Hadow. From the author's *Studies in Modern Music,* by permission of Seeley, Service, and Co.

Wagner by H. C. Colles. From the author's *The Growth of Music,* by permission of the Oxford University Press.

Brahms by J. A. Fuller-Maitland. From the author's *Brahms,* by permission of Methuen and Co.

Russian Musical History in Kaleidoscope by M. Montagu Nathan. From the author's *Contemporary Russian Composers,* by permission of Cecil Palmer.

Tchaikovsky by R. A. Streatfeild. From the author's *Modern Music and Musicians,* by permission of Methuen and Co.

Franck by Leland Hall. By arrangement with the author.

Debussy and Ravel by Paul Rosenfeld. From the author's *Musical Portraits,* by permission of Harcourt, Brace and Co.

Late Romanticism and Modern Trends by Paul Bekker. From the author's *The Story of Music,* by permission of W. W. Norton & Co., Inc.

Stravinsky by Leonid Sabaneyeff. From the author's *Modern Russian Composers,* by permission of International Publishers.

Harking Back and Looking Forward by Carl Engel. From the author's *Discords Mingled,* by permission of Alfred A. Knopf.

I
THE PERIODS OF MUSICAL HISTORY

THE PERIODS OF MUSICAL HISTORY

By Daniel Gregory Mason

THE modern view of history is vivified by a principle scarcely dreamed of before the middle of the last century; the conception which permeates all our interpretations of the story of the world, which illuminates our study of all its phases, was by our grandfathers apprehended either vaguely or not at all. For them, history dealt with a more or less random series of happenings, succeeding each other accidentally, unaccountably, and at haphazard; each single event, determined by causes peculiar to itself, was without relation to all the others. Political and social history, for example, was an account of battles, sieges, revolutions, governments; of kings, warriors, and statesmen. Its salient features were special occasions and individual men: Marathon and Waterloo, Alexander, Caesar, Alfred, Napoleon. Of pervasive social movements, tendencies of human feeling and thought, developments of industries, institutions, laws, and customs by a gradual process in which great numbers of personally insignificant men played their part, little account was taken. Facts were facts, and had no hidden significance, no mutual interaction, no cumulative force, momentum, or direction.

Far otherwise do we interpret the story of the world. Inspired by the great doctrine of the nineteenth century, the doctrine of evolution, first formulated by biology, but immediately applied to all realms of knowledge, we read in events a continuous movement, a coherent growth, a gradual, vast, and single process. For us, individual events and men sink into insignificance in comparison with the great drama of which they are only acts and actors. For us, great popular movements, instinc-

From the author's *Beethoven and His Forerunners*, by permission of The Macmillan Company.

tive strivings, of which the men and women under their sway were unconscious, vast blossomings of vital energy the roots of which were far below the surface of the human mind, rise into relief as the true interests of the historian, and we interpret all particular happenings and special persons in the light of these universal tendencies. In geology we trace the continuous formation of the earth through innumerable years; in zoölogy we study those slow but constant transformations of animals which are effected by natural selection and the survival of the fittest; in sociology we examine the painful yet inevitable crystallization out of the human spirit of such ideas as responsibility, liberty, justice; in philosophy we learn of the subtle implications of our nature, and so learning, substitute a human God for the idols of savages and the remote tyrannical deities of half-developed religions. There is not a branch of our thought in which this way of interpreting life as a process, this conceiving of it as dynamic and vital rather than static and inert, has not enlarged our outlook, deepened our sense of the sacredness and wonder of the universe, and filled our spirits with a new freedom, enthusiasm, and hope.

Peculiarly interesting is the application of this mode of study to the art of music. The expression of feeling through sounds combined in beautiful forms, gives us an opportunity, as cannot be too often pointed out,* for a much freer and more self-determined activity than we can enjoy in our other artistic pursuits. Because the art of music, both in its material and in its content, is less shackled, less thwarted in its characteristic processes, than the representative arts, its evolution is remarkably obvious and easy to trace. Its material, in the first place, is a product of man's free selection; that complex system of musical tones which he has constructed by many centuries of work, is his own, to use as he will, in a sense in which language, natural objects, and physical substances can never be. Whereas the growth of poetry, of painting, of sculpture, of architecture, is complicated and distorted by a thousand external conditions, that of music is determined by its own inner laws alone—by the laws, that is to say, of sound-production, of sound-perception, and of psychology. In the second place, the content of music, that which it expresses by means of these freely selected and composed tones, is purely internal. It is easy to see that the objects of musical expression, namely,

* See the author's *From Grieg to Brahms*, pp. 219–223.

human emotions in their essence, reduced, so to speak, to their lowest terms, are more fluid to manipulation than the comparatively fixed, in-docile, and external objects of the representative arts. By virtue, then, both of its material medium and of its ideal content, music enjoys, among human modes of expression, a unique freedom and autonomy. It grows, not under pressure from outside, but by its own inner vitality; its forms are determined, not by correspondence with anything in the heavens or on the earth, but, like those of the snow-crystals, by the inexorable laws that govern it; and the particular changes it undergoes in its evolution, marking merely successive incarnations of tendencies and potencies al-ways implicit in it, can be traced with comparative ease, clearness, and certainty.

But however unmistakably musical history may reveal an evolutionary process, it does not reveal that process as perfectly regular and uniform. That general tendency from a low toward a high state of organization, with increase in definiteness, coherence, and heterogeneity, which readers of Herbert Spencer expect in any evolutionary series, does characterize the growth of music as a whole; but within the large general process we also observe, as we do in many other cases of evolution of any degree of complexity, many momentary phases sharply marked off from one another, many separate and distinct periods, like the chapters in a book or the acts in a play. Each period, beginning tentatively, maturing slowly, and culminating in music which carries its characteristic effects to the highest possible pitch, is succeeded by another, presenting the same phases of growth, but seeking effects quite different. All the periods hang together in a large view; yet they are, after all, diverse in character, and therefore capable of being distinguished, and even dated.

An analogy offered by certain well-known chemical processes may help to make comprehensible this periodic nature of musical evolution. Chemists have a term, "critical point," by which they name a stage in the behavior of a substance, under some systematic treatment, at which it suddenly undergoes some striking change, some catastrophic trans-formation. Put, for example, a lump of ice in a crucible and apply an even heat by which its temperature is raised, say, one degree each minute. Here is a systematic treatment of the ice, a steady influence exerted upon it. Yet, curiously enough, this ice which is being so equably acted upon will not change its form in the equable, regular fashion we might expect.

It will seem to undergo little or no change until, at a given moment, suddenly, it passes into water, a liquid wholly different in appearance from the original solid. It has reached a "critical point." Continue the heating, and presently another critical point will be reached, at which, with equal suddenness, the liquid will be transformed into a vapor— steam. These catastrophes, in which the physical properties of the substance suddenly change, are conditioned, of course, by its chemical nature. They take place in the midst of a systematic treatment which we might expect to produce only gradual, inconspicuous effects, but which, as a matter of fact, produce a series of events as strikingly differentiated one from another as the acts of a drama.

It is in a similar way that, in the history of music, the tonal material used, under the systematic treatment of man's aesthetic faculty, has been constrained by its nature to undergo sudden changes, to recrystallize in novel ways, to take on unwonted aspects which initiate new periods. When the possibilities of one sort of tone-combination are nearly or quite exhausted, the keener minds of a generation, led by groping but unerring instinct, grasp an unused principle of organization, latent in the material, and inaugurate a new style. This in turn runs its course, develops its resources, reaches its perfection, and is succeeded by another, which, after due time, is also superseded. All these periods are but moments in one vast evolution, successive blossomings from the one root of human feeling expressible in music; yet each has its individual qualities, its peculiar style, its special masters. It is possible both to trace certain general tendencies through them all, and to define other special qualities in which each is peculiar; and it will be worth while to describe thus in general terms the salient features of the evolution as a whole, and to characterize, however briefly, the individual periods we can discriminate in it.

In the most general point of view, an evolution, of whatever sort, is a progress from what Spencer calls "indefinite, incoherent, homogeneity," to what, consistently if rather overwhelmingly, he calls "definite, coherent, heterogeneity." All low forms of life, that is to say, are so homogeneous in constitution as to be comparatively indefinite and incoherent; their parts, being all very much alike, cannot be built up into definite, strongly cohesive structures. A jelly fish, made up of thousands of but slightly differentiated cells, and without legs, arms, head, or any viscera worth mentioning except stomach, is doubtless a useful animal, but not one of pronounced individuality or solidarity. A savage tribe, consisting of many human beings almost indistinguishable from one another as regards character, strength, accomplishments, or powers of leadership, is a similar phenomenon in a different field, a sort of social jelly fish.

In higher forms of life, on the contrary, such as vertebrate animals and civilized communities, the elementary parts are sufficiently diverse to be interwoven into highly individual and compact organisms. The variety of the atoms or molecules make possible a great solidarity in the molar unit they compose, since the uniqueness and indissolubility of a structure is directly proportionate to the diversity of the elements that compose it. A man, if he is to attain the dignity of manhood, must be more than a stomach; he must knit into his single unity a bony skeleton, a circulatory system, a brain and nervous apparatus, complicated viscera, and heart, mind, and spirit. A state depends for its vitality on the varied characters and abilities of its citizens; it must have laborers, artisans, merchants, sailors, soldiers, students, and statesmen. In the second book of his *Republic,* Plato describes the differentiation of talents and pursuits in the citizens on which depends the advance in civilization of the society. Such an increase in differentiation of the parts, accompanied by increasing definiteness and coherence in the wholes, characterizes every process of evolution.

The history of music is the history of such an evolution. Music began with vague, unlocated sounds, not combined with one another, but following at haphazard, and but slightly contrasted in pitch or duration. Gradually, under the inconceivably slow yet irresistible influence of men's selective and constructive faculty, these sounds took on definiteness, were fixed in pitch, were measured in time, were knit into phrases and themes as words are knit into sentences, were combined simultaneously in chords as individuals are combined in communities:—became, in a word, the various, clearly defined, and highly organized family of tones we use in modern music. Two passages from Spencer's *First Principles* will bring before us very clearly the advance music has made towards heterogeneity in its elements, on the one hand, and towards definiteness and coherence in its wholes, on the other. "It needs," he says, "but to contrast music as it is with music as it was, to see how immense is the increase of heterogeneity. We see this . . . on comparing any one sample of aboriginal music with a sample of modern music—even an ordinary song for the piano; which we find to be relatively highly heterogeneous, not only in respect of the varieties in the pitch and in the length of the notes, the number of different notes sounding at the same instant in company with the voice, and the variations of strength with which they are sounded and sung, but in respect of the changes of key, the changes of time, the changes of timbre of the voice, and the many other modifications of expression: while between the old monotonous dance-chant and a grand opera of our own day, with its endless orchestral complexities and vocal combinations, the contrast in heterogeneity is so extreme that it seems scarcely credible that the one should have been the ancestor of the other." Of the corresponding increase in coherence and definiteness he writes as follows: "In music, progressive integration is displayed in numerous ways. The simple cadence embracing but a few notes, which in the chants of savages is monotonously repeated, becomes, among civilized races, a long series of different musical phrases combined into one whole; and so complete is the integration, that the melody cannot be broken off in the middle, nor shorn of its final note, without giving us a painful sense of incompleteness. When to the air, a bass, a tenor, and an alto are added; and when to the harmony of different voice-parts there is added an accompaniment; we see exemplified integrations of another order, which grow gradually more elaborate. And the process is carried a stage higher when these complex solos, concerted pieces, choruses, and orchestral effects, are combined into the vast ensemble of a musical drama; of which, be it remembered, the artistic perfection largely consists in the subordination of the particular effects to the total effect." In innumerable ways, which these passages will perhaps suffice to suggest, the material of music has undergone a continuous, orderly, and progressive process of development, from its earliest days down to our own. It has exemplified, in short, an evolution from "indefinite, incoherent, homogeneity" to "definite, coherent, heterogeneity."

Concomitantly with this special evolution of the sound-material of music, moreover, has gone on a more general evolution of human faculties, which has involved a gradual turning away of men's attention from comparatively low forms of musical effect to those higher forms which require for their appreciation a good deal of concentration, perception, and power of intellectual synthesis. What was the exclusive concern of the earliest musicians became, as time went on, but a factor in a more complex artistic enjoyment. In order to understand this aspect of the matter clearly, we shall have to distinguish as accurately as possible three kinds of musical effect, all indispensable to music worthy of the name, yet not of equal dignity and value.

There is, in the first place, the direct sensuous effect of the sounds, their deliciousness as sensations. Musical tones gratify the ear just as light and color gratify the eye, agreeable tastes the palate, aromatic odors the nose, and soft, warm surfaces the touch. A single tone from a flute, a violin, or a horn, is as delightful as a patch of pure color, white, red, or purple. To listen to music is, at least in part, to bathe in a flood of exquisite aural sensation. This immediate value for our sense of the "concord of sweet sounds" is a fundamental, legitimate, and important one, to deny or disparage which is to confess oneself insensitive or a prude. All music depends for a part of its appeal on its primary sensuous quality.

In the second place, music has what we call expressive value. Feelings, of surprising depth and variety, it can arouse in us, by inducing, through the contagiousness of rhythm and melody, tendencies to make those bodily motions and vocal sounds which are the natural accompaniment of our emotions.* These tendencies, of course, remain incipient; they do not discharge in actual movements greater than the tapping of the foot in "keeping time" and a slight contraction of the vocal cords; but even this faint organic commotion suffices to arouse those vivid feelings with which we listen to expressive music. It is worth while to note further that these feelings are in themselves necessarily most general and undefined, hardly more than moods of animation, excitement, apprehensiveness, solemnity, or depression. Their particular coloring is always imparted either by words or titles, or by the associations of the individual listener. On that very fact depend both the poignancy and the variety of musical expression.

The third and highest value of music is its aesthetic value, or beauty. This value, which springs from the delight we take in perceiving, or mentally organizing our sensations and ideas, is precisely analogous to the aesthetic value of the other arts, as, for example, the beauty of sonnets and other highly articulated poetic forms, of well-composed pictures, of

---

* For a fuller statement of this theory of musical expression, see *From Grieg to Brahms,* pp. 6–11.

finely-proportioned sculpture, of symmetrical and harmonious architecture. It depends, in general, on the perception of unity in a mass of
various impressions, and is but one example of a type of satisfaction we
are capable of finding in all the departments of our experience. Wherever, confronted by many objects, sensations, thoughts, or feelings, we
are able to gain a sense of their coherence, inter-relation, and essential
oneness, we get the characteristic aesthetic value. To win it is the highest
success we know. To perceive unity in the bewildering complexity of our
experience, is to possess, in the realm of knowledge, truth; in the realm
of practice, character; in the realm of art, beauty. Moreover, since perception is a far more active, self-directed process than either sensation or
emotion, which are in large degree passively suffered, its contribution to
our mental life has for us a deeper charm, a more far-reaching significance,
than that of any other faculty. Beauty transfigures all elements that may
coexist with it in the mind. In the intellectual sphere, for example, we
understand far more deeply the phenomenon when we know its species
and genus, and "science is but classified knowledge." In practical life,
all the little everyday events, the petty pleasures and pains, take on,
when we view them in relation to a conceived unity in our characters and
destinies, a new significance. Similarly in music, values of the first two
species, sweetness of sound and emotional expressiveness, can be trans-
figured by formal beauty; there is no tone that is not sweeter when it
embodies a lovely melody; there is no emotion that is not apotheosized
by association with others in a harmonious whole, or that does not
defeat itself when it stands out single, and will not merge itself in the
organism. No music is wholly devoid of any one of the three values; but
the greatest music uses the first two only as the materials of the third.

It is easy to see, however, that supreme as the aesthetic value of music
may be, men could arrive at an appreciation of it only after a long
novitiate and training. To enjoy the sensuous beauty of sweet sounds
one needs only ears; to be moved by melodies and rhythms that strongly
suggest those vocal utterances and bodily motions which are the natural
avenues of emotion, requires but a slightly more complex appreciative
mechanism, the mechanism of organic sensations and their associations
in the regions of naïve feeling; but to perceive the manifold inter-
relationship, and the final unity, of groups of tones combined together
by relations in pitch and in time, one needs a keen ear, an awakened

memory, a capacity for tracing unity under the mask of variety—in a word, a thoroughly trained and concentrated mind. Musical art could reach a stage in which all three of its values were associated in due proportion and proper adjustment, only through a gradual progress beginning with stages in which it was but the embodiment of sensuous, or at most of sensuous and emotional, values. That it did, as a matter of fact, go through these evolutionary phases, can be demonstrated by a brief and summary account of the actual periods in its history.

In the first periods that we can make out by theory and deduction—prehistoric periods that left no records—the values sought appear to have been preponderantly sensuous and expressive. The earliest savages, like all children even to this day, who make a noise for the mere joy of it, probably used their voices and their instruments chiefly as nerve-stimulants. As in the realm of color their tastes ran to vivid reds and greens and blues, barbaric hues that assaulted the eye with a potent stimulation, so in music they were addicted to the drums and trumpets, to shoutings, and wild contortions, to whatever gave them a generous measure of sensation, whether in ears or muscles. Their motto in art was doubtless the one which some unknown humorist, perhaps a Frenchman, has attributed to the Germans, in all departments from art to gastronomy —"Plenty of it." They did, to be sure, take a certain satisfaction in the expressiveness of their wailings and shoutings, and even in the crude formal designs into which they shaped them, generally by mere repetition of some easily recognizable formula; but their chief pleasure was to make a good rousing noise. Of these preliminary stages in the arts of dance and song it is impossible, however, to form any certain ideas. We can only rely upon conjecture and inference, supposing that something like them preceded the stages about which we have more reliable information.

The earliest music of which historic records remain is that of the Greeks. By painstaking study of the musical inscriptions on stone that have survived the centuries, of the instruments actually in existence, or described by ancient Greek writers, and of the technical treatises on music which are preserved, scholars have been able to substantiate a very few meager facts about the musical practices of the most artistic of nations. On the whole, these facts are singularly disappointing. Forgetting that music is the youngest of the arts, one is apt to expect of the Greeks that wondrous subtlety and maturity in it which they showed in sculpture, architecture, and poetry. A people possessed of so surpassing an artistic instinct, one is apt to think, must have carried its music to a high pitch of perfection. Investigation shows, nevertheless, that the reverse was the case. Indeed, no testimony could speak more eloquently for the deliberation and continuity of the growth of music than the childishness with which it was practised by a people so gifted as the Greeks with every fineness of nature, but at the disadvantage of living too near the time at which it emerged from savagery.

The Greeks used music chiefly as an adjunct to their poetry, and were accustomed to chant long epics in what would seem to us a monotonous sing-song, generally if not always without accompaniment. Their love for moderation and their avoidance of the passionate, harsh, or over-expressive, moreover, impelled them to exclude from their gamut both the lowest and the highest tones of the voice, so that even their tonal material was confined to a range of about two octaves. The tones included in this limited range, however, they classified and disposed with the greatest ingenuity. The intervals at which tone should follow tone were dictated by seven arbitrary schemes called modes, and each mode was supposed to have its peculiar quality of expression. Thus the Lydian mode, corresponding to our modern major scale, was considered voluptuous and enfeebling, while the Doric mode, an idea of which may be gained by playing a scale, all on white keys, beginning with E, was thought to breathe manliness, vigor, and dignity. They used no harmony, and introduced rhythm only by the meter of the verses sung. Consequently it is easy to see that they can have had from their music but little aesthetic delight, which depends on the grouping into harmonic or rhythmic forms of the tonal material; but must have valued it chiefly for its sensuous beauty, and for its power to enhance the expressiveness of their poetry.

It is nevertheless noteworthy that all three kinds of value did exist in the music of the Greeks, though the third was still in a rudimentary stage. As a result of the generally equal length of their verses or lines of poetry, the melody that accompanied them tended to be divided into equal sections remotely resembling our modern "phrases"; and these sections tended to balance each other, and so to give the sense of symmetrical form. Furthermore, it was customary to end each line with a fall of the voice analogous to the downward inflection of a speaking voice at the end of a sentence. These downward inflections, called cadences, from a Latin verb meaning "to fall," afforded a convenient means of dividing off the musical as well as the poetic flow into definite parts like segments in a piece of bamboo or the inches on a tape-line; and in the subsequent development of musical structure these divisions, marked by cadences, became the indispensable elements in a highly complex organism. Thus the Greeks, in spite of the immaturity of their music, considered in and for itself, did actually make valuable contributions to the progress of the art. Their period was one of promise rather than of fruition; but it contained the seeds of further growth. It is often called the Monophonic or "one-voiced" period, from the fact that their chants were purely melodic, employing but one voice at a time, without harmonic support.

With the simultaneous employment of more than one voice, music passed out of its infancy. The Polyphonic period, so called from Greek words signifying "many-voiced," extended, through all the Middle Ages, up to so recent a date as the end of the sixteenth century, there to culminate in the remarkable compositions of Palestrina. In duration it was the longest of all the periods; but this is not surprising when we consider, in the first place, the almost insuperable difficulties to be overcome before even two voices could be pleasantly and fluently conducted together; in the second place, the absence of all prototypes or models for the first experimenters to work from; and, above all, the surprising distance that separates Palestrina's ingenious, intricate, and beautiful tone-fabrics, written sometimes in as many as sixteen parts, from the rude and protoplasmic chants of two voices, singing an interval of a "fifth" apart, from which they were developed.

That type of chant in which two voices, one a fifth higher than the other, sang the same melody, primitive as it was, and intolerable to modern ears, was to its originators a convenient and pleasant device. It was convenient because, the natural range of soprano and tenor voices being about a fifth above that of contraltos and basses, choirs could chant at this interval more naturally than at the octave. It was pleasant because, while it left each of the two melodies distinctly audible, it produced by their combination a harmonic richness that must have fallen on mediaeval ears with an unwonted splendor. Organum, as this device of singing in fifths was called, must be ever memorable in the history of music as the beginning of harmony.

After musicians had once taken the plunge, and dared to make different melodies sound simultaneously, it took them but a comparatively short time (though eras in music, as in geology, are long) to combine the parts in other intervals than the fifth, to use varying intervals in successive chords, to add more voices, and in general to elaborate in every way their tissue of tones. Adopting, with some modifications, the Greek modes as the prescribed orbits of the individual melodies, they produced effects of harmony necessarily very unlike our modern ones, which are built upon the major and minor scales, but nevertheless novel and in their way extremely beautiful. The fabric of the mediaeval ecclesiastical music was made up of a succession of shifting chords, each very pure and sweet in itself, yet without those definite connections with its fellows that modern habits of thought demand. The whole effect was curiously kaleidoscopic, mysterious, and vague. Unity depended, not on the piece being in any one key, which it never was, but on the melodies being coherent and expressive. These were the salient features; the harmony was ancillary and incidental. One voice after another came out from the filmy background, sounded for a moment above the rest, and subsided again, to be replaced by another. Not only was there no attempt at a definite series of even sections, built up into recognizable rhythms, such as are indispensable to modern music, but any such effect was studiously avoided. The effort was rather to make the voices interweave inextricably and untraceably. The entire mass was in constant flux and change, a body of lovely and expressive sound, without a single distinct lineament, or any conceivable whence or whither. In Palestrina we have the style at its acme, vague, iridescent, beautiful with a mystical and unearthly beauty. Beyond the point it reached with him, pure polyphonic music, without rhythmic or harmonic definition, could not go. Another critical point was reached, another transformation was imminent.

By the beginning of the seventeenth century, moreover, there began to dawn upon men's minds various new principles of musical construction which were pregnant with possibilities for a far wider and more vital development than any that had gone before. The rapidity with which the art now began to grow, ramify, and mature, the variety of the new tendencies, and the multiplicity of different styles or orders of art, such as opera and oratorio, fugue and sonata, toward which they led, are surprising. In the countless centuries before Palestrina music grew slowly and uniformly, like a plant; in the short three hundred years between the birth of Palestrina in 1528 and the death of Beethoven in 1827, it had its inconceivably rich and various blossoming, and Monteverde and Gluck, Corelli and Scarlatti, Couperin and Rameau, Bach and Handel, Haydn, Mozart, and Beethoven, were the bright flowers it now put forth. Such a rapid and many-sided advance is fairly bewildering; but it is nevertheless possible to distinguish in the movement a few salient and dominant features, more significant and remarkable than all the others. From our present point of view, the labors of J. S. Bach in the fugue and suite forms, and of Haydn, Mozart, and Beethoven in the sonata form, are of supreme interest. These labors were guided and fructified by several new principles of musical effect.

The first step toward new fields was taken early in the seventeenth century by a set of daring reformers in Florence, who, boldly discarding the perfect polyphonic style of Palestrina, contrived a style of dramatic music, embodied in small operas, in which single voices sing more or less expressive melodies over an instrumental accompaniment in chords. Crude in the extreme as were necessarily the compositions of Cavaliere, Caccini, Peri, and their fellows, they opened up novel paths, because they had to rely for their effectiveness largely on the conduct of the harmonies employed. So long as the old church modes were adhered to, to be sure, the harmonic style remained necessarily vague, wandering, and mo-notonous; but gradually the composers began to see that, by altering their intervals, they could introduce variety and contrast into their cadences, making one line end on one chord, and the next on a different though related one, and that thus they could make coherent the successive phrases, punctuated by the cadences, and at the same time set them in an opposition that made for variety. In the interests of definiteness of cadence and an obvious distribution of contrasted yet complementary chords, therefore, the modes were slowly transformed into the modern scale, and music became at last harmonically definite and firm. All the tones came to be conceived as grouped around certain tonal centers, which could be manipulated and organized like the masses in a picture. Thus emerged the principle of tonality or key, and in the course of time the device of modulation by which one passes from one key to another. Still it remained difficult to get far away from the key in which one started out, because of the manner of tuning, which made only a few keys available at once; but J. S. Bach, modifying the system of tuning to what is called equal temperament,* which opens the doors simultaneously to the entire twelve keys, emancipated music entirely from the restrictions of the ecclesiastical modes, and in his great work, *The Well- [or Equally-] Tempered Clavichord,* demonstrated practically the use of all the twelve keys as an intimate and compact family. By his time the principle of tonality was firmly established.

A second principle vital to modern music is that of "thematic development." By this is meant, first, the existence in the music of certain salient, easily recognizable groups of tones, called motifs, subjects, or themes, which are presented to the hearer at the outset, and impressed upon him by their unique individuality of cut; and second, that subsequent elaboration of these themes, in varied but still recognizable forms, which corresponds closely with the process by which an essayist develops an idea, a mathematician proves a theorem, or a preacher elucidates a text. It is interesting to note that the German word *Satz,* often used by musicians to mean *a theme,* signifies primarily a thesis or proposition in logic, while *Durchführung,* used to describe the development of the theme, means primarily a leading-through or bringing to an issue. Thus the process of thematic development in music is much like any other process of intellectual statement and proof. Now it is evident that this process, which is indispensable to all the higher intellectual forms of music, requires in the first place definite, concise, and memorable themes, since it is impossible to discuss what one fails to grasp, or after grasping, forgets. As the proverb says, the preparer of a ragout of hare must "first catch his hare." Similarly musicians, before they could make their music logical, had to catch their themes. But as musical material up to the time of Palestrina never was definite or memorable, the first requisite of thematic music was some principle by which themes could be defined. This principle was found in the time-measurement of tones. So soon as a group of tones were placed in measured relations of duration to one another, an individual theme emerged, and could be elaborated. The second great conquest of modern music, then, was the conquest of the

*For a technical explanation of equal temperament, see Parry's *Evolution of the Art of Music,* pp. 187–188.

definite theme or motif, strictly measured in time, and of those devices by which it could be developed in an extended and logical discourse.

The third notable achievement of seventeenth century composers was the emancipation of music from servitude to poetry, and the establishment of it as an independent art. In one sense this was but a natural outcome of its new qualities of harmonic and thematic definition, lacking which it could never reach independence. So long as it remained in itself vague, amorphous, inchoate, it was constrained to be but a handmaid, to content itself with lending eloquence or atmosphere to the utterances of its sister art; but this condition of dependence, however inevitable for a time, was nevertheless unfortunate, and bound to be eventually outlived. Music is always fatally handicapped by association with words. In the first place, words impose upon it a concrete meaning immeasurably more trite, prosaic, and limited than that abstract and indefinable meaning to the heart and mind which is its proper prerogative; the expressive power of music really begins where that of poetry fails and ceases. In the second place, the limitations of all vocal music are in many ways serious. Not only are voices incapable of sounding readily and with certainty many intervals, but they are confined to a range of a little over three octaves, and to phrases short enough not to overtax the breath. Instruments are free from all these disqualifications. They produce pure tones, without words, the most celestial of artistic materials; they can sound any interval; they extend over a range of more than seven octaves, from the deep bass of the organ or contrabass to the shrill and immaterial treble of the piccolo; and the breadth of the phrases they can produce is limited not by their own mechanism, but only by the power of intellectual synthesis possessed by listeners. For all these reasons, instruments are the ideal media for producing music; and never until they supplanted voices could music reach its complete stature as a mature and self-sufficient art, leaning on no crutch, borrowing no *raison d'être,* but making by its own legitimate means its own unique effects.

The task of seventeenth century musicians was, then, in large part, the establishment of tonality and the hierarchy of keys, contrasted with one another, but accessible by modulation; the crystallization, by means of both harmonic and metrical definition, of individual themes out of the amorphous tonal matrix of previous eras, and the exploration of means for building up these themes into coherent organisms; and lastly the emancipation of the art thus brought into full life from the tyranny of association with words and voices. This was an immense task; and it is not to be wondered at that most of the men engaged in it never attained mastery enough to give them great personal prominence. Theirs was a time of beginnings, of preparation for novel and unprecedented achievements. The early opera writers, the Italian violinists, the German organists, and the clavichord and harpsichord writers of that period, men like Cavaliere and Caccini, Corelli and Scarlatti, Sweelinck and Frescobaldi, Purcell, Kuhnau, and Couperin, are chiefly known to us as preparers of the soil, and sowers of the seed, for a harvest which was gathered by later, and probably greater, though not more honorable men. The first composer after Palestrina who like him overtopped all his fellows, and brought to its culmination another great period, was Johann Sebastian Bach.

In Bach's style we find, in addition to the polyphonic or many-voiced texture of Palestrina, a thematic pointedness and logic and a harmonic structure which are entirely unforeshadowed in the older man. The fugue, a form which he carried to its highest pitch, and which was admirably suited to his genius, is in certain respects allied to the earlier style, though in others wholly modern. Like the ecclesiastical forms of Palestrina, it is of the basket-work type of texture. One voice begins alone, others enter in succession, and all wind in and out amongst one another almost as intricately as in a sixteenth century madrigal. On the other hand, the fugue as a whole begins and ends in some one key, and throughout its progress modulates from key to key with well-planned contrasts and firmly-controlled movement. Moreover, a single definite theme or subject appears at the outset of the piece, and stands prominently forth through its whole extent; it is announced by the first voice, repeated at a different pitch in the answer of the second, reiterated again by the third and fourth, and subsequently made the basis of an ingenious, varied, and extended development. Finally, although some of Bach's fugues are vocal, most of them are written either for organ or for clavichord. In all these respects his work is modern, and perhaps most of all is it modern in its inexorable logic, its subtlety and variety, and in its poignant, deeply emotional expressiveness, which is always held within the bounds necessary to supreme architectural beauty. The period of

Bach and his precursors, sometimes called the "polyphonic-harmonic" period, because in it the modern harmonic system was grafted upon the polyphony of Palestrina, remains to-day, from some points of view, the purest and noblest period of musical history.

All the time that Bach, in the privacy of an obscure German town, was writing his wonderfully intricate and beautiful polyphonic music, the world about him, oblivious, was seeking out a quite different type of art. It is a surprising fact that Bach's compositions were virtually unknown for fifty years after his death, and might have remained so permanently had they not been "discovered" by appreciative students, much as the receptacles of classical lore were discovered in the Renaissance after the long darkness of the Middle Ages, and made the basis of an intellectual revival. Bach's great works, too, were full of an undying vitality; but for a long time their potency had to remain latent, because men were occupied with another order of art, a different set of problems, an alien style. Ever since the Florentine revolution, when the polyphonic texture of mediaeval music was abandoned for a simple monodic or one-voiced style, in which a melody is accompanied by a series of chords, much of the musical genius of the world had been devoted to the development of eloquent single melodies, and of suitable harmonic backgrounds for them. With the systematization of harmony and the establishment of definite themes this type of art became mature. Composers discerned the possibility of building up whole movements to which interest could be given by the statement and development of one or more themes, contrasted both in character and in key. They saw that the whole could be unified by general qualities of style, by recurrence of the themes, and, above all, by being made to embody, in the long run, a single tonality, though with momentary departures from it for the sake of variety. Working out their idea, they devised a type of structure which has remained up to this day the highest and most widely useful of all musical forms. The essential features of "sonata-form," as it is called, are, in the first place, the Exposition of two themes or subjects of discourse, contrasting both in character and in key; in the second place, the Development of these themes, the exploitation of their latent possibilities; in the third place, Restatement of them, in the central key of the movement, bringing all to a point, and completing the cycle of Statement, Argument, and Summary. Sonata-form, of which it is easy to see the naturalness and beauty, depends for its unity, not on the equal interplay of many voices, like the older polyphonic forms, but on the saliency, cumulative development, and harmonic inter-relations, of single themes. We may, therefore, call the great period of Haydn, Mozart, and Beethoven, the period in which the sonata-form attained its full maturity, the "harmonic period," or, in view of the complete round or circuit of themes its forms exemplified, the "cyclical-form period." It culminated in the early years of the nineteenth century, in the grand works of Beethoven's maturity.

II
THE BEGINNINGS OF OPERA

THE BEGINNINGS OF OPERA

By Carl Engel

THE men who participated in the "creation" of opera were conscious of aiming at something new, at a departure in music as well as in drama. What they did not realize, what they could not have foreseen, was that they prepared the stage for a periodic renewal of both music and drama. It was from their stage, by them created, that such reformer-prophets as Rameau, Gluck, Wagner, Debussy, and Stravinsky, most effectively preached their "new" gospels. And the first operas, written at the beginning of the seventeenth century, bore in their kernel the essence of all "modern" secular music: the motival development of purely musical ideas for one player or a concert of instruments; the dance movements adopted as a basis of musical form and cyclic expansion; the poignancy and also the lurking tediousness of musico-dramatic utterance; the nobility and also the rampant lusciousness of musical lyricism; the foibles and fancies of "descriptive" or program music—in short, the whole apparatus composers have worked with for the last three hundred years.

What Western music would have turned into had opera not been invented is not the question; we must try to recognize that opera—when and where it began—was inevitably begotten by circumstances. We may quarrel with these circumstances, we may repudiate their child. But we cannot deny that, in the genealogy of music, its descendants were not only most prolific but extremely influential. And this in spite of the fact that the ancestor was far from being a "pure blood."

Opera represents the perfect union of the most delightful follies and absurdities committed in the name of art—not art for art's sake, but *all*

By arrangement with the author; hitherto unpublished.

23

the arts for pleasure's sake. It aims to please our eye and ear, it rouses our sympathetic imagination, and it flatters our social pride. To opera belongs the blue ribbon as the prize mongrel among artistic hybrids.

The mixed paternity showed clearly when the infant still lay in the cradle. Manifestly, opera sprang from the marriage between poetry and music; but the operatic family tree drops its roots deep into the ancient soil of the drama, while its spreading branches are hung with the fruits of painting, sculpture, architecture, pantomime, and the dance.

Opera need never have been invented, and yet we should have the whole of Bach, Chopin, and Brahms, the fullness of the greater Beethoven, the finest flower of Haydn, Schubert, Schumann, Mendelssohn, César Franck, Fauré, and others whose renown was not enhanced by the indifferent luck they had with opera. And this leaves out of the reckoning the musical giants who inhabited the earth before opera was born: Palestrina, Orlando, Vittoria, Morales, Byrd, to mention but the greatest of the contrapuntists. Yet all the absurdities, all the crimes of which the genus opera may be guilty, are pardoned, atoned for, and wiped out by the grandeur of Gluck, the exuberance of Mozart, the glamour of Weber, the tunefulness of Verdi, the glory of Wagner—men who have poured into their stage music all, or the best, they had to give. Our musical heritage, without these master operas, would be incalculably lessened. From the records of musical history would disappear the names of many composers whose fame rests upon one opera, or perhaps one aria from an opera, which has sung its way round the four quarters of the globe.

Opera is one of the few art forms for which we can actually name the place and date of birth. The place was Florence; the date, close to 1597. That, at least, is the year in which, according to the latest conclusions, the *Dafne* of Rinuccini and Peri was first performed. This "fable in music" is generally regarded as the first full-fledged specimen of the opera type. Poet and composer belonged to a group of men who—as O. G. Sonneck put it—"sought Greek drama and found opera."

Much has been done in recent years to uncover the antecedents of opera. The Italian, Angelo Solerti, and the Frenchman, Romain Rolland, have been particularly sedulous in this research. Our own countryman, Sonneck, who was one of the best authorities on operatic history, was of the opinion that this study has so far produced nothing that might rob the Florentine experimenters of their laurels. He maintained that "whether or not they [the Florentines] consciously or unconsciously utilized the traditional or progressive elements of their time, no historical subtleties will ever succeed in proving that opera really existed before the Florentine *camerata* stumbled on it."

To be sure, there existed nothing worthy of the name of opera before the *Dafne* of 1597, or the *Eurydice,* first given at Florence on the sixth day of October, 1600. It is the earliest opera of which the music (by Peri and Caccini) as well as the poem (by Rinuccini) has come down to us. Nevertheless, I should like to accept with certain qualifications Sonneck's phrase that the Florentines "stumbled" upon their discovery— the figure implying, as it does, too strongly the element of chance or unexpectedness. I rather think there is a good deal to be said for the belief that the chances were a hundred to one in favor of opera having been discovered just where and when it was stumbled upon. Indeed, I shall not attempt here a description of the first operas, or pile date upon date and name upon name in a chronological review of opera's infancy; these are facts made conveniently accessible in almost any book of musical history. What I should like to do instead, is to survey some of the "traditional or progressive elements"—as Mr. Sonneck aptly called them— and marshal them in close formation with the aim of making them converge upon one point: the inception of opera.

These elements may be divided into three main groups:

1.) the cultural elements
2.) the social elements
3.) the musical elements

The order is not an arbitrary one. I shall begin with the cultural elements, because they are the foundation and background for the others; I shall take up the social elements next, because opera is largely an outgrowth of certain social uses and abuses; that the musical elements should come trailing behind, in the third and last place, is not unnatural—they were the last to develop specifically operatic characteristics, and they have never stopped developing to this day.

It will help us in keeping present to our mind the cultural conditions in the last decade of the sixteenth century, if we measure the distance that separates the period from a few salient events. In 1597, when Peri's *Dafne* startled Florence, it was barely 150 years since the printing press had been invented; little more than a century had passed since the discovery of America; it was just 75 years since Martin Luther, in Wittenberg, had publicly burned the papal bull of excommunication; Michelangelo was dead only a little over 20 years; the graves of Palestrina and Orlando di Lasso—both dying in the same year, 1594—were still fresh.

With the invention of the printing press, with the diffusion of printed books, the seeds of human thought began to scatter in all the winds. They brought forth an unprecedented harvest. The eagerness of the reading public could not be satisfied by contemporary writers. There sprang up a demand for the authors of antiquity. Curiosity had been aroused about the life and history of ancient nations, especially of Greece and Rome. As the great admirals had set out upon their hazardous voyages over uncharted seas in quest of the gold of the Indies and had landed on unknown shores, so did the savants, philosophers, and poets scan the writings of the ancients for the treasures of the past, only to discover a new world which they found to be singularly in tune with their own times. It was not immediately that the shores of America were recognized as those of a new continent; it was not immediately that the true image of these old civilizations became apparent. Particularly ancient Greece was seen at first through the eyes of Rome and Roman writers, the writers of an opulent and decadent Rome, living in an era which represented the crest of a cultural wave, just as the towering swell was about to break up in a tremendous surf. What these writers touched, they imbued with reality. Even the gods, whose deeds and misdeeds they recounted, bore a striking resemblance to real human beings. Ovid in his *Metamorphoses,* Apuleius in his *Golden Ass,* had perpetuated stories which to the imaginative readers of the sixteenth century had the fillip of actuality. These tales of love, adventure, intrigue, murder, witchcraft, victory or defeat, were like so many "news items" of their own day. The poets quickly seized upon these resemblances. They unloosed a veritable deluge of allegorical poems in which the gods and goddesses of Greece and Rome served as a thin and flattering disguise for the great lords and ladies of the realm.

While these flocks of pagan deities appealed vividly to the imagina-

tion of the poets, the systems of pagan philosophy absorbed the specula-
tions of the thinkers. A humanistic awakening had deeply stirred the
world. The new learning was seeping through the fissures cleft into the
battlements of the church. Classic serenity and gaiety were bringing
solace to the minds perturbed by the loss of their faith. The heretic,
secretly or openly, took refuge in the dogmas of paganism. The artist
looked to pagan art for inspiration. The Gothic era, with its superb but
sombre cathedrals, had come to an end. The lacy spires could rise no
higher. Instead, St. Peter's dome, a magnified pantheon, was beginning
to raise its huge breast toward the heavens and to lift its colossal weight
with ease, by sheer perfection of shape and proportion. It was the crowning symbol of the rebirth, the revival of arts and letters—the Renaissance. And the new spirit gave form to the very church of the Vicar of
Christ.

In the sixteenth century man's inquiring turn of mind was wonderfully quickened; the interest in the fine arts was a vital concern to nearly
everyone. In consequence, the number of dilettanti—people earnestly
seeking to understand and foster art—grew enormously. The Renaissance produced an abundance of genius and virtuosity; but it is the age
par excellence of dilettantism. And it was not the sort of dilettantism
that sticks in the morass of mediocrity. As Jacob Burckhardt—perhaps
the greatest historian of the Renaissance—has said: "This dilettantism,
among the nobility as well as among the middle classes, was more widely
spread and came nearer to real artistry in Italy than in any other country."

In Italy, again, one of the liveliest art centers was Florence. For a
long time, it was the artistic capital of the Western World. Blest and cursed
with a government of enlightened despotism, under the rule of the
Medici family, it offered the ideal ground in which art and artists could
flourish. It was "the city of eternal movement," the magnet that attracted reformers and "progressives" of all shades. Florence counted
among its citizens many excellent musicians; many more were drawn to
it from other cities. Professionals and dilettanti soon banded together
in circles where questions of art were hotly discussed. They formed art
clubs—but called them by the more pretentious name of Academy.
These academies, cliques, and coteries fulfilled the functions which now
belong to our various poetry societies, drama guilds, composers' leagues,

and painters' associations. But they were not on so large a scale as that of our present-day defensive and offensive coalitions. It was oftener a small group of *beaux esprits,* of aesthetes, of theorists and artisans, gathered round some central figure who was their leader, perhaps for no better reason than that he was rich enough and willing to play the host.

The coterie that interests us most in relation to the beginnings of the opera is the Florentine *camerata.* The members of this group met in the house of Giovanni Bardi, Count Vernio, from about 1580 until 1594, the year in which Bardi was called to Rome. Stefano Arteaga, in his book on the *Revolution of the Italian Musical Theatre* (1783) characterized Bardi as "a virtuous cavalier, liberal, magnanimous, of excellent taste, highest gentility, great knowledge of every kind of letters, and consequently a just appraiser and devoted lover of the literati." In short, he was predestined to play the part of "angel" to his temperamental friends. The group included scientists, writers, artists who debated the aesthetic problems that confronted them, and criticized each other's work, probably with the same liberality that still prevails among brother-artists. Bardi's son, Pietro, wrote in 1634 a letter to Gianbattista Doni, musical theorist and first chronicler of early opera, in which he described these meetings at the house of his father. And in the course of this letter he refers to some of the preliminary experiments of one member of the group, Vincenzo Galilei, the father of the famous astronomer. Pietro Bardi relates that Galilei's experiment—a setting of the lament of Ugolino from Dante's *Divina Commedia* for a solo voice with an accompaniment of viols—excited the jealous criticism of most of the musicians, but pleased those who were "real lovers of music." Note the distinction.

Whatever their differences of opinion were, on one point all of them agreed—especially the poets and musicians—namely, that the polyphonic style of music had reached an intolerable complexity and that simplification was in order. The polyphonic music, for one thing, had made it impossible to understand the texts. Endless repetitions of sentences or single words broke up the sense of the poem. Let us admit that in most of these poems—especially in those of the Italian madrigals—the sense was so abstruse to begin with, the form so stilted, their metaphors were so far-fetched, their everlasting love-wails so inane and cloying, that no serious harm was done if these poetic pearls did remain hidden under the contrapuntal web of the music. But the poets themselves, of course, thought differently.

They encouraged a deliberate breaking away from the polyphonic style of music. They wanted their words to be heard when sung. In contrapuntal compositions of from four to sixteen voices, they counted themselves lucky if the hearers caught a final "Amen" or "amor." Even when a solo voice sang the top part of a madrigal and the rest of the parts were played on one or more instruments, the verses were hacked to pieces in stammering repetitions or dragged out in exaggerated prolongation of the vowel sounds. And here one of the cultural elements became a determining factor for the remedy that was applied—the humanistic creed that salvation lay in Hellas. The poets only followed the current of the times when they turned their faces toward the East and antiquity. If there was to be a union of words and music, they reasoned, it must be along the lines adopted by the ancient Greeks. They had wrought perfection in everything else; hence they must have known what to do when confronted with a similar problem.

Now, the only ancient art forms in which poetry and music were combined and of which samples had survived, were the plays of the old Greek authors. Unfortunately, of these samples only the texts were preserved; there remained not a note of music. To make up the deficiency, the numerous treatises by ancient Greek philosophers and musical theorists were diligently searched. The search was in vain, or what it produced was misunderstood by the searchers. Somewhere in Plato's writings someone had found a statement to the effect that music should first be words and rhythm, and only lastly musical sounds. This reversed the hitherto accepted order of importance. It upset all musical traditions. But so implicit was the faith in anything reputed to bear the hallmark of antiquity, that the musicians blindly followed a schoolman's narrow view, a philologist's illusion. It was their dream to out-Greek Sophocles. And the conception they had formed of Greek drama, could lead only to one thing: a chanted play.

Out of this obsession with antiquity, out of this Hellenistic fog emerged the first opera. Its steps were guided by people culturally disposed to walk in only one direction. The musico-dramatic explorers set their course for antique tragedy. What they discovered was new land—the opera. And yet, if they "stumbled" upon opera, they could no more have escaped it, than Columbus could have avoided stumbling upon America. Opera lay in their path. It was an organic and consequential up-shot of the humanistic trends to resurrect the stage of the ancients. It led to the reëstablishment of the public theatre. The play-house came to be the foremost assembling place of the populace. Society supported it, made a fad of it. Dramatic development in Italy went hand in hand with social development. The one becomes intelligible only if we look upon it in conjunction with the other. And the social elements we shall turn to next.

In antiquity the drama grew out of the "mysteries," the religious representations connected with temple worship. In the Middle Ages we witness a similar transition. By elaborating the religious ceremonies on feast days, the church gradually instituted a sort of sacred spectacle which proved a powerful attraction for the populace. From the twelfth century onward we can observe this practice. It began with miracle plays, with dramatized episodes from the lives of the saints. First performed within the church itself, these plays were later relegated to the square in front of the church. They had achieved the desired effect. More than that, they were attracting throngs too large even for the vast nave of the cathedral. The demand for them continued. But under the blue dome of the sky, with the cathedral portico for a proscenium, the character and the technique of these plays had to meet new conditions.

The removal from the hallowed interior of the church and the atmosphere of myrrh and incense to the open, and the more pungent aroma of the street, resulted in imparting a brisker air and a coarser flavor to the play. One of the favorite devices in building the stage for these "sacred representations" was to divide the structure into three sections: a middle or main section represented the earthly plane upon which were enacted the principal incidents of the story; rising above it was an upper section representing the heavenly abode or paradise; for reasons of symmetry as much as of theological doctrine, a lower section depicted the regions of hell. If Heaven and Paradise were peopled with actors in the guise of saints and angels, Hell had to have its lost souls and its devil. We may be sure that his part was not always a grateful one, and that upon many an occasion he was vigorously and indignantly hissed off the stage by the righteous spectators. Therefore we can only sympathize with the poor fellow if he tried to win favor with the public by fair means or foul. To render himself *dramatis persona grata* he resorted to the ingenious device of being funny. Now, a funny devil was perfectly harmless and not at all objectionable. In fact, he soon had the public on his side. He became "the hit of the show." The comic element made inroads. The grotesque and obscene little sculptures in which the cathedral masons gave vent to their spirit of hilarity and irreverence, had their echo on the stage in farcical antics and profane language. The church did not find it easy to lay the ghost it had called up. By 1548 the mystery plays had degenerated to such an extent that the "Brotherhood of the Passion," which long enjoyed a sort of monopoly in the giving of these performances, was ordered to stop them. If the spectacles ceased to be given as sacred performances, they continued in a different guise as secular entertainments. Carnival mummery and the *Commedia del arte* became national institutions. Theatrical performances found their strongholds at the courts of kings and princes. For the celebration of royal birthdays, nuptials, state visits—or on any plausible pretext—they were the ideal form of diversion, because they were the most lavish and the most picturesque. They pressed into service *all* the arts; they offered an opportunity for fantastic illumination, reckless pomp, and the glorifying of lovely women.

It is significant that the chief dates in the prenatal history of Florentine opera, and during the first stages of its infancy, coincide with wedding celebrations in the house of Medici. In 1539, Cosimo married Leonora of Toledo; in 1565, Francesco married Giovanna d'Austria; in 1589, Ferdinand married Cristina of Lorraine. These dates correspond to the Intermedi of Corteccia and Festa; to the *Psyche and Amor* of Corteccia and Striggio; and to the Intermedi of Malvezzi, Marenzio and others. Finally came the great family event, in 1600, when Maria de' Medici was given in marriage to Henri IV, King of France and Navarre. And that occasion is immortalized in the annals of music by the first performance of Rinuccini and Peri's *Eurydice*, the first opera of which we possess the entire score.

The whole period of the Italian Renaissance is dominated by the love of display, of military and civic processions—called *trionfi*—which were the joy of the rabble. The nobility had its private high days and high nights. Royalty indulged in whole weeks of revelries. The inventiveness of court poet, court painter, and court musician, could not work fast enough to produce ever new and startling surprises. The poet earned his wages by more or less delicate flattery of his employer, to which end he found mythological allegory most conveniently at hand. He turned Jupiter and Mars, Venus and Diana into complimentary disguises too easily pierced. Personal and political allusions stuck out everywhere in his poem. He was gone allegory-mad. There was nothing to stop him. The general culture, the wide acquaintance with the classic writers enabled everybody in the audience to penetrate the symbolism of character and actions. So when in 1513, as Vasari reports, a poet in Florence decided to present in his spectacle a young boy, naked but gilt from head to foot, there was probably not a person in the crowd who did not instantly recognize in the little fellow a personification of "the golden age." The poet was acclaimed. But the boy died; and Vasari does not tell us whether it was a cold or the gold that killed him.

In the libretti of the earliest operas, and far into the eighteenth century, the engineer of the stage contraptions is carefully mentioned, and a description of his handiwork is given; often we find his name when those of poet and composer were deemed not worth recording. In the preface to Marco da Gagliano's *Dafne* (1608) the composer specified that "the dragon (which Apollo fights) must be large; and if the painter, as I have seen it done, arranges it so that the animal flaps its wings and breathes fire and steam, it will be more marvelous to behold. But above all things the worm must wiggle and turn, and in order to do this, the man inside must have his hands on the ground and walk on all fours." These were some of the preoccupations that weighed on the first composers of opera—preoccupations largely imposed by the society that attended the opera. And after all, Wagner's Fafner in *Siegfried* is a direct descendant of Gagliano's worm.

Although nothing has been saved of Striggio's and Corteccia's music for *Psyche and Amor*, the intermedi of 1565, we are fortunate in having at least a description or synopsis of the action. And to read these accounts of sumptuous settings and trappings—serving only to set off in greater contrast Venus, "that loveliest of Goddesses, entirely nude," followed by the three Graces, "likewise recognizable by appearing wholly nude"—should remind us that the prevailing taste in spectacular stage productions has not materially changed since they were first attempted.

We should also remember that this was the age of Boccaccio, Aretino, Masuccio, Bandello, and all the other "gallant" novelists and satirists of the *quattrocento* and *cinquecento*. Private and public morals left much to be desired. The examples set by the princes of the realm and of the church were not always designed to raise the tone. And as regards the laxity of morals which the gods and goddesses of Greece exhibited, Ovid and Apulieus had seen to it that the Olympian "scandals" should tend, if anything, to lower the tone.

As their name implies, these early "intermedi," forerunners of the opera, were interpolations. The intermedi were inserted between the acts of a tragedy or comedy. In a Latin comedy of Plautus the Italian "intermedi" came as a relief from boredom, eagerly awaited by a yawning audience. It was nothing extraordinary for these "two in one" plays to last until three o'clock in the morning. Frequently the intermedi had nothing whatever to do with the play they interrupted. It was a practice artistically indefensible, and dramatically absurd. The only explanation of it was the demand for entertainment by a jaded society. Excuse for it there was none. And at the bottom of the whole astonishing procedure lay nothing but a perversion of taste brought on by social indulgence. Nor did the abuse stop with the beginnings of opera. For a long time the custom prevailed of interrupting the acts of an opera with the acts of a ballet, running two shows simultaneously, as it were; or a comedy was intercalated between the acts of a musical tragedy. To our minds the idea seems preposterous, incredible. But it persisted into the days of Handel. I quote from the letters of Baron Pöllnitz—notorious for having changed religions as easily and as often as his shirts—; he wrote from London: "The English . . . have an Italian Opera which is the best and most magnificent in Europe. . . . The music of these operas is generally composed by one Handel, who is esteemed by a great many people beyond all expression, but others reckon him no extraordinary man; and for my own part I think his music not so affecting as 'tis elegant . . . the room [that is, the Haymarket Theatre] is very large and well illuminated with wax candles. There's dancing between the acts when there is no burlesque Interlude."

In the early nineteenth century, when Stendhal used to haunt La Scala in Milan, the opera was still first a social event and the musical considerations came second. Stendhal tells us that the surest way of finding any man or woman in Milan society, was to look for them in their boxes at La Scala. The boxes were the rendezvous of foreign visitors as well as the Milanese. Stendhal was introduced to Lord Byron in the box of a mutual friend. The audience talked loudly, except when some special feat of vocal bravura claimed their attention. In Stendhal's day opera composers still provided for one or the other of the minor singers in the cast what was known as *l'aria del sorbetto*—the sherbet or ice-cream aria —which was timed so as to allow the people in the boxes to eat their ices to the accompaniment of a polite and colorless sort of music, too unimportant to disturb the brilliant chatter and the sipping of the cool dessert. "Diamond horseshoes" nowadays sparkle more by the wealth of jewelry than by the wit of conversation.

If the cultural elements had paved the way for the coming of opera, the social elements gave speed to its progress. The Italian Renaissance brought the end of the church as the civic center. There was nothing immediately to take its place. The princely courts remained the rallying points of society. Court life, court festivities, court adulation, engendered the allegorical masques, ballets, pantomimes, and intermedi which engendered opera. And opera is responsible for the creation of what became the new rallying points of the populace: the public theatres. In 1637 the first public opera house was opened, the Teatro San Cassiano in Venice. Only in 1651 did Naples follow; and Rome came next in 1652.

We now come to the musical elements. We come to them last, or rather they are the last to come to us. They invariably are. As one French critic has put it: *"la musique arrive toujours la dernière dans l'ordre de succession des arts"*—music always trails at the heels of her sister arts. To back up this opinion, those who hold it point to music as having followed the impressionistic painters; or, before them, the romantic poets; or, still earlier, the architects and interior decorators of the baroque period; and so down the line in alternate borrowing from one or the other of her thriving sisters.

As we have seen, it was chiefly the poets who prodded the first opera composers into changing the style of music. But there were others who wanted to help cook the broth or have a finger in the pie. Giulio Caccini in the important preface to his *Nuove Musiche* (1601) wrote: "In truth, at the time when flourished in Florence the eminent camerata of

the illustrious Count Bardi, in whose house not only a large part of the
nobility met, but the best musicians, men of talent, poets and philosophers of the town, I can say—having frequented them myself—that
I have learned more from their wise discussions than I did during more
than thirty years of studying counterpoint. For these highly enlightened
gentlemen have always urged me (and convinced me by luminous argument) to shun the kind of music which prevents the words from being
understood and does violence to the poem."

What these wise discutants and enlightened gentlemen tried to do,
was to set the clock back. It was indeed retrogression instead of advance.
To our present ears a duller, drearier, more dismal thing—musically—
than the first opera is not well conceivable. But the remarkable fact is
that, from this point on, the pendulum of the clock began to swing ten
times as fast as it had ever done before. In the three hundred years of its
association with the stage, music has progressed farther and more rapidly
than it did in the preceding three thousand years.

The Florentine experimenters rendered musical art one service which
cannot be too highly valued. With their demand that music pay greater
heed to the words and express more accurately the *sentiments* of the
words, they stressed the quality of feeling, of emotion in music. Music
should come from the heart as well as from the brain. Musical painting,
even program music, can be found in some of the madrigals. The only
actual invention of the Florentine musicians was their musico-dramatic
speech, the so-called *stilo recitativo* or *stilo rappresentativo*. What they
aimed at—even if they did not perfect it at once—was musical eloquence, molded over the prosody of the text. Their new style was intended to be "representative," indeed: that is, expressive of sentiments
which move the human breast, of different states of mind, of varying
moods of the soul. Emilio de' Cavalieri, in the preface of his *Rappresentazione di anima e corpo* (1600) speaks of the "great emotion" produced by the change from one sentiment to its opposite, from sad to
gay, from harsh to tender. And he shrewdly suggests that even the instrumental accompaniment should vary "according to the sentiments expressed by the singer." In a similar vein are some of Caccini's remarks in
the preface to his *Nuove Musiche,* namely, that "in order to well compose and sing in this style [the representative], the sense of the idea
and words, the flavor and image of the thought reproduced by the use

of expressive notes (*corde affettuose*) and by an interpretation full of sentiment, are far more important than is the counterpoint."

To-day we can hardly comprehend what the deliberate infusion of sentiment into music must have meant at the time it was first practised. The wonder of it had not worn off when Mattheson, in 1713, published *Das neu-eroeffnete Orchester,* really one of the earliest guides to the "appreciation of music." In it he says: "Among secular things the theatrical ones are undeniably the most popular, and among these again the esteemed operas, because in them may be encountered a conflux, so to speak, of all musical beauties. There the composer has the very chance of giving rein to his invention. There he can very naturally picture, with a thousand variations and graces, in innumerable ways, such things as love, jealousy, hatred, gentleness, impatience, eagerness, indifference, fear, revenge, valor, timorousness, generosity, horror, nobility, meanness, pomp, poverty, pride, humility, joy, laughter, tears, gaiety, sorrow, beatitude, despair, storm, calm, yea! heaven, earth, sea, and hell." A rich field, indeed, for any composer. And when the composer happened to be a man of genius, such as Monteverde was, the novel effects produced by him were simply overpowering. In his *Combat in Music of Tancred and Clorinda* (to the words of Tasso) he employed for the first time in musical history the quickly repeated strokes of one and the same note, known as "tremolo." Monteverde reports that at the performance of this music in the house of Girolamo Mocenigo in Venice, in 1624, the whole nobility was present, and was so moved by compassion as to shed tears. Monteverde called this manner the *stilo concitato*—the agitated style— as opposed to the "tender" and the "temperate" style. He wrote: "In none of the works by composers of the past have I been able to find an example of this agitated style, only the tender and temperate ones."

Naturally, to ears overfed on polyphonic music all these novel devices of the *stilo recitativo* and *stilo concitato* came as a relief and as a new thrill. The devices had not only the merit of novelty, but that of comparative simplicity. It did not require learning to appreciate them, only plain, everyday sensibility. Hence the appeal they had for the layman; hence the immediate success that the Florentines reaped with their dramatic compositions in which the voice was supported by a simple, though often harmonically daring, accompaniment of a homophone nature. Each player was left to mix the ingredients of the accompaniment from a shorthand recipe which was called the *basso continuo*—the continuous or figured bass. Musicians lived on this slender fare for over one hundred and fifty years, and music managed to thrive exceedingly.

Yet, it would be erroneous if credit were given—as it often is—to the Florentine experimenters for having *invented* the solo song, or monody, as opposed to the singing in parts. There has always been solo singing. The Gregorian chant, the liturgical songs of the synagogue, and, last but not least, the secular songs of the common people long antedated the Florentine camerata. Furthermore, liturgical chanting and folksongs were not the only kinds of solo singing that preceded the "recitative." Italy had its *cantori a liuto*—singers who accompanied themselves on the lute—about the same time that Germany had its minnesingers. Some of the old lute tablatures contain solo songs, the signs for the voice part being printed in red over the black lines and symbols of the lute tablature. But these voice parts were not yet freed entirely from a contrapuntal interdependence. Similarly, only a "pseudo-solo" was obtained when the upper part of a vocal madrigal was given to one singer while one or more instruments played the other voice parts.

Note that we are still speaking of voices and voice parts. That is precisely what the Florentines objected to. And their objections sprang not from purely musical considerations. Beneath the musical considerations lay something else, something far more compelling. The objection arose from a new consciousness, a new mentality, produced and shaped by the Renaissance. The ego had learned to assert itself. The personality, the individual was in the ascendant. The individual refused to submit to a musical employ in which it had no other function than to take an impersonal share. In the part-song the individuality of the singer must be submerged, the blending of the separate voices must be complete. And to this self-effacement the musician of the Renaissance would no longer assent.

Our own day is furnishing us with a striking example of how the mentality and temper of a generation can act upon the arts. "Jazz" is a term which connotes more than a noisy, blaring lot of saxophones and traps. It may well come some day to mark an epoch. And the future historian of that epoch need not waste his time in trying to find the particular back-alley or saloon where the first "jazz-band" worthy of the name exercised its uncanny and unholy skill. No doubt, it would form

an interesting bit of information. But more to the point will be his in-
quiry into our present state of mind, morals, and materialism, if he
wishes to prove that what flared up in one spot could have assumed the
dimensions of a conflagration only because the fuel was there, waiting to
feed the flame.

The first "jazz-band" may have been a calamity; but it was no more
a local accident than was the first opera. Those Florentine experimenters
were moved by the spirit of their times, by the ardent desire to express
their personalities. Dante's *Vita nuova* had shown the way; John Adding-
ton Symonds has called it "the first complete analysis of personal emotion." Petrarch, in his letter to posterity, had laid bare his inmost self
which, as he believed, no one before him had done so unsparingly.
Greater and farther-reaching than the discovery of new or old worlds was
man's discovery of himself. That was the crowning achievement of the
Renaissance. And when man realized that such a thing as personality, as
individual sentiment and emotion might be expressed in music, he had
to take but one step in applying his theory to a form of art in which in-
dividualization and personification had been accomplished—that form
was the drama. Thus the *dramma per musica,* the drama for music, became the natural vehicle for the singing voice which ceased to be an
impersonal part merged into a complex whole, but took on a character
and sensibility of its own. Giordano Bruno (in *Della causa,* 1584) had
written that "the soul is not individual or particular, as a point might be,
but in a certain way it is like the voice." The soul of Dafne, the soul of
Orpheus, each with its individual voice, would henceforth utter no more
vague generalities, but a specific thought, a particular emotion, expressed
in the words of Dafne or Orpheus. By investing these words of the individual with their proper emotional inflexions and a heightened melodic
intonation, the Florentines created their "recitative" or musico-dramatic
speech. Because this speech involves words as well as music, a fine pair
of vocal cords is most effective when supplemented by brains.

Epigrammatic brevity cannot always be depended upon to hit the
nail on the head, or to hit more than one nail at a time. Yet, I should
like to squeeze the gist of this brief survey into the following concise, if
not exhaustive, summary: the cultural, social, and musical elements that
combined in bringing about the creation of opera correspond to the Hel-

lenistic, hedonistic, and realistic tendencies of the men of the Italian Renaissance. The Hellenistic tendencies were responsible for the character and subject of the text, the hedonistic tendencies for the display of scenery, the realistic tendencies for the style of the music. Together, text, scenery, and music make up the essential parts of an opera.

In the very decade during which the Florentines were trying to rediscover the Greek drama and experimented in their "musico-dramatic" laboratory, an English actor in London was writing plays for himself and his fellow actors to appear in, and was doing it rather well. By 1597 he had written, among other things, *Richard III, A Midsummer Night's Dream, Romeo and Juliet,* and *Henry V.* In 1598 he added to his repertory *The Merchant of Venice.* By the time the Florentines got all excited over a mild little "favola in musica" on the touching connubial fidelity of a mythological Orpheus and Eurydice, the Englishman had quietly finished a rollicking comedy entitled *The Merry Wives of Windsor* and two rather gloomy tragedies, one with *Macbeth* as hero, the other with *Hamlet, Prince of Denmark.*

Think how very much alive those plays still are to-day, how much they mean to us, into how many languages they have been translated; and then reflect upon the hopeless distance that separates us from those first experimental operas of the Florentines, indeed, from practically all the operas that hold for us little more than an historic interest—until we come to Rameau, Handel, Gluck, and Mozart. The reason for this difference lies not in the fact that Shakespeare was a genius such as opera was not favored with until the advent of Wagner; rather is it because the Florentines had elected to shape an art work out of *theories,* while Shakespeare carved his plots and characters out of the very stuff of *life.* Life, human nature, may take on varying shades in its constant process of adjustment to new conditions. But fundamentally it does not change. On the other hand, theories dictated by cultural, social, and musical elements of a particular period must lose their validity with the passing of that period. Shakespeare disposed over an inadequate stage and had no scenery to speak of. What music he used, consisted in an occasional flourish of trumpets or a simple ditty. The Florentines had more scenery, machinery, and fire-works than was altogether good for them. The elements that gave birth to opera also afflicted it with the hereditary maladies and congenital abnormalities that have made of it the extraordinary mongrel—the child of all the arts—which we know it to be. And yet, the crown reposes safely on the brows of those admirable Florentine poets, philosophers, and musicians of the "camerata"; for, after all, it is to them we owe the prototype from which eventually sprang Gluck's *Orpheus,* Mozart's *Magic Flute,* Rossini's *Barber of Seville,* Bizet's *Carmen,* Wagner's *Tristan and Isolde,* Debussy's *Pelleas and Melisande,* and Stravinsky's *Petrushka* and *The Nightingale.* Hail to their future progeny!

III

BACH

JOHANN SEBASTIAN BACH

Born March 21, 1685, at Eisenach in Thuringia; the most eminent member of a distinguished musical family. His career is usually divided into three epochs during which his most important compositions were created: Weimar 1708–1717, where as church organist he composed the bulk of his organ works; Coethen 1717–1723, where as kapell-meister to Prince Leopold he composed his principal works for orchestra and chamber ensemble; Leipzig, 1723 until his death in 1750, where he served as director of the St. Thomas Schule for choir singers and organist of the St. Thomas Church. During this period he composed the majority of his choral works. Bach's fame was limited to a small circle until the middle of the nineteenth century, when thanks to the efforts of Mendelssohn and Schumann his principal works were performed and the Bachgesellschaft was formed to publish his complete works. Several of his sons achieved fame as composers: Wilhelm Friedemann Bach, Karl Philip Emanuel Bach (kapellmeister to Frederick the Great) and Johann Christian Bach (known as the English Bach for his success as opera composer in London).

PRINCIPAL WORKS

CHORAL: Mass in B minor; 4 small masses; 5 passions, of which the *St. Matthew* and the *St. John* have survived; 5 sets of church cantatas, besides single cantatas for special occasions, also secular cantatas including the comic *Bauern* and *Caffee* cantatas; *Christmas Oratorio;* 2 magnificats, motets, etc.

INSTRUMENTAL: Principal works for clavichord and harpsichord include the 48 preludes and fugues of *The Well-Tempered Clavichord* (Books I and II); inventions in two and three parts; 6 French suites; 6 English suites; 6 partitas; the 32 "Goldberg" Variations; *The Art of the Fugue,* for harpsichord; *Chromatic Fantasy and Fugue; Concerto in the Italian Style;* 6 sonatas for violin and piano; solo sonatas and partitas for violin and other instruments; 6 Brandenburg Concertos for orchestra; *Musicalisches Opfer* for harpsichord and accompanying instruments; 4 overtures or orchestral suites. Principal works for organ include toccatas, preludes, fugues, choral preludes, trio sonatas (9 volumes).

BACH

By C. Sanford Terry

CHRONOLOGICAL exactitudes are generally misleading in measure as they are precise. Still, it is a tenable thesis that modern music begins with Bach and Handel. For of the masters before the Vienna dispensation they alone speak a language we entirely comprehend. That they were born in the same year is one of History's happy coincidences; that they never met, one of Chance's most quippish pranks. Emerging together, they dominated a musical sphere not otherwise impressive. Gluck was under forty when Bach died, his highest achievement unfulfilled; Haydn was eighteen. When Handel followed his contemporary to the grave, Mozart was a child of three and Beethoven's birth was eleven years distant. So, the earlier half of the eighteenth century belongs to Bach and Handel. They shine with uncontested brilliance from a sky that holds no other suns.

It is a commonplace, that to comprehend a genius we must approach him through the circumstances that surrounded his birth. For, as Emerson remarked, the truest genius is "the most indebted man," or colloquially, "Genius is one part inspiration, and three parts perspiration." Bach himself, when asked the secret of his mastership, replied simply, "I worked hard." The explanation is inadequate; but it is his career in eleven letters. Among the masters of music he was, by circumstances and of his own volition, "the most indebted man." Compared with Handel's, his career was monastic in its seclusion, experimental in its habit. Before he was ten he was furtively copying compositions of the masters of the keyboard for his own instruction. Later, he transcribed the acces-

From the author's *Bach: An Historical Approach,* by permission of the Oxford University Press.

sible scores of Palestrina, Caldara, Lotti, Vivaldi, and Legrenzi; and, of the French school, studied those of Couperin, Grigny, Dieupart, Raison, and Gaspard le Roux. England, too, came within the orbit of his curiosity. Indeed, there is little music from Palestrina onwards of which there are not copies in his industrious script. Handel, too, quarried, but with how different a purpose, appropriating themes his indolent Muse found it inconvenient to provide! But Bach, from our earliest introduction to him, confronts us as a student, almost demoniacally urged to unravel and discover the principles of his art. In no other of the great masters was this call so insistent, none who faced such obstacles to answer it. He paid his adventurous visits to those giants of the North, Böhm and Reinken, while he was still in his teens. He was hardly settled in his first employment at Arnstadt before he took French leave, and risked dismissal, in order to receive lessons from Buxtehude at Lübeck. Even in the maturity of his genius the neighborhood of a fellow craftsman drew him always to seek his acquaintance, and haply his instruction. Twice, and vainly, he sought Handel's conversation. His famous Dresden encounter with Marchand is but an example of his eagerness to learn from any who had knowledge to impart. Unremitting study and self-criticism fashioned his individual style. Indeed, if the early neglect that obscured his memory was due in part to his failure to explore the art forms then coming to birth, it was no less the result of meticulous self-discipline that refined his work beyond the comprehension of the generations that knew and followed him.

What, then, were the conditions out of which his genius emerged? Why did he express himself in the forms in which he is familiar to us? How comes it that, while Handel was fluent in opera, Bach was careless, even contemptuous, of the stage? How is it that, unlike the other masters of his period, we associate with him no new musical form? And why do we group him as the last portent of the old dispensation no less than the first of the new? These are questions which invite a historical retrospect.

In the middle age of European civilization music was the handmaid, one might say the slave, of religion. Hence its earliest expression was ecclesiastical plain-song, monodic, unisonal. But, at an early period it achieved a complex technique distinguished as polyphonic or contrapuntal, in which several melodies impose themselves on a fixed theme or *cantus,* in such a way that each voice—for the original art was vocal—adds a strand of accompanying melody to the main theme, parallel to it, consonant with it, and yet in itself complete and melodic. That it was practicable, and also agreeable, to sing two melodies together at a fixed interval, instead of one in unison or at the octave, was a discovery which sprang, we must believe, from circumstances rather than deliberate design. For men's voices, of which the mediaeval choir was composed, fall naturally into two categories, tenor and bass, pitched roughly a fourth or fifth apart. Consequently a plainsong *cantus* low enough to suit the basses might be inconvenient for the tenors, while a melody fitted to the tenors might soar too high for the basses. Hence, perhaps in the ninth century, an "inspired precentor," a recent pen has called him, had the happy thought to invite his singers to recite the *cantus* at the convenient pitch of their individual voices: a cacophony in consecutives we probably should find it, but not disagreeable to the innovator, who, unknowingly, made the first approach towards the art of weaving simultaneous melodies into a coherent whole.

So, here was a primitive descant, the chief of the strands of complex polyphony. And, since dissonance resulted where before there was consonance, the new art was named *diaphonia* (dissonance), or *organum,* after the organized voice (*vox organalis*), which sang at the fourth or fifth, while the principal voice (*vox principalis*) declaimed the foundation melody or *cantus.* Thus was brought to birth the scheme of woven melody, of vocal polyphony, of which Bach's scores afford the supreme example. It is not convenient here to trace its development in the interval, from the tiny seed to the spacious tree. But its general course is clear. In time, by experiment or accident, other intervals, the third and sixth, were found as agreeable as the fourth and fifth on which to pitch the organized voice. Or, the organized and principal voices were duplicated at the octave, thereby producing *four* moving themes. But always their motions were parallel to the *cantus;* if the *cantus* rose or fell, the *vox organalis* did so sympathetically by a precisely similar interval. But eventually, after a further interval of experiment, the *cantus* ceased to put chains on the organized voices. Strict parallelism was abandoned, free motion was attempted, the *vox orga-*

nalis moving up when the *vox principalis* moved down, and vice versa, till at length composers were able to treat the *organum* as the vehicle of independent and agreeable melody.

But, even at this stage of its development, music was separated from Bach by a chasm we might suppose unbridgeable. For to him, as to us, it predicated the correlation of three complementary factors—melody, rhythm, harmony. In elementary form the first two are as ancient as man's earliest vocal sounds. But harmony is an almost recent ingredient. For the early polyphonists did not analyze music vertically, as we do. Their preference was to build horizontal or parallel melodies, capable of simultaneous utterance, linked rhythmically, exhibiting acoustic smoothness (i. e., harmony) at certain points or cadences of repose, but elsewhere displaying a lack of harmonic relevance which, to us, is disagreeable. Still, in the sixteenth century a closer approximation to our modern harmonic system was gradually achieved, until the polyphony of the Middle Ages found its highest expression in Palestrina, a master unsurpassed by Bach himself in the noble sincerity of his art.

With Palestrina we enter a Golden Age, when musical culture was never so widespread, nor its votaries lit by a holier flame. Vocal polyphony began to move in melodious obedience to rules; and harmony, though still immature, became ordered and expressive. And yet, in their artistry, how immense an interval separates Palestrina's *Stabat Mater* from Bach's *Magnificat!* It could not astonish us if the space between them was measured in centuries. In fact, only ninety years, three generations, divide Palestrina's death in 1594 from Bach's birth in 1685. Thus, in the equipment Bach was familiar with, music reached him after a surprisingly short period of incubation. For Palestrina was barely in sight of the forms Bach employed. Music was still obedient to the limitations of religious usage and tradition, though no longer exclusively ecclesiastical in its uses. It was sung *a cappella* and was exclusively vocal; it lacked instrumental accompaniment; it demanded a choir of singers, it ignored a solo voice; the vocal aria was not invented; neither organ nor clavier had developed their technique, and the orchestra was not yet constituted. Moreover, key-consciousness had not been attained, nor was the principle of measured time comprehended. These developments were revolutionary, and they were the achievement of the bustling ninety years that separate Palestrina from Bach, in broad terms, the seventeenth century, that age of turmoil and yet of swift progress. It invented new forms of musical expression. It set instrumental music on an independent course. Beginning in bondage to the old modes, it ended by preferring the Ionian and the Aeolian—the keys of C major and A minor—and transposed them to various pitches to build our major and minor scales. A pulsing century of rapid, organized growth, perfected and crowned by the absorptive genius of Bach.

The first and crucial advance along this path of high adventure was the so-called monodic revolution, conveniently synchronous with Palestrina's death. Its impulse was the intellectual stirring we call the Renaissance, that overpowering inclination of the individual to express himself, to look out on the universe from his own windows, and no longer through the spectacles tradition and authority had fixed on his nose. Thus impelled, and seeking to become the vehicle of individual emotion, music demanded fresh modes of utterance, new forms in which to interpret the aspirations and accomplishments of the human mind. Concretely, the pioneers of the "New Music," as these sixteenth century rebels against tradition styled it, asked that music should no longer decorate only the unemotional corporate worship of the Church Catholic, but should equip itself to interpret secular themes, no longer in the staid formulas of the ecclesiastical *cantus,* but in dramatic periods as naturally inflected as the tones of an actor. In a word, the individual, who so far had been submerged in the collective voice, now claimed a medium appropriate to his self-expression.

But the distinction of Giovanni Bardi and his fellow innovators is not so much that they introduced unisonous dramatic forms—the recitative and aria—as that they sponsored them in the Academies, in which till now polyphony alone was admitted and taught. So here is the convenient starting point of modern music. Only six years after Palestrina's death, Jacopo Peri produced (1600) his *Eurydice* at Florence, the first notable work of an operatic school which maintained its continuity, though not its monopoly, thenceforward till the era of Verdi and Puccini. And, with suggestive coincidence—for the two forms are scarcely distinguishable—the same year witnessed the Roman production of Emilio de' Cavalieri's *Rappresentazione di anima e di corpo,* with scenery, dresses, action and recitative, closely similar to Peri's work in form and style. Thus in Italy modern opera and modern oratorio came to birth simultaneously. And in Italy opera survived. But oratorio, deserting the land of its origin, fared northward, and eventually mated with the genius of Bach.

Meanwhile, the potentialities of instrumental music were not overlooked by the revolutionary Florentines—indeed the word Sonata, signifying music mechanically sounded, came into simultaneous vogue with Cantata, the new music sung by the human voice. Monteverde (d. 1643) boldly employed every instrumental resource at his disposal to elaborate his operatic scheme, and for purely instrumental effects. So, the orchestra discovered an independent rôle. And conveniently and coincidently, superseding the antique viols, the violin family presented it with its most cherished and effective member.

Probably few of us realize how recent was the vogue of the violin in Bach's lifetime. It is not found in a music score before 1587. Andrea Amati, who first gave it a form distinguished from the treble viol, died (c. 1580) a century before Bach's birth. But Antonio Stradivari, the greatest of the Cremona makers, was his contemporary and predeceased him (d. 1737) by only thirteen years. Giovanni Battista Vitali, the earliest master of violin sonata-form, died (1692) when Bach was a schoolboy at Eisenach. Giuseppe Torelli (d. 1708), whose *Concerti grossi* established the features Bach himself accepted, published (1709) them actually after Bach had reached manhood. Arcangelo Corelli died (1713) while Bach was in service at Weimar, and his favorite Antonio Vivaldi (d. 1743) preceded him to the grave by only seven years. With his contemporary, the brilliant Giuseppe Tartini (1692–1770), Bach, perhaps, was not familiar. But the Italian school of violin-playing culminated in him, and greatly surpassed the prevalent standards; to what an extent is revealed by the fact that, when Corelli's sonatas reached Paris in 1753, three years after Bach's death, not a violinist is said to have been found there with ability to play them! The statement, if correct, permits us to relate Bach's technique to that of his period.

If Bach's instrumental music largely declares an Italian parentage, his clavier works associate him with another national school. For their models he looked principally to France, and his introduction to them at Celle was an early experience of his career. France's musical Renaissance expressed itself in the clavier Suite. The word is French, but the music it denotes was not localized. It everywhere comprehended a string of dance measures whose characteristics were their profusion and diversity. Their contrasts, no doubt, originated the idea of bringing a number of them together in what became the earliest cyclic art form. At the outset no rigid principle selected the movements admitted to the suite. But, by the middle of the seventeenth century, four had established a universal claim for inclusion—the German *Allemande*, the French-Italian *Courante*, the Spanish *Saraband*, and the Italian *Gigue*. You find them, and in that order, in Bach's suites and partitas, in the whole eighteen of which the gigue is only once missing as the final movement. Arrangements of this kind bore no general title. In England they were called "Lessons" (as by Handel and John Christian Bach); in Germany "Partitas" or "Partien" (as by Bach); in France "Suites" and "Ordres"; in Italy "Sonatas." But the French composers, especially François Couperin and Jean-Baptiste Lully, so identified the form with their own country that Bach not only took them as his models, but distinguished his own compositions with a French label.

On other grounds Bach was attracted to Couperin, though hardly indebted to him. As he demonstrated in the famous "Forty-Eight," his adoption of equal temperament for the clavier enabled him to play in every key, minor and major, and so brought the neglected black notes into use. But this innovation, along with the complexity of his music, necessarily jettisoned the old system of fingering, which kept the thumb and every finger but the second and third on each hand normally out of action. Bach, on the contrary, gave the thumb its regular function in the scale and made the neglected fourth finger pull its weight. Couperin also devised a system which brought the thumb into use, though in a less methodical way. But his treatise was not published till 1717, and Bach cannot have been indebted to it. Yet, there are clear proofs that his French contemporary—Couperin died in 1733—interested him deeply and had his admiration.

France's influence on Bach is otherwise revealed. His Suite or Overture in B minor, published in 1735, consists, like his French Suites, of dance movements. But it differs in that it opens with a slow introduction followed by a fugal allegro, as do his orchestral overtures and those Handel wrote for the stage. The form is that of the classic opera overture as Lully wrote it, and as it continued till Gluck reformed it after Bach's death.

Bach's intellectual curiosity was insatiable, and, excepting Beethoven, unique among the masters. The compulsion of curiosity which dragged him as a youth to Hamburg and Lübeck, invited him to his contest with Marchand, and twice set him on the road in pursuit of Handel, moved him as urgently to investigate the music of other countries. And his larger suites for the clavier appear to indicate that the English school was not unfamiliar to him. They were known to his sons as the "English Suites," Forkel gathered, because they were written for an Englishman of rank, an obvious conjecture but improbable solution. Another explanation has been found in the fact that the first Suite opens on the theme of a Gigue by Charles Dieupart, a popular French harpsichordist in London during Bach's early manhood. But I think a more satisfactory explanation can be deduced from the fact that, unlike their French fellows, each English Suite begins with a prelude, as do those of Henry Purcell and his precursors. Since Bach was acquainted with Dieupart, Purcell would hardly be unknown to him—indeed attributed to him in the Bachgesellschaft Edition is a Toccata and Fugue by Purcell, the only Englishman whose place among the great masters is universally conceded. It is agreeable to reflect that Bach knew English music at a period of distinction it has never excelled, but to-day boldly and confidently soars to approach.

So, with one reservation, the ancestry of Bach's keyboard and instrumental music is French and Italian. But that of his vocal works is uncompromisingly German. They reveal him, indeed, as the very flower of the German Renaissance, the greatest voice out of Germany after Luther, and, in his most serious aspect, Luther's corollary. That he should have emerged at this period is the more remarkable when we reflect on Germany's musical insignificance to this point. Herself an unwieldy system of noncohering states, lacking a common pivot, political or artistic, and controlled by no national instinct, she had so far reacted feebly to those impulses shaping musical culture elsewhere. Moreover, early in the century of Bach's birth she plunged into the vortex of the Thirty Years' War, and emerged from it less than forty years before he saw the light. Yet, so soon as the Treaty of Westphalia gave peace, even a nebulous unity, to her disjointed system, at a bound she achieved sovereignty in the realm of music. It was, however, not in Handel's operas and operatic oratorios that her new voice was heard, but in utterances of noble elevation in which Bach's genius displayed itself—the passion, cantata, choral. Let me indicate concisely the paths by which they reached him.

Sir Hubert Parry once deduced, from her late submission to it, that Germany was less apt for music than her neighbors. Charles Burney came to that conclusion twenty-five years after Bach's death. In truth, music tardily fired Germany's soul, not as an aesthetic experience, but as the vehicle of religious emotion. It has been said that the German Renaissance is only another name for the German Reformation. Certainly it is so in the sphere of music, where the choral and cantata as clearly express Germany's Renaissance culture as the galleries of Italy or the drama of England reveal the peculiar genius of their peoples.

The Reformation stemmed the tide of church music in Germany along the channels it so far had followed. For the Evangelical Church rejected the musical apparatus of the ancient creed along with its dogma and ritual, preferring its music, like its liturgy, to be congregational in form and utterance. Luther set the new course in his *Achtliederbuch*, the first Lutheran hymn-book, published in 1524, the source of an expanding stream of dignified hymnody which is Lutheran Germany's proudest heritage—"the *Feste Burg* of German music," Sir Charles Stanford appropriately called it. Thus, reaching out on one side to the severe plain-song of the Latin Church, and, on the other, to popular folksong from which it did not disdain to borrow, the choral was deep rooted in the affection of the German people within a century of Luther's death, and fed the genius of her composers. Set in four-part harmony, it assisted the development of a new harmonic structure. And, since it was essentially the apparatus of religion, it aided and inspired the organist to develop and perfect his technique.

So, in the critical ninety years between Palestrina's death and the birth of Bach the choral became the most vital factor in Germany's musical experience. Of the cantata, passion, oratorio, motet, organ prelude, fugue, and variation, it controlled the form and supplied the material. Bach's art is inextricably associated with it. His earliest and his last work as a composer was based on it. All the chorals in common use he harmonized with matchless skill. They are rarely absent from his cantatas and oratorios. They provide the core of his passions, the most intimate part of his motets. His organ technique was developed on them, and they are the theme of the bulk of his music for that instrument. In brief, he associated them with all he did in the service of God, embellishing them like precious jewels in a holy shrine.

Historically, as its name declares, the cantata was Italian. But for the composition the word came to denote Bach preferred the term "Concerto," invented early in the seventeenth century to distinguish new style concerted music from plain-song monotone. To Giacomo Carissimi, who died only eleven years (1674) before Bach's birth, are referred its distinctive features—the association of declamatory recitatives, solo arias, and orchestral interludes in a short work suitable for the Church or concert room. In this shape it passed from Italy to Germany, where it was forthwith admitted to the Lutheran liturgy, in which, at first, its use seems to have been restricted to festival occasions. But it soon established itself as the *Hauptmusik* of the Sunday morning service. The earlier German cantatas, however, those of Albert, Schütz, or Hammerschmidt, for instance, were modeled rather on the chamber cantata and had little affinity with Bach's massive compositions, except in their use of the choral. For he brought to their creation the elaborate technique he had acquired already on the organ. Yet, their virtuosity is not their most distinctive characteristic. For, they were heard in a form of public prayer closely coördinated. It pivoted on the Gospel for the Day; the opening motet anticipated it, the hymns were based on it, so was the sermon, whose text was taken from it, and so was the cantata that preceded it. Thus, Bach's cantatas are not wholly intelligible to us unless we realize that, when writing them, he placed himself in the pulpit, as it were, to expound the Gospel text in terms of music. To the task he brought a mind well versed in theological dialectics, and, with it, a devout spirit as profound as it was sincere, resolved to give his exposition the most persuasive force of which his art was capable. His cantatas might aptly be termed his sermons; for, in intention, they are no less.

The masses have the design and derivation of the cantatas—they apply the new style to portions of the liturgy formerly polyphonic. Bach's Mass in B minor, in effect, consists of three cantatas, the "Kyrie,"

"Gloria," and "Credo," with an epilogue. The *Magnificat,* also, is an elaborate cantata, and in its first state actually was punctuated with chorals. But the motets and passions are in another category. Their ancestry, in the one case, is patently German, and, in the other, that strain predominates. Bach's motets are distinguished from his cantatas in form and in purpose. They are *a cappella* music, exclude the solo aria, dramatic recitative, operatic orchestra, and are the finest flower of his polyphonic technique. But their austerity was the consequence of their usage. For, with one possible exception, they are funeral music, *Trauermusik.* Bach's talented relatives Johann Christoph and Johann Michael wrote similar motets, and so did his predecessors in the Leipzig Cantorate. As we have it in Bach's authorship, therefore, the motet is patently of German ancestry, an interesting association of the polyphonic tradition with the Lutheran ritual.

The passion music also sprang from a German source. For the custom of chanting the passion story in Holy Week was ancient, and Luther's conservatism retained it. At Leipzig its performance took place at Vespers on Good Friday afternoon, either in St. Thomas's or in the sister church of St. Nicholas. But the elaborate compositions Bach wrote were only in Leipzig's very recent experience. Until 1721 the setting used was contemporary with Luther! Leipzig heard the first "musicirt Passion" (a composition which, like Bach's, employed the resources of the new style) only two years before Bach came to St. Thomas's. His *St. John Passion,* performed in 1723, was but the second of its kind performed at Leipzig, where conservative feeling was scandalized by the trespass of opera upon a domain so sacred.

Assuredly Bach did not merit this resentment; it is his distinction to have rescued the passion from the trappings of the theatre, and to have placed it, in its noblest form, at the service of religion. For the spirit that animated Palestrina passed from Italy when opera was born, and the modern oratorio, of which Bach's are the perfect example, was begotten of the exiled Italian tradition by its union with the passion music of Germany. They first met in Heinrich Schütz, the earliest German composer to free himself from Italian conventions and so to evolve a national style. Born exactly one hundred years before Bach, he exhibits in his passions a reverent emotionalism which makes him Bach's direct ancestor. He admits no arias, uses no reflective chorals.

But his recitative is flexible, his choruses are terse and dramatic, and, like Bach, he sets forth his text with reverent restraint. In a word, we first detect in him the serious purpose which is the characteristic of German music. But a generation later the influence of opera, established and vigorous at Hamburg, threatened to deflect the passion from its dignified and appropriate course. In 1704 Reinhard Keiser, a man eleven years Bach's senior, produced there a dramatic passion which contemptuously discarded the Bible text, ejected the choral, and unfolded the narrative in conventional rhymed stanzas. Some of his imitators even inserted stage directions in the text! Thus, when Bach took office at Leipzig in 1723 the German passion was in critical peril. It is not the least of his achievements to have rescued it from Hamburg's contaminating secularism and completely to have vindicated the German tradition. He reinstated the Bible text, infused a religious intention into the secular forms oratorio borrowed from opera, elevated the choral to a height of emotional appeal it had not yet attained, and produced a masterpiece, dramatic, but essentially devotional. Its technical majesty excites our homage. But chiefly we bow before the fact that it affords a presentation of the Bible story deeply pondered, supremely reverent, fundamentally devotional.

Of all the forms in which Bach expressed himself oratorio and fugue were the modes of utterance most attuned to his nature. His fugues are unique because, among his predecessors and contemporaries, he alone fully realized the romantic and artistic possibilities of the fugal form. His personality is behind every bar of them. They are the poetry of a master who found it natural and congenial to express himself in that form. His relation to the fugue, in fact, is that of Beethoven to the sonata, or of Haydn to the quartet.

A natural adaptation of the vocal canonic form, the fugue reached Bach through German models, though Forkel names the Italian Frescobaldi among those he studied. In an earlier generation the contrapuntist Andrea Gabrieli (d. 1586) had been remarkable. Through his pupil Pieter Sweelink his technique passed directly to Georg Böhm and Johann Reinken, and so to Bach, who sat at the feet of both of them. Bach was also in intimate contact with the two masters of his early years, Johann Pachelbel and Dietrich Buxtehude. Of the former his eldest brother and teacher was the pupil, and to hear the second he journeyed to Lübeck in his teens, might indeed have succeeded him there if the charms of Fräulein Buxtehude had sufficiently assisted her father's design! From these mentors he received the principles of his own more brilliant art. But, till he expounded it by rule and example, the fugue was a contrapuntal, soulless exercise. Among its masters Bach had high regard for Johann Josef Fux of Vienna, whose *Gradus ad Parnassum,* published in 1725, was a standard manual. But in Fux's hands the fugue was a mechanical and lifeless exercise. "First choose a subject suitable to the key you intend to compose in," he directs, "and write it down in that part in which you propose to begin. Then repeat the subject in the second part, either at the interval of a fourth or fifth, adding such notes in the first part as will agree with it." And so on, with the prosaic precision of a cookery-book! Still, sanctioned in the generation that preceded Bach's birth, these elementary prescriptions afforded the foundation on which he reared his more splendid art. Applying the expanded key-system of his *Well-tempered Clavier,* and enriching his themes with a wealth of melody and contrapuntal resource the fugue had never experienced, Bach evolved a nervous organism out of Fux's skeleton and fashioned a poem from an exercise.

We have reviewed, very inadequately, the language in which Bach worked. And what is our conclusion? He spoke in forms that are now archaic. He invented no new one. None was more firmly linked with the past than he, none more obedient to its conventions. No other of the great composers was so mediaeval in the circumstances of his life. He spent it in one corner of Germany, and for the last twenty-five years of it never, save once, travelled above a hundred miles from his center. Indeed, he worked in such artistic isolation, was so shut in upon himself, had such little opportunity to test his genius by experiment, that we must suppose him driven to compose by sheer compulsion from within.

But, mediaeval though he was in the forms in which he expressed himself, his technical skill in them remains unique and unsurpassed. No one has approached him in the miraculous complexity of his part-writing, or in his ingenuity in weaving melodic strands into a single fabric. No one equally displays his gift of melody, his sense of form, the virile quality of his themes, the boldness of his technique, even the daring of his harmonic coloring. Thus, even within the forms he used,

Bach is dateless, his art perennial, immortalized by the intense individualism that informed it. Directed by a faith childlike in its simplicity, he used it to interpret the infinite, saw the heavens opened, and was prophetically oracular. Only Beethoven approaches him in this quality, and both stand upon a peak of wonder. From Mozart onwards his peers have done homage to his example, even in forms he never knew. So, he belongs to no age, at once remote from us and yet intimately close. Schumann summed him up in a sentence: "Music owes as much to Bach as a religion to its founder."

IV
HANDEL

GEORG FRIEDRICH HÄNDEL

Born at Halle, February 23, 1685. Early career as organ virtuoso and composer of operas in the Italian style in Italy and Germany. Settled in London c. 1716 where his patron was George I; naturalized in 1726 and anglicized his name to George Frederic Handel. Director of Royal Academy of Music; as the vogue for his operas declined he turned to oratorio in English c. 1740, restoring himself to fame and fortune. Died April 14, 1759, and was buried in Westminster Abbey.

PRINCIPAL WORKS

VOCAL: 40 operas, including *Rinaldo; Radamisto* (Zenobia); *Lotario; Xerxes* (Serse); *Faramondo; Dedamia; Julius Caesar.* 19 oratorios, including *The Messiah; Athalia; Deborah; Esther; Saul; Israel in Egypt; Samson; Semele; Joseph; Belshazzar; Heracles; Judas Maccabaeus; Joshua; Solomon; Susannah; Theodora; The Choice of Heracles; Jephtha.* Other vocal music includes the settings of Dryden's *Ode for St. Cecelia's Day*, Milton's *L'Allegro* and *Il Penseroso;* the masque *Acis and Galatea;* early oratorios, operas, and a passion.

INSTRUMENTAL: 12 organ concertos; 12 concerti grossi for strings; suites for full orchestra, including *Water Music, Fireworks Music,* etc.; concertos for various instruments; sonatas for violin, viola, oboe, etc.; many preludes, fugues, etc., for organ.

HANDEL

By Romain Rolland

NO great musician is more impossible to include in the limits of one definition, or even of several, than Handel. It is a fact that he reached the complete mastery of his style very early (much earlier than J. S. Bach), although it was never really fixed, and he never devoted himself to any one form of art. It is even difficult to see a conscious and a logical evolution in him. His genius is not of the kind which follows a single path, and forges right ahead until it reaches its object. For his aim is no other than to do well whatever he undertook. All ways are good to him—from his early steps at the crossing of the ways, he dominated the country, and shed his light on all sides, without laying siege to any particular part. He is not one of those who impose on life and art a voluntary idealism, either violent or patient; nor is he one of those who inscribe in the book of life the formula of their campaign. He is of the kind who drink in the life universal, assimilating it to themselves. His artistic will is mainly objective. His genius adapts itself to a thousand images of passing events, to the nation, to the times in which he lived, even to the fashions of his day. It accommodates itself to the various influences, ignoring all obstacles. It weighs other styles and other thoughts, but such is the power of assimilation and the prevailing equilibrium of his nature that he never feels submerged and overweighted by the mass of these strange elements. Everything is duly absorbed, controlled, and classified. This immense soul is like the sea itself, into which all the rivers of the world pour themselves without troubling its serenity.

The German geniuses have often had this power of absorbing

From the author's *Handel*, by permission of the author and of Henry Holt and Co.

thoughts and strange forms, but it is excessively rare to find amongst them the grand objectivism, and this superior impersonality, which is. so to speak, the hallmark of Handel. Their sentimental lyricism is better fitted to sing songs, to voice the thoughts of the universe in song, than to paint the universe in living forms and vital rhythms. Handel is very different, and approaches much more nearly than any other in Germany the genius of the South, the Homeric genius of which Goethe received the sudden revelation on his arrival at Naples. This capacious mind looks out on the whole universe, and on the way the universe depicts itself, as a picture is reflected in calm and clear water. He owes much of this objectivism to Italy, where he spent many years, and the fascination of which never effaced itself from his mind, and he owes even more to that sturdy England, which guards its emotions with so tight a rein, and which eschews those sentimental and effervescing effusions, so often displayed in the pious German art; but that he had all the germs of his art in himself, is already shown in his early works at Hamburg.

From his infancy at Halle, Zachau had trained him not in one style, but in all the styles of the different nations, leading him to understand not only the spirit of each great composer, but to assimilate the styles by writing in various manners. This education, essentially cosmopolitan, was completed by his three tours in Italy, and his sojourn of half a century in England. Above all he never ceased to follow up the lessons learnt at Halle, always appropriating to himself the best from all artists and their works. If he was never in France (it is not absolutely proved), he knew her nevertheless. He was anxious to master the French language and musical style. We have proofs of that in his manuscripts, and in the accusations made against him by certain French critics. Wherever he passed, he gathered some musical souvenir, buying and collecting foreign works, copying them, or rather (for he had not the careful patience of J. S. Bach, who scrupulously wrote out in his own hand the entire scores of French organists and the Italian violinists) copying down in hasty and often inexact expressions any idea which struck him in the course of reading. This vast collection of European thoughts, which only remains in remnants at the Fitzwilliam Museum at Cambridge, was the reservoir, so to speak, from which his creative genius continually fed itself. Profoundly German in race and character, he had become a world citizen, like his compatriot Leibnitz, whom he had known at Hanover, a European with a tendency for the Latin culture. The great Germans at the end of that century, Goethe and Herder, were never more free, or more universal, than this great Saxon in music, saturated as he was with all the artistic thoughts of the West.

He drew not only from the sources of learned and refined music—the music of musicians; but also drank deeply from the founts of popular music—that of the most simple and rustic folk. He loved the latter. One finds noted down in his manuscripts the street cries of London, and he once told a friend that he received many inspirations for his best airs from them. Certain of his oratorios, like *L'Allegro ed Il Penseroso,* are threaded with remembrances of his walks in the English country, and who can ignore the *Pifferari* (Italian peasant's pipe) in *The Messiah,* the Flemish carillon in *Saul,* the joyous popular Italian songs in *Hercules,* and in *Alexander Balus?* Handel was not an artist lost in introspection. He watched all around him, he listened, and observed. Sight was for him a source of inspiration, hardly of less importance than hearing. I do not know any great German musician who has been as much a visual as Handel. Like Hasse and Corelli, he had a veritable passion for beautiful pictures. He hardly ever went out without going to a theatre or a picture sale. He was a connoisseur, and he made a collection, in which some Rembrandts were found after his death. It has been remarked that his blindness (which should have rendered his hearing still more sensitive, his creative powers translating everything into sonorous dreams) soon paralyzed his hearing when its principal source of renewal was withdrawn.

Thus, saturated in all the European music of his time, impregnated with the music of musicians, and the still richer music which flows in all Nature herself, which is specially diffused in the vibrations of light and shade, that song of the rivers, of the forest, of the birds, in which all his work abounds and which have inspired some of his most picturesque pages with a semi-romantic color, he wrote as one speaks, he composed as one breathes. He never sketched out on paper in order to prepare his definite work. He wrote straight off as he improvised, and in truth he seems to have been the greatest improviser that ever was. He wrote his music with such an impetuosity of feeling, and such a wealth of ideas, that his hand was constantly lagging behind his thoughts, and in order to keep apace with them at all he had to note them down in an abbreviated manner. But (and this seems contradictory) he had at the same time an exquisite sense of form. No German surpassed him in the art of writing beautiful, melodic lines. Mozart and Hasse alone were his equals in this. It was to this love of perfection that we attribute that habit which, despite his fertility of invention, causes him to use time after time the same phrases (those most important, and dearest to him), each time introducing an imperceptible change, a light stroke of the pencil, which renders them more perfect. The examination of these kinds of musical *eaux-fortes* in their successive states is very instructive for the musician who is interested in plastic beauty. It shows also how certain melodies, once written down, continued to slumber in Handel's mind for many years, until they had penetrated his subconscious nature, were applied at first, by following the chances of inspiration, to a certain situation, which suited them moderately well. They are, so to speak, in search of a body where they can reincarnate themselves, seeking the true situation, the real sentiment of which they are but the latent expression; and once having found it, they expand themselves with ease.

Handel worked no less with the music of other composers than with his own. If one had the time to study here what superficial readers have called his plagiarisms, particularly taking, for example, *Israel in Egypt,* where the most barefaced of these cases occur, one would see with what genius and insight Handel has evoked from the depths of these musical phrases, their secret soul, of which the first creators had not even a presentiment. It needed his eye, or his ear, to discover in the serenade of Stradella its Biblical cataclysms. Each read and heard a work of art as it is, and yet not as it is; and one may conclude that it is not always the creator himself who has the most fertile idea of it. The example of Handel well proves this. Not only did he create music, but very often he created that of others for them. Stradella and Erba were only for him (however humiliating the comparison) the flames of fire, and the cracks in the wall, through which Leonardo saw the living figures. Handel heard great storms passing through the gentle quivering of Stradella's guitar.

This evocatory character of Handel's genius should never be forgotten. He who is satisfied with listening to this music without *seeing* what it expresses—who judges this art as a purely formal art, and who does not feel his expressive and suggestive power, occasionally so far as hallucination, will never understand it. It is a music which paints emotions, souls, and situations, to see the epochs and the places, which are the framework of the emotions, and which tint them with their own peculiar moral tone. In a word, his is an art essentially picturesque and dramatic. . . . The intimate sense of his works was falsified in the century which followed his death by the English interpretations, strengthened further still in Germany by those of Mendelssohn, and his numerous following. By the exclusion of and systematic contempt for all the operas of Handel, by an elimination of nearly all the dramatic oratorios, the most powerful and the freshest, by a narrow choice more and more restrained to the four or five oratorios, and even here, by giving an exaggerated supremacy to *The Messiah,* by the interpretation finally of these works, and notably of *The Messiah,* in a pompous, rigid and stolid manner, with an orchestra and choir far too numerous and badly balanced, with singers frightfully correct and pious, without any feeling or intimacy, there has been established the tradition which makes Handel a church musician after the style of Louis XIV, all decoration —pompous columns, noble and cold statues, and pictures by Le Brun. It is not surprising that this has reduced works executed on such principles, and degraded them to a monumental tiresomeness similar to that which emanates from the bewigged Alexanders, and the very conventional Christs of Le Brun.

It is necessary to turn back. Handel was never a church musician, and he hardly ever wrote for the church. Apart from his *Psalms* and his *Te Deum,* composed for the private chapels, and for exceptional events, he only wrote instrumental music for concerts and for open-air fêtes, for operas, and for those so-called oratorios, which were really written for the theatre. The first oratorios he composed were acted. And if Handel resolutely abstained from theatrical representation—which alone gives the full value to certain scenes, such as the orgy and the dream of Belshazzar, expressly conceived for acting—on the other hand he stood out firmly for having his oratorios at the theatre and not in the church. There were not wanting churches any less than dissenting chapels in which he could give his works, and by not doing so he turned against him the opinion of religious people who considered it sacrilegious to carry pious subjects on the stage, but he continued to affirm that he did not write compositions for the church, but worked for the theatre—a free theatre.

It remains for us, after having attempted to indicate the general characteristics of Handel's art, to sketch the technique of the different styles in which he worked.

To speak truly, it is difficult to speak of the opera or of the oratorio of Handel. It is necessary to say: *of the operas or of the oratorios,* for we do not find that they point back to any single type. We can verify here what we said at the commencement of this chapter, about the magnificent vitality of Handel in choosing amongst his art forms the different directions of the music of his times.

All the European tendencies at that time are reflected in his operas: the model of Keiser in his early works, the Venetian model in his *Agripina,* the model of Scarlatti and Steffani in his first early operas; in the London works he soon introduces English influences, particularly in the rhythms. Then it was Bononcini whom he rivalled. Again, those great attempts of genius to create a new musical drama, *Guilo Cesare, Tamerlano, Orlando;* later on, those charming ballet-operas inspired by France, *Ariodante, Alcina;* later still, those operas which point towards the *opéra comique* and the light style of the second half of the century, *Serse Deidamia.* . . . Handel continued to try every other style without making any permanent choice as did Gluck, with whom alone he can be compared.

One sees what a variety of forms and styles he used. Handel was too universal and too objective to believe that one kind of art only was the true one. He believed in two kinds of music only, the good and the bad. Apart from that he appreciated all styles. Thus he has left masterpieces in every style, but he did not open any new way in opera for the simple reason that he went a long way in nearly all paths already opened up. Constantly he experimented, invented, and always with his singularly sure touch. He seemed to have an extraordinary penetrating knowledge in invention, and consequently few artistic regions remained for him to conquer. He made as masterly a use of the recitative as Gluck, or of the *arioso* as Mozart, writing the acts of *Tamerlano* which are the closest and the most heartrending dramas, in the manner of *Iphigénie en Tauride,* the most moving and passionate scenes in music such as certain pages of *Admeto* and *Orlando,* where the humorous and the tragic are intermingled in the manner of *Don Giovanni.* He has experimented very happily here in new rhythms. There were new forms, the dramatic duet or quartet, the descriptive symphony opening the opera, refined orchestration, choruses and dances. Nothing seems to have obsessed him. In the following opera we find him returning to the ordinary forms of the Italian or German opera of his time.

Still less can we say that he held to a rigid form with his operas, which were continually adapted to the changing tastes of the theatre public of his age, and of the singers which he had at his disposal, but when he left the opera for the oratorio he varied no less. It was a perpetual experiment of new forms in the vast framework of the free theatre (*theatre en liberté*) of the concert drama; and the sort of instinctive ebb and flow in creation seems to have caused his works to succeed one another in groups of analogous or related compositions, each work in a nearly opposite style of feeling and form. In each one Handel indulged momentarily in a certain side of his feelings, and when that was finished he found himself in the possession of other feelings which had been accumulating whilst he was drawing on the first. He thus kept up a perpetual balance, which is like the pulsation of life itself. After the realistic *Saul* comes the impersonal epic of *Israel in Egypt.* After this colossal monument appear the two *genre* pictures, *The Ode for St. Cecilia's Day* and *L'Allegro ed Il Penseroso.* After the Herculean *Samson,* a heroic and popular tragic comedy sprang forth, the charming flower of *Semele,* an opera of romanticism and gallantry.

But if the oratorios are so wonderfully varied they have one characteristic in common even more than the operas; they are musical dramas. It was not that religious thought turned Handel to this choice of Biblical subjects, but as Kretzschmar has well shown, it was on account of the stories of the Bible heroes being a part of the very life-blood of the people whom he addressed. They were known to all, whilst the ancient romantic stories could only interest a society of refined and spoilt dilettanti. Without doubt, these oratorios were not made for representation, did not seek scenic effects, with rare exceptions, as for instance the scene of the orgy of *Belshazzar,* where one feels that Handel had drawn on the direct vision of theatrical representation, but passions, spirits and personalities were represented always in a dramatic fashion. Handel is a great painter of characters, and the Delilah in *Samson,* the Nitocris in *Belshazzar,* the Cleopatra in *Alexander Balus,* the mother in *Solomon,* the Dejanira in *Hercules,* the beautiful Theodora, all bear witness to the suppleness and the profundity of his psychological genius. If in the course of the action, and the depicting of the ordinary sentiments, he abandoned himself freely to the flow of pure music, in the moments of passionate crises he is the equal of the greatest masters in musical drama. Is it necessary to mention the terrible scenes in the third act of *Hercules,* the beautiful scenes of *Alexander Balus,* the Dream of *Belshazzar,* the prison scenes in *Theodora,* or in the first act of *Saul,* and dominating all, like great pictures, certain of the choruses of *Israel in Egypt,* in *Esther* and in *Joshua,* and in *Chandos Anthems,* which seem veritable tempests of passion, great upheavals of overpowering effect? It is by these choruses that the oratorio is essentially distinguished from the opera. It is in the first place a choral tragedy. These choruses, which are nearly eliminated in Italian opera during the time of the Barberini, held a very important place in French opera, but their rôle was limited to that of commentator or else merely decorative. In the oratorio of Handel they became the very life and soul of the work. Sometimes they took the part of the ancient classical chorus, which exposed the thought of the drama when the hidden fates led on the heroes to their destinies—as in *Saul, Hercules, Alexander Balus, Susannah.* Sometimes they added to the shock of human passions the powerful appeal of religion, and crowned the human drama with a supernatural aureole, as in *Theodora* and *Jephtha.* Or finally they became the actual actors themselves, or the enemy-people and the God who guided them. It is remarkable that in his very first oratorio, *Esther,* Handel had this stroke of genius. In the choruses there we see the drama of an oppressed people and their God who led them by his voice superbly depicted. In *Deborah* and *Athaliah* also, two nations are in evidence. In *Belshazzar* there are three, but his chief work of this kind, *Israel in Egypt,* the greatest choral epic which exists, is entirely occupied by Jehovah and His people.

The oratorio being a "free theatre," it becomes necessary for the music to supply the place of the scenery. Thus its picturesque and descriptive rôle is strongly developed and it is by this above all that Handel's genius so struck the English public. Camille Saint-Saëns wrote in an interesting letter to C. Bellaigue, "I have come to the conclusion that it is the picturesque and descriptive side, until then novel and unreached, whereby Handel achieved the astonishing favor which he enjoyed. This masterly way of writing choruses, of treating the fugue, had been done by others. What really counts with him is the color— that modern element which we no longer hear in him. . . . He knew nothing of exotism. But look at *Alexander's Feast, Israel in Egypt,* and especially *L'Allegro ed Penseroso,* and try to forget all that has been done since. You find at every turn a striving for the picturesque, for an effect of imitation. It is real and very intense for the medium in which it is produced, and it seems to have been unknown hitherto."

Perhaps Saint-Saëns lays too much weight on the "masterly way of writing his choruses," which was not so common in England, even with Purcell. Perhaps he accentuates too much also the real influence of the French in matters of picturesque and descriptive music and the influence which it exerted on Handel. Finally, it is not necessary to represent these descriptive tendencies of Handel as exceptional in his time. A great breath of nature passed over German music, and pushed it towards tone-painting. Telemann was, even more than Handel, a painter in music, and was more celebrated than Handel for his realistic effects. But the England of the eighteenth century had remained very conservative in music, and had devoted itself to cultivating the masters of the past. Handel's art was then more striking to them on account of "its color" and "its imitative effects." I will not say with Saint-Saëns that "there was no question of exotism with him," for Handel seems to have sought this very thing more than once; notably in the orchestration of certain scenes for the two Cleopatras, of *Guilo Cesare,* and of *Alexander Balus.* But that which was constantly with him was tone-painting, the reproduction through passages of music of natural impressions, a painting very characteristic, and, as Beethoven put it, "more an expression of feelings than painting," a poetic evocation of the raging tempests, of the tranquillity of the sea, of the dark shades of night, of the twilight which envelops the English country, of the parks by moonlight, of the sunrise in springtime, and of the awakening of birds.

Acis and Galatea, Israel in Egypt, Allegro, The Messiah, Solomon, all offer a wondrous picture gallery of nature, carefully noted by Handel with the sure stroke of a Flemish painter, and of a romantic poet at the same time. This romanticism struck powerfully on his time with a strength which would not be denied. It drew upon him both admiration and violent criticism. A letter of 1751 depicts him as a Berlioz or Wagner, raising storms by his orchestra and chorus.

"He cannot give people pleasure after the proper fashion," writes this anonymous author in his letter, "and his evil genius will not allow him to do this. He imagines a new *grandioso* kind of music, and in order to make more noise he has it executed by the greatest number of voices and instruments which one has ever heard before in a theatre. He thinks thus to rival not only the god of musicians, but even all the other gods, like Iöle, Neptune, and Jupiter: for either I expected that the house would be brought down by his tempest, or that the sea would engulf the whole. But more unbearable still was his thunder. Never have such terrible rumblings fallen on my head."

Similarly Goethe, irritated and upset, said, after having heard the first movement of the Beethoven C minor Symphony, "It is meaningless. One expected the house to fall about one's ears."

It is not by chance that I couple the names of Handel and Beethoven. Handel is a kind of Beethoven in chains. He had the unapproachable manner like the great Italian artists who surrounded him: the Porporas, the Hasses; and between him and them there was a whole world. Under the classic ideal with which he covered himself burned a romantic genius, precursor of the *Sturm und Drang* period; and sometimes this hidden demon broke out in brusque fits of passion—perhaps despite itself.

The orchestral music of Handel comprises twelve *Concerti Grossi* (1740), the six Oboe Concertos (1734), the Symphonies from his operas, oratorios, and his open-air music—*Water Music* (1715 or 1717), *Firework Music* (1749)—and *Concerti* for two horns.

Although Handel was in art a visualist, and though his music had a highly descriptive and evocatory power, he made only a very restrained use of instrumental tone-color. However, he showed on occasion a refined intelligence in its use. The two oratorios written at Rome when he found himself in the society of the Cardinal Ottoboni, and his great virtuoso works, *The Triumph of Time* and *The Resurrection* of 1708, have a fine and well-varied orchestration. In London he was one of the first to introduce the use of the horn into the orchestra of the opera. "He was the first," says Volbach, "to assert the expressive personality of the violoncello." From the viola he knew how to secure many curious effects of indefinite and disquieting half-tones, he gave to the bassoons a lugubrious and fantastic character, he experimented with new instruments, small and great, he used the drum (*tambour*) solo in a dramatic fashion for Jupiter's oath in *Semele*. For special situations, by instrumental tone-colors, he secures effects not only of dramatic expression, but also of exotism and local color. It is so in the two scenes from the two Cleopatras, *Guilo Cesare* (1724) and *Alexander Balus* (1748).

But great painter as Handel was, he did not work so much through the brilliancy, variety, and novelty of his tone-colors as by the beauty of his designs, and his effects of light and shade. With a voluntarily restrained palette, and by satisfying himself with the sober colors of the strings, he yet was able to produce surprising and thrilling effects. Volbach has shown that he had less recourse to the contrast and mixing of instruments than to the division of the same family of instruments into different groups. On the other hand, Handel, when he considered it advisable, reduced his instrumental forces by suppressing the viola and the second violin, whose places were taken by the harpsichord. All his orchestral art is in the true instinct of balance and economy, which, with the most restricted means in managing a few colors, yet knows how to obtain as powerful impressions as our musicians of to-day, with their crowded palette. Nothing, then, is more important, if we wish to render this music truly, than the avoidance of upsetting the equilibrium of the various sections of the orchestra under the pretext of enriching it and bringing it up to date. The worse fault is to deprive it, by a useless surplus of tone-colors, of that suppleness and subtlety of nuance which is its principal charm.

Let us consider his *Concerti Grossi*. None of his works is more celebrated and less understood. Handel attached to them a particular value, for he published them by subscription, a means which was usual in his day, but which he himself never adopted except under exceptional circumstances.

One knows that the kind of *Concerti Grossi,* which consists chiefly in a dialogue between a group of solo instrumentalists (the *Concertino*) and the full body of instruments (*Concerto Grosso*), to which is added the cembalo, was, if not invented, at least carried to its perfection and rendered classical by Corelli. The works of Corelli, aided by the efforts of his followers, had become widely known in Europe. Geminiani introduced them into England, and without doubt Handel did not hesitate to profit by the example of Geminiani, who was his friend; but it is much more natural to think that he learnt the *Concerto Grosso,* at its source at Rome, from Corelli himself during his sojourn there in 1708. Several of the concertos in his Opus 3 date from 1710, 1716, 1722. The same feature shows itself right up to the time of his apprenticeship at Hamburg: in any case he might have already known the Corellian style, thanks to the propaganda of George Moffat, who spread this style very early in Germany. After Corelli came Locatelli, and especially Vivaldi, who singularly transformed the *Concerto Grosso* by giving it the free character of programme music and by turning it resolutely towards the form of the sonata in three parts. But when the works of Vivaldi were played in London in 1723, and the works which aroused such a general enthusiasm became thoroughly known to Handel, it was always to Corelli that he gave the preference, and he was very conservative in certain ways even about him. The form of his concerto, of which the principal movements varied from four to six, oscillated between the suite and the sonata, and even glanced towards the symphonic overture. It is this for which the theorists blame him, and it is this for which I praise him. For he does not seek to impose a uniform cast on his thoughts, but leaves it open to himself to fashion the form as he requires, so that the framework varies accordingly, following his inclinations from day to day.

The spontaneity of his thought, which has already been shown by the extreme rapidity with which the *Concerti* were composed—each in a single day at a single sitting, and many each week—constitutes the great charm of these works. They are, in the words of Kretzschmar, grand impression pictures, translated into a form, at the same time precise and supple, in which the least change of emotion can make itself easily felt. Truly they are not all of equal value. Their conception itself, which depended in a way on mere momentary inspiration, is the explanation of this extreme inequality. One ought to acknowledge here that the Seventh Concerto, for example (the one in B flat major), and the last three have but a moderate interest. They are amongst those least played; but to be quite just we must pay homage to these master-pieces, and especially to the Second Concerto in F major, which is like a Beethoven concerto: for we find there some of the spirit of the Bonn master.

Let us now come to that class of Handel's instrumental music to which historians have given far too little attention, and in which Handel shows himself a precursor, and at the same time a model. I refer to his open-air music.

This took a prominent place in the English life. The environs of London were full of gardens, where, Pepys tells us, "vocal and instru-mental concerts vied with the voices of the birds." Handel wrote pieces especially intended for these garden concerts. Generally speaking, he attached very little importance to them. They were little symphonies or unpretentious dances, like the *Hornpipe,* composed for the concert at Vauxhall in 1740.

But he composed on these lines some works tending towards a much vaster scale: from 1715 or 1717 the famous *Water Music,* written for the royal procession of barges on the Thames, and the *Firework Music* made to illustrate the firework display given in Green Park on April 27, 1749, in celebration of the Peace of Aix-la-Chapelle.

The *Water Music* has a grand serenade in the form of a suite com-prising more than twenty movements. It opens with a pompous opera overture; then come dialogues, with echoes of horns and drums, where the brass and the rest of the orchestra, which are arranged in two sec-tions, respond. Then follow happy and soothing songs, dances, a bour-rée, a hornpipe, minuets, popular songs, which alternate and contrast with the joyful and powerful fanfares. The orchestra is very nearly the same as in his usual symphonies, except that considerable importance is given to the brass. One even finds in this work certain pieces written in the chamber-music style, or in the theatrical manner.

With the *Firework Music* the character of open-air music is even more definitely asserted, quite as much by the broad style of the piece as by the orchestration, which is confined entirely to the wind instru-ments. The composition is divided into two parts: an overture which was to be played before the grand firework display, and a number of little pieces to be played during the display, which corresponded to certain allegorical set pieces. The overture is a sort of stately march in D major, and has some resemblance to the overture of the *Ritterballet* (Huntsman's Dance) of Beethoven, and which is, like it, joyful, equestrian, and very sonorous. The shorter movements comprise a bourrée, a *Largo a la Siciliana,* entitled *Peace,* of a beautiful, heroic grace, which lulls itself to sleep; a very sprightly allegro entitled *The Rejoicing,* and two minuets for conclusion. It is an interesting work for the organizers of our popular fêtes and open-air spectacles to study. If we have said that after 1740 Handel wrote hardly any other instrumental music than the *Firework Music,* and the two monumental concertos, *a due cori* (for two horns), we have the feeling that the last evolution of his thought and instrumental style led him in the direction of music conceived for the great masses, wide spaces, and huge audiences. He had always in him a popular vein of thought. I immediately call to mind the many popular inspirations with which his memory was stored, and which vivify the pages of his oratorios. His art, which renewed itself perpetually at this rustic source, had in his time an astonishing popularity. Certain airs from *Ottone, Scipione, Arianna, Berenice,* and such other of his operas, were circulated and vulgarized not only in England, but abroad, and even in France (generally so unyielding to outside influences).

It is not only of this popularity, a little banal, of which I wish to speak, which one could not ignore—for it is only a stupid pride and a small heart which denies great value to the art which pleases humble people;—what I wish to notice chiefly in the popular character of Handel's music is that it is always truly conceived for the people, and not for an élite dilettanti, as was the French opera between Lully and Gluck. Without ever departing from his sovereign ideas of beautiful form, in which he gave no concession to the crowd, he reproduced in a language immediately "understanded of the people" those feelings in which all could share. This genial improviser, compelled during the whole of his life (a half-century of creative power) to address from the stage a mixed public, was like the orators of old, who had the cult of style and instinct for immediate and vital effect. Our epoch has lost the feeling of this type of art and men: pure artists who speak *to* the people and *for* the people, not for themselves or for their confrères. Today the pure artists lock themselves within themselves, and those who speak to the people are most often mountebanks. The free England of the eighteenth century was in a certain measure related to the Roman republic, and indeed Handel's eloquence was not without relation to that of the epic orators, who sustained in the form their highly finished and passionate discourses, who left their mark on the shuddering crowd of loiterers. This eloquence did on occasion actually thrust itself into the soul of the nation as in the days of the Jacobite invasion, where *Judas Maccabaeus* incarnated the public feeling. In the first performances of *Israel in Egypt* some of the auditors praised the heroic virtues of this music, which could raise up the populace and lead armies to victory.

By this power of popular appeal, as by all the other aspects of his genius, Handel was in the robust line of Cavalli and of Gluck, but he surpassed them. Alone, Beethoven has walked in these broader paths, and followed along the road which Handel had opened.

V

HAYDN

JOSEF HAYDN

Born at Rohrau, lower Austria, March 31, 1732. Went to Vienna, 1740, and studied music there, lived principally in Vienna, and from the age of 20 held various musical appointments, notably as kapellmeister to the Esterhazy family. His career was long and brilliantly successful, both in Vienna and on the tours he made throughout Europe. He died at Vienna, May 31, 1809.

PRINCIPAL WORKS

VOCAL: *The Seven Words from the Cross;* oratorios including *The Creation* and *The Seasons;* the cantatas *Ariana a Naxos, The Ten Commandments;* some 14 masses and other sacred and secular compositions. 1 German opera; 4 Italian operas; 4 Italian comedies; 22 arias; 36 German songs; etc.

INSTRUMENTAL: Some 125 symphonies and overtures (including the "Clock" symphony, the "Farewell" symphony, the "Surprise" symphony, and many others frequently performed). Some 31 concertos for various instruments with orchestra, chiefly harpsichord, violin, cello; also for double-bass, flute, horn, etc. Chamber music: 77 string quartets; 38 piano trios; 4 violin sonatas; 66 various compositions for wind and strings; 12 collections of minuets; 30 trios; 6 duets for violin and viola. Piano music (originally composed for clavichord or harpsichord) includes over 50 sonatas, divertimenti, etc., and numerous smaller pieces.

HAYDN

By W. Oliver Strunk

IN Haydn's London diary, among the entries for 1791, there is this
note: "On December 5 there was a fog so thick that one might
have spread it on bread. In order to write I had to light a candle as early
as eleven o'clock." Could Haydn have known what had happened in
Vienna on that critical morning, he would not have cared to write at
all. As it was, he wrote on; two weeks later he received news of Mozart's
death. "I am as pleased as a child at the thought of coming home and
embracing my good friends," he writes to Marianne von Genzinger on
the 20th. "My one regret is that the great Mozart will not be among
them, if it be true, as I trust it is not, that he is dead. Not in a hundred
years will posterity see such a talent again."

Though the Haydn who penned these lines was no longer a young
man, his vitality was unimpaired, his productivity unabated. "I am still
sprightly and in the full possession of my strength," he had assured
Mozart before leaving Vienna; early in 1792 he reports with evident
satisfaction to Frau von Genzinger that he has never written so much
in one year as in that just passed. His reputation, already distinguished,
now assumed such proportions that, in later life, he often insisted that
he had become famous in Germany only by way of England. Strangers
stopped to stare at him, exclaiming: "You are a great man!" Within
less than a year three fashionable artists had painted his portrait.
Honored with a Doctor's degree conferred by Oxford University, fêted
by professional and amateur musicians, sought after by peer and com-
moner alike, Haydn took most satisfaction, perhaps, in his new-
found independence. "How sweet a little liberty tastes!" he writes. "I

By arrangement with the author; hitherto unpublished.

used often to sigh for freedom—now I have it, in a measure. I appreciate it, too, though my mind is burdened with a multitude of tasks. The
knowledge that I am no longer a hired servant repays me for all my
trouble." For thirty years Haydn had written for a select group of con-
noisseurs; now, at fifty-nine, the opportunity to address a wider audience
had come to him at last. The change brought with it a new sense of
responsibility—to art and to society—a sense of responsibility that
found ultimate expression in his great oratorios, *The Creation* and *The
Seasons*.

As Mozart's biographer, Otto Jahn, once observed, the difficult task
is to portray the Haydn of the fifties, sixties, and seventies. "Thus far
we know little, if anything, about him and about the conditions and
influences to which he was subject. The Haydn everyone knows is not
Mozart's forerunner, but his contemporary and successor." Our knowledge of the musical environment from which Haydn sprang goes
further than Jahn's, but for most of us the works of his earlier years still
remain uncharted territory. Let us begin, then, on familiar ground—
with the music of the post-Mozartian Haydn. We will follow him the
more easily through the vicissitudes and complexities of his upward climb
if we have first seen the goal at which he aimed. And we will recognize
the more readily that his music is something more than an introduction
to Mozart and Beethoven, that his rôle in musical history is something
more than that of a pioneer, if we take as our starting point the works
of his last period.

During the London years Haydn is preoccupied with instrumental
composition; after his return to Vienna "the father of the symphony"
tends more and more to write for voices. Up until the time of the composition of *The Seasons* there is no slackening of his pace. The piano
variations in F minor; the last three piano-sonatas; a set of three piano-
trios dedicated to the Princess Dowager Maria Theresa Esterhazy; a
second set dedicated to Princess Marie; a third set for Mrs. Schroeter,
his "invariable and truly affectionate" correspondent; a fourth set for
Mrs. Bartolozzi, the wife of the London engraver; the single piano-trio
in E-flat, afterwards rewritten as a piano and violin sonata for Madame
Moreau; the six "Apponyi" quartets; and the twelve "London" symphonies: these thirty-five major instrumental works are the fruit of the
first five years alone, surely no mean achievement for a man in his

sixties. To the next five years belong the eight quartets dedicated to Count Erdödy and to Prince Lobkowitz; four of the last six masses; the revision of *The Seven Last Words;* the Te Deum in C; and the two oratorios. With the composition of *The Seasons* Haydn's creative activity is practically ended. In 1801 he writes the "Schöpfungsmesse," in 1802 the "Harmoniemesse." Then, in 1803, he completes two movements of his last quartet, dedicated to Count Fries. It was never finished. "I am no longer able to work at anything big," he writes to Thomson in the following year. "My age weakens me more and more." Yet for a time his imagination remains as keen as ever: in 1806, on his seventy-fourth birthday, he expresses the conviction that there are no limits to music's possibilities, that what may still be accomplished in music is far greater than what has been accomplished in the past. Often, he says, there come to him ideas through which the art might be advanced much further; his physical limitations, however, no longer permit him to undertake their expression.

"The secret of music's effect lies essentially in this: that in composition everything comes as it must come, yet otherwise than we expect." However one-sided his view of the romantic scene may have been, Eduard Hanslick was a shrewd judge of classical values; in its application to the music of the last quarter of the eighteenth century this brilliant aphorism of his comes very near the mark. The kind of effect he has in mind is not possible in every stage of the development of a style. In the experimental stage its presence is inconceivable; in the conventional stage, which follows, we seldom meet with it. Only when the rules of the game are well established is it feasible for the composer to play on the expectation of his listener. And even then, to play on expectation he must first arouse it. To secure emphasis he must first exercise self-control. He cannot afford to be continually surprising his listener. He must be simple before he is complex, regular before he is irregular, straightforward before he is startling. The composer of the "Surprise" symphony understood the working of these first principles. He could be simple, regular, and straightforward; this is a point that need not be brought home to the modern reader, who is only too apt to exaggerate the extent—or misunderstand the purpose—of this side of Haydn's writing. He could also be original without being eccentric; this the more generous among his contemporaries were always ready to concede. "That sounds queer," Kozeluch once remarked to Mozart, startled by a bold transition in a Haydn quartet, "would you have written it that way?" "Scarcely," Mozart replied, "but do you know why? Because neither you nor I would have hit on the idea."

Eminently suited to the display of the particular sort of originality that consists in playing on the expectation of the listener is the sonata form, as Haydn saw it toward the end of his career. In this type of movement the climax of interest regularly coincides with the beginning of the third part—the return of the principal tonality and the principal idea; artistic success or failure depends largely on the way this climax is hastened or delayed and on the angle from which it is approached. Once the third part has begun the listener's recollection of what has gone before leads him to anticipate the composer's every step; in this part of the design each deviation from the familiar path is a potential source of aesthetic pleasure or disappointment.

The compositions Haydn wrote for London are so full of this kind of originality that it is difficult to single out any one work to illustrate it. Let us choose one of the most familiar—the last of the three symphonies of 1795, the last of all Haydn's symphonies, the so-called "Salomon" symphony in D. Turn to the finale and observe how skillfully Haydn prepares the "return," growing more and more deliberate as he approaches the critical point, wandering further and further from the key at which he intends to arrive, then thinking better of it and making an unlooked-for close that is at once the end of the second part and the beginning of the third; before we have realized it, the "return" has been accomplished. Or turn to the first movement, compare the third part with the first, and observe how artfully Haydn delays restatement of the "second subject"—as is quite usual with him, it is the "first subject" all over again;—only when we have almost given up hope of hearing it does he bring it in at last. It is in the original treatment of just such details as these that the superiority of the London Haydn over the rank and file is most evident. In the compelling audacity of their design, the compositions Haydn wrote for London represent the final development of form in classical music. While he was writing these compositions, plans were already taking shape in his mind for a work that was to make his name last in the world.

"Since time immemorial the Creation has been regarded as the most exalted, most awe-inspiring picture that mankind can contemplate. To accompany this great drama with suitable music can surely have no other result than that of intensifying these sacred emotions in men's hearts and of making them more submissive to the benevolent omnipotence of their Creator." These lines from a letter Haydn wrote in 1801 —three years after he had completed *The Creation*—throw a revealing light on the frame of mind in which the aging master approached this most exacting of all the tasks he set himself. For the devout Catholic who habitually began and ended his manuscripts with the words "In nomine Domini" and "Laus Deo," the subject was made to order. The work of composition occupied him for two full years. "I spend much time on it," he said, "because I intend it to last a long time." For once, the composer who "never wrote until he was sure of himself" made systematic sketches. To Griesinger, his first biographer, he confessed that he had half finished his score before its success was apparent to him. "I was never so devout as during the time I was working on *The Creation*," Griesinger quotes Haydn as saying. "Every day I fell on my knees and prayed God that he might give me strength to bring this work to a satisfactory conclusion." Early in 1798, shortly after the composer's sixty-sixth birthday, that satisfactory conclusion was announced. Before the oratorio had been publicly performed, Haydn was at work on *The Seasons*.

"With the decrease of my mental powers, my inclination and the urge to work seem almost to increase," Haydn wrote in June, 1799, to the publishers Breitkopf & Härtel. "Every day I receive many compliments—even on the fire of my last works; no one will believe what trouble and strain I endure to produce them." Goethe's friend Zelter called *The Seasons* "a work of youthful vigor and mature mastery." Schiller's friend Streicher came nearer the truth in 1809 when he called it "a musical debauch." "Without it," he added, "Haydn would assuredly have enjoyed ten more years of activity." Haydn himself said that *The Seasons* had "finished" him.

Haydn often regretted that he was never able to visit Italy. But it is a question whether he would have profited half as much from such a visit as he did from his two visits to England. Without them neither *The Creation* nor *The Seasons* would have been written. The two oratorios owe something to English poetry—one is based on an adaptation from Milton's *Paradise Lost,* the other on Thomson's *Seasons.* They owe more to the English audience and to the Anglicized Handel, whose music was virtually new to Haydn when he arrived in London. The Handel Commemoration in 1791 and the "Concerts of Ancient Music" were revelations. To the English composer, Shield, who asked his opinion of "The Nations Tremble" in Handel's *Joshua,* Haydn replied that he had long been acquainted with music, but never knew half its powers before he heard it; when Shield praised the recitatives in Haydn's early oratorio *Il Ritorno di Tobia* (1775), Haydn declared that the recitative "Deeper and Deeper Still" in Handel's *Jephtha* surpassed them in pathos and contrast. Power, pathos, and contrast—these are the secrets of Handel's greatness, and when Haydn returned to Vienna he took them with him. Written for the concerts of the "Society of Noble Amateurs," *The Creation* and *The Seasons* speak to the plain man.

One type of artist is concerned with design, another with expression. Haydn is concerned with both. The classic perfection of the "London" symphonies and the "Apponyi" quartets has its counterpart in the romantic intensity of the works of his last years in Vienna. In the light of later developments Haydn's romanticism may appear somewhat restrained to us; to his contemporaries it was bold and even startling. The rich sonorities of his last quartets and orchestral accompaniments point to Beethoven and to Weber. The simple piety of his *Creation* is no less affecting than the artless realism of his *Seasons.* The ordered lawlessness of his "Representation of Chaos" breaks down old barriers. "It is impossible and contrary to rule that so excellent a piece should be accepted, universally and at once, for what it is and alone can be," Zelter wrote in Breitkopf's journal. "Certain deep-rooted theories, derived from the works of an earlier period, remain eternally at odds with the spirit of progress, leading inevitably to the kind of criticism that is always demanding, but does not know how to accept." Haydn thanked Zelter for praising the "Chaos" by saying: "You could and would have written it just as I did." To which Zelter replied, modestly and with perfect truth: "I could never have written it as you did, great master, nor shall I ever be capable of doing so."

As he approached the end of his career, Haydn became increasingly sensible of the social responsibility of the artist, and of all the testimonials showered on him during his declining years he prized those most that bore witness to his honorable discharge of this obligation. He took particular pride, Griesinger tells us, in the honorary citizenship conferred on him by the municipal authorities of Vienna, seeing in this an illustration of the old saying, "Vox populi, vox Dei." Another tribute of the same kind, simpler, perhaps, but no less sincere, moved him to write what is at once the most revealing and the most touching of all his letters. From the little town of Bergen, capital of the island of Rügen in the Baltic, a society of amateurs wrote to thank him for the pleasure that performing his *Creation* had given its membership.

"Gentlemen: (Haydn replied) It was a truly agreeable surprise to me to receive so flattering a letter from a quarter to which I could never have presumed that the productions of my feeble talent would penetrate. Not only do you know my name, I perceive, but you perform my works, fulfilling in this way the wish nearest my heart: that every nation familiar with my music should adjudge me a not wholly unworthy priest of that sacred art. On this score you appear to quiet me, so far as your country is concerned; what is more, you give me the welcome assurance—and this is the greatest comfort of my declining years—that I am often the source from which you, and many other families receptive to heartfelt emotion, derive pleasure and satisfaction in the quiet of your homes. How soothing this reflection is to me!

"Often, as I struggled with obstacles of all kinds opposed to my works—often, as my physical and mental powers sank, and I had difficulty in keeping to my chosen course—an inner voice whispered to me: 'There are so few happy and contented men here below—on every hand care and sorrow pursue them—perhaps your work may some day be a source from which men laden with anxieties and burdened with affairs may derive a few moments of rest and refreshment.' This, then, was a powerful motive to persevere, this the reason why I can even now look back with profound satisfaction on what I have accomplished in my art through uninterrupted effort and application over a long succession of years."

The fifty most active years of his life—the fifty years between his first compositions and his *Seasons*—coincide with one of the most restless and fruitful half-centuries in all musical history—the half-century between Bach's death in 1750 and Beethoven's first symphony in 1800. Old forms and old methods had gone the way of old ideals; pathos had yielded to sentiment, severity to informality; music had become less comprehensive, more individual, less uniform, more many-sided, less intellectual, more spontaneous. Tastes had changed, and a combination of forces—social, cultural, and artistic—had brought about a complete reversal of musical values. Before the pre-classical movement had reached its height in the music of Bach and Handel, these forces were already working toward its dissolution; by the middle of the century they had undermined the old structure and laid out in bold outline the ground plan of the new.

"We have gradually rid ourselves of the preconceived idea that great music is at home only in Italy. Respect for those illustrious names in *ini* and *elli* is disappearing, and Germans, formerly occupied with the modest business of accompaniment, have raised themselves to the first place in the orchestra of the powers. We no longer listen to the swaggering foreigners, and our scribes, who only yesterday were so bent on propagating fair copies of the empty eccentricities of Italians devoid of ideas, now vie with one another for the honor of making the works of their countrymen known."

So Marpurg wrote in 1749, and it is noteworthy that this somewhat rhetorical declaration of his, far from being a random observation, stands at the very beginning of his *Critical Musician*. That just at this time there should have been a belated reawakening of national feeling among German musicians is highly significant. Having assimilated all that Italy could give, Germany was ready to strike out for herself, and in her leading musical centers—Berlin, Mannheim, and Vienna—native musicians were even now contending for the supremacy.

It was at this moment that Haydn, dismissed at seventeen from the cathedral choir-school in Vienna, faced the problem of shifting for himself. His immediate musical environment, while not precisely dominated by the Italian tradition, was less aggressively German than that of Berlin or Mannheim; what is perhaps more important, it was an eminently popular environment, related in a variety of ways to the everyday life of the community. The popular theatre was in a flourishing condition. Wagenseil, Starzer, and Reutter were putting the music of the street and the dance-hall to artistic uses in their serenades and divertimenti; Monn, another Viennese musician of the older generation, is thought to have been the first to introduce the minuet in a symphony. Haydn, true to his surroundings, began by composing music of just this kind. One of his earliest experiments was a serenade, and, according to one account, it was an improvised performance of this piece that brought him his first commission and led to the composition of his first "opera," *Der krumme Teufel.* To the same category belong his earliest quartets, written for his first patron, Baron Fürnberg in Weinzierl, and the numerous divertimenti for various combinations that he wrote before and during his brief service as musical director to Count Morzin in Lukavec. "Le Midi" (1761), one of his first symphonies, already contains a minuet. To recognize the Haydn we know in the compositions of this early period is no easy matter; at no other time in his life is the Italian influence more marked. While contemptuously repudiating the "scribbler" Sammartini, whom Mysliweczek had called the father of his style, Haydn was always ready to acknowledge his debt to Porpora. Berlin and Mannheim are negligible factors, so far, though by 1760 Haydn was not only a fervent admirer of Bach's son Carl Philipp Emanuel, but had already gone so far as to dedicate one of his compositions to Stamitz's patron, the Elector Karl Theodor. "I wrote industriously, but not quite correctly," Haydn said himself, and when in 1805 a score of his first mass was discovered and brought to him after fifty-three years, his comment was: "What pleases me most in this work is a certain youthful fire."

The next few years brought important changes in Haydn's outward circumstances and in the kind of music he was called upon to supply. In 1761, on his appointment as second *Kapellmeister* to Prince Paul Anton Esterhazy at Eisenstadt, he found himself in a responsible and highly desirable position exceedingly favorable to the development of his gifts and reputation; in 1762, on Paul Anton's death and the arrival of his brother and successor, Prince Nicholas, his responsibilities were materially increased, for the new employer was not only an ardent music-lover, but an amateur performer as well, and the demand for new compositions was relentless and almost unlimited. Then, in March, 1766, Haydn was made first *Kapellmeister,* and a few months later the opening of the magnificent residence Prince Nicholas had built at Esterhaz—with its opera house seating four hundred and its marionette theatre—again increased his responsibilities, obliging him to devote serious attention to operatic composition, a branch of music in which he had thus far had little experience.

Haydn's first fifteen years at Eisenstadt and Esterhaz constitute a period that is surely one of the most interesting of his long career: it is the period during which the foundation of his later reputation was laid; during which the works of his first maturity were written; during which he ceased to feel the influence of his lesser contemporaries and, abandoning their conventions, became himself a determining influence in the career of the younger Mozart. Entering the Esterhazy service an almost unknown musician, Haydn began at once to attract attention, not only in Vienna, but in other musical centers. In 1763, Breitkopf's catalogues announce eight "quadros" and six trios for strings, with two concertos and a divertimento for the harpsichord, as available in manuscript; from the same year dates one of the earliest notices of Haydn on record, a manuscript note in an interleaved copy of Walther's *Lexikon* now in the Library of Congress: "Haydn, an incomparable musician and composer, lives in Vienna and distinguishes himself in the writing of fine quartets, trios, and symphonies." The first recorded publication of a work of Haydn's occurred in March of the following year, when the Paris publisher Venier advertised an edition of one of the early quartets in his series "Sinfonie a più Stromenti Composte da Vari Autori" (Opera Decima Quarta) under the title "Les noms inconnus bons à connoitre" (Unknown names worth knowing) in company with compositions by Van Maldere, Beck, Pfeiffer, Schetky, and Fränzl. By 1775 a formidable array of Haydn's sonatas, duos, trios, quartets, and symphonies had been engraved (apparently without the composer's authorization!) in Paris, Amsterdam, and London; the Vienna editions began in 1774 with Kurtzböck's printing of six sonatas. As early as 1766 Haydn is mentioned in magazines published in Leipzig and Hamburg, while in Vienna he was already being called "the darling of our nation." So universal, in fact, was the recognition accorded Haydn by the end of this period that in responding in 1776 to a request for an autobiographical sketch he could write: "In my chamber music I have had the good fortune to please almost everywhere, save in Berlin!"

Successively considered, the compositions of the decade 1765 to 1775 reveal Haydn's steadily increasing mastery of form and content. Not satisfied with the facile polish of his fourth series of quartets (Opus 9, 1769), he strove in those that followed toward greater refinement of workmanship, toward more intense formal concentration, toward the suppression of the episodic and conventional (Opus 17, 1771), resorting in the last series written during this period (Opus 20, 1772) to time-honored contrapuntal devices to enhance the interest and insure the balance of his texture. At the same time Haydn contrived to give his music a more individual note. In their book on Mozart, Wyzewa and Saint-Foix draw attention to certain particularly striking examples of this tendency in the works of the early 1770's—the C minor piano sonata, the quartets Opus 20 ("à la fois pathétiques et savants"), the "Trauersymphonie," the "Farewell" symphony—and speak of the year 1772 as the "romantic crisis" of Haydn's artistic career. A year or two later, the same writers tell us, still another change took place in Haydn's manner. Now he surrenders to the "galant" style, and henceforward his principal aim is to impress us agreeably or to amuse us with ingenious turns of musical rhetoric.

Then, in 1781, came the publication of the "Russian" quartets (Opus 33), the series that ushered in the style Haydn himself described as "entirely new." Here is the turning-point in his career. Until now Karl Philip Emanuel Bach had been Haydn's principal model; with the appearance of the "Russian" quartets Mozart began to take Bach's place. In the "Paris" symphonies (1786), the "Oxford" symphony (1788), and the two sets of quartets written in 1789 and 1790 for the Viennese wholesale merchant Johann Tost, Haydn attained full maturity, and the transition to the works of the last decade was only a step.

While Haydn had been at work, a new kind of music had grown from tentative beginnings to conscious maturity; his own music had itself passed through every stage in that growth, now following in a path cleared by others, now leading the way. With the possible exception of Handel, no great composer was ever more prolific; with the possible exception of Beethoven, no great composer ever maintained so fresh an outlook. Keeping pace with contemporary developments and more often anticipating them, Haydn ended even more progressively than he had begun.

VI

MOZART

WOLFGANG AMADEUS MOZART

Born at Salzburg, January 27, 1756, a son of the court composer Leopold Mozart, with whom he began his studies at the age of three. His talent was uniquely precocious in performance, composition, and musicianship; he taught himself to play several instruments, as well as to compose. His first appearance as a pianist was at the age of six, his first works published the following year. Was taken as a child on concert tours of England, France, Italy; spent many years in travel. Settled in Vienna, 1780, and lived there chiefly. Throughout his life he composed prolifically in all forms; made many concert tours with varying success. Died a pauper in Vienna, December 5, 1791.

PRINCIPAL WORKS

VOCAL: Choral: 15 masses; *Requiem* (completed by his pupil Süssmayr); cantatas, including *Davidde Penitente, Maurer-Freude,* etc., and other church music; 27 arias, 1 rondo for soprano with orchestra; 34 songs; 20 canons. Operas in Italian: *Don Giovanni; Cosi Fan Tutte; The Marriage of Figaro; Idomeneo;* earlier operas, including *La Finta Giardiniera,* etc. Operas in German: *The Magic Flute; The Abduction from the Seraglio.*

INSTRUMENTAL: 41 symphonies, of which the best known are those in C major (The "Jupiter"), K551; G minor, K550; E flat major, K543. 31 *divertimenti,* serenades, etc.; 25 dances; 9 marches; 25 piano concertos; a concerto for 2 pianos and one for 3 pianos; 6 violin concertos; concertos for flute, for flute and harp, for horn, for clarinet; *Eine Kleine Nachtmusik* (suite in four movements). Chamber music: Some 26 string quartets; 7 string quintets; 42 sonatas for violin and piano; quintet for clarinet and strings; many *divertimenti* and other pieces for various combinations of strings and winds. Piano music: 17 sonatas; Fantasie and fugue; 3 fantasies; 15 variations; 18 shorter pieces, including minuets, rondos, etc.; 5 sonatas for four hands; Andante and variations for four hands; sonata for 2 pianos; fugue for 2 pianos. Organ music includes 17 sonatas.

MOZART

By W. J. Turner

MR. BERNARD SHAW once remarked that nothing could be more uncharacteristic of Mozart than the portraits of the beautiful young man exhibited above his name in all the music shops of the world to-day. These portraits show Mozart as the most handsome, the most regular-featured of all great composers. These "classic" proportions seem at first sight to be peculiarly appropriate to a composer who is to-day universally admired as the classic of classics. Where else in music shall we find those qualities of serenity, limpidity, simplicity, lucidity, which we concentrate in one adjective: Mozartian? It is impossible to find a parallel to that flawless perfection. Whether we take a whole opera—such as *The Marriage of Figaro*—or a mere scrap scribbled impromptu on the page of a visitors' book—such as the Gigue written in 1789 for the Leipzig organist, Engel—we are confronted with a completely finished musical composition in which there is not a superfluous bar, not a redundant or meaningless note. There is no waste in Mozart—no overlapping, no exaggeration, no strain, no vagueness, no distortion, no suggestion. He is so simple that he is meaningless. His music *disappears,* like the air we breathe on a transparent day. Everybody who has really appreciated Mozart will admit that at one time or another they have felt a Mozart masterpiece as one would feel a still, bright, perfect, cloudless day. Such a day has no meaning, none of the suggestiveness, the "atmosphere," the character of a day of cloud or storm, or of any day in which there is a mixture of warring elements whose significance has yet to appear. Such a day does not provoke or in the faintest degree suggest one mood rather than another. It is in-

From *The Heritage of Music*, by permission of the Oxford University Press.

finitely protean. It means just what you mean. It is intangible, immaterial—fitting your spirit like a glove.

Thus, as Sir Charles Stanford has said, when you are a child Mozart speaks to you as a child—no music could be more simple, more childlike—but when you are a man you find to your astonishment that this music which seemed childlike is completely adult and masculine. At every age this pure pellucid day, this intangible transparency, awaits you and envelops you in its unruffled light. *Then* suddenly there will pass through you a tremor of terror. A moment comes when that tranquillity, that perfection will take on a ghastly ambiguity. That music still suggests nothing, nothing at all; it is just infinitely ambiguous. Then you remember the phrase of a German critic who wrote of the "demoniacal clang" of Mozart. Then you look at a genuine portrait of Mozart, and instead of that smooth Praxitelean young beauty, you see a straight jutting profile with a too-prominent nose and an extraordinary salience of the upper lip, and for an instant you feel as if you have had a revelation. But that revelation escapes you as suddenly as it came, and you are left face to face with a mask whose directness and clarity is completely baffling.

In endeavoring to explain Mozart to oneself, it is well to remember first of all that he was the most remarkable example of a child prodigy that has ever been known. He played the harpsichord in public at five years old. At seven he composed, and played on the harpsichord, the organ, and the violin. In 1764, at the age of eight, after touring Europe, he came to London and played before the Royal Family; in London he published his third set of sonatas and wrote an anthem for four voices entitled *God is Our Refuge,* which was presented to the British Museum. At the age of ten he wrote an oratorio which had a great success in Holland, and a year later, in Vienna, he wrote an *opera buffa, La Finta Semplice,* for the Emperor Joseph II. At fourteen he was taken to Italy by his father, and in Rome during Holy Week he went to the Sistine Chapel to hear the famous *Miserere* of Gregorio Allegri. Immediately on returning to his lodging he wrote down the *Miserere* from memory, note for note. The same year he was subjected to the severest possible examination by the Bologna Accademia Filarmonica, passed it successfully, and was awarded the degree of "compositore," although the regulations did not admit of any candidates under twenty years of age.

This exercise is Number 86 in Köchel's catalogue, and, in Professor Donald Tovey's words, is "written in the severe ecclesiastical style of the sixteenth century," and abounds in "points of ingenious imitation and device." In 1770, at the age of fourteen, he wrote an opera entitled *Mitridate Re di Ponto* for La Scala, of Milan. The orchestra of La Scala was at that time the largest in Europe; Mozart directed it seated at the harpsichord as the fashion then was. The opera was received with enthusiasm and ran for twenty nights.

From the age of fourteen onwards Mozart poured forth a constant stream of compositions of all kinds. What is astonishing is that this immense early productivity seems in no way to have harmed the natural growth of his mind, for although there are pieces of church music written before the age of fifteen which the best critics claim as masterpieces, yet there is perceptible in his music a real development of his natural powers which ends only with his death.

It is suggested by some writers that the fact that Mozart acquired at the age of fourteen a technique equal to, if not surpassing, that of any living composer explains why he was able to pass through the critical years of adolescence from fourteen to twenty in ceaseless musical composition without straining his mind. For Mozart had to acquire the usual education, and his letters suggest—as later his invention in the *Seraglio* of the character of Osmin, words and all, proves—that he had great literary ability and possibly the same inexhaustible fertility in language that he had in music. But Mozart's intellectual force was a quality inherent in the structure of his mind. One day the physiologists will be able to show us in a physiological generalization Mozart's peculiar gift for form. Many writers on aesthetics think music is the most abstract of the arts, but it is certainly true that Mozart's are the purest works in music. One may speak of a movement of Mozart just as a mathematician might speak of a beautiful proposition of Euclid. Whereas in the music of most composers it is a case of content *and* structure, it is with Mozart a case of structure only, for there is no perceptible content —*ubi materia ibi geometria*. Nowhere, perhaps, is this more strikingly shown than in the overture to *The Marriage of Figaro*. I would suggest to the reader that he should buy the gramophone records of this overture and of Rossini's overture to *The Barber of Seville,* and compare them. The difference is astonishing. Rossini was born the year after

Mozart's death; he also had the advantage of following instead of preceding Beethoven, and he was a composer of striking natural genius. But, after *Figaro,* listen to the *Barber of Seville* overture, with its alluring tunefulness over its easy *tum-ti, tum-ti, tum-ti, tum-ti* bass, and you will be struck with its straggling formlessness. Its tunes are very engaging, but you can carry them away with you and hear them mentally on a penny whistle, a cornet, or any instrument you like. They are like bright threads in a commonplace piece of stuff, which you can pull out without compunction as there is no design to spoil. But you can do nothing of the sort with the *Figaro* overture. There are no bright threads to pull out. There is no melodic content as such. You cannot even hear the music in your memory apart from the rush of the strings and the accents of the wood wind. It cannot be played upon the piano. Take away a note of it and the whole is completely disintegrated. Nor can anyone put his hand upon his heart and say what feeling that music arouses in his breast. It is completely without expression, as expression is vulgarly understood; but the oftener you hear it the more excited you become, the more passionate grow your asseverations that there was never music like this before or since. Its effect upon the mind is out of all proportion to its impingement on the senses. To hear it is as though one had been present at a miracle and had seen a mountain of matter blown into a transparent bubble and float vanishing into the sky. Your desire to hear that overture again and again and again is the simple but intense desire to see the miracle repeated. It is an astonishing experience, and it is an experience which only Mozart can give us.

It would be useless to attempt to explain this peculiar intellectual gift which was Mozart's in a degree that separates him from all other composers. It must just be stated and left. But there are certain facts known about Mozart which are so relevant to this point that they should be mentioned now. He was exceptionally good at dancing and playing billiards, which were his two chief pleasures. He was small, but his limbs, feet, and hands were beautifully proportioned. He composed away from any musical instrument, entirely in his head, and could complete the whole of a work, from the first note to the last and then write it down—often some weeks or more later—from memory. Thus the overture to *Don Giovanni,* written on the night of October 28th, 1787, for the first performance of the opera in Prague on the next day, while his wife kept him awake by telling him fairy stories, was not composed on that night but merely copied out from memory. He would often compose at meals, and while composing would take his napkin by two corners and continually fold and refold it very neatly and exactly. To me this is all extraordinarily illuminating. Conciseness—even conciseness so unparalleled and amazing as Mozart's—is not surprising in a composer who could work in this way. One also cannot but think that his invariable serenity and good temper—upon which all who knew him have left comment—was yet another sign of perfect physical and mental poise. It is on record that Mozart never used glasses and that his eyesight was perfect at his death in spite of the strain which manuscript music imposes. This, also, is not without significance. Mozart may be bracketed with Schubert as one of the two composers whose fertility in melodic invention exceeds all others, but the listener never feels that Mozart is being swept along the current of his own emotions as he feels Schubert is. In listening to such works as Schubert's Octet or his "Unfinished" Symphony, one is conscious sometimes of a dissolution, almost a liquefaction, of the composer's sensibility, which streams into the music like treacle. It is this that makes Schubert's music often so formless. The composer is simply melting helplessly away, and it seems as if only death can conclude the process. Yet melting, tender, exquisitely sweet as Schubert's melodies can be, they are never in themselves intrinsically sweeter or tenderer than Mozart's, but only in their effect. They seem sweeter because of the absence of that intellectuality, that lucid precision which was so integral a part of Mozart's mind. There are passages in Mozart's pianoforte concertos which are so piercing in their intense sweetness that I have often stopped playing and laughed aloud with excess of pleasure; but Mozart's mental grip never loosens; he never abandons himself to any one sense; even at his most ecstatic moments his mind is vigorous, alert, and on the wing. It is from this astounding elasticity that his conciseness largely derives. Most artists are unable to tear themselves away from their most delightful discoveries; they linger on them and handle them fondly, but not Mozart. He dives unerringly on to his finest ideas like a bird of prey, and once an idea is seized he soars off again with undiminished power.

Yet impossible as it is in Mozart's music to separate form from content—which is his great, his unique intellectual distinction, the quality in which he surpasses all other composers—we can range his forms in a hierarchy of value. The overture to *Figaro* is perfect. There is nothing to be altered, there is not a note we could wish different, and nobody but Mozart could have written it; but, nevertheless, the overture to *The Magic Flute* is a finer work. It also is perfect, but it is artistically greater than *Figaro*. Wherein is it greater? Well, I believe we shall go least astray if we make the comparison in purely quantitative terms. The overture to *The Magic Flute* is a greater composition than the overture to *Figaro* because while form and content are equally one, while "matter" has once again been turned to "form," more matter has been involved in the operation. It was a bigger and more difficult bubble to blow.

I am conscious that some readers will dislike the manner in which I have put this comparison of *Figaro* with *The Magic Flute*. They will wonder why I do not use the familiar terms: *Figaro* is a comic opera, *The Magic Flute* is a more serious work. It expresses Mozart's religious feeling, his idealism; that is why, they will say, *The Magic Flute* overture is superior. Such expressions, I admit, are not without meaning, but they are misleading. The world is full of music which is none the less worthless because it is "serious" or "religious." What we can say is that there is present in the music of *The Magic Flute* a quality which is not present in *Figaro*, and a quality which we instinctively feel to be infinitely more precious. That "infinitely" is a concession to my own feeling. I hope it will appease the fanatical admirers of Beethoven, but my reason urges me to take it out. However, it must be recognized that Beethoven almost consistently attempted to blow bigger bubbles than Mozart. That he so frequently failed, that his bubbles so often burst instead of sailing off beautifully, as Mozart's do, into the upper regions of the mind, will not prevent his admirers ranking him instead of Mozart as the greatest of all musicians. I do not really object to this very seriously, because one or two of Beethoven's biggest bubbles do float off successfully, although I confess I always watch them with anxiety, never with that utter confidence which Mozart inspires. But when we remember that Mozart died at the age of thirty-five, and reflect upon such works as *Don Giovanni,* the *Requiem,* the *Magic Flute,* and much of his earlier church music, it is permissible to believe that he would have successfully achieved even bigger things.

Personally, I would go farther. I very much doubt if Beethoven or any other composer has exceeded Mozart in vital energy. The last movement of Beethoven's Seventh Symphony has been called the "apotheosis of the dance," and in actual "sound and fury" it far exceeds anything Mozart ever wrote; but I do not feel there is as quick, as tense a "rush" in it as there is in the *Figaro* overture; there is only a bigger volume of noise. It is the rumble of thunder compared with the flash of lightning. Nor is there in all Beethoven's great and intensely dramatic overtures anything more impressive, more dramatically effective than the use made of the opening chords in *The Magic Flute* overture; but Mozart secures this dramatic intensity with a far greater economy of sound. He never bludgeons the senses into recognition of his powers, as so many inferior composers do; he appeals directly to the imagination.

It is not astonishing that a mind so well-balanced as Mozart's should show so great a sense of humor. In this he surpasses all other composers, and as the sense of humor is essentially intellectual, it is natural that Mozart, the most intellectual of composers, should be the greatest master of comic opera. But what is altogether unexpected is his power to make one's flesh creep. Nothing has ever been written of such truly diabolical verve as the aria for the Queen of the Night in the *Magic Flute*. It is the rarest event to find a light soprano who can sing this at all; it is certain that we shall never have it sung so as to do full justice to its startlingly coldblooded ferocity. And yet that aria has the smooth, glassy surface of a mere bit of coloratura virtuosity; but it is the surface of ice beneath which is a fathomless black water. This sinister ambiguity is a quality quite apart from the more familiar power of striking the imagination which he shows in the music which announces and accompanies the entrance of the statue at the supper-party in the last act of *Don Giovanni*. This is the most famous of Mozart's dramatic touches, and nobody can deny that there is not a more thrilling moment than this in the whole of Wagner's *Ring*, or, indeed, in any opera that has ever been written.

Yet I would like to insist that there is another and even more troubling quality in Mozart's music. Linked with the "demoniacal clang" which is probably the result of that bareness which makes Mozart's music appear a mere rhythmical skeleton beside the work of more sensuous composers such as Brahms and Wagner (but a skeleton of electric vitality!), there is a profoundly disturbing melancholy. It is never active in Mozart's work as it is frequently in the work of Tchaikovsky, in Brahms, in Chopin, and even in Beethoven. It is a still, unplumbed melancholy underlying even his brightest and most vivacious movements. It is this which gives his music that ambiguity to which I drew attention at the beginning of this essay. It would be an interesting psychological study to try to discover its meaning. It may be that Mozart's life was a profoundly unhappy one—he was certainly unfortunate in his environment, far more unfortunate than Beethoven, for he never had Beethoven's comparative financial security, nor did he ever enjoy such appreciative and discriminating friends. It is probable that his extreme sensitiveness in unfavorable surroundings caused him great suffering, and that he was unfortunate in his relations with women; but such in varying degree are the trials of all artists of genius, and I do not think they will account for the peculiar, all-pervading, transparent gloom of Mozart's music. I am not even sure that "gloom" and "melancholy" are the right words to use. Mozart is very mysterious— far more mysterious than Beethoven, because his music seems to express much less of his human character. I believe that Mozart's personal life was a failure. In his last years he abandoned himself to frivolous gaiety. Without being dissipated, he wasted his time and strength upon masked balls, dancing, feasting, and idle gallantry. It is impossible to believe that he found such a life satisfactory. Why, then, did he pursue it?

Mozart was not without that sense of spiritual life which we call religious. On the contrary, he had this sense as highly developed as his sense of humor—he was no La Rochefoucauld. The *Requiem, The Magic Flute, Don Giovanni,* the *Twelfth Mass,* and a great deal of purely instrumental music exist to prove it. If it were not so, Mozart would be enormously less important. But Mozart obviously lacked that quiet, steady, flaming faith which burns so intensely in Bach and Beethoven. This is the secret of that all-pervading gloom, that quiet hopelessness. I do not mean, merely, that Mozart was a child of the eighteenth century and consequently a realist and a skeptic. The true eighteenth century man of the world is not troubled by any religious feelings at all; he entirely lacks spiritual sensibility. All men are materialists, because all life is "matter," even if that "matter" resolve itself into positive and negative electricity—though God alone knows what that means! But "matter" varies in its sentient power. One piece of matter "Mr. A" can see but cannot hear: he is deaf, for him sounds do not exist; another piece of matter "Mr. B" hears but cannot see; another, "Mr. C" hears *and* sees, but he is color-blind: for him colors do not exist, yet he, living among the blind and deaf, may easily convince himself that he misses nothing, and that these "colors" of which a few odd people talk, are fantastic or sentimental illusions. This is the position of the true eighteenth century "materialist." Mozart was not one of these; he was vividly aware of the spiritual colors of life, they were to him as concrete as heat and cold.

But something else was lacking. I am conscious of it, but I do not quite know how to describe it. I can only point to Beethoven's Ninth Symphony and declare that I find it unmistakably present there. Mozart could not have written the last movement of that symphony. He was not capable of it. It expresses an emotion he had never felt. To describe this emotion as "joy" is utterly inadequate and ridiculous. It is a spiritual sublimity which surpasses in value all other human emotions, and which only the few supreme spirits of this earth have ever expressed. In many millions of years from now, men—if there are still men or descendants of men living on this planet—may be able to explain in biological terms the value of this emotion; or, rather, it will have become intelligible to them—as the value of the abstract feeling for justice is to-day becoming intelligible. At present it is the rare emotional possession of the few, but nothing can prevent its slowly dominating mankind. Its power is irresistible because it is latent in us all. Bach and Beethoven knew this, and therefore—to use the extraordinarily apt and suggestive words of the Jacobean translators of the old Hebrew folk-tales—they "walked with God." Mozart did not. Mozart danced with the masked daughters of Vienna and wasted his spirit, not in passion or in sudden excesses of lust—which might not have harmed him, which might even have been beneficial to him—but in the aimless dissipation of the man without faith. This spiritual "faith" in which Beethoven and Bach lived is altogether different from that romantic faith in themselves which came into fashion for artists and men of genius in Europe at the beginning of the nine-teenth century, when Napoleon began to talk about his "star" and Byron set the fashion of extravagant, egoistic gestures. Bach had none of this, and in so far as Beethoven indulged in it it did him harm. Mozart was not handicapped through having lived before the invention of that comfortable padded cell of the soul, that lotus-island, the Nietzschean vanity of the superman-artist; and of all artists who have ever lived Mozart was least likely to fall a victim to such a snare. He had too penetrating an intelligence, too keen a sense of humor. No, he was deficient in an active power which Beethoven and Bach possessed, and I think he was deficient in nothing else. In all else he was indeed superior to Beethoven and Bach, and, consequently, to all others.

But now that I have put my finger on what I believe to be the radical weakness of Mozart, and have given my explanation of the melancholy of his music—namely, that Mozart had extreme spiritual sensitiveness but no spiritual faith in life (and by that I do not mean acceptance of any theological dogma)—I think I can give a different interpretation of one of Mozart's apparent failures. In Professor Donald Tovey's brilliant article on "Sonata Form" in the *Encyclopædia Britannica,* he says: "The sonata style never lost with him (Mozart) its dramatic character, but while it was capable of pathos, excitement and even vehemence, it could not concern itself with catastrophes and tragic climaxes." He then goes on to say that the G minor Symphony shows poignant feeling, but that it is not an embodiment of sad experiences. So far Professor Tovey, although writing about the "sonata form," is accusing Mozart of a lack of emotional content, but then he continues: "In the still more profound and pathetic G minor Quintet we see Mozart for once transcending his limits. The slow movement rises to a height not surpassed by Beethoven himself until his second period; *an adequate finale is unattainable with Mozart's resources, and he knows it.*" But in what way, may one ask, has Mozart transcended his limits in this work if the slow movement only rises to a height surpassed by Beethoven in his *second* period and his resources do not admit of his writing an adequate finale?

That the slow movement of the G minor Quintet is surpassed by Beethoven in his second period I should be inclined to deny. That the technical resources of the man who wrote that wonderful allegro, that astonishing minuet, that rich and tragic slow movement, and those poignant introductory bars, were inadequate to a satisfactory finale is to me unbelievable. That Mozart—whose technical mastery at every point surpasses Beethoven's in the opinion of, I should imagine, ninety-nine per cent of scholars—should have been incapable of satisfactorily *concluding* an admitted masterpiece through lack of technical resource is completely unconvincing. What, then, does Professor Tovey mean? Let us examine that last movement of the G minor Quintet. What is wrong with it? In my opinion, this: Mozart has written a really great work, he has taken plenty of room, the design of the quintet is magnificently spacious, and he can fill it. Not only has he all the technical resources necessary— to talk of Mozart ever lacking technical resources seems to me ludicrous —but he is in the rich, abundant, creative mood to fill it, and so to fill it that it strikes Professor Tovey as "profound and pathetic"—words which he does not use lightly. The third movement, *adagio,* is tragic in its intensity. But what, then, happens? Mozart concludes with a finale, light, sparkling, and gay, but once more masking an abyss of black melancholy. A finale that is utterly inadequate—admitted! But why inadequate? It is not technically inadequate. To spin that light-hearted gossamer *allegro* so that, after what we had heard, it should captivate and delude, not shock and disgust, the listener, called for that technical skill which Mozart alone possessed. But, still, inadequate! That finale is beyond all denial inadequate. Why? Because after the poignant, heart-breaking intensity of the slow movement some affirmation of the soul is inexorably demanded. *Mozart could not make that affirmation.* He could not even attempt to make it. If he had attempted but had failed, *then* we could speak of inadequate resources. But he had no faith, he could not lift up his heart and sing from the bottom of that abyss, he could not stretch his wings and rise up out of it, he could only shrug his shoulders and blow us another bubble. Therefore, and therefore only, he is not the world's greatest composer.

VII

BEETHOVEN

LUDWIG VAN BEETHOVEN

Born at Bonn, December 16, 1770. Studied briefly with Haydn; lived principally in Vienna. Beethoven's life, both musically and personally, was extraordinarily rich and varied; the most important events are treated in the accompanying chapter. He died at Vienna, March 26, 1827.

PRINCIPAL WORKS

VOCAL: 2 masses, in C and D (*Missa Solemnis*); oratorio, *Christ on the Mount of Olives;* 10 cantatas; opera: *Fidelio.* Over 250 songs, including *Adelaide, In Questa Tomba, An die Hoffnung, An die Ferne Geliebte.*

INSTRUMENTAL: 9 symphonies (the last with chorus); overtures to *Egmont; Coriolanus; Leonore* (nos. 1, 2, 3, and 4); *Fidelio, King Stephen, Ruins of Athens;* 5 piano concertos; fantasie for piano, orchestra and chorus; 1 violin concerto; 2 romances for violin and orchestra; triple concerto for piano, violin and cello; ballet, *Prometheus.* Chamber music: 16 string quartets; *Grosse fuge* for string quartet (originally composed as final movement of the quartet in B flat, Opus 130; published separately as Opus 133); sextet for strings and winds; 8 trios for piano, violin, and cello; 5 trios for other instruments; 2 string quintets; 10 sonatas for piano and violin; 5 sonatas for piano and cello. Piano music: 32 sonatas; one sonata for four hands; over 100 smaller pieces, including variations, rondos, preludes, etc.

BEETHOVEN

By C. Hubert H. Parry

BEETHOVEN was born in 1770 at Bonn, where both his father and grandfather had musical posts of some rather insignificant kind in the service of the Elector of Cologne. His early life must have been rough and bracing; for the family had to exist upon a wretchedly poor income, and the father was a man of dissipated habits, which grew upon him more and more as he grew older, till his drunkenness and irregularities made him utterly unfit to perform either his musical or domestic duties any longer. It was, however, from his father that Beethoven had to get the earlier part of his musical education till he was nine years old. By that time the extent of his father's knowledge was fairly well exhausted, and he began to pick up stray fragments of knowledge from anyone he could find who was fit to teach him anything. Neefe, the organist of the court chapel, helped him to learn something of the organ, and he soon got on well enough to act as deputy when his master had to be away. When he was a little over twelve he was given the post of "cembalist" in the orchestra of the theatre; and this must have been a great advantage to him, as he had to take an active part in the production of many of the most successful operas of the time, and was able to gain something by the experience which would be serviceable for composition. He could scarcely have had any regular instruction beyond that, as none of the musicians he seems to have been in contact with at Bonn were likely to have much idea of teaching composition. But he nevertheless tried his hand at writing occasionally, and produced works like sonatas and rondos for the pianoforte, which were of no very great im-

From the author's *Studies of Great Composers,* by permission of George Routledge and Sons, Ltd.

portance. But his playing and general musical gifts began to strike many people, and made them think he was likely to make some mark in the world.

When he was seventeen years old he somehow managed to get to Vienna, the greatest musical center of that time; and there he had the good fortune to be brought into contact with Mozart, who was very much struck by his extemporizing, and seems to have given him some lessons. Beyond that his journey did not produce any remarkable result, and he had to hurry back in a few months on account of the illness of his mother, who died in July, 1787. This must have made the condition of affairs at home worse than ever, as the mother was of a kind and gentle disposition, and her death left the young Beethoven to manage his dissipated father and the domestic concerns of the family as best he could. Fortunately he began to make friends among a class of people who were well fitted to help and brighten his life. Under the trying conditions of his early existence his character was evidently developing, and showing those qualities which all through his life exerted an extraordinary fascination upon people of all grades of society and intelligence. Among his earliest friends were a family of von Breunings, people of better position than himself, and of higher cultivation and refinement than most of those of his own rank. He gave lessons to the younger members of the family, and the mother, who was a widow and a woman of considerable intelligence, had a most excellent influence upon him, and gave him that turn for general cultivation and an interest in literature which soon more than made up for the scantiness of his early education in general subjects. Another important friend he made about the same time was a Count Waldstein, an enthusiastic amateur, who helped him and did most friendly offices for him in various ways, and was well repaid by the immortality Beethoven conferred on his name by dedicating to him one of his greatest piano sonatas.

In the same year that he came back from Vienna the music at the theatre in Bonn was put on a better footing than it had been before. Several distinguished players were engaged—Neefe, Beethoven's old master, was made pianist, and Beethoven himself was appointed to play the viola in the band, besides his other duties. This gave him opportunities of hearing better music better performed than had been his fortune previously, and his standard of ideas probably improved under the circumstances. But his position in art was still a very curious one, and very ill-defined. What struck people most was his extemporizing, which seems to have been daring and vigorous, and full of interesting ideas and surprising strokes of genius. His playing can hardly have been very perfect or finished, for he had no opportunity of learning any keyed instrument systematically, or of hearing first-rate performers. But throughout his life it seems to have been the style of expression which made his playing so impressive, rather than any gifts of facility or dexterity. His character and behavior and his musical performances must have been rather of a piece in these respects; and people were attracted by both one and the other notwithstanding roughness and want of polish, for the depth of earnestness and absolute sincerity there was in him, and the absence of anything like affectation.

Of composition up to this time there was very little to show, and, in fact, people had not begun to regard him as a composer, though he every now and then brought out a work of some sort. When Haydn passed through Bonn on his way to England in 1792, Beethoven took him some work that he had been writing, and Haydn praised it and advised him to go on composing. It may have been partly the result of this that the Elector, his master, began to think of sending Beethoven to Vienna again to be under Haydn for regular instruction in composition. It seemed rather late in the day to be taking such a step, when Beethoven was already well past twenty; but it was evidently well worth trying, and in the latter part of 1792 the arrangements were completed and Beethoven left his native Bonn for Vienna, after most affectionate partings with the von Breunings and Waldstein and others who had learnt to appreciate him at his true worth.

He began to work with Haydn as soon as possible after his arrival in Vienna, and the old master set him to do the usual, dry, technical studies in counterpoint which are the orthodox means of gaining facility in composition. Beethoven worked with a will and produced a great deal more of this sort than Haydn had time to look at. It does not, indeed, seem that the old master can ever have given him regular and systematic teaching at any time; and before long Beethoven began to be restless and to think that he might do better with someone else. He felt that Haydn was too busy to attend to him properly, and he was getting old too, and was not by any means ready to appreciate the bent of Beethoven's mind.

So when he started on another of his journeys to England in 1794, Beethoven looked about for some other master who could drill him more thoroughly, and he certainly found a man as fit to do mechanical and rigid drilling as anyone known to history.

The name of Albrechtsberger is still well known to musicians as one of the most famous of theorists, and one of the strictest and most mechanical of musical pedants. To this man Beethoven attached himself, in despite of the obvious fact that he would necessarily be more antagonistic and unsympathetic to him than even Haydn had been; and for him he ground through reams of technical exercises, out of which it is probable that he could not quite contrive to keep his characteristic qualities from displaying themselves. The master, for his part, did his duty thoroughly, and conducted his willing pupil through the most arid wastes of ingenuity; which Beethoven bore as patiently as a perfect novice, though he was by this time twenty-four, and a man of some experience and great power in some branches of his art. Albrechtsberger had the most hearty contempt for his pupil, and told some inquiring person to have nothing to do with him, "for he had never learnt anything, and would never do anything in a decent style," a criticism of genius which is characteristic of pedants of all times and places.

From a man like Albrechtsberger this was to be anticipated, but it is more disappointing to find that Haydn's feelings towards Beethoven were not by any means sympathetic or appreciative. Their intercourse was naturally rendered difficult by the peculiar independence and unhesitating contempt for conventionalities of all sorts, which was one of the most striking marks of Beethoven. He detested pretension and shallow pedantry in almost equal measure, and never hesitated to express himself clearly on such subjects, whoever happened to be his company. An old and established musician nearly always has an extraordinary quantity of empty and dried-up formularies hanging about him, and looks upon them as articles of faith. The school of the time before Beethoven and the musicians who followed it in later times have had even more of this about them than any other set of musicians in history, and Beethoven, who was born to be the first and greatest exponent of a different order of things, was brought at once into antagonism with a great representative of the old order. He at first made some few works quite after the old models, and as long as he did that Haydn was satisfied with him. But even in one of the earliest compositions which he produced after going to Vienna there were things which were thoroughly characteristic of him, and then Haydn sadly shook his head and recommended Beethoven to suppress the work that contained them, and not allow it to appear in print. Beethoven was quite certain that this was the best of his works so far, and posterity has thought the same; so he must have felt that there was something radically wrong in Haydn's views of art, or else that he was jealous of him. Beethoven always felt the truth and rightness of a thing he had made up his mind about so thoroughly that it was difficult for him to realize the position of people who could not follow or agree with him; and so his quick and impatient temper sometimes led him to think other people had bad motives for judgments and actions when they were thoroughly sincere.

It is not therefore so very surprising that Haydn should have looked on Beethoven's ways with dislike. The younger musician had as yet made no mark whatever in composition, and there was not enough work of his before the world to enable a critical man to judge how much of the new departure was the result of caprice and recklessness, and how much was the result of well-balanced judgment and genius. Haydn had in reality a great deal in common with Beethoven, though the things which seemed like needless violations of his rules of art were too prominent to allow him to judge of him with equanimity; and the result was that their relations with one another did not run quite smoothly and equably at any time. They did not quarrel decisively, but Beethoven sometimes said rude things to Haydn, and Haydn for his part spoke slightingly of Beethoven. But at bottom Beethoven had a great reverence and admiration for the old master, and at least one burst of enthusiastic feeling for him is recorded even about this time; and in later days, when Beethoven was shown a picture of the place where Haydn was born, he said— "To think that so great a man should have been born in so humble a cottage."

Beethoven's relations with other musicians were for the most part worse than with Haydn. There were a few liberal-minded and intelligent men whom he liked and who behaved reasonably to him, but there were also numbers of self-sufficient professionals who had won success chiefly by imposing on the public with tricks of technique or by exceptional powers of self-confidence, and these naturally detested this real true man when he came amongst them, just as similar pharisees have always done. These Viennese pharisees had a very good subject to mock at, for Beethoven's appearance was peculiar and his dialect was different from theirs; his behavior was not of the kind affected by polite Viennese; his style of music, especially in extemporizing, no doubt seemed like perfect impudence to the taste of a real well-bred pharisee of the old school; and it is no wonder they threw his compositions on the floor and trampled on them, and otherwise showed what nature they were of at his expense. To Beethoven this was of little consequence. It happened with him as it happened with Wagner since; he found amongst intelligent amateurs and such public as was in those days, the cordial sympathy and appreciation which a large body of his own fellow musicians denied him.

Among the distinguished and cultivated amateurs in Vienna at that time he soon found enthusiastic admirers, and his music and his force of character so deeply impressed them that they overcame the usual habits of the courtly classes in a capital where aristocratic rank is almost made more of than anywhere else in Europe, and placed him on equal terms with men and women of the highest position—or at least, if not on equal terms, it was with the advantage on his side; for many of them carried their admiration for him to such a pitch that they would bear anything from him; and rudeness and bearishness and ill-temper that they would not have endured for a moment from an equal, were taken with perfect patience and quietness when they came from him.

Almost the earliest of these aristocratic friends was a Prince Charles Lichnowsky, whose name is associated, by dedications, with some of Beethoven's best-known compositions. They were soon on intimate terms, and the prince induced Beethoven for a time to accept rooms in his house. But Beethoven could not conform to the ways of such people, or keep their hours, and before long the arrangement came to an end. But it does not seem to have produced any sort of breach between them, and though Beethoven occasionally broke into wild tempers with his generous friend, it was long before their familiar intercourse was materially affected. Beethoven used frequently to play to the people who met together at Prince Lichnowsky's house, and at the houses of other musical aristocrats of like disposition, and the character and interest of his performances rapidly gained him more and more friends among them. But still for a good while after he came to Vienna he was known more as a player than as a composer, and even as a player he was known only to the aristocratic circles who met in private houses. The first occasion when he made his appearance in anything like a public concert was in 1795, when he had been three years in Vienna; and then he played his own concerto in C major, which had been finished just before. Very soon after this he appeared in public again at a concert given for Mozart's widow, when he played one of Mozart's concertos. From this time he continued to make his appearance in public more frequently, either as performer or composer, and his reputation soon went up to a very high point. He also began to show himself in other towns besides Vienna, and in 1796 he went as far as Berlin, where he played before the king, and was treated with appreciative distinction.

In the year which followed he continued steadily working at composition, but he still did not begin the line of grand works which has been his special triumph. It was not till he was almost thirty that he produced his first symphony, and this was first performed in 1800. Moreover, his style did not yet approach to anything like the full measure of his independent originality, and even the first symphony, which made its appearance so late in his life as compared with the great works of Mozart and many other famous composers, was still very much more like, in general character, to the works of his predecessors than it was to his own maturer style. He seemed cautious and reserved in the production of the works about which he had a full sense of artistic responsibility, and began tentatively; and only as he made sure of his ground and tested the power of his hand to express exactly what he wanted, did he venture to give fuller rein to his inspiration. Every now and then there came out a work which had all the force of his character in it, and then sometimes he went back again and wrote another work more after the style and manner of thought of Mozart or Haydn. But to his contemporaries even the works which seem to musicians of the present day to be the most slender and obvious of his productions, appeared amazingly daring, and delighted them or revolted them in proportion to their feeling for poetry and powers of expansion.

The next work on a large scale which he was engaged upon after the first Symphony in C was the *Mount of Olives,* his first great choral achievement. On this he was at work in 1801, and its first performance took place in 1803. Almost at the same time he was busy with a second symphony, which had much more of his own fire and independent style in it than the first; and several other works of considerable importance, such as sonatas and chamber music, were in progress. His ideas came so profusely that he always had several works going on at once, and he always meditated and thought over them for a long while before he brought them to completeness. His practice was to jot down the ideas roughly as they came into his head in little sketch-books which he carried in his pocket, and he then polished and improved these original ideas time after time, sometimes for years, before he worked them up into complete works. He was very fond of the country and of open-air exercise, and the ideas used sometimes to come to him as he was walking or wandering in the woods, or sitting on the branch of a tree, and when they laid hold of him he was thoroughly like one inspired. His eyes are said to have dilated, and his whole being seemed to be possessed by the fervor of his thoughts, and he became altogether careless of time or engagements as long as the excitement lasted. This must have been a characteristic trait even in the early days before he left Bonn, for his friend Madame von Breuning described him as "being in his *raptus*" at times, and then it was quite impossible to manage him. In later times he used to stamp and stride about, and sing and shout passages that were passing through his brain, or thrum them in a wild way on the pianoforte.

It is altogether an extraordinary contrast to the ways of the earlier composers, with whom emotion counted for less than good workmanship. Haydn appears to have been quite quiet and self-possessed when he was producing his music, and liked to be tidy and neat and to have his best clothes on when he was at work upon anything serious; and Mozart wrote many of his works as quickly as most people would write an ordinary letter, and was so far from being wildly impassioned that he could quite well listen to or take a share in talking at the same time. But Beethoven could not produce his best work except under the influence of some such powerful emotion as his music represents. He considered that the emotion and poetical or dramatic effect of the music was of the highest importance and the title that he valued most was *Ton-Dichter*, or "tone poet." This was one of the characteristics of his work which showed the way in which art was moving; for it is its emotional power and variety which mark it as the highest expression of that expansion of the sympathies of mankind which began in the latter part of the eighteenth century.

The third of his symphonies, at which he was working about this time, was the result of his feelings on the great questions at issue between kings and aristocracies on the one side, and peoples on the other. He had developed an immense admiration for Napoleon Bonaparte, who seemed to him the very ideal of a hero of the people. Napoleon's career had not yet arrived at the point when he appeared in his full lineaments as an insatiable conqueror, and the very impersonation of imperial attributes; he was still regarded as the extreme opposite of kings and monarchical traditions; to Beethoven he seemed to be the liberator of down-trodden peoples from old despotisms, and the benefactor who would give new laws to the peoples of the world for the peoples' benefit and not for the advantage of despots or privileged aristocracies. In this mood he set about writing a symphony in his honor, and produced by far the grandest and longest and most powerful work of its kind that had ever appeared. It made altogether an epoch in the history of the symphony, for all the greatest works which had appeared before it were mere shadows by its side in point of emotion and breadth and poetical interest. Many had been perfect in respect of artistic workmanship, and balance of beautiful form, but composers of the previous century had never even aimed at such degrees of force or such variety of interest. His enthusiasm for his ideal hero brought out the greatest music he had in him at that time, and by 1804 the work was finished, and the title-page bore the name of Napoleon Bonaparte. He was even preparing to send it to Paris, when the news was brought to him by his pupil Ries, that Napoleon had taken the title of emperor. His ideal hero was dashed from his pedestal in an instant; the man he had believed in had, after all, joined the ranks of the despots. He tore off the page which bore the detested name, and, according to the commonly accepted story, the symphony itself narrowly escaped destruction for its connection with such a gigantic impostor. But fortunately for the world the election of the new emperor did not produce such grievous results as that, and by way of denoting the ideal circumstances under which it was produced, it received the name of *"Sinfonia Eroica* in memory of a great man." The word "memory" carries a mountain of meaning.

This whole story illustrates very happily Beethoven's strong and independent views about great social subjects. His sympathies were all on the side of the masses, and against privileges and class distinctions and artificial dignities of all sorts. He could hardly be patient at the conventional subservience expected of ordinary people when they were brought into contact with aristocrats, for he felt that the common people were often worthier and more useful members of society than the individuals they were expected to bow down to. He himself ignored their claims to special respect even ostentatiously, and many curious stories are told of his behavior to them. On one occasion, for instance, when he was playing to a party of aristocratic people, some of the younger ones went on talking, just as people often do to the sound of good music in modern drawing-rooms. Beethoven flew into a great rage and stopped the music, saying loudly he "would play no more to such hogs." Another time as he was walking in the street he met a group of people of rank, among whom was an especial friend of his; and the revulsion against empty formalities was so strong in him at the moment, that he kept his hat tight on his head and did not even give the company any sign of recognition. It is very much to the credit of the aristocratic people in Vienna, that in spite of his well-known views on the subject of rank and commonalty, and his brusque and unrestrained manner of speech and behavior with them, they were his most constant friends and supporters. It is curious, too, to think that they should have entered into music which was so very different in many respects from the quiet, self-contained kind which had been prepared for their especial amusement by the composers of the previous generation. It proved at least that their humanity was larger and more generous than the restrictions they had to submit to by etiquette and custom allowed to appear. At the same time it is probable they did not in those days realize what Beethoven was doing. They felt the greatness and impressiveness of what he said, but did not guess what it all meant; and if they had appreciated the fact that it was an appeal from their influence on art, and their exclusive patronage, to a wider and more independent public, they might not have been so ready to fall in with it.

In this respect, as in the character of his music, Beethoven is a link between the old and new order of things. The rich German princes and nobles had always been remarkable for their great love of music, and they had been so long accustomed to regard it as a sort of appanage and property of their own, that even when such an independent creature as Beethoven appeared in the world, they still regarded him as their particular care, and as a person for whom it was their prescriptive duty to provide. Their generosity and helpfulness to him is so surprising that it can hardly be explained on any other grounds. The offer of Prince Lichnowsky to take him into his house has before been mentioned; another man of rank, called Baron Pasqualati, reserved rooms for him in a house on the ramparts of Vienna, in what was called the Mölk Bastion, from which there was a beautiful view; and here he used often to shut himself up when he was busy composing. Another patron, Count Browne, gave Beethoven a horse, in return for a set of variations on a Russian air which Beethoven wrote for his wife; and Beethoven characteristically forgot all about it, and was very much enraged when the bill came in for its keep. Similar generosity was shown by one of the Apponyi family, who proposed to Beethoven to write his first string quartet and said he might propose what terms he would for the work. But the most striking piece of generosity came later in his life, when three noblemen, Archduke Rudolph, Prince Kinsky, and Prince Lobkowitz, clubbed together to secure him a regular income, which would have amounted to £400 a year but for the unfortunate condition of monetary affairs in Austria at the time, owing to long and ruinous wars, which reduced the value of the amount paid in notes to about £210. And they not only did this, but when the depreciation of notes became worse and worse, and a measure had to be passed which substituted a new means of exchange for the old one at a very much lower value, they made good the difference to him as well as they could at their own loss.

Nevertheless Beethoven was rarely in a prosperous condition. He could not give his mind to practical matters, and his ordinary affairs were generally in pitiable confusion. He forgot almost everything: sometimes it was his washing, another time he forgot that he had engaged rooms which he was not living in, at another time he forgot to eat his dinner, at another time, as before said, he forgot he had a horse. He was so often profoundly absorbed that things which were outside the range of his musical thoughts had to go by chance. It was altogether a most happy-go-lucky and uncertain existence: flying from lodging to lodging, falling out with his servants, fancying all sorts of grievances with his friends, and breaking out into wild transports of rage, and pouring insults upon them; and then, if he found out he was wrong, writing the most affectionate and self-accusing letters of repentance. All his life long it was the same, and showed a childlike and transparent simplicity, combined with a force of character and nobility of soul, such as is always one of the most attractive compounds in human nature.

People's interest in him was also enhanced by his troubles and misfortunes. Chief among these was his deafness, which began to show premonitions of its approach as early as 1798 by singings and buzzings in his ears. By 1800 it had become serious enough to require the attention of doctors; and its progress from bad to worse was so steady and unmistakable in its march, that he foresaw himself that it must end in total deafness. To a man whose whole organism was centered in the beauties of sounds it must have appeared a most fearful prospect; and the anticipation tortured him. He endeavored to face it with determined courage. He looked forward to moments when he would be the most wretched of God's creatures, but he made up his mind "to grapple with fate, and not allow it to drag him down."

There is something very tragic in the whole story of his life. He had a most sensitive and excitable disposition, and was in a constant state of suffering, either from his own headlong mistakes, or from the troubles which fate brought upon him; and as he grew older the net seemed to get closer round him, and the worries and misfortunes more desperate and to be less often relieved by brighter moments; till at last he was shut out from all communication with the outer world by means of sounds, and from all sensation of his beloved art.

But though he was also pressed upon incessantly by poverty and bad health, and harassed by the baseness of the nephew in whom he had centered his affections, yet he always went on rising to nobler heights of art and greater and more powerful achievements, with a Titanic power and endurance, and a spirit which misfortune seemed rather to purify and exalt than to subdue.

The indications of approaching deafness which were becoming more and more conspicuous about the beginning of the century, appeared only to increase his ardor for work; as if in anxiety to get as much completed as possible before the time when he should no longer be able to hear himself what he had made for all the world to hear. Among the most important things which he set to work upon soon after the *Eroica* symphony was the opera *Fidelio*. He had long been wishing to try his powers in opera writing, and had even accepted engagements from managers to write works for them, as, for instance, for Mozart's old friend, Schikaneder; but these had all fallen through. One of his difficulties was very characteristic of him. The opera writers of previous generations had been content to set the most inconceivable and idiotic rubbish to music; and so long as there were some points which were effective for the stage, or which gave opportunities for the show of qualities of voice or acting, for prima donnas and famous tenors, the public did not mind the dramas being unintelligible nonsense. The patrons of the earlier operas went to the theatre to be amused, and if such a thing as a variety entertainment had been invented in those days, it would have been quite sufficient to give the performance an imposing name and the pretence of a story to make it answer all the purposes of a high-class opera, and satisfy its highly cultivated audiences that they were listening to a work of art. Even Mozart, whose dramatic sense and power of character-drawing in music was of the highest kind, did not inquire too minutely into the nature of the stories upon which his librettos were founded, but accepted the silliest and most empty things to set to music. Beethoven's point of view was altogether different. He felt that in an artistic sense, the dramatic side of the matter was as important as the music; and that to be worthy of the name of a work of art, an opera must be complete and intelligible in all respects, and not like the creatures of old Norse fable—a face and front with neither back nor substance underneath. And this was not all. He felt the need of the thing being sound throughout; and he felt also that the subject must be of the noblest and broadest kind to be worth setting to music. He knew that silly and empty commonplaces could be set consistently only to silly and empty music. The connection between the music and the words and dramatic situation was so close in his mind that he could not bring himself to write music to anything ignoble; or to deal with anything as opera which was not a great type of some sort.

In the end he fixed upon a story of brave and unconquerable womanly devotion, and this was embodied in the libretto of *Leonora,* or *Fidelio* as it was afterwards called; and by the end of 1805 the work was ready for performance. He took enormous pains over it, and tried and tested the various parts of it with even more than usual patience. It is said that he made as many as eighteen different versions of one famous passage, and ten of another, and similar changes and experimental improvements throughout. The result was a work thoroughly worthy of him and of the labor he had given to it. To modern musicians it has a unique place in the whole province of opera; and in nobility and truth of sentiment, and depth of musical feeling, and insight into the possibilities of operatic art, it is beyond rivalry among the works produced before the present generation. But unfortunately, when it was brought out in its first form, it had all sorts of unfavorable circumstances against it. The first performance actually took place when the French army was in possession of Vienna, and had just driven out the high society of the place, among them many of Beethoven's most faithful friends and admirers. Besides this it was evidently too long, in its earliest form, for the endurance of any average audience, and he was so determined not to alter anything when he had once thoroughly made up his mind, that it was almost hopeless to try to get him to cut it down. The singers complained that some passages were unsingable, but he simply refused to make any changes for their benefit. He had come to a decision as to how the music ought to go, and so it was to remain. It was the same with the difficulties that troubled the band, and when his friends protested that it was too long it threatened to be the same with them. But after long wrangling, which made Beethoven violently angry, he finally gave in and agreed to reduce the length of the work materially. The impression it produced seemed to improve after this, though its success was evidently not striking or enthusiastic; and after no very great number of performances disagreement between Beethoven and the intendant brought them to an end early in 1806; and no more were given anywhere for many years.

Beethoven thenceforward gave up opera writing, and went back to the lines of art for which he found more sympathetic audiences. He was by this time arriving at the full maturity of his power; and the traces of the formal style of the composers of the previous generation which had again and again presented themselves, even in *Fidelio,* were by degrees being pushed altogether out of sight by the growth and increase of his own individuality. He was one of those rare men whose energy and vitality continue so constantly unabated through life, that they grow and improve even up to the days of their old age. Neither weariness nor excess of labor could make him write conventionally or formally. Formality is often the fruit of indolence and want of earnestness, which makes men put empty phrases, which cost them nothing, in the place of the real ideas which exhaust their nature. Beethoven was always possessed with such thorough enthusiasm for art that every work he wrote served as a stepping-stone in some way to further advance. He would rather not write at all than write things without any artistic or emotional point in them; and now that he had arrived at complete mastery of the resources of art, after the manner of his predecessors, he turned all his energies to the improvement of the emotional qualities of his work.

The chief works which he was engaged upon immediately after *Fidelio* were symphonies, the famous Violin Concerto, a Mass in C, and some overtures. The most important of these is the Symphony in C minor, which has in later times had the greatest popularity of all his larger works for orchestra. It was almost the first in which the full force of his originality came out untrammeled by conventions or by traces of the old formal traditions. It had no external name or association, like the Third Symphony, to define to the public the kernel of poetical meaning upon which it turned; but it seemed to tell its own tale without that. Every movement in it expressed something as a whole which the public could grasp and feel, apart from the mere technical development of the work of art, and each successive movement set off and illustrated what had gone before it, and the last of all was at such a pitch of grandeur, and weight, and force, as the world had never heard in a last movement before. The people who clung to the old traditions, the conservatives by inclination from their birth, often found its originality intolerable; but it sometimes happened that even those who began with mocking ended with enthusiasm.

A similar wealth and power of imagination now began to make its appearance in all his instrumental works, and gave them the peculiar character which is now recognized as belonging to his most vigorous and warmly poetical middle age; before sorrow and trouble and the isolation coming from deafness had given his music the peculiar cast which it bore throughout the later years of his life. In these works the character of a new line of music is completely fulfilled; the prominence of art from the craftsman's point of view has given place to a high poetical conception, and from this starting point the whole course of modern music has since flowed. He seemed now to have thoroughly matured his plan of operations, and new works followed one another rapidly. Some of them merely appeared with the usual formal names, Symphony No. 4, or No. 5, or Sonata, Opus 54; and some had descriptive names given them, such as the *Pastoral Symphony* and the sonata called *"Les Adieux, l'Absence et le Retour,"* which was inspired by a parting with his friend, the Archduke Rudolph.

But Beethoven was not altogether in favor of the practice of giving definite names to musical works to fix their meaning. He probably knew that the public was attracted by such a procedure, but he felt that it was not without its risks. It happens very often that music can express things which words have not the subtlety to describe; and the practice of tying a composer down by a definite program sometimes leads him to try to express things which are not fit to be said by music, and may prevent his rising to those heights in which music must be superior in the matter of expression to the most subtle and refined language. The impulse which led him away from the old formal methods of composing made him often conscious of the connection between his music and some poetical idea external to music, and at certain points it was possible to state the connection in words; but his feeling and judgment set him against trying to paint scenes or events in musical sounds. The vulgar conception of program music, which consists of actually reproducing scenes or events in music, was naturally repugnant to him. If he had to make music to any idea or scene he would try to express not what was seen by the eye, but what was felt inwardly. Music, to be true to itself, must refer to the inner emotional working, and not the outer sensation; and, if that were kept in view, program music might always be admirable but for the fact that words would too often be behindhand in the race.

The power of music to express subtle gradations of feeling is so much greater than language, that in most cases the attempt to describe the meaning of the former by the latter is almost hopeless. It can often give no more than the baldest suggestion of the outline, and leaves all the more characteristic elements of the music and its internal working untouched. Nevertheless, Beethoven seems to have had an inclination towards defining the feelings he expressed in his music, and he allowed it to sway him occasionally; as appears from the names he gave to a few of his works, and the manner in which he developed some of them in connection with words. But many of the familiar names by which his works are known, such as the *Pastoral Sonata,* the *Moonlight Sonata,* the *Sonata Appassionata,* were neither given nor authorized by him, but were either invented by publishers, who knew the value a name has with the ordinary public, or else by admiring amateurs; and a general impression of their usefulness has kept them on in defiance of the protests of good judges, and the fact that one at least is perfectly inappropriate. In the case of the *Pastoral Symphony* the name was given by Beethoven himself, and the plan was deliberately worked out by him, and it contained some things which certainly came very near being attempts at musical scene-painting, as, for instance, in the movement which represents the storm. But Beethoven was careful to point out that he intended it all to be more as feeling than painting; *"mehr Ausdruckder Empfindung als Malerei,"* as he himself wrote. Actual imitation of birds' notes, and of the whispering of the brook, does come into it, it is true, but such things only enter as accessories, and the removal of what is implied would make very little difference to the effect of the work as a whole. The music is perfectly intelligible and complete of itself, and does not depend upon the coloring or influence of the external idea on the minds of the audience.

This may serve to illustrate the position of Beethoven as the greatest composer of pure instrumental music. The object of the successive generations of composers who had worked on this branch of composition before him, was evidently to produce works which should be perfectly interesting and intelligible of themselves without the help of words or explanatory names or text. They had to content themselves at first with very simple and slender works, as the whole scheme and system upon which music could be made intelligible of itself had to be found out. They put dance tunes together, and found that their contrasts were effective, and they spun out the time by making variations and so forth. Each generation improved a little upon the work of the generation before, and found out how to do more with the instruments, and how to make the movements longer and more interesting. So it went on till the time of Haydn and Mozart, who produced very perfect works of art in the form of symphonies and sonatas, trusting to the principles upon which they were constructed, as the means of making them intelligible. Then Beethoven came and added a greater element of interest and a stronger bond of connection in all parts of the work by bringing ideas and moods and various means of arousing impressions more strongly forward. He filled his music as full of emotion as it would hold without upsetting the balance of those qualities upon which the existence of pure unadulterated instrumental music depends. The fact that he did adopt a name in the case of the *Pastoral Symphony* gives a sort of clue to his principles in making works without names; but his art was perfectly pure in so far as it was completely interesting and intelligible of itself.

The story of the middle period of his life is altogether centered in his art. It would have been impossible for him to produce works so full of deep and earnest feeling without giving all his vitality to them. And even though he concentrated all his energies upon them, he produced very much less than his predecessors had done. The conditions under which he worked were altogether different from theirs, and much more exhausting. They had been able to produce little elegant works to please their refined public without much exertion, but he wanted to appeal to his hearers and move them in a deeper way. To him art was not an amusement, or a means of passing hours that might otherwise hang heavy on men's hands, but a means of elevating them, and giving them interests and feelings which should take them away from the sordid and material cares of everyday life, and supply a counterbalance to their hardening influences. He worked essentially for the same ideals as a poet, and he put his whole soul into his work in a way which no composer before, except perhaps Bach, had thought of; and the result naturally was that the vital force was concentrated into fewer works, instead of being diffused in a thinner stream in many.

Besides this there was much more actual exertion in making his works than there had been in those of his predecessors, both in the matter of thought and mere manual labor. Composers had gone on increasing the number of instruments they used for their symphonies, and they had gone on trying to increase the force and fullness of sound of their works even when they wrote for only one instrument. The symphonies which numberless forgotten composers used to write for the delectation of aristocratic patrons in the earlier part of the eighteenth century, just before or about the beginning of Haydn's career, had usually been written for little bands of eight instruments, such as two violins, a viola, a cello, and two flutes, or two haut-boys and two horns; to which a harpsichord was allowed to supply a sort of accompaniment and filling-in at the discretion of the conductor. At first composers used this little band very roughly, and did very little in the way of refined or delicate expression. But as time went on musicians were impelled to attempt more finish and artistic effect, and to experiment with more instruments. Stamitz earned a good title to be honorably remembered for the way in which he taught the band at Mannheim to play in a more finished and intelligent way, and to use more subtle shades of *piano* and *forte* than had been thought of before. Mozart profited by this when he went to stay at Mannheim, and devised his symphonies with much more attention to such matters afterwards; both he and Haydn did an immense deal to make the treatment of the band more refined and thoroughly artistic; and they also increased the usual size of it by adding several more instruments, such as trumpets and drums, and bassoons, and sometimes clarinets. Beethoven in his time began at once to make the band larger and more powerful, and to treat the instruments with more artistic independence. In some cases he introduced trombones, and sometimes he used four horns instead of two, and he constructed the works altogether upon a more elaborate and grander scale. So of course there was much more work to do in even the actual writing of such works, than in the early symphonies; in which there had not been half the number of instruments which he employed, and the labor of writing out their parts had been greatly lessened by the simple device of directing several to play the same passages together for whole pages in succession.

A similar change came about also in works written for solo instruments. Beethoven's career corresponds with the regular adoption of the pianoforte by the musical world in general in place of the old harpsichord. Both Mozart and Haydn had been brought up to the harpsichord, and wrote many of their sonatas for it. And even when Mozart took to playing and writing for the pianoforte he continued to treat it in a harpsichord style, which was subdued and very quiet; and he very much disliked the energetic and muscular kind of playing which was necessary to get the proper and characteristic effect out of the pianoforte. The first great representative of genuine pianoforte playing was Clementi, and he did the world some service by leading the way in the development of a proper treatment of the new instrument. By Beethoven's time the requirements of the instrument were becoming much better understood. The prejudices and conventions of the old harpsichord school were giving way before the rising school of regular pianoforte players, and music was devised in a way better suited to the character of the new instrument. The result was a much grander scale of writing in sonatas, just as there was in orchestral symphonies, and Beethoven was the composer to whose share the work of bringing this branch of art to perfection also fell. Mozart's and Haydn's sonatas were even slenderer and more unimportant in proportion than their symphonies. The larger portion of them were the merest trifles, neatly put together, but containing the very slightest amount of interest or matter of striking character. They both of them wrote a few tolerably large works of the kind, but harpsichord traditions and their craftsman-like point of view prevented their producing anything very impressive or striking in this kind. Beethoven began from the first to put his full energies into the writing of his pianoforte sonatas. In his early days he was so much drawn in this direction that a good deal more than half of his first fifty works were in this form. He soon developed an extraordinary insight into the nature of the instrument, and produced new and deep and noble effects with it. He found out how to express his own individuality completely in this branch of composition earlier than in any other; and he gave such color and character to what he wrote for it that the whole standard of pianoforte music has been raised thereby to a higher level. He continued writing pianoforte sonatas for nearly twenty-five years of his life, always endeavoring to add to their interest and to improve the form of art; and in no branch of music can the course of his musical life be more clearly traced, from the beginning under the influences of Mozart and Haydn, to the mature richness and warmth of his middle age, and on to the great and unsurpassable utterances of his wisest and deepest latter days.

As years went on his fame spread abroad. In England his works were brought to a hearing, and up to a certain point met with enthusiastic appreciation. The appearance of his new works was looked forward to with eagerness, and overtures were made to him now and then to write things especially for publishers or audiences in this country. Among these invitations was one from a publisher called Thompson, in Edinburgh, for settings of Scotch national tunes, for which he was ready

to give Beethoven very liberal remuneration. Beethoven accepted the
task, and arranged over 150 of them after his own fashion—a labor which
it took him a great many years to get through. The result illustrates
rather his views of art and his own idiosyncrasies than anything Scotch.

In the year 1814 the opera *Fidelio* was revived. Though Beethoven
had been difficult to persuade to make any alterations in it at first, the
lapse of time made him regard such changes from his settled intentions
with more patience. He allowed the libretto to be revised, and set to work
himself to make considerable alterations in the music throughout. In its
new form it was performed in May, and seems to have been received
with much more appreciation than at first. In the same year he brought
out one of his most interesting and romantic symphonies, which was
received with enthusiasm. The position he had attained in public estimation was also shown in the same year by the way he was made much of
by the crowds of grand people who came to Vienna for the Congress. A
great hall was lent him by the authorities, and here he gave two grand
concerts, to which he himself invited crowned heads as well as aristocrats.
The first concert was attended by fully 6,000 people, and Beethoven met
with all the sympathy and appreciation he could have desired, and got a
certain amount of substantial profit out of it as well. So for a time
things seemed to be prosperous with him.

But the tide turned again very soon, and from the year 1815 troubles
constantly thickened round him till the end. In that year his brother
Caspar died. This was unfortunate for him, in the first place, because
Caspar had been very useful to him in respect of those worldly affairs
which he was so utterly unfit to deal with. But there were other and
heavier misfortunes which followed from the same occurrence. Caspar
left behind him a son who was confided to the care of his brother, and
Ludwig took the charge upon him with more than paternal assiduity.
His first difficulties were with the widow, whom he could not endure;
and he was entangled in several successive lawsuits in the endeavor to get
sole custody of the son. They went on from year to year, sometimes in
his favor and sometimes in hers, and his sensitive nature was harrassed
and tormented with anxiety, and his time wasted in letter-writing and
conferences with his advisers and friends on the subject; and when finally
the case was decided in his favor, the object of all his solicitude turned
out to be desperately unworthy, and showed a thoroughly bad and un-

lovely nature. But Beethoven's affection had become centered in him, and nothing could destroy it. It was a sort of infatuation which made him seem to beg tenderly for forgiveness whenever he was obliged to take the object of his devotion to task for incessant wrong-doing. In one part of a letter he found fault with him, and then, as if afraid that it would make a bar between them, went on—"Only come to my arms: not one harsh word shall you hear. You shall be received as lovingly as ever— only come." Letter after letter is in the same style; but the only effect it had upon the unworthy object was to make him thoroughly callous.

The fruit of all this worry and distress of mind was naturally to increase Beethoven's irritability, and to aggravate the ill-health which troubled him more and more as he grew older. He was frequently obliged to resort to doctors for matters of general health, while his deafness became so serious that in 1816 he began to use an ear-trumpet. He gave up playing in public in 1814, and everything which depended to any extent upon hearing, such as conducting or superintending rehearsals, had in like manner to be brought to an end. After a time it became difficult even to take part in ordinary conversations; and he had to carry a notebook and a pencil about with him, and people who wanted to talk to him had to write their part of the conversation. Another misfortune which came upon him at the end of 1816 was the death of Prince Lobkowitz, one of the three aristocratic friends who had guaranteed him a fixed income. No arrangements seem to have been made for the continuance of the payments after the prince's death, so Beethoven's income was from that time seriously diminished.

But no amount of pinching or distress for funds would make him sacrifice his art, or try to make musical sham and pretty twaddle to catch the pence of the public. At the very time when want of money was beginning to tell most heavily upon him, he devoted all his best energies to the production of works which were even more than usually unsaleable. The worry and waste of time arising from the guardianship of his nephew seems to have prevented his working at any large orchestral works for a while, but he set to work instead to produce the finest and grandest of his pianoforte sonatas, which were so terribly difficult that there was no chance of any but very able and experienced players attempting them; while they were constructed at such a high pitch of art, and the things they expressed were so noble and exalted, that there was no chance of any but the few who were gifted with musical sense being able to understand them. It shows how entirely the impulse to compose was an artistic and poetical one with him. His gift was too sacred to be desecrated for ignoble uses. He was often driven to try very hard to get money's worth for what was done, but such a thing as altering or lowering the standard of his art with the object of making it more saleable seems never to have been allowed to enter into his head. In this he is the greatest type of high and unyielding honor; for the idea of degrading and cheapening his precious art seems to have been so entirely impossible to him that he probably never allowed himself to consider it for a moment. In this respect German musicians have always been patterns to all the world. In all other countries composers have been too easily led by cheap sophistries to escape from the taint of dishonoring their art, and publishing what they knew to be bad, vulgar, and commonplace, because it is easiest to get the ignorant public to pay for what pleases them most easily. The public is, in fact, helpless in matters of taste if it is not led and directed by true artists and sincere judges; and it is so difficult for ordinary people to understand in what real art consists, that it is no wonder they often seem not to appreciate the devotion of those whose true love and feeling for the honor of their art is stronger than their desire for popularity and well-fed ease. But nevertheless in Beethoven's case the sense of his perfectly heroic determination to work for art and art alone, and to make his music as perfect as possible without one thought for profit or fame, must have given the people of his time a very exalted notion of his true-heartedness; and was no doubt one of the sources of the great admiration in which he was held in the latter part of his life by musicians throughout the world; for, as far as appreciation of his works went, it is quite obvious he was leaving musicians more and more behind. It took many people some time even to understand his early works, and while they were coming to that point he was going on to more and more perfectly original and grand conceptions, so that the people who really understood him grew fewer, instead of more plentiful, as time went on. Most people found his latest sonatas and quartets hopelessly unintelligible, and it was only in later times, through the power and devotion of such men as Liszt and Bülow and Joachim, and a few less widely known but hardly less able and earnest performers, that these greatest of musical works were put within the reach of the public. In Beethoven's own time even works which now seem perfectly natural to ordinary musical amateurs were regarded as chaotic extravagances; and people only pardoned things, which seem like master-strokes now, as the "eccentricities of genius." It went even so far that some well-intentioned amateur wrote to him and offered him a good round sum if he would write something in the style of his early days, thinking thereby that Beethoven would benefit humanity as well as himself.

But Beethoven was not to be turned aside, and devoted himself to carrying out works according to his own highest ideals of art in all forms; and two of the greatest of all his works were yet to come. The first of these is the great Mass in D which he wrote for the installation of his friend the Archduke Rudolph as Archbishop of Olmütz. The sacred music of the Roman Church had long been suffering under various degrading influences, and had passed through a meretricious and theatrical phase, which was altogether unworthy of the depth and seriousness of the words of the Mass, and other ecclesiastical literature. Beethoven had given one earlier example of his notion of how such things ought to be treated, and he now attacked the matter again from a still more exalted point of view. He idealized religious emotions of the broadest and most comprehensive kind, as things belonging to all men, and all creeds and forms of religion; and he endeavored to express them in music of the most vivid, powerful, and earnest kind. He became extraordinarily absorbed in it, and more wildly possessed by inspiration than ever. A characteristic account of his ways of working at this time has been given by his friend Schindler, who saw a great deal of him, and wrote a book which is not considered entirely trustworthy, but has plenty of characteristic matter in it. In 1818 Beethoven had gone for the summer, according to custom, to a country place near Vienna, for fresh air and the country scenes which he loved. Here he used to be shut up in his room, sometimes all day, shouting, stamping, and tearing about the room under the influence of the excitement of the emotions which he was trying to express in his music. He used to forget all about time and rest and food for whole days at a stretch, and to come out dishevelled and haggard and exhausted at the end. But notwithstanding the vehement way he worked at it, the Mass took a long while to finish and was actually not complete till two years after the installation for which it was intended.

When that was finished all his attention was directed to the completion of the greatest of all his works. He had long been attracted by Schiller's *Ode to Joy;* and ever since his youthful days he had been meditating a setting of it in some form or another, and many years before this time ideas for it had been roughly indicated in his sketchbook. At last, when he was over fifty, he set his hand definitely to the task of embodying it all in a grand symphony. Again the composition took possession of him, and he seemed to forget all the comforts and conveniences of life, and even ordinary necessaries, in the wild fervor of inspiration. The symphony which resulted is entirely unique. It all turns upon Schiller's poem, though the first portion—consisting of three movements like the ordinary first three movements of symphonies —is purely instrumental. In this part he seems to express various conditions in man's existence while searching for the truest and highest form of joy, and being denied step by step. At last after several attempts the true conception wanted seems to be found, and with the entry of the voices come varying forms of utterance—sometimes wild and exuberant, sometimes gay, sometimes earnest and serene—of the ideal of joy as conveyed by the great and noble melody he at last developed to express it.

The reception which the great work had from the public in general was disappointing. It was fearfully difficult to perform, and even in Vienna it was not understood; while in London it was looked upon as a distressing failure. A critic of the day went so far as to discuss the causes for the falling off and failure of the powers of so great a master, as shown in this work, to parts of which he applied such epithets and expressions as "odd" and "almost ludicrous rambling," "chaos come again," "obstreperous roaring of modern frenzy"; and endeavored to account for it as the result of the deafness which cut Beethoven off from the rest of the world of music; and one of the most painful inferences he draws is, that Beethoven found "that noisy extravagance of execution and outrageous clamor in musical performances more frequently insured applause than chastened elegance and refined judgment, and that he wrote accordingly." Anything so diametrically opposite to fact could hardly have been proposed. If Beethoven ever thought of a public at all it was of an ideal public gifted with like insight and like feelings with himself. He knew that the public had to be considered, but he felt also that the public could be led; and his belief has proved right. In the course of the time that has elapsed since, the public has so far advanced under his guidance that this great symphony has become a special feature of all series of concerts of the highest class, and the work to which conductors and performers address themselves with most ardor and eagerness; and the one which most intelligent amateurs and professed musicians alike look upon as the highest and most noble and enduring enjoyment which can be presented to them.

This was Beethoven's last work in a grand scale. After it he only wrote string quartets * and other works of less dimensions. His aspirations were as great as ever. He hoped to write yet another opera; and to set Goethe's *Faust* to music, and to write more symphonies and other works still greater than those he had already done. He went on sketching ideas into his notebook, and even got on some way with fresh works; but nothing more on so grand a scale was destined to be finished. In 1826 he went with his nephew to stay with a brother who had a little property at a place called Gneixendorf, not far from Vienna. An account of his daily ways there was given by a Michael Krenn, which is so characteristic of him that it is worth quoting. "At half-past five he was up and at his table, beating time with his hands and feet, singing, humming, and writing. At half-past seven was the family breakfast, and directly after it he hurried out of doors, and would saunter about the fields, calling out, waving his hands, going now very slowly and now very fast, and then suddenly standing still and writing in a kind of pocket-book. At half-past twelve he came in to dinner, and after dinner he went to his own room till three or so, then in the fields again till about sunset, for later than that he might not go out. At half-past seven was supper, and then he went to his room and wrote till ten, and so to bed." But his brother did not make him comfortable or treat him well, and the whole conditions of life were such as he could not endure for long, so he started with his nephew to go back to Vienna on December 2, 1826.

* Since this article was written, Beethoven's last quartets have come to be regarded among his greatest works.

Unfortunately they could not get a closed vehicle to travel in, and the journey had to be done in an open carriage. The condition of his health rendered him quite unfit for such exposure, and when he arrived home he became very ill with cold, which developed into inflammation of the lungs, and was followed by dropsy. The illness lasted long; but it did not at first alarm him or his friends enough for them to think there was any serious danger. His most faithful attendants were two members of that same von Breuning family who had been almost his first friends in the old Bonn days; and Schindler, who left the account of him before referred to. He was not allowed to compose, so he took to reading, both literature and music. He tried Sir Walter Scott, but could not get on with him, as he thought "that he wrote for money." He also read some of Schubert's songs, and thought they were real music; and he had a great quantity of Handel's works by him, apparently for the first time in his life. About the middle of March, 1827, he got seriously worse, and was unable to go on even with writing letters, and now foresaw that the end was coming. He said to his friends in a grimly humorous way, characteristic of him, *"Plaudite, amici, comoedia finita est*—Applaud, friends, the comedy is ended." The struggle with death was long and terrible. His strength was so great that he seemed to wrestle with it. On the evening of March 26, there came on a sudden storm of thunder and lightning, and in the midst of the rattle of hail and wild commotion of the elements he died.

The funeral, which took place on the 29th, was attended by an enormous crowd of people, mourning in real earnest; and masses were performed, and addresses on his memory were read, and every token was given of the immense admiration in which he was held. All over the civilized world it was felt that a man of the most powerful character and unique genius was gone; and yet to the public of that day his music was not a tithe of what it is to musicians of the present. His far-reaching mind went beyond their understanding; and even now there is still a vast store of beauty of the most exalted and noble kind which the public has not attained to. He is one of the few great creators of art whom a man, though he be ever so blessed with musical intelligence, may study for a lifetime and never exhaust.

VIII

THE ROMANTIC MOVEMENT

CARL MARIA VON WEBER

Born at Eutin, Oldenburg, December 18, 1786. From his youth made frequent concert tours as pianist and conductor; reorganized Opera at Prague, 1813, and at Breslau, 1816. Died in London, June 5, 1826, after finishing the opera Oberon, *commissioned for Covent Garden.*

VOCAL: Operas: *Der Freischütz; Euryanthe; Oberon.* Some 90 songs; part songs for men's voices, etc. Choral music including masses, cantatas, etc.

INSTRUMENTAL: 2 symphonies; 2 piano concertos; *Concertstück* for piano and orchestra; 2 clarinet concertos; 1 bassoon concerto. Piano: 4 sonatas; 1 sonata for 4 hands; many smaller pieces including the famous waltz, *Invitation to the Dance;* 6 sonatas for piano and violin.

FELIX MENDELSSOHN

Born at Hamburg, February 3, 1809. A precocious musician and prolific composer; at seventeen he wrote the incidental music to A Midsummer Night's Dream. *He took a leading part in the* Bachgesellschaft, *discovering and publishing the works of Bach; at 20 he conducted the first performance of Bach's* St. Matthew Passion *since the composer's death. Lived chiefly in Berlin, Düsseldorf, Leipzig; held numerous conductorships. He died at Leipzig, November 4, 1847.*

VOCAL: 3 oratorios, including *Elijah;* the symphonic cantata, *Lobgesang,* etc.; 83 songs. Opera: *Lorelei* (unfinished) and several others.

INSTRUMENTAL: 4 symphonies, the C minor; the "Scotch" in A minor; the "Italian" in A major, the "Reformation" in D major; overture and incidental music to *A Midsummer Night's Dream;* overtures to *Hebrides, Fingal's Cave, Ruy Blas,* etc.; 2 concertos for piano; other pieces for piano and orchestra; violin concerto in E minor. Chamber music: including 7 string quartets, 3 piano quartets, 2 piano trios, 2 trios for piano, clarinet and basset horn; a sonata for violin and 2 cello sonatas. Piano music includes 3 sonatas; 6 preludes and fugues; *Songs without Words* in 8 books; *Variations serieuses;* 6 *Children's Pieces;* 4-hand variations, etc. Organ music includes 3 preludes and fugues, 6 sonatas.

THE ROMANTIC MOVEMENT

By Paul Bekker

EARLY ROMANTICISM

THE German classical period is the last in which we find a unifying cult music. With the death of Goethe and Beethoven this period comes to an end. What happened before now happens again. There is a splitting up into national groups, emphasis is laid no longer upon universality but upon national distinctiveness. This new attitude is called *romanticism*. It intensifies the subjective element in classical idealism, stressing what is actually unique in the individual. It sets forth to give expression to those particular qualities only which happen to determine the characteristics of a personality. But in so doing, it seeks to impress everything else with this same unique stamp. It is the impossibility of realizing such an illusory aim that leads to the tragical mood, the pessimistic temper of this age in which passionate, surging conflicts, dissatisfaction with life, resignation, flight from the world, and retreat into the solitude of self, are characteristic symptoms. A critical *intellectual* and *psychological* attitude is responsible for these conditions and manifests itself in art by making possible a new intensity of dynamic impulses. Herein lies the new creative stimulus in music.

The disintegration into separate national expressions of forces which had been held together by the cult of the ideal is characteristic of earlier similar processes. The catastrophic *rapidity* of the decay in this case, however, is astonishing. The absence of any opposition shows that the religion of "the Enlightenment"—the belief in the idea—was, even more than orthodox religion, the work of man. Based on intellect alone,

From the author's *The Story of Music* by permission of W. W. Norton & Co., Inc.

it lacked the uniting corporeal strength which the church possesses in its dogma, a body of beliefs which may help men to weather spiritual crises and itself gain new strength in the process. Belief in ideas was bound to go under the moment the intellect itself failed. This process began while Schiller was still alive, at the turn of the nineteenth century, during the first quarter of which it proceeded with such rapidity that Goethe and Beethoven, reaching over into the new century, seemed almost like relics of the old. With their death, romanticism held undisputed sway.

Goethe, Schiller, Mozart, and even Gluck and Haydn, indeed, already showed certain elements of the romantic, for romanticism, having been born of classicism, must have been contained within it. But it is Beethoven who points the way to romanticism most clearly in his ruthless individualism, in the stress he lays upon the symbolic significance of music and upon its power of expression—that is, upon all its dynamic values. With him, however, these are but means of expressing an impersonal unifying idea; the emphasizing of the particular is never an end in itself, but points toward the larger aspect of the universal. The structure of the Ninth Symphony, crowned by the *Ode to Joy,* is in this respect a model of the classical attitude in art, in which romantic egotism is transformed into a broad human spirit. The romantic composer would have brought this symphony to a close not with a chorus expressing joy but with some form of self-glorification. Thus Goethe's words relate as much to Beethoven as to himself: "The classical I call healthy, and the romantic sick. Most of the new is romantic not because it is new but because it is weak, sickly and infirm, and the old is classical not because it is old, but because it is strong, fresh, joyous and healthy." Goethe is not differentiating here between the classic and romantic *styles*. He is describing the emphasis upon the *pathological* as characteristic of romanticism, and he calls it weak and sick. Yet all nineteenth century art was influenced by this very quality. So that after all Goethe's definition does apply in a general way to the classic and romantic styles in art, as he, the classical genius, inevitably saw them.

It is difficult for us to speak of the art of the nineteenth century. We have reached a point to-day where we are as well aware as Goethe was of the pathological character which he thought fundamental to romanticism, and feel the same objection toward it. This was not true of the nineteenth century, where this pathological quality, on the contrary, was considered indispensable to the creation of works of art. Inasmuch as we are turning away from it, back from exaggeration of the particular toward fundamental general types, we necessarily assume a *critical* attitude toward the nineteenth century, the attitude of sons toward their fathers. This attitude is unavoidable where two periods follow each other in such close succession, and it is justified in so far as it indicates an urge toward continued productivity and is not meant to be deprecatory. But there is some danger lest, on account of our opposing point of view, we look less objectively at this time and its people than at earlier times; just as the generation after 1750, because of its easily comprehensible opposition to the contrapuntal style, failed to do full justice to Bach and Handel, while with the appearance of harmonic melody about 1600, the polyphonic composers were very critically handled.

This sort of antagonism, therefore, while easily explained and forgiven on human grounds, is apt to create a wrong point of view of which we should beware in our present study. As children of the nineteenth century and grandchildren of the eighteenth, we find our grandparents more sympathetic than our parents. Our children will perhaps think differently. The element in romanticism which we call pathological will no longer strike them as so disturbing. Already most of us find a composition like Wagner's *Tristan* very clear, transparent and smooth in form. Our whole power of perception changes also. What in its own time seems wild and irregular may be considered artistic, well balanced and pleasing a century later. We have not yet arrived at this more mature attitude with regard to the nineteenth century, being still somewhat antagonistic toward it. I shall therefore avoid entering into a detailed discussion of its music as it would entail a special sort of criticism.

It is necessary to differentiate between two kinds of music, *cult* music and *secular* music. One of the two always dominates: cult music in times of a universal spiritual culture, secular music in times of divergent spiritual tendencies. The nineteenth century is one of disparity in every field. It is an age without religion, even an irreligious age, and therefore an age of secular music. Church music exists but it is secular in character. Neither religion nor philosophy is able to create a community of interest. Instead there appears an influence which is an unknown quantity and scarcely to be defined, in the *public character* which now attends all musical activity. This constitutes a purely utilitarian social bond. It provides two outlets for the nineteenth century composer, the opera house and the concert hall, and through these he writes for the public interest. No other sphere any longer exists for his activity. The music of the nineteenth century is thus entirely secular; it is either opera or concert music. The composer may awaken or make use of that universal appeal which is characteristic of the cult, but even so the cult spirit is confined to expression in the secular forms of opera or concert music.

Both concert and opera music are stamped with the creative individuality of the composer. The whole character of musical style, indeed, is now determined by this individual quality. Romanticism as a whole we have seen to be a process of disintegration, developing the psychological to a pathological degree and setting up an individualistic ethical attitude in its philosophy. A corresponding process takes place in romantic music. The harmonic complex splits up under the influence of intellectual and psychological tendencies. The chord is reduced to atoms, as it were, and the active elements of harmony become finer, more delicately ramified. The tendency toward disintegration, toward diffusion from within, more and more takes the place of centralized activity. It is expressed in composition in the increased use of *modulation* and of *chromatics,* and in a corresponding diffusion of *tonal color*. Melody itself now becomes only a part of the whole harmonic activity of tone and color. While the active impulse lay with Bach and Handel in the basses, and with the latter classic composers in the melody, it is now concentrated in the middle voices. Harmony breaks up from within, as it were, is forced asunder. Not only is melody swept away in this whirl of tone colors produced by modulation; the importance of the bass in supporting the tonality also vanishes. The composer now bestows all his attention upon modulation and variety of tone color. To him, harmony is the continuous play of consonant tones and the orchestra makes possible the amalgamation of all available tone colors. The development of these two factors in concert and opera music constitutes the main contribution of the nineteenth century.

Beethoven and Goethe seemed almost like spirits of the eighteenth century carried over into the nineteenth. They are the rivets that bind the two centuries, that hold classicism and romanticism together. The rise of romantic music actually took place under Beethoven's very eyes. When Beethoven died, Spohr had already written his two most famous operas, *Faust* and *Jessonda,* and Mendelssohn his overture to *A Midsummer Night's Dream,* Marschner was about to compose his *Vampire* and *The Templar and the Jewess,* and Berlioz was working at his *Fantastic Symphony.* And of the two leading figures in early romantic music, Carl Maria von Weber had died at the age of forty, one year before Beethoven, while Franz Schubert, who was eleven years younger than Weber, died only one year after Beethoven. So we may say that the first two great romantic composers in the field of opera and concert had completed their life's work just as Beethoven finished his, while their successors had practically reached their highest achievement at the time of Beethoven's death.

At the mention of Weber, we think first only of his *Freischütz,* which, biographically speaking, is of course hardly accurate. Weber wrote several other operas, of which *Euryanthe* and *Oberon* are still performed. He also wrote a considerable number of instrumental compositions, largely for his own use as a piano virtuoso. Some of his songs, furthermore, have passed into the class of popular melodies. Yet for posterity *Der Freischütz* is still Weber's *great* work. It occupies a place of its own in German opera. Not only are all Weber's excellences happily displayed here and all his weaknesses at their least noticeable. *Der Freischütz* signifies more than the composition of an opera; it is Weber's great *cultural* contribution. Despite the *Abduction from the Seraglio, The Magic Flute* and *Fidelio, Der Freischütz* is the first *German* opera, German in the new sense, which means that it is limited by national characteristics but at the same time inspired with the young romanticism of this new age. *Der Freischütz* was not only an opera in the German tongue, it was an opera of the German people. In its story it characterized their most intimate feelings, and in form it went back to the old German song-play, being in the main an apotheosis of folk-song, or at least of song in the folk manner. For these reasons, and not for any outstanding artistic quality in Weber himself, *Der Freischütz* achieved a success sensational to a degree we can scarcely imagine nowadays. With it national opera triumphed for the German public. It was the battering-ram which shattered the hold of Spontini, the Italian, who was then general musical director in Berlin, and of Italian opera in Dresden.

The real folk quality of *Der Freischütz* lies in the naturalness and simplicity of the music and the combination of gaiety, sentiment, and phantasy in the text. It acquires its particular musical character from the picturesque treatment of orchestral color, as in the wood-wind and horn effects, and from the contrasting of unadorned and simple solo parts with the Huntsmen's and Bridesmaids' choruses. The exalted lyric types of Max and Agatha, the roguish Aennchen, the evil figures of Caspar and Samiel, with the descriptive music of the huntsmen's carousal at the village inn, of the ravine of the wolves, of forest scenes by night and by day—all these features bespeak the establishment of a fundamentally German type of opera. Germans everywhere, from city or countryside, were enchanted by its faithful reflection of their own inner life. The typically German character is represented to perfection, as the Italian character is in Rossini's *Barber of Seville* and the French in Bizet's *Carmen*. With *Der Freischütz* German romantic opera was not only established but also strictly defined. Weber himself was never able to step beyond the confines here laid down, and those who came after him simply developed certain details more particularly, like Spohr and Marschner, or, like Wagner, expanded into an entirely new field.

As Weber created German romantic opera, so Schubert created German romantic *concert music*. A schoolmaster and teacher of music living in Vienna, he was overshadowed by the gigantic figure of Beethoven, for which reason his contemporaries and successors scarcely knew him as an instrumental composer. In the beginning his fame was founded on the *lied*, a type of composition which had been comparatively little cultivated. If German romantic opera never went beyond Weber's *Freischütz*, a like situation holds good with regard to Schubert's songs. Both the sacred or spiritual and the secular or social forms of the lied may be traced back to the minnesingers. The music, being set to the verse form of the lied, was naturally dependent upon the literary level of the day. Among Schubert's predecessors and contemporaries, who wrote songs of this type in which the music was an aid to the poetry, the Berlin school in particular, with Peter Abraham Schultz, Reichardt and Zelter, is worthy of note. But the *romantic* lied, being a musical composition to a certain extent independent of the poem, presupposed that subjective quality in musical expression which first appeared in the post-classical period. This form of the lied was indeed the most original, the most independent, the finest creation of romantic music. Here all the romantic elements converged in a great art form which could only have come into being with the fulfillment of all the possibilities inherent in these elements. Here, too, intensified individuality found its most direct and ideal form of expression. While the classical composers had been but incidentally interested in the lied, Schubert, the first great romanticist, was also the first to voice the new type of self-expression in this form.

NATIONAL ROMANTICISM IN CONCERT AND OPERA

In saying that romantic music voiced the composer's own experience, I do not mean to imply that the composers of the romantic period had experiences different from their predecessors, which they proceeded to interpret directly in their art. We may assume that experience is the same for all men at all times; only the forms of experience are modified under the influence of different cultures. The significance of experience for *art* is another matter. An attitude which considers the particular as but a transitory phase naturally attaches little importance to the experiences of the individual, and regards them merely as means to the understanding of the whole. An attitude, on the other hand, which sees the general typified in the particular must tend to intensify the capacity for experience in the individual. It must take experiences themselves seriously because they reflect life and the world as a whole. In short, it is not the experience that is new, but the significance that is attributed to it.

When we say that art expresses experience, people usually think that the artist goes through some sort of human trial, a love affair or a great sorrow, and so acquires an idea for a work of art. This notion seems to be confirmed by Goethe's words:

> *"And when Man in his anguish grows mute*
> *A God it is gives words to tell the pain,"*

and by Heine also when he says:

> *"Out of my great, great sorrow*
> *I make my little songs."*

But we should beware of so interpreting these lines, lest we confound cause and effect. A work of art does not grow out of an experience, is not the result of accidental circumstances. The desire to create always comes first and it is the creative urge which *impels* the necessary experience. With the increased importance of individual experience in the new romantic attitude, the composer's whole life is forced into the service of his art. He has to induce his own adventures in joy and sorrow in order to bring to light the work that is latent within him. Bach did not need to bring experience thus directly into his composing; he could outwardly lead the life of a worthy citizen without harming his art. But as the creative process becomes more and more subjective, the personal life of the composer is *drawn into* it. The influence of the ideal nature of their art is apparent in the lives of Mozart and Beethoven; but with the romanticists the exclusive domination of the subjective leads, as it were, to the opposite extreme. Personality is completely absorbed, swept along in the creative process. It almost ceases to exist on its own account in becoming the end and aim of artistic expression.

Romantic art now passes into a new phase. Through an excessive subjectivism it reduces real human values to naught and becomes a theatrical art. In regarding man as but an instrument for the accomplishment of artistic ends, in setting the resistless urge of the individual creative spirit above life itself, it robs that life of its value. Thus romanticism comes to *overrate* art. And art is no longer an elevating influence, no longer a bearer of the joy and the deeper awareness of living. It becomes an end in itself, a law unto itself, a fount of all understanding, a religion. This holds true in varying degrees with romantic artists everywhere.

The national characteristics in romantic art were also connected with this urge toward expression of personal experience, for in them the artist found his nearest medium for a fuller individual expression. Thus we see how the music of the nineteenth century increasingly divides into national schools. In the first half of the century Germany, France, and Italy are the leading musical nations. In the second half, the Scandinavians branch out independently, the Russians, the Czechs, the English, the Spanish, the Americans, and the divisions and subdivisions become always more numerous. The process goes hand in hand with political developments, and is still active to-day. It is impossible to take up each of these national branches here, and we shall therefore only attempt to indicate the main tendencies and to mention some of the most outstanding personalities.

I have said that opera and concert music were the two fundamental types of romantic composition and that Weber and Schubert were the first German representatives of these forms. Contemporaneously with these two, and also immediately after them, a number of kindred composers appeared in Germany, France, and Italy. Though they differed from each other individually, they had in common the tendency to deviate from the unifying aspirations of classical art and to accentuate national characteristics. In opera, as *Der Freischütz* showed, this was evident in the choice and treatment of subject matter. In concert music, apart from the lied which remained an essentially German form, national character could not be so obviously expressed in subject matter, but it appeared, nevertheless, in diversity of form and in the varied development of instrumental technique and expression. This last was the contribution of the *virtuosi* who now appeared upon the scene— German, French, Polish, Spanish, Belgian, Norwegian, English, Italian —violin or piano players for the most part. Among these virtuosi two came to the fore whose influence in music history was far-reaching, Paganini and Liszt.

We incline to-day to underrate the cultural significance of virtuosity because we know it only as a reproductive activity. True virtuosity, however, as represented by Paganini and Liszt, is creative. It expresses itself in *improvisation,* where all effects are concentrated upon the moment of performance, to which end all the charms of instrumental tone are exploited. It was in these fanciful revelations that the fascination of virtuoso playing, its magic effect upon the listeners, lay. Technical dexterity was a secondary matter and was first intentionally practised when the virtuoso no longer improvised but exhibited his skill in some given composition. If a violinist plays the Paganini Caprices to-day, that is in itself an accomplishment, for they are among the most difficult compositions in violin literature. But even the most perfect reproduction is not to be compared with Paganini's own playing of them. The remarkable thing was not that Paganini could play these pieces but that he was the first to make such pieces possible. The extraordinary effect, the ecstatic transports that gripped people when they heard him play, were caused by his revealing of possibilities in the instrument which had never been dreamed of. Paganini's violin gave voice to the spirit of romanticism itself, individual, subjective, displaying all the dynamic forces of the music, all the expressive nuances of a singing tone, all the characteristic color of the instrument.

What Paginini did for the violin, Liszt did for the piano. He called attention to all its possibilities of modulation and color, reformed piano-playing, in other words, in accord with the specific characteristics of romantic style. Liszt was not unique. Chopin, the Pole, was very like him; also Hummel and Thalberg, who belonged, respectively, to the older and younger generations of Mozart's pupils. But Liszt had the widest range of interest of them all. Not satisfied with the piano alone, he proceeded to transmit to the orchestra all that he had learned from it in the way of modulation and color effects.

The romantic orchestra was an outgrowth of this same stimulus of virtuosity. It was first developed in France by Berlioz, who very much resembled Liszt. Berlioz was also a virtuoso, but from the very outset his instrument was the orchestra. Like Liszt, he was profoundly influenced by Paganini; but he carried the inspiration into his compositions, and here Beethoven was his model. With Berlioz, Beethoven's spiritual idea is changed into the realistic *programmatic* idea, which now becomes the leading thought in the virtuoso orchestra. The programmatic idea is strictly personal, self-revelatory. The composer himself, the subjective quality of the idea he expresses in his program, takes the place of the actual instrumental virtuoso. The program is an idealized personal expression, so to speak. Here lies the difference between the old, purely pictorial program music and romantic program music, which is the exposition of personal experience, of an individual interpretation.

In their leaning toward the programmatic idea, which aimed to achieve the utmost brilliance of orchestral harmony and color, Berlioz and Liszt were alike. But they put the idea to different uses. With Berlioz, the Frenchman, it was always associated with the visual, with action, as in the opera; while Liszt strove for abstract expression, passing into the realm of thought. Hence Liszt's inclination toward the German romanticism of Mendelssohn and Schumann and, in particular, of Schubert.

German instrumental music also was influenced by the stimulus of
virtuosity, the real significance of which was the rôle it played as a means
of developing expression. Music became a *tone-language* in which *emotional experience* was interpreted in poetic form. Characteristic examples
are to be found in Mendelssohn's *Songs Without Words* and in his overtures to *A Midsummer Night's Dream, Fingal's Cave, Calm Sea and
Prosperous Voyage,* and in certain piano works of Schumann, the
Davidsbündler Dances, Kreisleriana, Carnival, Scenes of Childhood.
The poetic idea was taken for granted as the inspiration and setting
for the music. Schumann's writings give us to understand that to him
the inner relation between music and poetic experience was beyond
question. But the German romanticists showed no liking for the naturalistic interpretation of Berlioz nor the breadth of form for which
Liszt strove. Their art was simple, inclining towards the intimate, the
contemplative. Hence their preference for smaller chamber music forms
and for the lied or part-songs. They even treated the orchestra with a
view less to full and glowing color than to the display of delicate pastel
shades. They avoided great pathos in favor of a gentle, pleasant spirit
of revery. This tendency to *introspection,* to absorption in their own
dream-world, was peculiar to the German romantic composers.

Individuals differed, of course. Mendelssohn's form is notable for the
clearness of construction, the polish and symmetry which characterize
him as the most classical of the romanticists. Schumann's, on the other
hand, is typical for its unevenness, its breaking up of outline, its fantastic spirit overflowing here and fading there. The lives of these two
composers corresponded with their natures. Mendelssohn, passing from
success to success as a piano virtuoso and founder of modern orchestral
conducting, died at the height of his activities, celebrated everywhere
as a leading composer. Schumann, who had a long struggle for the
recognition which he was never unstintingly accorded, became mentally
deranged. It is a strange coincidence, perhaps not unconnected with the
type of music they wrote, that the four greatest of the early German
romanticists—Weber, Schubert, Mendelssohn, and Schumann—died
young, or at least did their best work in early life. They were all children of spring. Their physical constitution lasted only until early manhood. Where, as with Schumann, it endured longer, the mind wearied
and at last gave out.

The same holds good for the German romantic opera composers, inasmuch as their main works were written during the first half of their lives. Spohr was only fourteen years younger than Beethoven. A violinist of the grand style, he represents German romantic virtuosity at its height. He is remembered, apart from his violin concertos, especially for his operas *Faust* and *Jessonda*. But in his own time he also had far-reaching influence as a composer of symphonies and oratorios, and being a conductor, he belongs, like Mendelssohn, among the practical organizers of public musical life. Heinrich Marschner, who was nine years Weber's junior, devoted himself to conducting and composing when still young. His great successes were *Vampire, The Templar and the Jewess,* and *Hans Heiling* which appeared in 1833, all written before his fortieth year. Marschner and Weber have some traits in common; for example, the popular vein and forms of their music, and the leaning towards the fantastic, which with Marschner rises to the gruesome, the uncanny, and leads to new harmonies and color combinations. Spohr, on the other hand, is primarily the lyric spirit, the composer of ingeniously melodious music. But he lacks the robust folk-style, especially in his rhythm, and therewith the direct simplicity of the popular manner. His *Jessonda* is noteworthy for its leaning toward the exotic, expressed in the play of chromatics and an unusual treatment of color.

Italian and French opera ran parallel with German opera in their own definite national strains. In opera before Gluck's time, the most characteristically Italian type was the opera buffa. This form was just as inimitable, in its way, as the German lied and the romantic opera of the *Freischütz* type which sprang from it. Such forms can only emanate from a definite national psychology. For this reason, again, their influence is limited. Thus we can scarcely picture the real charm of opera buffa properly unless we hear it sung by Italians in Italian. This type, which various composers had brought to universal recognition in the second half of the eighteenth century, reached its height in Rossini's *Barber of Seville,* first performed in 1816. Rossini was then twenty-four years old. He had begun composing at sixteen and continued until he was thirty-seven, when he definitely concluded his career as an operatic composer with *William Tell*. He lived almost forty years longer, but wrote only small piano pieces and a few religious works, among them the famous *Stabat Mater*. Thus it happened with Rossini as it happened with the German romanticists: his productive power ceased towards the end of his fourth decade. His younger contemporary, Bellini, who was famous especially for his wealth of melody, lived to be only thirty-four years old, while Donizetti, the third of this generation of Italians, like Schumann, suffered a mental breakdown on the threshold of his fortieth year.

With these three Italians of the first third of the eighteenth century, Italian opera, both seria and buffa, was carried on in undiminished freshness. The operas of the great Italianized Germans, Gluck and Mozart, were not considered nationally characteristic. Mozart's operas, indeed, always met with least response in Italy. The Italian is always a singer, whether in comic or in tragic mood; he *sings* and derives dramatic form from the laws of singing alone. For this reason the works of Rossini, Bellini and Donizetti show no important difference in form from those of the eighteenth century. They simply absorbed into the realm of vocal expression the stimulus derived from virtuosity in instrumental music. The voice continued to dominate until the middle of the century when a new master, Giuseppe Verdi, appeared, who, fusing the art of his three predecessors and reaching beyond the idea of *bel canto,* gave to the singing voice the natural human quality of individual expression.

In France *opera comique* and grand opera offered a contrast similar to that of opera seria and opera buffa in Italy. Opera comique was the expression of popular sentiment, while grand opera stood primarily for dramatic representation. Hence the individuality of French art is more striking and more characteristic in opera comique. In the operas of Adam, Auber, Méhul, Boieldieu and many others, we have a long list of pleasing and delightful examples of typically French art. In these the work of the smaller composers of the eighteenth century—Monsigny, Philidor, Grétry—is carried over into its romantic phase. Founded on the fundamental forms of the lyric *chanson* and the metrical *couplet,* opera comique is the French representative of the German song-play.

The less intimate *grand opera,* with its rhetorical pathos and dramatic emotion, was not intended to be particularly national in character or subject matter. Many of the composers who wrote in this form were themselves not French. Gluck was a German. After him came the Italians Cherubini, Spontini and, after Auber's great success with *La*

Muette de Portici, Rossini with his *William Tell.* The Frenchmen,
Méhul, Halévy, Hérold, naturally turned to grand opera as well as to
opera comique, but they were all outstripped by the German, Jacob
Meyer Beer, or, as he later called himself, Giacomo Meyerbeer. In his
operas, of which *Robert le Diable, les Huguenots, le Prophète* and
l'Africaine still live, virtuosity triumphs. The rôles are written for singers
who are both highly trained virtuosi and consummate actors. The
decorative setting demands expert handling of technical apparatus, and
Meyerbeer's treatment of the orchestra reveals him as an instrumental
composer ranking with Berlioz in skill, while his wealth of melody
shows an inventiveness equal to that of the Italians. He is one of the
ablest composers in the history of music, the type that masters everything, knows everything, does everything correctly, and has at his command both taste and an unerring instinct. Thus he was one of the
greatest, even among all the virtuosi of his time—the Paganini, Liszt
and Berlioz of opera, the great composer-virtuoso. In this capacity he
conquered from Paris the stages of the world until he was succeeded
by another, who strove for the same domination and who now precipi-
tated the dramatic wars of the nineteenth century. This man was Richard
Wagner.

IX
SCHUBERT

FRANZ SCHUBERT

Born January 31, 1797, at Lichtenthal, near Vienna, one of fourteen children of a schoolmaster. Taught at his father's school, 1814–1816; in his spare time he studied with Salieri, and composed. Wrote 144 songs in 1815, including Der Erlkönig. *After 1817 lived chiefly in Vienna, supported by the generosity of his friends; he was never able to support himself as a musician, and did not give his first concert of his own works until the year of his death, 1828.*

PRINCIPAL WORKS

VOCAL: Over 650 songs, sometimes as many as eight in one day. It is impossible to list here even the best known. Among the earliest were *Erlkönig, Gretchen am Spinnrade, Heidenröslein, Der Wanderer.* Song cycles, including, *Die Schöne Müllerin,* 20 songs; *Die Winterreise,* 24 songs; *Ossian,* 9 songs; *Schwanengesang,* 6 songs. Several operas unfinished and unproduced. Choral: Several masses, an oratorio; 2 cantatas; part-songs, hymns, etc.

INSTRUMENTAL: 8 symphonies, of which those most frequently played are No. 7 in C major, and No. 8, "Unfinished," in B minor. 7 overtures (including overture to *Rosamunde;* 2 overtures "in the Italian style," etc.); Rondo for violin with orchestra; ballet-music from *Rosamunde.* Chamber music: some 15 string quartets, of which those most frequently played are the A minor, Opus 29; D minor (*Death and the Maiden*) posth.; G. major, Opus 161; a quartet for flute, guitar, viola, and cello; quintet for piano and strings (*Forellenquintet,* with double bass); string quintet (2 cellos) Opus 163; octet for strings and winds, Opus 166; 2 string trios; 2 piano trios. For piano and violin: a Fantasia, a Duo, a Rondo Brilliant, and 3 sonatinas. Piano music: 24 piano sonatas (3 for 4 hands) and a vast quantity of lesser pieces: impromptus, moments musical, dances, marches, etc.

SCHUBERT

By C. Hubert H. Parry

FRANZ SCHUBERT was born on January 31st, 1797. The stock he came from was a thoroughly plebeian one, for his grandfather had been a Moravian peasant. His father had come from the country to Vienna, where he became a parish schoolmaster. He married a woman by the name of Elizabeth Vitz, who was a cook, and had fourteen children, several of whom died young. Franz was the youngest son of the first family, separated from his eldest brother Ignaz by a space of twelve years, and from the brother Ferdinand, to whom he was most deeply attached, by three years. Schoolmastering was a characteristic occupation of the family. Franz's uncle was a schoolmaster, and these two brothers became so also, as soon as they were old enough, and Franz himself, in his turn, had for some time to adopt the same calling. The family also had musical tastes. Both Ignaz and Ferdinand played the violin and the father played the cello, and they were fond of making music together. The brothers became Franz's first masters, and as soon as he got beyond their capacities, which did not take long, he was passed on to the parish choir-master, Michael Holzer, who taught him the violin and pianoforte, and organ, and some harmony. Holzer was immensely impressed with the boy's powers, and said afterwards, "If ever I wished to teach him anything new, I found he knew it already. I cannot be said really to have given him lessons at all; I merely amused myself, and looked on." The truth of the matter appears to have been, that Franz's friends and neighbors were scarcely thorough musicians enough to know what to do with him, and many people consider that it was

From the author's *Studies of Great Composers*, by permission of George Routledge and Sons, Ltd.

a great misfortune that he was not more thoroughly drilled in his youth in the mechanical part of the art. But at least it can be said that mechanical drilling and discipline could not have improved the sensitive impressionableness which was the source of his masterpieces in song writing; and it might have taken away some of his spontaneity and originality for the sake of what a theorist would consider correct and well-balanced treatment.

He developed a beautiful voice as a boy, and was taken first into the choir of the Lichtenthal, the parish where the family lived; and from there he was advanced at the age of eleven years to the school that was called the Convict, where boys were educated for the choir of the Imperial Court chapel in Vienna. In this school his musical opportunities were a good deal improved. Besides singing, the boys had a regular little band in the school, which was good enough to play the simpler kinds of symphonies that were popular in those days. Franz took his place in the band at once, as his violin practice at home and his natural ability gave him some advantages; and it is also recorded that they won him at once a good friend. At the time he arrived in the school a boy called Spaun was the best violin player and led the band; and one day hearing some one playing unusually well behind him he turned round to see who it was, and found it was "a small boy in spectacles called Franz Schubert." Spaun was nine years older than Schubert, but the latter's ability bridged over the gulf which often separates boys of such different ages, and Spaun became one of his truest and most helpful friends. Franz was very poor, and Spaun appears to have been rather better off, and did not neglect any opportunities to help his small friend. The impulse to try his hand at composition seems to have taken possession of Franz by this time, but it was hindered by the difficulties of getting anything to write on. Among other kindnesses Spaun helped him in this respect, and when he found what Franz's talents were took good care they should not be wasted for want of paper.

As time went on Franz rose to be quite an important individual in the school. He became first violin in the boys' band, and his schoolfellows looked upon his compositions as marvelous. But he had no one to direct him or advise him, and his early works were for the most part wild and irregular attempts to express himself with no better guidance than his own instincts, and the knowledge he had of such models as

the works they performed at the school. He wrote hugely long pianoforte pieces, and songs, overtures, quartets, variations, and church music; and in 1813 he produced his first orchestral symphony, which was
his last composition as a boy at the Convict, for his time there came
to an end in that same year, and he went to live at home again. . . .

When he got home he found one great change; for his mother had
died the year before, in 1812. But there is very little recorded of the
effect it had upon him or upon the ways of living at home, and before
long his father was married again; and the new wife did not come up
to the conventional and traditional reputation of a stepmother, but
treated Franz well, and appears to have been regarded by him with
affection.

It was now necessary that he should do something definite for his
living, and being somewhat in dread of being taken off as a soldier, he
shortly became a schoolmaster at his father's school, where he taught
the lowest class. This, of course, entailed a considerable amount of
drudgery, but he somehow managed to find time to pour out a constant
flood of new works, and even to have lessons in composition from old
Salieri, who was then *kapellmeister* of the Viennese Court, and had a
great reputation among his contemporaries. Salieri was a man of the
old school, and went to work to try and get Schubert into the traditional ruts, wherein respectability prefers to go leisurely along. He
naturally thought most of Schubert's productions to be wild vagaries,
and cautioned him against the great lyrical poets of Germany, Goethe
and Schiller, whose thoughts and words seemed to him too wild and
irregular for music. He even tried to make Schubert write vocal music
in the old conventional forms after the Italian manner, and to Italian
words. This, fortunately, had very little effect upon Schubert, and if
Salieri had any influence upon him at all it probably was in lines which
were less vital to his position as a representative composer. On the
other hand, it must be confessed that Salieri was not a stubborn pedant
altogether, and had enough vital expansion in him to win a good word
even from Beethoven; and he was not really incapable of seeing how
great Schubert's genius was, though he naturally tried to direct it into
channels more congenial to his own tastes.

The extraordinary impulse to compose, which seems to have possessed Schubert more powerfully than any other composer known to

history, drove him to try his hand in various directions. The year after he left the Convict school he produced a mass for the Lichtenthal church, where his old master Holzer still reigned over the choir. The work was well performed under the boy's own direction, with some very good musicians among the performers, and was received with enthusiasm by his friends and relations, including Salieri, who appears to have been very complimentary, and to have publicly recognized Franz as his own pupil. Another large work soon followed, which was no less than an opera called *Des Teufels Lustschloss,* and this was followed by another mass, and various other works of large caliber.

But among these, and in some ways more important than any of them, are the first great songs, which made their appearance about this time. A most extraordinary thing about them is that in this line he seemed to require no preparation or education; for some of his very finest songs were produced within the year of leaving the Convict and while he was still endeavoring to imbue infantile minds at his father's school with the elements of knowledge. In some branches of art, such as symphonies, he began at rather a low and uninteresting level, and went on growing and gaining in mastery all through his life. But the tamer style of his instrumental works was probably owing to the same causes which made his song-writing so very remarkable. In instrumental music he was rather at sea at first; and from lack of education and advice he did not know what to aim at, or how to carry on the music in an interesting way. But in relation to songs the want of discipline had its advantages, for it left him all the more open to the impression which the poet produced upon him, and the music seemed to come out as a natural reaction from it. The poems themselves seemed to supply him with the principle of form upon which to construct his music; and with the best musical ideas to intensify the situations; and even with a characteristic style. So he needed no guidance but the receptiveness of his nature to lead him at once to his goal.

It was as early as 1815 that he produced one of his most famous and most powerful songs. The subject is a weird ballad by Goethe called the *Erl King;* in which a father is represented carrying his child on horseback through a wild night in winter. The terrified child fancies it sees the Erl king, and that he is calling it to come to him. The father tries to pacify the child, and assures it that there is nothing but waifs of cloud and howling of wind. The fancied voice of the Erl king mockingly calling the child to come to him is heard, and the excitement waxes wilder as the child's terrors increase, and the despairing father urges on his horse and folds the child closer to his breast. In vain. For when he arrives at his own door the child is dead.

It was a splendid opportunity, and splendidly did Schubert master it, and gave it an impressiveness and a power which no reading of the poem by itself could approach. He gives the impression of the wild elements, and of the headlong career through the night; the terror of the child, the anxiety of the father, and the mocking summons of the Erl king; and combines it all in sounds which rush with excitement ever increasing from moment to moment, till with their arrival at the door of their home, the music, like their headlong career, stops suddenly, and in a stillness of despair the father's horror at finding his child dead in his arms is simply told in six quiet words, which supply exactly the dramatic effect that is wanted. This was one of Schubert's earliest songs, and it contains all the marks of the artistic song in complete maturity. Such an effect of course cannot be obtained by the voice alone on the old methods, but the most elaborate resources of instrumental music have to be employed to express the terrors of the situation, while the voice at times does little more than declaim the words. But Schubert never meant to degrade the voice to a secondary position, or let the song be a pianoforte piece with a voice to explain what it was about. His instincts brought him to make use of all the opportunities at his disposal to convey the poet's meaning in musical terms. Sometimes in other songs the voice is far more musically prominent, and the pianoforte has little more than a subordinate accompaniment, in the usual sense of the term; but that is in cases where it seemed right and possible to him to treat the poem in such a way. In most cases where he is dealing with an impressive poem the balance between the voice and the instrument is such as to give to each the full share in conveying the poet's meaning that it is capable of.

The story of the first appearance of the *Erl King* has been told by Schubert's friend Spaun, who called upon him at his home one afternoon in 1815, and found him in a state of excitement over Goethe's ballad, which he had only just come across. The song was finished and written out before the evening, and they took it to the Convict, where some of the old friends were gathered, and they tried it together. As was very natural, they were rather bewildered than pleased with it. Everything thoroughly genuine and original puzzles people at first, and in this instance the work was not only very much out of the beaten track, but extremely wild and dramatic into the bargain; so it is not to be wondered at that his audience did not take it all in at once. But they admired and loved Schubert too well to discourage him, and before long all his friends had learnt to understand and delight in it.

The rapidity with which he wrote this famous song is characteristic of him. He devoured everything that came in his way in the line of lyrics, and scarcely ever paused to consider whether the poetry was good; but if it conveyed any impression to his mind, he set it at once. At one time he lived with a poet, by the name of Mayrhofer, whose acquaintance he made in 1815, and they used to sit in their room together, the one writing poetry and the other music; and as Mayrhofer finished a poem he would toss it across to Schubert, who read it through, and began to make the music for it directly. As a rule this speed was almost a necessary condition of Schubert's work in all branches of art. He had no taste for the patient balancing, considering, and rewriting again and again, which was characteristic of Beethoven. The thought possessed him, and must go down on paper, and luckily, in the matter of recording what was in his head he was tolerably certain of the effect he wanted. What he wrote expressed what he meant, and that was enough for him. At the same time, though he did not often alter works when once written with a view to improving them, he improved immensely in successive works; especially in such more arduous kinds of composition as symphony and quartet, because there was in his nature an appreciation of possibilities beyond his first efforts in such lines. In song writing it was difficult to find how to do better than he did even before he was twenty years old.

He was still slaving at the school, and pouring out ceaseless floods of music in the intervals of work, when a new friend sought him out, and at least for a time helped to put him in a position more suitable for his genius. This was a certain Franz von Schober, a young man of some means, who had met with his songs, and had been very much struck by them. He called upon Schubert, and was very much impressed by the apparent unfitness of things in a composer of such extraordinary powers devoting his strength and many hours daily to the education of small infants; and proposed that Schubert should go and live with him, and pursue his art more freely and with less interruption. This generous proposal was accepted, and as Schubert's temperament was for the most part easy and accommodating, the arrangement answered very well as long as it lasted. Schubert devoted himself to composition and congenial company, and his moderate wants were provided for chiefly at von Schober's expense. He never troubled himself to think much about providing for the future.

Meanwhile his compositions were not making any great way. His friends appreciated him fully, but the public knew next to nothing about him, and publishers would not so much as look at his works, or even accept them as a gift. The friends he had made hitherto had scarcely been in a position to help him before the public, but soon after making von Schober's acquaintance, he had the good fortune to make friends with a famous singer and actor called Vogl, whose position in the world as a highly cultivated, enthusiastic, and intelligent man, gave him the very best opportunities of serving any one in whose abilities he believed. Spaun has given an account of their first meeting in Schober's rooms. Vogl had been persuaded by Schubert's friends to see him, and arrived one evening. Schubert with shuffling gait and incoherent stammering speech received his visitor. Vogl, the man of the world, was quite at his ease, and taking up a sheet of music paper, which lay close by, began humming the song Schubert had written on it. Then he tried one or two more, and ended by saying, "There is stuff in you, but you squander your fine thoughts instead of developing them." He was not carried away by enthusiasm all at once, and made no promise that he would come back again. But he made the acquaintance of more of the songs, and became more and more impressed with the style of the music; and then he began to go and see Schubert oftener, and Schubert in turn began to pay Vogl frequent visits. Vogl gave him excellent advice, and helped him in the choice of poems, discussed and criticized, and—practically more useful than all—he began singing Schubert's songs in the many houses in Vienna where he was welcome, and sometimes took Schubert with him to accompany him. In this way began the friendship which had the most important effect upon Schubert's career.

To this same period, or near it, belong some of the few remains which exist of written expressions of Schubert's own, which throw some light on his character. Fragments of a diary of 1816 contain the most curious passages, such as aphorisms, exclamations, criticisms, and but few biographical details. One passage which gives a clue to his musical mood at the time is interesting. It is of June 13th. "This day will haunt me for the rest of my life as a bright, clear, and lovely one. Gently, and as from a distance, the magic tones of Mozart's music sound in my ears. With what alternate force and tenderness, with what masterly power did Schlesinger's playing of that music impress it deep, deep in my heart. Thus do sweet impressions, passing into our souls, work beneficently on our inmost being, and no time, no change of circumstances, can obliterate them. In the darkness of life they show a light, a clear, beautiful distance, from which we gather confidence and hope. Oh, Mozart! immortal Mozart! how many, and what countless images of a brighter, better world hast thou stamped on our souls!"

Three days afterwards come the words, "To-day I composed for the first time for money—namely, a cantata for the name-day festival of Herr Professor Watteroth von Dräxler. The honorarium 100 florins, Viennese currency." Then follow a whole string of general remarks which have nothing to do with one another, and tell nothing of his life except in so far as they illustrate the state of his mind. Such as, "Natural disposition and education determine the bent of man's heart and understanding. The heart is ruler; the mind should be. Take men as they are, not as they ought to be. Town politeness is a powerful hindrance to men's integrity in dealing with one another," and so on, whole pages in a single day. The marvel of it is that he could find time to write so much, when he was incessantly producing one composition after another, and at such a pace that it is wonderful how he could even put it all down.

He made an attempt every now and then to get some fixed musical appointment which might bring him in a little money regularly. In 1818 he was invited to go with the family of a Count Johann Esterhazy, to their country-house at Zelesz in Hungary, to make himself generally helpful in musical ways, and to give the daughters music lessons. All the members of the family were musical. The Count and Countess and their two daughters all sang, and the two latter also played on the pianoforte; and they had with them a friend, the Baron von Schönstein, who had a fine voice and sang well, and soon entered into Schubert's songs. The opportunity had in it some decided advantages for Schubert; the country was beautiful and healthy; and the company was good; and, moreover, he had opportunities of hearing Hungarian music in its own home. He was naturally attracted by the style of it, as many other great musicians have been; and he wrote down many of the tunes which he heard sung or played by gipsies or servants. Among other results was a very fine *Divertissement à la Hongroise,* which is said to have been founded on some tunes he heard a kitchen-maid singing as he and the Baron von Schönstein were coming in from a walk. . . .

Owing to Vogl's advocacy, Schubert's name was brought more and more before the world; and in 1820, a comic operetta called the *Zwillingsbrüder* was performed in one of the Vienna theatres, and a work called the *Zauberharfe* was also performed later in the same year; so things must have seemed to be growing a little brighter for him. In the next year a more important event occurred, which was the first publication of some of the songs. This consummation was at last brought about owing to some concerts which were given in the house of people called Sonnleithner, one of whom had been at school with Schubert, and had cherished his friendship, as all men seem to have done when they had once won it. At these concerts many of Schubert's works were performed, and among them some of his finest songs. The audience was so much pleased that every one began to think a decided effort ought to be made to enable people to possess such treasures. Schubert's friend Leopold Sonnleithner, and Gymnich, an amateur who sang the songs admirably, made up their minds to try and find a publisher. They searched in vain. The publishers thought the works too difficult, too uncommon, and that the composer's name was not known enough. Finally, in despair of succeeding any other way, Schubert's friends determined to publish sets of songs on their own account, and get the copies subscribed for among the people who came to the Sonnleithners' concerts, and other friends. A selection was made, and the publications began in April, 1821, and continued for the rest of the year at intervals. The friends did all they could to bring the songs before the public and keep the interest alive, and the result was that sufficient copies were sold to encourage the cautious publishers to go on bringing out more of them at their own expense. This to a certain extent improved Schubert's position as a composer, and the sale of copies even put him for the moment in funds; and this was perhaps the most successful financial result his compositions ever brought him, for in the whole course of his life the publishers could never be induced to give him more than the most absurdly trifling sums, even for his most attractive songs. . . .

Not long after the successful launching of his first compositions into print he went for an expedition round about the country with his friend Schober, to visit certain of Schober's relatives and friends. The principal result of this journey seems to have been the composition of a large opera called *Alfonso and Estrella,* to words written by Schober during their journeyings together. It was finished early in 1822, and then came the usual disagreeable operations necessary to get it performed. He seems to have brought it to the notice of all sorts of people at various periods in succeeding years, but met with nothing but excuses or rebuffs. One well-known passage of arms between him and Weber is reported to have arisen from it. Schubert certainly criticized Weber's opera *Euryanthe* rather unfavorably, and it appears to have got to Weber's ears, who was annoyed about it. Schubert, meaning no evil, afterwards took his score of the *Alfonso and Estrella* to show to Weber; whereupon Weber expressed his opinion of that work by saying that it was "usual to drown the first puppies, and the first operas," under the supposition that it was Schubert's first attempt in that line. Later he repented of his sharp speech, and is even said to have thought of performing the work himself at Dresden. Schubert made another attempt by sending his work to Berlin to a friend called Anna Milder, who was a great singer. She returned him a very friendly answer, but held out no hope of getting a performance, as she said, "It pains me to remark, but I must do so, that the libretto does not suit the taste of the people here, who are accustomed to the grand high tragic opera, or the comic opera of the French." At the Vienna theatres he had no chance of getting a performance, as two of them were in the hands of a thoroughly mercenary man, who would not dream of undertaking anything that was not sure to bring him in good profits. Schubert's friends would have got up a performance but for the fact that the difficulties of the work were beyond their powers of execution. In the end all hopes had to be given up, and the work was never performed till long after his death, when Liszt brought it out at Weimar, among several other apparently forlorn hopes which he gallantly led, in 1854. But even then its success was doubtful, less from the characteristics of the music than from bad arrangement of the story, and ineffectiveness on the stage. A few years ago it was again revived in Vienna, and having been elaborately revised by the conductor, met with more success.

Of course the failure to get a performance must have been trying to him, but he was always too busy and too merry with his genial friends to allow such rebuffs to weigh heavily upon his spirits; and he still had his heart set on doing something in the same line. In 1823 he wrote a little one-act opera called the *Conspirators*, and this, too, after being in the hands of the licensers of plays for a year, was returned to him, and was never performed in his lifetime. He followed up this work by yet another in the same line, but on a larger scale—a regular full-sized romantic opera, in three acts, called *Fierabras*. The words were put together by a man called Josef Kupelwieser, and were all about contests of Franks and Moors, and kings and knights and noble ladies. Of this Schubert really had some hopes of getting a performance, as the libretto, foolish as it seems, was already accepted by the manager of one of the theatres before he began to write the music. As soon as the words came to him he set to work and wrote at a most astounding speed. According to the dates given he wrote the whole of the first act, which is 300 pages of manuscript, in seven days, and the whole opera, which filled up more than three times as many pages, was composed and finished in every detail between May and September; though he appears to have been so ill at some time between those two dates that he had to go to a hospital. As soon as it was finished, and before the fate of its performance was decided, he was engaged upon yet another work for the stage, called *Rosamunde,* the words of which were supplied by that absurd old poetical aspirant, Wilhelmina von Chezy, who wrote the words of Weber's *Euryanthe.* The story was called *Rosamunde, the Princess of Cyprus,* and was of the same preposterous romantic texture as Weber's opera, and had the same pernicious effect upon the fortunes of the music associated with it. It was not so much an opera as a play with incidental music to it, and it did not take Schubert long to write his share; but his share was a beautiful contribution, and far too good to be dragged down into oblivion by the foolishness of the words. It was performed in 1823, and the music was well appreciated; but so much depended upon the play that the combination was an inevitable failure, and the music as well as the literary part was laid aside and forgotten. Long after, in 1867, the work was found in the cupboard where it had been left, by Sir George Grove, when he was hunting for relics and forgotten beauties of Schubert in Vienna; and much of the music has subsequently been revived in concert-rooms, and is always received with delight by all lovers of Schubert. In the same year he wrote many more beautiful songs, among which the most celebrated are a set of twenty, called the *Schöne Müllerin,* upon which he was engaged at different times in intervals of work upon the opera *Fierabras*—some of the songs being said to have been written while he was ill in the hospital.

Early in the next year the fate of *Fierabras* also was decided. It was returned to him unperformed, and without any prospect being held out of his ever hearing a note of it. These repeated disappointments seem at last to have seriously depressed him. Several written expressions of his about this time show how he felt them. In a letter to the brother of the friend who had put the poem of *Fierabras* together he pours out his grief: "I feel myself the most unhappy, the most miserable man on earth. Picture to yourself a man whose health can never be re-established; who, from sheer despair, makes matters worse rather than better; a man whose most brilliant hopes have come to nothing, whose enthusiasm for the beautiful (an inspired feeling at least) threatens to vanish altogether; and then ask yourself if such a condition does not represent a miserable and unhappy man. Your brother's opera was declared impracticable, and no demand of any sort was made for my music. Thus I have composed two operas to no purpose whatever." . . .

The next year seems to have been a brighter one for him. Its chief incident was a country excursion which he took with his friend Vogl; when, for five months, he enjoyed the delights of travelling through beautiful scenery, mixing with pleasant company at the various places where they stayed, and finding thorough sympathy and appreciation for his music on all sides. Vogl used to sing his songs to the people wherever they met congenial friends, with Schubert to accompany him; and, as Schubert wrote to his brother, "The way Vogl sings these things and I accompany him—so that whilst the performance lasts we seem to be one—is quite an unheard-of novelty amongst these people." They indeed took a great fancy to him, and made much of him, and everything combined to make him happy and hopeful. When the summer came to an end Vogl went off to Italy, and Schubert came back to Vienna and resumed his usual ways of life there.

Nothing occurred to mark the course of his life for some time after this beyond the appearance of fresh compositions. The chief events which happened in the following years were two more attempts to gain a definite musical post, such as might supply him with a small but regular income and a definite position among his fellow artists, but they both came to nothing. Another interesting event was the visit to Beethoven's bedside just before that great master died. Schindler, Beethoven's admirer and biographer, was a great believer in Schubert, and tried to bring them together, but had failed till the end was manifestly approaching. When Beethoven was laid up with his last illness Schindler got some of Schubert's best songs to show him. Beethoven became very much interested in them, and was much surprised when he heard what an enormous quantity of such works Schubert had produced. He is reported by Schindler to have said, "Truly Schubert has the divine fire in him." It is probable that it was owing to these favorable expressions that Schubert was persuaded to visit the great man's bedside. Very few words were said, but they must have been such as to show Schubert that Beethoven had found out his gifts and appreciated them. He went again later, but at that time Beethoven was not able to speak, and could only make signs with his hand, and within three weeks he was dead. At the funeral Schubert was one of the torch-bearers. When he and two of his friends were returning they stopped at a *gasthaus,* and Schubert and his friends each drank one glass of wine to the memory of the great man departed, and a second to the one of the three who should first follow him. Schubert little thought then how short his own time was destined to be.

About this time he began to receive communications from publishers with a view to bringing out more of his music, and also some encouraging proposals to write works especially for sundry societies; and in the same year he was elected a member of the representative body of the Musical Society of Vienna, which he regarded as a pleasant honor. He went on with composition with even greater ardor than ever, and by the spring of 1828 had finished his greatest symphony, the only one which was destined to be thoroughly characteristic of him and also complete; and other instrumental works, such as sonatas, and a very fine quintet for strings, a cantata called *Miriam's War Song*, and a number of songs, succeeded one another rapidly. He seemed to think it was time to give less attention to songs and more to works on a larger scale; as he said to a friend: "he hoped to hear no more about songs, but to devote himself to opera and symphony."

In March, for the first time in his life, he gave a public concert in the hall of the Musik-Verein of Vienna; the program included part of a string quartet of his, a trio for pianoforte and strings, music for men's chorus, and several fine songs. Many excellent performers came forward to help him, among them his old friend Vogl; and it shows how his genius was beginning to become known and appreciated, that the hall is said to have been fuller than ever was remembered before, and the people were delighted. The good attendance also brought about £32 into his pocket, which must have made him feel quite rich. As was usual with him, his friends got the benefit of his prosperity, and he spent his wealth royally as long as it lasted, and by summer-time he was as badly off as ever. The idea of going for another excursion into the lovely country of Styria was again entertained, but had to be given up because of the low state of his funds, and he had to remain in Vienna all the year round.

Early in September he went to live with his brother Ferdinand in a house in the suburb called the Neue Wieden. He had been bothered with an old trouble of inclination of blood to the head, and giddiness, and it was thought it would do him good to be nearer to the country, and to have readier opportunities of getting away for exercise and fresh air. The house they occupied was a new one, and it is supposed this aggravated his unhealthy and over-strained condition. He became decidedly ill, and doctors had to be called in. Then he picked up a little, and went for a five days' excursion with some friends into the neighborhood of Vienna, visiting among other places the grave of Haydn at Eisenstadt. He seems to have regained some of his usual gaiety for the time, but when he got back to Vienna the illness returned.

One evening, when having supper with some friends at an hotel, he suddenly threw down his knife and fork, saying the food tasted like poison. He still walked about a good deal after this, but he took scarcely anything to eat and got steadily worse. But he did not seem to have any anxiety about himself, and spoke to the composer Lachner, who came to see him, of his intended work on a new opera he had in hand called *Graf von Gleichen.* He went to hear music, and was very much excited over a performance of one of Beethoven's latest quartets. Among other ideas he had one of developing his mastery of counterpoint more thoroughly; a purpose which arose from his becoming acquainted with Handel's works so late in life; and he applied to a man called Sechter, who was considered an authority in that branch of art, to give him lessons; and the matter even went so far that he went to see Sechter and discussed what would be the best books to work upon, and arranged dates for the lessons. The last music he heard publicly performed was a mass by his brother Ferdinand which was done in the church at a village called Hernals on the 3rd of November.

When he got home again he was very tired and ill, and grew worse day by day. He wrote to his old friend Schober, "I am ill. I have eaten and drunk nothing for eleven days, and am so tired and shaky that I can only get from the bed to the chair and back." And he asked for some books to amuse him, suggesting some of Cooper's novels. Some of his friends came to see him, but there seems to have been a dread of infection, and he had not so much company to cheer him as was desirable. He occupied some of his time correcting proofs of the latest set of his songs, called the *Winterreise,* and still had hopes of doing more work. But after a few days he became delirious, and the doctors announced that he had typhus fever. The faithful brother Ferdinand attended him constantly. Franz was possessed with strange fears, and asked: "Brother, what are they going to do with me? I implore you to put me in my own room, and not to leave me in this corner under the earth. Don't I deserve a place above the ground?" Ferdinand did all he could to quiet him, and assured him he was in his own room; but Franz only shook his head, saying, "It is not true, Beethoven is not here." He never became himself again, but died on Wednesday, November 19, 1828, only thirty-one years old. Two days afterwards the funeral took place, and his body was borne, accompanied by many friends and admirers, to the cemetery at the village of Währing, where Beethoven had also been buried; and it was deposited as near as possible to the last resting-place of that great master, towards whom in his latter years he had been so strongly drawn by sympathy and admiration. Many performances were given and articles written in honor of his memory; and the proceeds of concerts and subscriptions were enough to pay for a monument over his grave, upon which were appropriately inscribed the words:

> *"Music has here entombed a rich treasure,*
> *But still fairer hopes."*

Several great musicians have been cut off even before what might be fairly considered the prime of their life and vigor, but of all the greatest ones Schubert's time was shortest; yet in those few thirty-one years of life he produced such an enormous quantity of music that the amount would have been noticeable even if his life had been rather longer than most men's. He wrote over 500 songs; at least seven entire symphonies, and two incomplete ones, of which latter, one is among his most beautiful and popular works; over twenty sonatas; numbers of string quartets, six masses, and other large and fine examples of church music; several operas, part songs, cantatas, overtures, and so forth. His rapidity of thought and of writing must have been marvelous. As fast as he finished one thing he generally began another, and often wrote several songs in a single day; and those not songs of the cheap, ephemeral description, familiar in modern times, but works of art, with real thought and point and good workmanship in them.

Of all these various works comparatively few came before the public before he died, which may be partly accounted for by the shortness of his life. But when he was dead the interest in his music began steadily to grow, and the publication of songs went on unceasingly for such a long time that one critic, in facetious terms, suggested that some one was trading on the popularity of Schubert's name, and passing off as posthumous works of his, things that were written by somebody else. . . .

The revival of his last great symphony was due to Schumann, who did more than any other man of his time to bring before the public works by all sorts of composers, living and dead, who, without his advocacy, might have been ignored, or at least have had a very long fight to win recognition. Schumann went to Vienna in 1838, ten years after

Schubert's death, and found an enormous quantity of manuscripts which were still in the possession of the faithful brother Ferdinand, and among them was the last symphony in C which he had written in the year that he died. Schumann soon recognized what a splendid work it was, and sent it to Mendelssohn, who was then conductor of the famous Gewandhaus concerts at Leipzig, and it was performed there early in 1839 for the first time. Mendelssohn had but little sympathy with Schubert's large instrumental works, but he was, nevertheless, willing to champion a work on such a grand scale, and brought it to England with him to have it performed under his direction at the Philharmonic in 1844; but the band failed to understand it at the rehearsal, and behaved so badly that Mendelssohn withdrew it; and the prominent English critics of the day not only pronounced their verdict against this and other instrumental works of his, but even against his songs. For instance, the song known as the *Junge Nonne,* which is one of his most impressive works, was sung at a Philharmonic concert in the same year, 1844, and was described by the critic who was considered to have the greatest ability and judgment in the country "as a very good exemplification of much ado about nothing—as unmeaningly mysterious as could be desired by the most devoted lover of bombast." For many years the same tone was kept up; but in defiance of critics, Schubert's music grew more and more into favor: the public felt that what it said to them was true, and it moved them as genuine music should; and in the end it was accepted as a regular feature, even in places where little but well-tried classics are admitted; and nowhere has it been better received than in England, where at first it met with such contemptuous opposition.

The position which Schubert's larger instrumental works have won in the end is rather a significant one; for, judged by comparison with the great works of such masters as Haydn, Mozart, and Beethoven, they certainly have artistic defects. The nicety of adjustment of details of form, after the manner of such masters, is defective, and self-restraint, concentration, conciseness, and judgment are too often absent; and yet the works have taken their place among things which are most delighted in, through the beauty of their ideas, and their color, character, and spontaneity. It is this state of things which makes his instrumental works especially interesting, as pointing to the position occupied by the intrinsic qualities of music in this century compared with the prominence of formal qualities in the last century. The success of Haydn's and Mozart's work depended to a great extent upon beauty of form, and not very much upon strong individuality. Beethoven alone balanced form and idea upon equal terms, and made strong character one of the essentials, and after him instrumental music began to move into more erratic forms, and to depend much more upon ideas and character; and Schubert was one of the first composers of mark who gave point to this tendency. There only exists one symphony and a half of his which represent him thoroughly, and yet that is enough to outweigh a whole dozen of symphonies by composers whose works were looked upon with complacency by his contemporaries at a time when his were ignored. But though the symphonies and the masses, and the operas and the sonatas and pianoforte pieces, have a place in history, they all must yield in importance to his songs, and it is as the first great representative song-writer that he must be chiefly remembered. With him begins that wonderful flow of songs which are as characteristic of Germany as the symphony and the sonata; for no other nations have been able to produce a natural kind of art-song like theirs, any more than they have been able to produce symphonies. Symphony and song fill up the extreme limits of the picture, and the thoroughness of the German people in musical matters has won for them the first place all through.

Schubert is another example, like Beethoven, of that supreme devotion to art which makes all convenience and comfort of daily life of secondary importance. His, too, has that singular and untarnished honor of persistently writing what he felt to be best and most beautiful, without ever thinking of what he might get by accommodating his music to his hearers. Popular sophisms could have no hold upon him, because there was no weak place in the armor of his belief. He believed in what was good and not in what was convenient, and it was quite impossible for him to act against his feeling. If other nations could show a few such men among their composers they might rise in time to equal musical honor with the great Germans.

X
CHOPIN

FREDERIC CHOPIN

Born near Warsaw, March 1, 1809. A concert pianist from the age of 9; played in many German cities, and at 19 had composed his 2 piano concertos. A brilliantly successful pianist throughout Europe. Settled in Paris, 1831. Was in poor health after 1838, and seldom played in public; but led an active social life, travelled widely; his friends included Liszt, Berlioz, Bellini, Balzac, Heine, Mendelssohn, George Sand—with the last of whom his association was long-continued and intimate. He died in Paris October 17, 1849.

PRINCIPAL WORKS

Chopin composed almost exclusively for the piano. The chief exceptions are the orchestral parts of his two piano concertos, a piano trio, a sonata for piano and cello, and his songs. Aside from their musical value, his works were of the greatest importance in developing the resources of the piano as an instrument. Compositions include: 2 sonatas (B minor and B flat minor); 4 ballades; 2 series of *Etudes* (12 each, Opus 10 and Opus 25); 19 nocturnes; 11 polonaises; 24 preludes (Opus 28); Prelude in C sharp minor; 13 waltzes; 4 fantasies (most frequently heard, the *fantasie in F* minor); 54 mazurkas. Many other piano pieces, including impromptus, rondos, scherzos, variations, 17 Polish songs (Opus 74).

CHOPIN

By J. Cuthbert Hadden

THERE is no style of music that is better known to the musician and the amateur than that of Chopin. Yet when one sits down to write of it, to try to analyze it, to say exactly what are its essential characteristics, to what it owes its peculiar fascination, it is then that one feels the inadequacy of the language. True, the grammarian might go through it, classify all its progressions, and label all its chords. There is no more reason why this analytical process should not be possible with Chopin's music than with Bach's or Mendelssohn's. But the result of such a process would be mainly a negative one. It would show that Chopin was not a great master of form in the larger sense, not a skilled contrapuntalist, not a deep thinker with a "message." It would show, indeed, that he was a master of melody and an innovator in harmony, but it would help us not a whit to understand the qualities which make him unique. His spirit is "too volatile for our clumsy alembics, too intangible for our concrete methods of investigation. It eludes our glance, it vanishes at our touch, it mocks with a foregone failure all our efforts at description or analysis."

To some who know it only superficially it may seem easy enough to characterize the music of Chopin in general terms. Its extraordinary beauty and finish are perhaps the leading qualities. One thinks instinctively of Tennyson—the Tennyson of the *Princess* in which we have the best words best placed and that curious felicity of style which strikes us instantly and without cavil as the perfection of art. "Load every rift with ore" was the advice which Keats gave to Shelley. In Chopin it is as if every rift had been consciously loaded with ore. Not

From the author's *Chopin*, by permission of E. P. Dutton and Co.

a single bar seems to be wanting, not a single bar seems to be redundant. There is no commonplace, nothing stale, nothing hackneyed,
nothing vulgar. The perfection of form, the complexity of figure, the
delicate elaboration of ornament, the rich harmonic coloring, the fine
polish of phrase, the winning melody, the keen vital quality of passion,
the grace and the tenderness—these at least can be pointed out in terms
of everyday vocabulary. I have mentioned Keats and Shelley. In the
music of Chopin there is something of the spirit of both. Chopin's
world, like Shelley's, is a region "where music and moonlight and feeling are one"—a fairy realm where nothing seems familiar. Both look
upon a night of "cloudless climes and starry skies." The warmth, the
spirituality, the color of the romance spirit is in the one as in the other.
We note the ethereal grace of both, the beautiful images, the exquisite,
if sometimes far-drawn, fancies. Like Keats, too, Chopin often sees

> Charmed magic casements, opening on the foam
> Of perilous seas, in faery lands forlorn.

His philosophy is of the beautiful, as is Keats's; and while he "lingers
by the river's edge to catch the song of the reeds, his gaze is oftener fixed
on the quiring planets." He is Nature's "most exquisite sounding-board,
and vibrates to her with intensity, color, and vivacity that have no
parallel." A whole volume might be written about Chopin the composer. The essence of the matter is here. Chopin is pure emotion. "Make
me thy lyre," he might have prayed the spirit of Poesy. His music is
all expressive of moods, of phases of feeling, now strenuous, now morbid,
now tender, now simply tricksy. There is nothing of Bach's calm dignity or Beethoven's titanic energy; you find no traces of intellectual
wrestling, of thoughts too deep for tears, you find instead tears that
are, perhaps, a little too facile, like the tears of women, the cause not
always commensurate with their copiousness. There is gaiety, yearn-
ing, pathos, but nothing that even touches sublimity, little that stirs
one to the beautiful activity that is the true life of man. Chopin's music
is, first and last, emotion surcharged, not intellectualized, not finding
its legitimate development into action. As with Chopin the player, so
with Chopin the composer; he stands alone. He is the one master *sui
generis,* a genius for whom the musical critic and historian has no pigeon

hole in his bureau of "classified" composers. His art ended with him. As he sprang from no existing school, so he founded no school. It is this absolutely unique quality of his music which has preserved him so effectually against the flattery of imitation. His work is entirely beyond the reach of the imitator. Its charm is so wholly personal to himself that only another Chopin, like in all things—in temperament, in bias, in environment, in emotion, in experience—could hope to reproduce it. "None but himself could be his parallel." Followers he no doubt has had. But the follower can at best copy only the method, and Chopin had practically no method. What he had was a manner.

It has been remarked that as a pianist Chopin was less successful on the concert platform than when playing to a select circle of friends. The conditions may be said to apply to his music, though not to the same extent. That Chopin's music makes a large part of the stock-in-trade of the concert pianist is, of course, true. Yet it can hardly be denied that even in the hands of the same interpreter the emotional effect of many of the compositions is greater when these compositions are heard in a private room than in a concert hall. Much of the subtle and sensuous harmony seems to be lost in large surroundings and in the presence of a large audience. A British composer of the younger school, Mr. Learmont Drysdale, writes in a private note: "To me it has always seemed that the proper atmosphere for the due appreciation and true enjoyment of Chopin's magic strains is that of a darkened or softly lit chamber, with a select few listeners *en rapport* with this particular style of music and with one another. Then, under such congenial conditions, one is carried away into another world—a world of strange things—by the wonderfully mysterious and weird dreaminess of the music, so full of meaning, and charged with such poetical suggestion."

And here I am reminded of the fact that Chopin's strongest appeal can only be to certain natures. Beethoven, Mozart, even Wagner, appeal to all minds in all moods. Chopin appeals chiefly to one class of mind and to one mood of that mind. "He is," writes the late Dr. Hueffer, "the representative of a decaying nation, and his individual genius is tinged with melancholy to a degree which to a robust and healthy nature might well appear in the light of a disease." He has been bracketed by some writers with the "sick men"—whoever they may be—and his entire musical product has been called morbid, sickly, unwholesome. "It may be feverish," says a prominent English critic, "merely mournful, *cadavre,* or tranquil, and entirely beautiful. . . . It is marvelous music, but all the same it is sick, unhealthy music." Heinrich Pudor, who describes Wagner as a "thorough-going decadent," declares that the figure of Chopin the composer comes before one "as flesh without bones—this morbid, womanly, womanish, slip-slop, powerless, bleached, sweet-caramel Pole."

This is the sort of person who would look for genius only in the full red cheeks and the expansive waistcoat. But even for invalidism one might find something to say. Some of the finest things in art and literature have been done by people who are in more or less delicate health. Pope spoke of "that long disease, my life." Mere valetudinarianism seems to have been the inspirer of much that is admirable in prose and verse. Invalidism has been the motive cause, or at any rate, the marked accompaniment, of a great deal that is effective and even charming in art and literature. It is from the minds of women poets not physically robust that have come most of those "airs and floating echoes" which "convey a melancholy unto all our day." *Wuthering Heights*— one of the strongest pieces of fiction ever done by a woman's pen—was conceived and written while the shadow was waiting with the keys. That Chopin was consumptive is nothing. Perhaps, if he had *not* been consumptive, oblivion would long ago have covered him with her poppies. But that is another of the ineffectual "ifs"!

Personally, I think that far too much is made of Chopin's melancholy. "Chopin," said one of his own friends, "had a cheerful mind but a sad heart." Chopin's music is a compound of the same contradictions—of cheerfulness and sadness. Without doubt, nature had tuned him in the minor key; but just as in everyday life he had his gay moments, so in his music we find moments of light-heartedness, moments of humor I had almost said, when life seems worth living, and this world something better than a charnel-house. If we knew all the circumstances connected with the inception of his various works we should probably find that what is *triste* in them was written during his gloomy, sentimental moods. When he composed in a bright mood he could be as bright as anybody.

His early works in particular show sprightliness and vivacity—the Variations on *Don Juan,* for instance. Look at the Rondos of Opus 5 and Opus 16, at the Fantasia on Polish Airs, at the two Concertos. There is no sadness or despair in these; rather youth, exuberance of life, happiness and elation, love of mankind. In the Fantasia Opus 13 there is a note of melancholy, but the impression is not lasting: a long shake, a few chords, and we are in a brisk country dance. There is fire and cheerfulness in the grand Polonaise in E Flat Major, written at Paris; and the Concert Allegro Opus 46 is full of life and "go." The mazurkas, the national dances of Poland, are in a minor key. But it does not follow that Chopin's mazurkas are sad. On the contrary, some have quite a warlike ardor. The minor key of the Polish dances is neither unhappy nor *macabre*. "A fig for wretchedness!" says a national proverb. The Polish peasants are happiest when they sing in the minor mode. The nocturnes, again, have a character at variance with the idea that the composer, from first to last, was the enervated, broken creature so often depicted. No doubt they are heavily charged with sentiment, but it is not a sickly sentiment. Similarly with the preludes. Many people imagine that they see in these evidences of his misery in Majorca. But, suppose he was unhappy in what may be called his "domestic" relations: so were Haydn and Mozart, and yet they are not found, if the expression may be allowed, washing dirty linen in their works. There is too much reading into Chopin's compositions of the personal states and physical condition of the man. "Poor fellow! he was a consumptive!" That is the key which unlocks the alleged melancholy. There is melancholy in Chopin, certainly. But what I mean is that a great many people find him all melancholy who would have found no melancholy in him at all if he had been a portly, roast-beef Englishman (how impossible is the supposition!) with a vigorous constitution that carried him to the fourscore.

But, when all is said and done, we come back to our original assertion that Chopin's strongest appeal can only be to those of strongly sensuous, emotional, impressionable temperament. "I do not care for the ladies' Chopin," said Wagner, "there is too much of the Parisian *salon* in that." The statement involves no reflection on Wagner, any more than it involved a reflection on Chopin that he did not care for the occasionally boisterous gaiety of Schubert. Even as long ago as 1841 the conditions necessary for a full appreciation of Chopin were understood. In that year a Parisian critic wrote: "In order to appreciate him rightly one must love gentle impressions and have the feeling for poetry." That puts the matter in a nutshell. And just as Chopin can only appeal to certain natures, so Chopin can only be interpreted through the keyboard by players who, in addition to the peculiar temperament demanded, have the special kind of technique and touch which is necessary. It was remarked by a Frenchman of his own time that to hear Chopin rightly interpreted was to read a strophe of Lamartine. But how seldom do we hear him rightly interpreted! The "conscientious and heavy-handed pianist" attacks him and crushes him out of all recognition. "Solidity of execution" may serve for several composers on the virtuoso's list, but solidity of execution must prove absolutely fatal in the case of Chopin. The daintiest delicacy of touch is requisite for these airy creatures of his, for that filigree work which decks his scores. They are conceived in the poetic, let us even say in the troubadour spirit, and are no more to be rendered with scientific exactness than are the gipsy songs of the Hungarians. You cannot make the ideal Chopin interpreter. Like the poet, he must be born.

To trace the influences which helped to form Chopin's style as a composer for the keyboard is a work of almost futile supererogation. His style was his own from the beginning. As one may see the Tennyson of *In Memoriam* and the *Idylls* in the early poems of his Cambridge days, so in the first of the Chopin compositions we recognize the peculiarities of the Chopin manner. Practically there was no development. We talk of Beethoven's "three styles"; and the merest amateur knows that the Wagner of *Rienzi* is not the Wagner of *Tristan*. In the Verdi of *Il Trovatore* and *La Traviata* who would have thought to find the Verdi of *Otello* and *Falstaff*?

Chopin presents no such study of evolution. Of all the great masters —the adjective may be allowed for the present—he is the one who showed the most originality from the start. Handel, Beethoven, Haydn, Schumann, Schubert, Mendelssohn—in the tentative works of all these one can clearly discern the influence of their predecessors. Wagner wrote his first and only symphony with his model before him, and his first operatic works betrayed allegiance to Meyerbeer. From the first Chopin struck out his own path. As by a natural intuition he "seized at once on the most adequate mode of expressing his thoughts, and never changed it." No doubt, if it were worth while attempting the task, one might make him out a debtor in certain small details. Schumann said of him: "He studied from the very best models": he took from Beethoven "temerity and inspiration, from Schubert tenderness of feeling, from Field, manual dexterity." But this can be accepted only in the most general way, as one would accept the statement that Beethoven was indebted to Bach, or Pope to Spenser and Dryden. "We are all literary cannibals and feed on each other," says Oliver Wendell Holmes. Chopin fed upon those who had gone before him, but the assimilation was so perfect that, to carry the metaphor a little further, his music shows no more of its original constituents than did Dr. Holmes's physical body of the sheep and oxen on which it was sustained. His obligations to Hummel and to John Field have often been insisted upon, but I think this can only apply to the very earliest of his compositions. From Field he got his idea of the Nocturnes, but the limpid style of that neglected composer would have come out in Chopin though Field had never written a bar of music.

It is more to the point to trace the influence on his style of his beloved Poland's folk-song. In his young days he was much in the country listening to the fiddling and the singing of the peasants. In this way he indirectly laid the cornerstone of his art as a national composer. I say a national composer advisedly, for so Chopin regarded himself. It was an aspiration with him from the first to put Poland, as it were, into his music. "I should like," he said, "to be to my people what Uhland is to the Germans." To be sure, the external qualities of his music are all his own. But the texture is essentially of native growth and native substance. Mr. Hadow brings this out more clearly and with more detail than any other writer who has touched on the subject. He shows that there are three separate ways in which the national influence affected Chopin's work. In the first place, it determined the main forms of his art-product. The popular music of Poland is almost invariably founded on dance forms and dance rhythms: more than a quarter of Chopin's entire composition is devoted ostensibly to dance forms, and throughout the rest of it their effect may be seen in a hundred phrases and episodes. A second point of resemblance is Chopin's habit of "founding a whole paragraph either on a single phrase repeated in similar shapes, or on two phrases in alteration." This is a very primitive practice, for which no artistic value can be claimed when standing by itself. But "when it is confined to an episodical passage, especially in a composition founded on a striking or important melody, it may serve as a very justifiable point of rest, a background of which the interest is purposely toned down to provide a more striking contrast with the central figure." It is in the mazurkas that we find this practice most successfully employed—particularly in the first (in F sharp Minor), the fifth (in B flat), and the thirty-seventh (in A flat). Thirdly, Chopin was to a considerable extent affected by the tonality of his native music. The larger number of the Polish folk-songs are written, not in our modern scale, but in one or other of the mediaeval Church modes—the Dorian, the Lydian, and the rest. Moreover, some of them end on what we should call dominant harmony. Of this tonal system, as Mr. Hadow shows, some positive traces may be found in the mazurkas, the cadences of the thirteenth, seventeenth, and twenty-fifth, the frequent use of a sharpened sub-dominant, and the like; while on the negative side it may perhaps account for Chopin's indifference to the requirements of key relationship. The latter is an unusually interesting point. In several of his works widely-divorced keys are brought into the closest relationship; and many of his modulations are as inexplicable on theoretical grounds as those of the average church organist who, in his flights of "improvisation," smothers the tone in the swell-box and allows the new key to emerge from the obscurity. Something of all this might perhaps be set to the account of the romantic movement. But I think Hadow is right in seeing a special reason beyond the fact that Chopin approached our Western key system from the outside and never wholly assimilated himself to the method of thought which it implies.

This seems to be the place for some remarks on what may be termed the theoretical aspect of Chopin's works. The perfection of his form has already been hinted at, and, indeed, there is little to add on the point. Chopin was as finical about the form of his compositions as he was about his dress and personal appearance; and when one has said that with him there is no padding, no commonplace, that "every effect is studied with deliberate purpose and wrought to the highest degree of finish that it can bear," one finds it unnecessary to step over to the grey borderland of pedagogy. His harmonies must have been the horror of the old school-men. Genius makes its own laws, but never did genius flaunt the formulas of the theory books as Chopin did. He was in many ways distinctly in advance of his time. The great chords in the B Minor Scherzo (Opus 20) are Wagnerian before Wagner. In one of the Studies (D flat, Opus 25, No. 8) there is a remarkable passage of consecutive fifths which must have staggered its pundits more than anything that Beethoven or Wagner ever dared. Consecutive major thirds appear in a second study—the one in A flat without opus number. In certain of the other compositions there are combinations which, far as we have travelled on the theoretical road since Chopin's day, still excite marvel. Established distinctions between concord and discord are ignored with an audacity that has no parallel in the history of the art. It has been hinted in explanation of these and other vagaries that Chopin's theoretical training was imperfect. There is no ground for a suggestion of the kind, but if there were we should reject it, and that simply because the end in Chopin justifies the means. There is not a solitary instance in which his infractions of accepted rules fail of their effect. They ought to be ugly; in his hands they are beautiful. Doubtless in another style of music they would be less welcome to the ear. The Chopin harmonic system goes with the Chopin manner. It is not to be regarded in the orthodox fashion. Rather may we liken it to a river—"its surface wind-swept into a thousand variable crests and eddies, its current moving onward, full, steadfast, and inevitable, bearing the whole volume of its waters by sheer force of depth and impetus."

It is a subject of remark with all writers on Chopin that he never once attempted choral composition and such of the larger forms of his art as the symphony, the overture, and the opera. With some this is regarded as a reproach. It is really no reproach. Chopin knew his own *métier* and he stuck to it. Shelley once said that it was as vain to ask for human interest in his poems as to seek to buy a leg of mutton in a gin-shop. It is all but certain that as a composer of opera Chopin would have been a total failure; it is entirely certain that if he had attempted the symphony he would have altogether overstepped the bounds of his genius. He was no "mighty mouthed inventor of harmonies." His genius was essentially lyric—elegiac, not epic, nor even truly dramatic. As his character was deficient in virility so his Muse must have broken down under a big undertaking. Technique aside, he lacked the power of concentrated effort, that sustaining quality, which must be the possession of the composer who would successfully work out primary ideas to their logical and inevitable ending on a large scale. His thoughts were excellent, and his original ideas in the way of themes were excellent, but they depended greatly upon the clothing given them on the keyboard and on the peculiar genius of the instrument. They could never have been heard to advantage in an orchestral dress. The delicate embroideries, the pedal effects, the broken arpeggios and scale passages, are all quite unsuited to orchestral work and totally unfitted for orchestral treatment. Chopin always thought in terms of the piano: he had nothing of the orchestral sense, comparatively little of the orchestral technique. In his two concertos the piano is everything; the orchestration is such as might have been written by a Bachelor of Music. It is crude and absolutely unorchestral. Deficiency of technique, it must be insisted, does not account entirely for this: the main reason is that Chopin's *ideas* were not orchestral. His orchestration has been re-scored by adepts of the art, and yet it remains unsatisfactory.

The point need not be labored. In these things there are compensations. Had Chopin been a great master of the orchestra it is more than probable that his pianoforte music would not have been the unique product it is. If one may dare say it, even Beethoven was often too orchestral in his piano music, especially in his later sonatas. Brahms's heavy chords in the lower register of the piano may have been intended as an attempt at certain orchestral effects, but the attempt cannot be called successful. Liszt scarcely counts, because he was a performer's composer; and besides, however beautifully written his works for the instrument may be, they have no great thematic value. He, too, had severe limitations, and in the larger works which he essayed proved that he lacked the technical training necessary to develop in a natural way. Like Chopin in his concertos, he was out of his depth. To Chopin is really due, as von Bülow has said, the honor and credit of having set fast the boundary between piano and orchestral music, which through other composers of the romantic school, Schumann especially, was in danger of being blotted out, to the prejudice and damage of both species.

If Chopin was small in great things, he was great in small things. He was a composer for the piano and for the piano alone. His style is suited to it and to no other instrument whatever. He cannot be "arranged," as most of the great masters from Handel to Wagner have been "arranged." Divorce him from the keyboard and you rob him of his native tongue. It is as if Paganini had been set to play the oboe or the French horn. Rubinstein said finely: "The piano bard, the piano rhapsodist, the piano mind, the piano soul is Chopin. Tragic, romantic, lyric, heroic, dramatic, fantastic, soulful, sweet, dreamy, brilliant, grand, simple: all possible expressions are found in his compositions, and all are sung by him upon his instrument." In a lesser man this oneness of theme would have led to monotony: in him it led to concentration of the very highest order. He scaled no Alpine heights of art. He worked in a small field, as Edvard Grieg worked. As we see in Grieg, so we see in him—a personality graceful without strength, romantic without the sense of tragedy, highly dowered with all gentle qualities of nature, but lacking in the more virile powers, in breadth of vision, in epic magnanimity, in massive force. We may not call him a "great" composer: we cannot deny his claim to genius. The great composers went their way; Chopin went his. He lived his life, gave what was in him, and died with a name destined, like the name of Mary Stuart, to exert over unborn generations a witchery and a charm unique in the history of his art.

XI

SCHUMANN

ROBERT SCHUMANN

Born at Zwickau, Saxony, June 8, 1810. Settled in Leipzig, 1830; ten years later married Clara Wieck, distinguished pianist. Active as composer, conductor, critic and essayist; founded and edited the Neue Zeitschrift für Musik. Lived at Dresden, 1844–1850; after 1850 at Düsseldorf as music-director. An early champion and friend of Brahms. Incipient insanity developed; attempted suicide, 1854, and died at Eudenich, July 29, 1856.

PRINCIPAL WORKS

VOCAL: Choral: *Paradise and the Peri;* music for *Faust; Requiem for Mignon;* 2 masses; cantatas, choruses with orchestra, including *Adventlied; Abschiedslied.* Many choruses *a capella.* The opera, *Genoveva.* Many songs, of which scores are familiar to-day, including the song cycles to Heine's *Liederkreis* and *Dichterliebe;* 9 songs from *Wilhelm Meister;* etc.

INSTRUMENTAL: 4 symphonies; Overture, scherzo, and finale for orchestra; piano concerto in A minor; cello concerto; fantasia for violin with orchestra; music to Byron's *Manfred* for orchestra; overtures, *Die Braut von Messina, Festouverture, Julius Caesar, Hermann und Dorothea.* Chamber music: piano quintet in E flat; 3 string quartets; 3 piano trios. A great variety of piano music, much of it important in the development of the instrument; including *Abegg variations, Papillons, Davidsbündlertänze, Carnaval, Fantasiestücke, Etudes Symphoniques, Faschingswanke aus Wien, Fantasia Opus 17, Toccata, Kinderscenen, Kreisleriana, Noveletten* (4 bks); 3 sonatas, 3 sonatas for the young; etc.

SCHUMANN

By W. H. Hadow

SCHUMANN'S whole life was an endeavor to unite two ideals. In spirit he is a romantic of the romantics, directing his music towards the outside world with a hundred hints and explanations. In form he recognized Bach as his master, and strove to express his ideas in the most elaborate language of the old polyphony. He does not, like Berlioz, splash on his colors principally with an eye to effect. On the contrary, he pays the utmost attention to detail and finish. In a word, his Davidsbund, like the Pre-Raphaelite Brotherhood, was an attempt to adapt ancient methods to modern subjects, with this difference, that whereas the English Pre-Raphaelitism sometimes lost its hold of the theme in its attention to the treatment, Schumann regards the theme as paramount, and adapts the treatment to it as best he can. Hence the first requisite in estimating his work is to examine the character of his ideas, and especially to explain the contention, already advanced, that in forming them he was much influenced by the romantic movement in literature.

Now, as among the musicians of his time, Schumann was exceptionally well read. His classical attainments were probably allowed to rust during his long life as composer and journalist; but as late as 1854 he was ransacking Greek authors for passages about music, and, even if he took Voss's Homer instead of the original, must have gained some acquaintance with the spirit of the *Iliad* and the *Odyssey*. Among the English poets he was a thorough student of Byron and Shakespeare, and knew something at least of Burns and Scott. Of the Italians he certainly read Dante and Petrarch, and possibly others as well; while the romantic

From the author's *Studies in Modern Music,* by permission of Seeley, Service and Co.

writers of his own country were almost as familiar to him as his own works. He knew his Richter as some Englishmen know Dickens, his Heine as some Frenchmen know Musset. He not only studied Goethe, but interpreted him. Of Rückert, Geibel, Eichendorf, Chamisso, and many other contemporary poets, he was the closest reader and the most valuable commentator. Further, he was himself endowed with some not inconsiderable talent for authorship.

It has been already stated that in his earlier days music and literature divided his allegiance; at Heidelberg he could astonish his friend Rosen with verse translations of Petrarch's sonnets. During his Russian journey in 1844 he kept an intermittent "Poetical Diary," which must at least have implied some facility in meter. His projected romance on the Davidsbund never seems to have come into existence, but in the *Neue Zeitschrift* he treats that society in a manner which shows that he possessed something of the novelist's gift. Florestan, Eusebius, and Raro are distinct living characters, drawn, it may be, from life, but still "seen through a temperament," and contrasted with remarkable skill and consistency. To the last he retained his appreciation of style. The essay on Brahms which closed his career as a journalist is written with the same care as the essay on Chopin which began it. Throughout the whole course he uses his medium like an artist, and endeavors not only to say what he means, but to say it in accordance with the best literary traditions of his time.

Again he acknowledges the debt which his music owed to the study of his favorite author. "I learned more counterpoint from Jean Paul than from my music-master," he tells Simonin de Sire; and writing to Henrietta Voigt *à propos* of the *Papillons* he adds, "I might tell you a good deal about them had not Jean Paul done it so much better. If you ever have a moment to spare, please read the last chapter of the *Flegeljahre,* where you will find it all in black and white, down to the seven-league boot, in F-sharp minor. (At the end of the *Flegeljahre* I always feel as if the piece was over but the curtain still up.) I may further mention that I have adapted the text to the music and not vice versa. Only the last of all, which by a happy chance became an answer to the first, owes its existence to Jean Paul." It is difficult for us to see in the last number of the *Papillons* Wult's departure or Wult's fantastic dream, but the point is that Schumann saw it. The mind that conceived that dainty finale was brought into its particular mood by a literary influence.

Thirdly, in one important point Schumann's method of composition stands in closest relation to the earlier romantic movement in German poetry. "The plastic figures in antique Art," says Heine, "are identical with the thing represented. The wanderings of the *Odyssey* mean nothing more than the wanderings of the man called Odysseus, the son of Laertes and the husband of Penelope. It is otherwise in Romantic Art: here the wanderings of the knight have an esoteric signification; they typify, perhaps, the mazes of life in general. The dragon that is vanquished is sin: the almond tree that wafts its fragrance to the hero is the Trinity. . . . Classical Art had to portray only the finite, and its form could be identical with the artist's idea. Romantic Art had to represent, or rather to typify, the infinite and the spiritual, and therefore was compelled to have recourse to a system of traditional parabolic symbols." So it is with music. The tunes in a sonata of Mozart are satisfied to be beautiful melodies and nothing more: no question arises as to their meaning or character. The tunes of Schumann, like the colors of Rossetti, are always trembling on the verge of symbolism. Not, of course, that music can be tied down to any definite signification: on this point the failure of Berlioz is complete and conclusive. But though it cannot work on the same lines as articulate thought, it may possibly work on parallel lines:—that is to say, it may express some broad generic type of emotion with which the articulate thought may be brought into sympathy. For instance, a great many of Schumann's pianoforte pieces have specific names—*Warum, Erster Verlust, Botschaft,* and so on. It would be impossible for us to supply the names from hearing the piece; but if we know the names already we shall recognize that the musical treatment is appropriate. This was precisely what Schumann intended. He writes to Dorn, "I have never come across anything more absurd than Rellstab's criticism of my *Kinderscenen.* He seems to imagine that I got hold of a crying child and sought for inspiration from its sobs. I don't deny that certain children's faces hovered before my mind while I was composing, but the titles were of course added afterwards, and are, as a matter of fact, merely hints as to the treatment and interpretation." At the same time his indications are curiously detailed. He distinguishes the *Kinderscenen* from the *Weihnachts Album* on the ground that the former are the recollection which a grown man retains of his childhood, while the latter "consists of imaginings and expectations of young people." He finds the story of Hero and Leander in the fifth of the *Fantasiestucke:* he accompanies two of the *Davidsbundlertänze* with a running commentary of Florestan and Eusebius; while as climax he declares that in one of Schubert's pianoforte works he and a friend discovered exactly the same pageant, "down to the name of the town in which it was held." Even his directions for performance show something of the same tendency. In the ordinary indications of *tempo* he is notoriously careless; it is a well-known joke against him that the finale of the "Concerto without Orchestra" begins, *So schnell als möglich* and ends *piu presto,* while there is still a controversy whether the coda of the slow movement in his F major quartet should be marked *piu mosso* or *piu lento.* But on the other hand he often suggests the manner of interpretation by such phrases as *Etwas kokett,* or *mit humor,* or *mit innigkeit.* Once he gets as far as *Etwas hahnbuchen,* a hint which pianists must find some difficulty in taking. The great pianoforte Fantasia in C has a motto from Schlegel, the fourth of the *Waldscenen* has one from Hebbel, and similar texts were appended to the earliest edition of the *Davidsbundlertänze* and of one of the *Novelletten.* Everywhere we find the evident intention of establishing a parallelism between music and some influence from outside. In one word, Schumann did not wish his melodies to tell a definite story or paint a definite picture, but he did wish to bring his hearers into a condition of mind from which they could "go on romancing for themselves."

One example of this parallelism deserves a special word of comment, partly from its intrinsic importance, partly because hitherto it has been somewhat underrated. The *Kreisleriana* certainly owe more than their title to Hoffmann's fantastic sketches. Critics who tell us that Schumann "is expressing his own sorrows, not those of Dr. Kreisler," and that "he might just as well have called his pieces 'Wertheriana,' or any other name," have missed a point which it is of some moment to observe. Among Hoffmann's *Fantasiestücke in Callot's manier* there are two sets of Kreisleriana, loose, disconnected papers, dealing with music and musical criticism very much in the style which Schumann afterwards adopted for the *Neue Zeitschrift.* The essay on Beethoven might have been signed "R. S.," Florestan and Eusebius might have been members of the Musico-Poetical Club, the Musikfeind was a well-known figure in the editorial sanctum at Leipzig. Even Dr. Johannes Kreisler himself—"the little man in a coat the color of C-sharp minor with an E major colored collar"—is not far removed in spirit from the party who listened to Chopin's Opus 2, or tried experiments with the "psychometer." In short, of all German artists Schumann approaches most nearly to Hoffmann in standpoint. Both deserted law for music, both were at the same time composers and journalists, both employed the manner and phraseology of Richter to the advancement of the new school of composition. The differences between them, which no doubt are sufficiently wide, lie mainly outside the domain of the art: within that domain they fought for the same cause with the same weapons. Hence in calling his pieces *Kreisleriana* Schumann is expressing a real connection of thought, a real recognition of alliance. They are, in fact, *Fantasiestücke in Hoffmann's manier,* and bear more intimate relation to the creator of Dr. Kreisler than all the copper-plates that ever issued from Callot's studio.

The connection is interesting because it illustrates the attempt to relate musical to literary influences under the most favorable of conditions. We have here two men possessed of somewhat similar gifts and united by a common aim. Hoffmann is enough of a composer to have a full understanding of music; Schumann enough of an author to be closely in touch with literature. Both desire to reconcile the two, so far as such reconciliation is possible; each sets himself to the work from his own side. Hence in estimating the result of their efforts we shall see once for all the limitations of musical romanticism. It is a unique opportunity for determining in what sense effects of tone and effects of word can be held to react upon one another.

Now in the second series of Hoffmann's *Kreisleriana* is described a meeting of the Musico-Poetical Club, a precursor of the Davidsbund, which assembled in the Kapellmeister's rooms to hear him play, and to profit by his instructions. Unfortunately at the outset there is an accident to the piano, attempts to remedy it only make matters worse, and at last so many of the strings are broken that the instrument becomes practically useless. But the doctor is equal to the occasion. He seats himself at the keyboard, and striking at intervals such notes as are still available, supplies the place of his fantasia with a long rhapsodical description of its poetical meaning. The performance, in fact, is the exact reverse of a song without words:—it is a pianoforte piece without music. We may notice that Hoffmann is wise enough not to attempt any definiteness of outline. There is no portraiture of hero or heroine, no detailed description of incident, all is left vague, shadowy, indeterminate. Literature has become all but melodic, it is standing on the extreme verge and stretching out its hands over a gulf which it cannot cross. In like manner the *Kreisleriana* of Schumann are all but articulate. In no other of his pianoforte works is the expression of emotion so clear and so intelligible; the voice is eloquent even though we cannot catch the precise words of its utterance. Here also is no attempt to depict any specific scene or occurrence; the music is suggestive, not descriptive; the end is attained purely and simply by the indication of broad general types of feeling. This, then, would seem to be the conclusion of the whole matter. The most determinate effects of tone produce in the hearer a mental impression analogous to that caused by the least determinate effects of word. As language becomes more definite, as music becomes more abstract, so the two recede from one another until they arrive at poles, which have as little in common as a page of Macaulay with a melody of Mozart. At their nearest they can never be brought into contact, for music is in more senses than one a universal language, and cannot be adequately translated by the concrete particulars of our accustomed speech. But, near or far, their closest points of convergence are the two *Kreisleriana*.

It may be added that Schumann himself had a clear view of the extent and limits of his position. "People err," he says, "if they think that a composer puts pen to paper with the predetermination of expressing or depicting some particular fact. Yet we must not estimate outward influences and impressions too lightly. . . . The more elements congenially related to music which the tone-picture contains within it the more poetic and plastic will be the expression of the composition, and in proportion to the imaginativeness and receptivity of the composer will be the elevating and touching quality of his work." And again, more boldly: "The ill-educated man can scarcely believe that music possesses the power of expressing particular passions, and therefore it is difficult for him to comprehend the more individual masters. We have learned to express the finer shades of feeling by penetrating more deeply into the mysteries of harmony." No doubt Schumann is here claiming too much. Music cannot "express the finer shades of feeling," it can only suggest the broader types and universals. But in any case we have here the words of a composer who approaches his art from the poetical side, who is as far as possible removed from the abstract, unconscious, unreflective methods of the earlier masters. Mozart and Haydn were musicians; Schumann was in the fullest sense of the term a tone-poet.

So far we have considered the character of Schumann's ideas, and the external or literary influences by which his mind was trained for their conception. It would now follow to complete the account of his education by pointing out the influence exercised upon him by the work of previous composers. Among these, of course, Bach was paramount. Schumann almost passes over the great triumvirate to whom we owe the sonata, the quartet, and the symphony. Mozart and Haydn hardly affected him at all; Beethoven "mainly in his later compositions"; it is to Bach that he looks as the second fountain-head of his inspiration. "Bach and Jean Paul had the greatest influence upon me in former days," he writes to Kossmaly, and as late as 1851 he makes the same acknowledgment. "There are three to whom I always go for advice: the simple Gluck, the more intricate Handel, and the most intricate of all—Bach. Only study the last-named thoroughly and the most complicated of my works will seem clear." Half his admiration for Mendelssohn was devoted to "the master who was the first, by the strength of his own enthusiasm, to revive the memory of Bach in Germany"; almost the last work which occupied his failing powers was a set of pianoforte accompaniments to the violin and violoncello sonatas of the great Cantor. No doubt he gained something from Weber and Schubert, but his relation to them was far less intimate. From first to last his ideal in musical expression was "the great and lofty art of the ancestor of harmony."

Bach and Jean Paul—polyphony and romance—these are the two keys which unlock the mystery of Schumann's work as a composer. His own individuality remains unimpugned; all artists are in some degree indebted to the continuous growth and development of previous work; and Schumann's method is no more derivative than that of Beethoven or Handel. The formative conditions of genius are those by which it is trained, not those by which it is created, only in all cases the training must be efficient if creation is to lead to maturity. At the same time it is of considerable interest to notice three main points in which his education told upon his style. It may be impossible to explain the life; it is both possible and profitable to dissect the organism.

First, his career as a composer is unique in the history of music. There is no other instance of a musician who applies himself successively to each department of his art, masters it, and passes on to the next. Almost all his great pianoforte works were written before 1840; then came a year of song writing, then a year of symphony, then a year of chamber music, then *Paradise and the Peri*. Schubert's songs cover the whole period of his productive life; Beethoven's first piece of concerted music is Opus 1 and his last Opus 135; Haydn's symphonies extend over nearly half a century. The other great masters, in short, seem either to have had the forms always at hand, or, like Wagner and Berlioz, to have left some altogether untouched. Schumann employs every medium in turn; but he fetches it from outside, and puts it back when he has finished with it. No doubt he wrote songs after 1840, and orchestral compositions after 1841; but it is none the less noticeable that he devoted himself exclusively to the different forms when they first came under his hand, and that almost all his best work may be divided into a series of detached groups, each produced in one particular manner at one particular time. Surely we have here the indirect working of a logical, deliberative mind—a mind that has been trained into special habits of purpose and selection. In the very character of his method Schumann is actuated by psychological forces different from those of his predecessors in the art.

The second distinctive point is his system of melody. All tune implies a certain fundamental unity—otherwise it would be chaotic; and a certain variation of detail—otherwise it would be monotonous. This identity in difference can be attained in two ways, which we may call respectively the Continuous and the Discrete. In the former a series of entirely different elements is fused into a single whole: no two of them are similar, yet all are so fitted together that each supplies what the others need. In the latter a set of parallel clauses are balanced antithetically: the same rhythmic figure is preserved in all, and the differences depend entirely upon qualities of tone and curve. The former is the typical method of Beethoven, the latter that of Schumann. Take, for instance, the opening subject of Beethoven's violoncello sonata in A. No two bars present the same figure, yet the whole is a unity. Take the longer melody which opens the slow movement of the *Sonata Pathétique*. It contains almost as many figures as there are bars, yet the effect is of a single and perfect sentence. Of course Beethoven employed both methods, as he employed every other mode of musical expression, but it is incontestable that in the power of varying and developing his figures is to be found one of his greatest claims to supremacy as an artist. This power Schumann seldom or never brought into active operation. In the opening movement of his pianoforte quintet, to take an instance from the most familiar of all his works, the first four bars contain two clauses, upon which are built the whole of the first subject and the transition; while the first two bars of the second subject contain the clause upon which the whole of the succeeding melody is constructed. In the last movement of the D minor trio, in the cantabile tune of the first *Novellette,* in the well-known theme of the *Bilder aus Osten,* in a hundred other examples we find a definite square-cut scheme, exactly analogous to the structure of a stanza of verse. There are very few of Beethoven's instrumental melodies to which it would be possible to adapt metrical words; there is scarcely one of Schumann's which could not be so treated. His relation to poetry extends even to the fact of versification.

Hence his melodies are much easier to analyze than those of Beethoven. Indeed it often happens that the melodic phrase is obvious—almost commonplace—and that the value of the tune depends upon the skill of its treatment, and especially the richness of its harmonization. The charming little waltz in the *Papillons* is simply an ascending and descending diatonic scale; the very effective opening subject in the slow movement of the pianoforte quartet is a series of sevenths; and similar instances may be found in the scherzo of the pianoforte quintet and in many of the songs. Sometimes, too, he took his theme from the "musical letters" in a word, witness the Abegg variations, the *Carnaval,* and the fugues on the name of Bach, and though this has been done by other composers, yet none have treated the matter so seriously or with such earnestness of purpose. The *Carnaval,* in particular, is an astonishing instance of the effects that can be produced out of five notes. But it is only very rarely that Schumann's tunes approach the "divine unconsciousness" of the *Appassionata* or the A major symphony. They have their own character, their own vitality, but the genius that gave them birth was to some degree affected by the preoccupations of an external interest.

The third point is Schumann's comparative indifference to what is technically known as musical form. When he writes about the constituent elements of music he almost always specifies them as melody and harmony—the "king and queen of the chess board"—without any mention of that relation of subjects and distribution of keys by which the laws of structure are constituted. This indifference is still more noticeable in his estimate of other men's work. Schubert's C major symphony, Schunke's pianoforte sonata, Bohme's string quartet are discussed with little or no reference to their construction; while, strangest of all, Berlioz's *Symphonie Fantastique* is treated as the legitimate outcome of the system established by Mozart and Beethoven. So it is with his own compositions. Except the symphony in B flat all his orchestral works are in some degree experimental, and in one of them, the symphony in D minor, he practically abandons the old scheme altogether; his pianoforte sonatas are only sonatas in the sense in which *Don Juan* is an epic; his quartets, although they keep the elementary laws, yet show that there is much difference between obeying rules and mastering them. His two finest examples of structure are the pianoforte quintet and the overture to *Manfred;* and even these exhibit a sense of effort which place them on a lower level than the concealed art of Beethoven or Brahms. No doubt it is perfectly admissible to seek after new forms. In this respect, as in every other, music must be allowed free permission to advance. But, if we are to acquiesce in a substitute for the earlier methods, we must be assured that it is at least as capable as they of satisfying our requirements. And at present it is not too much to say that, except in the one detail of the "transference of themes," classical structure has not seen any discovery of importance since the publication of the Rasoumoffsky quartets. It must be remembered that in this respect there is a marked difference between Schumann and Berlioz. The latter simply shows a want of acquaintance with the laws of construction. The former knows the laws, but underrates their importance. Schumann is far the greater musician of the two, but though his error is less apparent it is not less existent.

There are three possible reasons why a composer of such brilliant genius and such unwearied industry should have displayed this weakness. First, that Bach wrote before the great cyclical forms were established and could therefore give his devoted student little or no assistance in dealing with them. Second, that of all modes of musical expression form is the most abstract—the most essentially musical. Melody and harmony may have some rough analogues outside the limits of the art: the laws of structure have none. Hence they constitute an inner shrine to which only the most single-hearted musicians can penetrate; and he who visits the Temple with any other prepossession— even of poetry itself—must be content to worship among the people. Third, that the whole tone of Schumann's thought was lyric. A very large number of his works consist of short detached pieces, in which there is neither need nor scope for any elaborate system of construction. Hence he grew habituated to the methods of conciseness and concentration, and his sustained efforts were hardly more congenial than the tragedies of Heine or the historical dramas of Uhland.

In one further respect the character of his work was affected by his general habit of mind. No other composer has ever submitted his music to so much alteration and recension. The later editions of the *Davidsbundlertänze,* the *Etudes Symphoniques,* the *Impromptus on a Theme* of Clara Wieck's, and other of the piano compositions, are full of variant passages, which range in importance from the correction of a detail to the complete restatement of a whole number. No doubt this form of self-criticism has existed to some extent among artists of all ages: Handel rewrote part of the *Messiah,* Berlioz of the *Symphonie Fantastique,* and Brahms, late in life, gave to the world a new version of his first pianoforte trio; but in no other case has the faculty manifested itself so persistently or attached itself so frequently to the printed page. Here again we have evidence of a mind trained in a different school from that of Haydn and Mozart. They made their point once for all with an unerring certainty of intuition: Schumann weighs, deliberates, and finally revises.

As a writer for the pianoforte he may be said to rank beside Schubert. He has less melodic gift, less sweetness, perhaps less originality, but he appreciates far more fully the capacities of the instrument, and possesses more power of rich and recondite harmonization. His polyphony was a new departure in the history of pianoforte music, based upon that of Bach, but exhibiting a distinctive color and character of its own. The beauty of his single phrases, the vigor and variety of his accompaniments, the audacity of his "bitter sweet discords," are all so many claims on immortality: hardly in the whole range of art have we such intimate household words as *Warum,* and *Träumerei, Carnaval* and *Humoreske,*

Kreisleriana and *Novelletten*. His spirit, too, is essentially human. No composer is more companionable, more ready to respond to any word and sympathize with any emotion.

Among minute points may be mentioned his frequent use of syncopation, sometimes picking out the melody for emphasis, sometimes retarding it to half-speed, oftener traversing the rhythm altogether; his fondness for long sustained organ chords, as in the *Humoreske* and at the end of the *Papillons;* and his peculiar habit of placing his theme in the middle of the harmony and surrounding it on both sides with a "transparent fabric" of arpeggios. Of more importance is his employment of new lyric and narrative forms for the pianoforte: the former of which may be illustrated by the detached yet interconnected numbers of the *Blumenstück,* a Liederkreis without words; the latter by the structure of the first *Novellette,* in which the distribution of keys is based upon the interval of a major third, instead of the old stereotyped relations of tonic and dominant.

A special word should be said on Schumann's position as a writer of variations. There are two points of view from which this device can be regarded. The composer may consider the melody as the essential feature of the theme, and occupy himself solely with embroideries and arabesques; or he may take his stand upon its harmonic structure, and reproduce the thought that it contains in different modes of expression and phraseology. The one is, roughly speaking, the method of Mozart and Haydn—it is simpler, more rudimentary, more easily exhausted; the other, which is practically inexhaustible, is the method of Brahms. Beethoven represents the turning point between the two. In the slow movement of his pianoforte trio in C minor (Opus 1, Number 3) he gives us a developed example of the earlier form; in the Diabelli variations we have the finest existing instance of the later. Schumann, of course, is an uncompromising exponent of the second system. Indeed he is sometimes over-zealous in his anxiety not to adhere too closely to the melody of his subject. The set of variations for two pianos, though it atones for its freedom by its extraordinary beauty and charm, yet contains two episodes in which the theme is practically abandoned. It is in the *Etudes Symphoniques* that his power of variation is shown at its best. They also push freedom to its utmost limit, but they never lose touch with their original text, and in richness, brilliance, and vitality they are almost worthy to rank beside the highest efforts of Schumann's great successor.

After the pianoforte works come the songs. Here again Schumann's position can be stated by a single contrast. As absolute music his songs have less value than those of Schubert, he has never given us a tune like the *Litanei* or *Sie Mir Gegrüsst;* as illustrations of lyric poetry they are unsurpassed in the whole history of the art. With him the terms "words" and "setting," "melody" and "accompaniment," lose their distinctive meanings; all are fused into a single whole in which no part has the preëminence. He follows every shade of the poet's thought with perfect union of sympathy, he catches its tone, he echoes its phrase, he almost anticipates its issue. It is not too much to say that no man can understand Heine who does not know Schumann's treatment of the *Buch der Lieder.*

His songs are interesting also in certain matters of form. He was the first composer who ventured to end with an imperfect cadence, if the words were abrupt or inconclusive, as for instance *Im wunderschönen Monat Mai* and *Anfangs wollt' ich fast verzagen.* Often, too, he ends his earlier verses with a half-close, and so makes the song continuous throughout, as in *Mondnacht* and the *Lied der Zuleika.* Another point is his curious use of declamatory passages, neither exact melody nor exact recitative, as in *Ich grolle nicht.* But no analysis can do justice to the beauty, the variety, and the profusion of his lyrics. The composer of *Frühlingsnacht* and *Widmung,* of *Die Löwenbraut* and *Die Beiden Grenadiere,* of *Schöne Wiege* and *Er der herrlichste von allen,* has assuredly some claim to be considered the most poetical of musicians.

The qualities required for a successful treatment of the orchestra are precisely those in which, comparatively speaking, Schumann was most deficient, and it is not therefore surprising that his orchestral compositions should be of less value than his works for the voice or the pianoforte. The symphony stands to music as the epic to poetry; it is the broadest, most sustained, most heroic of all forms of expression. Hence it cannot easily be attained by a composer whose gift is for short flights and rapid movements, whose manner of thought is concrete, whose best writings are those which give most scope for the display of brevity and concentration. No doubt Schubert has left us one brilliant instance of a lyric symphony, but, apart from the difficulty of judging a work by two movements, it remains an exception. Schumann, at any rate, seems to lose his bearings among the "swelling and limitless billows." In the opening allegro of his C major symphony, for instance, the exposition is vigorous and concise enough, but before the end of the movement his boat has refused to answer to the helm and gone drifting off into strange and unknown regions. Again, in the finale of the same work, he finds that the materials presented at the outset are inadequate, discards them half-way through, and introduces an entirely fresh subject. It is hardly unfair to say that the only thing which holds the movement together is a single two-bar phrase containing a diatonic scale. The same vagueness of outline is to be found in his symphony in D minor, originally called by the more appropriate name of *Symphonische Fantasie*. And it may be submitted that these are not really new forms, since they lack the organic unity which the form implies. If they are to be taken as experiments it must be in Bacon's sense of *mero palpatio*.

On the other hand the lyric movements—the scherzos and adagios— are always beautiful. Here Schumann was in his element, he was dealing with forces which he knew how to control, and his success was complete and indisputable. It is only necessary to recall the larghetto of the first symphony, or the exquisite romance from the second, or the *Volkslied* from the third, to see that within the limits of a narrower form Schumann could well display his power of musical expression. Indeed his first symphony is almost a masterpiece throughout, and his others, even the most indeterminate, contain separate thoughts and phrases for which we may well be grateful. It is only when we compare him with the great symphonic writers, Brahms and Beethoven and Mozart, that we see evidence of weakness and imperfection.

It is usual to depreciate Schumann's power of orchestration, and indeed there can be little doubt that the general texture of his scoring is somewhat thick and heavy, and that he too frequently writes for the band passages that seem to owe their inspiration to the pianoforte. Still, he has supremely good moments—the bassoon in the adagio of the C major symphony, the trumpets in the *Manfred* overture, the violin solo of the symphony in D minor—and often what he loses in transparency he supplies in warmth and richness of color. Among his mannerisms may be mentioned a persistent habit of breaking up his string phrases into rapid repeated notes, and an almost restless change of pitch in his use of the transposing instruments.

Three of his concerti are published, one for the pianoforte, one for four horns (a curious revival of the old *concerto grosso*) and one for violoncello. Of these the pianoforte concerto is the best known and the most valuable. It consists of a brilliant opening fantasia, a light, graceful intermezzo in which the second subject is ingeniously developed out of a phrase in the first, and a stirring finale in Schumann's best style of composition. The concerto for four horns is seldom or never given, owing to the extreme difficulty and compass of its first solo part; but it may be noticed that the allegro is more regular in form than the general run of Schumann's orchestral works, and that the romance is scored with unusual care. The violoncello concerto has a fine manly first movement, a very beautiful though very short adagio, and a rather diffuse finale, in which, however, the capacities of the solo instrument are treated with considerable skill.

A composer who writes pianoforte passages for the orchestra has but an ill augury in approaching the special technique of the string quartet. No form of composition demands more exact perfection of style, more intimate sympathy with the medium employed. Every phrase is salient; every note shows through; there is no possibility of covering weak places or condoning uncertainty of outline. Hence there is little wonder that Schumann's three essays in this field should rank among his comparative failures. The three opening allegros have great charm of melody, and in two of them the structure is firm and solid; the sectional movements exhibit Schumann's usual power of dealing with lyric forms, but the rest show a continuous sense of effort which is inadequately repaid. Many passages, too, even in the more successful numbers, are alien to the style of the quartet, and recall methods of treatment which would be more appropriate to the orchestra. The case is very different in the concerted works for pianoforte and strings. Here the medium is pastel in place of water-color; the new instrument brings with it an entirely new means of expression, and one, moreover, of which Schumann was a consummate master. At the keyboard he was once more at home, and his work in this department of the art may rank among the most genial of his inspirations. Indeed, this particular form lay most emphasis on the qualities of romance and least on the technical gifts of absolute music. Mozart's pianoforte trios are weaker than his string quartets; Schumann, who is beaten by the strings alone, has only to add the pianoforte and his victory is assured.

As a dramatic writer he displays the same strength and weakness as Byron, with whom he has often been compared. Both possessed a considerable gift of description; both were steeped in romanticism; both were too intensely subjective to succeed in that essential of the drama—characterization. In *Genoveva,* for instance, the whole background of the opera is vividly depicted in the strong chivalrous overture, but the *dramatis personae* are drawn with an uncertain hand and even the situations are imperfectly presented. Golo's first song is far too beautiful to be wasted on a villain; the supernatural element is clumsily treated throughout; Siegfried, except for one moment, is a mere lay figure; and even the heroine fails to retain the interest which ought to center about a title-rôle. No doubt in this, as in Weber's *Euryanthe,* much allowance must be made for a weak libretto, but it may be remembered that Schumann himself chose the subject and modeled the words. He treated it, in short, as a psychological study, than which the stage can follow no more fatal ideal.

Much may be said of *Manfred.* The incidental music is most successful where it deals with description, least so where it deals with action, and at best does not approach the superb force and splendor of the overture. In this Schumann's orchestral writing reaches its highest point. From the first note to the last, it is as magnificent as an Alpine storm, somber, wild, impetuous, echoing from peak to peak with the shock of thunder-clouds and the clamor of the driving wind.

In *Faust* we rise above the tempest. The overture and the earlier scenes need not here be considered, for they were written when Schumann's powers were beginning to fail under the stress of disease, and so cannot justly be estimated in relation to his normal work. But in the scene of Faust's salvation, we have an incontestable masterpiece. It may be, as some critics have asserted, that the last half of the *Chorus Mysticus* is something of anti-climax, that in neither of its two alternative versions does it "breathe the pure serene" of the other numbers. In any case the whole work is noble music, vast in scale, lofty in spirit, a worthy interpretation of the great poem that summoned it into being. The only fit analogue with which it may be compared is the third act of *Parsifal,* opening with the solemn quietude of the Hermitage and closing with the Eucharistic strains that ascend to the gate of Heaven itself.

Among Schumann's cantatas *Paradise and the Peri* stands preëminent. It is easy to see how readily he would be attracted by the subject, and how fully he would avail himself of the opportunities afforded by its warm imagery and its suggestions of Oriental color. The artificial glitter of Moore's verse is mercifully obscured in a translation: only the thought is left for the composer to decorate as he will. Nowhere is Schumann's treatment of a libretto more thoroughly characteristic. All his favorite devices are here—long rhetorical passages, hovering between tune and recitative, single melodic phrases of great beauty, rich, almost sensuous, harmonization, even the broad sustained chords which form such a distinctive feature in his pianoforte music. It is, in short, an abstract and epitome of the romantic movement, a scene of fairyland admirably painted against a background of human interest and emotion. Of other choral works for the concert room two deserve special mention: the exquisite *Requiem for Mignon,* and the bright, tuneful *Pilgrimage of the Rose.* The rest belong to Schumann's period of exhaustion, and lie outside the limits of fair criticism.

At the same time no account of his compositions would be complete without some reference to the sacred music, which he declared to be the "highest aim of every true artist." Yet his own work in this field is singularly scanty. The two so-called motets are rather inconspicuous, the *Altkatholisches Requiem* is but a beautiful song not much larger in scale than Schubert's *Ave Maria,* and besides them we have only two works— the Mass and the Requiem—left for examination.

Of these the Requiem is undoubtedly the finer. In the Mass Schumann is approaching too closely the unfamiliar region of absolute music; its style demands an austerity, a self-repression to which he had never grown accustomed. Further, with all his experience as a song writer, he had not concerned himself with the peculiar capacities of the voice, and hence was unprepared for the special treatment of counterpoint which all tradition has connected with the kyrie and the credo. Hence, although his Mass contains some good episodes, notably the offertorium, which he added to the orthodox text, it cannot be regarded as certainly successful. In the Requiem, on the other hand, we have two of the finest things that Schumann ever wrote: the opening number, and the portion which contains the *Qui Mariam absolvisti,* the *Confutatis* and the *Lacrymosa.* It is hard to believe that the mind which conceived that wonderful music was already tottering to its fall.

It may be that much of his work will not survive the attack of time. There are few men who do not find that the greater part of their life's record is written in water. But something at least will remain. He is not only the best representative but the virtual founder of a distinct style in music; his sense of beauty is often exquisite; his feeling pure, manly and chivalrous. So long as melody possesses the power to soothe, to comfort, to sympathize, so long shall we turn in gratitude to one who could transmute the sorrows of his own heart into an elixir for the cure of others. After all we have no right to require that an artist's whole gift should consist of masterpieces. We do not judge Wordsworth by his stories of the nursery, or Shelley by his two attempts at burlesque; we take the ode and the sonnets, *Prometheus* and *Adonais,* and let the failures go. In like manner we can discard some of Schumann's compositions as uninspired, but when we have done so there will still be left a legacy that may enrich music to the end of the world. It matters little whether his monument be large or small; in either case it is imperishable.

XII
WAGNER

RICHARD WAGNER

Born at Leipzig, May 22, 1813. Throughout his life Wagner was a man of extraordinary and varied activity: as composer, conductor, librettist for his own operas, pamphleteer and author of numerous works ranging from autobiography to drama. Travelled, more or less constantly, throughout Europe; went to Paris, 1839; conducted Dresden Opera, 1843–1849, when he was banished from Germany as a revolutionist. Lived chiefly in Zurich, 1849–1855; went to London, Paris, and Vienna producing his operas; returned to Germany, 1861. Under the patronage of Ludwig II of Bavaria achieved his first great success at Munich. Married in 1870 Cosima, daughter of Liszt and divorced wife of the conductor von Bülow. Permanent Wagner theatre inaugurated at Bayreuth, 1872. Wagner died at Venice, February 13, 1883.

No brief sketch could begin to trace even in outline the succession of events which contributed to Wagner's career: his struggles with fortune, his attempts to obtain hearings for his works, from Riga to London; his incessant succession of ideas and writings on every conceivable topic; his vivid personal associations, entanglements, and adventures, some of which contributed subject matter to his librettos.

PRINCIPAL WORKS

Before he was 20 Wagner had written a symphony, a string quartet, and piano sonatas. Other early works include his first operas, *Die Feen* and *Das Liebesverbot.*

OPERAS: *Rienzi, Der Fliegende Holländer, Tannhäuser, Lohengrin, Tristan und Isolde, Die Meistersinger von Nürnberg, Der Ring des Nibelungen (Das Rheingold, Die Walküre, Siegfried, Götterdämmerung); Parsifal.*

ORCHESTRAL MUSIC: *Siegfried Idyll* (in celebration of the birth of his son); *Faust* overture and other overtures; *Kaisermarsch, Huldigungsmarsch,* and other marches.

WAGNER

By H. C. Colles

WILHELM RICHARD WAGNER, the youngest of a large family, was born at Leipzig on May 22, 1813. His mother, left a widow a few months after Richard's birth, soon married again an actor named Geyer; the event caused a removal of the family to Dresden, where Richard was put to school at the age of nine. His cleverness soon asserted itself. It is recorded that at the age of thirteen he translated the first twelve books of the *Odyssey* out of school hours. Poetry of all kinds attracted him immensely. He wrote voluminous verses, read Shakespeare in German translations and learnt enough English to attempt some translation on his own account, and stimulated his fancy by trying to write tragedies modeled partly on the Greek drama, partly on Shakespeare.

In these years Weber was at Dresden, and was on friendly terms with the Geyer family. He became a hero to the young Wagner, who knew *Der Freischütz* by heart. Soon after Weber's early death the family moved back to Leipzig, and there Richard added to his limited musical experiences his first hearing of the symphonies of Beethoven and the music to *Egmont*. He immediately determined that poetry and drama, even the great tragedy which he had designed to write, would be barren without music of the heroic Beethoven-like kind, so he resolved to write such music, and got hold of a book on harmony from which to learn the few technical facts which he thought it necessary to know. In this incident one sees Wagner in a flash. What he willed to do he was quite certain that he could do; he brushed aside every impediment. With supreme self-confidence everything and everybody throughout his life

From the author's *The Growth of Music*, by permission of the Oxford University Press.

was made to conform to his will, and he never doubted the rightness of his will.

Needless to say, the great tragedy and the great music to it came to nothing, but this much came out of his enthusiasm: that some definite musical teaching was procured for him. He was now fifteen, his schooling went on at Leipzig, and it is of passing interest to know that for a time he attended the "Thomasschule." That, however, did not bring him the acquaintance with Bach's music that one might expect, for in 1830 Bach was not treasured in Leipzig as he was at a later time when Mendelssohn had revived the *Matthew Passion* and begun the great research among the manuscripts which Bach had left behind him.

Wagner, however, was taught music by Theodor Weinlig, who, as Cantor of the "Thomasschule," was actually a successor of Bach. He entered the university in 1831 and wrote music, including a symphony in C major, with a good deal of diligence; but all the time, even though he allowed himself to be guided by Weinlig into the regular forms of instrumental music, he was inclined to revolt against them. It was in 1833, when he was twenty years old, that his career as a musician began with an engagement as chorus-master at the small theatre of Würzburg in Bavaria. Here he wrote an elaborate opera *Die Feen* (The Fairies); both words and music were his own composition, and the story, considerably altered, was taken from an Italian play by Gozzi. Though this opera was put aside for many years, and has only been published since Wagner's death, there is a good deal in its melody and in its imaginative treatment of the fairy story which suggests his own style. In some ways it is more characteristic than the later and better-known *Rienzi*.

From this time began the period of more or less transitory theatrical engagements, tentative compositions, continuous difficulties largely made by himself, which lasted until his resolve to go to Paris in 1839. Another opera, *Das Liebesverbot* (Forbidden Love), founded on Shakespeare's *Measure for Measure*, belongs to this time. Among his many moves from place to place the appointment as conductor to the opera at Magdeburg, where he met and married Minna Planer, is the most important. The difficulties were largely connected with money. Wagner was always getting into debt because of his rooted assurance that what he required he must have, that if he could not get it for himself other people ought to supply it for him.

This does not give a very agreeable picture of Wagner's character, and many phases of it were far from being agreeable; but it must be remembered that his extreme egotism rested on the conviction that he had the ability for great things. He never saw that other people could not be expected to take him at his own valuation until he had given proof of the justness of that valuation. The better side of him may be compared to Beethoven in his early days in Vienna; one can see now that he no more than Beethoven was playing a gambling game when he claimed to be given a chance to express himself freely. Like Beethoven, he only needed time to justify his artistic claims; but, unlike Beethoven, he made large material claims upon those about him while he was gaining time, and he had no scruples in pressing those claims to the detriment of others.

In 1839, having got nothing but small theatrical appointments in Germany, which chiefly meant the duty of producing other composers' operas, Wagner determined upon a great bid for fortune. He planned a visit to Paris, where he hoped to get a new opera performed by securing the good offices of Meyerbeer, then one of the most popular operatic composers of Paris, and one whose word would carry weight with the directors of the Paris opera. Again he was doomed to disappointment, but this Paris visit, nevertheless, had a great effect upon his career.

Wagner, his wife, and a huge Newfoundland dog (at that time his constant companion) all shipped on board a sailing vessel bound for London at the port of Pillau on the Baltic, and on the voyage he had his first experience of the sea and an exceedingly severe one. In the storm which they encountered the legend of the Flying Dutchman, which he had read as Heine told it, was graphically brought to mind, and his impressions became subsequently translated into music in the overture which remains one of the most vivid sea-pieces ever written for the orchestra. They landed in London and stopped there a week, but, quite unknown, did little beyond wandering about the streets and gazing at the Houses of Parliament. Thence they went to Boulogne, where Wagner met Meyerbeer, obtained the introductions which he wanted and proceeded to Paris. Meyerbeer's introductions did little for him, and during the two years spent in Paris hopes of a performance on a large scale were continually held out to him and as continually fell through. He went on with his work and finished *Rienzi,* scoring it boldly for a large orchestra in the manner popular with Paris audiences. He tried all sorts of means of getting work to support himself; some songs written to French words include the charming *Dors, mon enfant.* He did a quantity of journalistic work both for French and German papers; for the former he wrote on the nature of German music, for the latter various reports on the music which he heard in Paris. He undertook to make piano arrangements from operatic scores, especially from the popular operas of Halévy, and was even reduced to arranging suites of pieces for the cornet from operas.

Painful as such work was for a man of genius, his genius enabled him to gather a good deal of useful experience from it. There was much which he could learn from the orchestras of Paris even apart from the example of Berlioz. Certainly, he learnt to know how operas were made; technique, which as a boy had seemed to him a trivial matter, became the groundwork on which he was to build. Moreover, in Paris he met both Liszt and Berlioz, and though he began by falling foul of Liszt for being a successful virtuoso, the foundations of a friendship which later was to be of immense value to him were laid at this time. He could not fail to be impressed by Berlioz's extraordinary command of instrumentation.

As his prospects in Paris became more hopeless, Wagner began to press for the performance of his opera *Rienzi* in Dresden, and when at last he heard of its acceptance he determined to leave Paris and return to his own country. The acceptance of *Rienzi* was soon followed by his appointment as conductor to the opera at Dresden, and it was here that Wagner had his first successes in the performances of both *Rienzi* and *Der Fliegende Holländer* (The Flying Dutchman).

Here in 1842 he settled down to work with a consistency and enthusiasm which the opportunities called out. He came across a number of folk-tales in simple German versions—the story of Tannhäuser and the contest of song; legends of the knights of the Grail, including stories of Lohengrin, Titurel, and Parsifal, and these soon worked upon his imagination. He began to mold them into material for drama with music, writing his own poems as usual, choosing from the stories those incidents which appealed to him, altering details in order to make the story consistent with his philosophic and ethical theories. For Wagner could never see a work merely as an artistic production; it always had to represent to him, and through him to his audience, some part of his philosophy of life: the redemption of Tannhäuser by the devotion of Elizabeth, the failure of Elsa to trust completely in the moral grandeur of her knight Lohengrin—in these things Wagner had a moral purpose which to him seemed the very essence of artistic expression. He is almost if not quite a solitary instance of a great artist in music who viewed his art primarily from the preacher's point of view. In every department of life he was convinced of his own mission as a teacher. That fact in itself was enough to make his enemies (and no one ever had more enemies than Wagner) ready to point to discrepancies between his teaching and his life.

Tannhäuser was completed in 1844, and followed *Der Fliegende Holländer* on to the stage at Dresden in 1845. It is interesting to notice that these years at Dresden included at least the beginnings in Wagner's mind of all the big music-dramas of his life. *Lohengrin* was the next one to occupy him fully, and we have seen that it and *Parsifal*, the last to be actually written, began to germinate in his mind soon after his leaving Paris. The idea for a comedy on the subject of a contest of song as a sort of counterpart to the tragedy of *Tannhäuser* also suggested itself to him, and was eventually fulfilled, though again many years later, in *Die Meistersinger von Nürnberg*. And it was in 1848 that he first began to dramatize the myths of the Nibelungen Saga which materialized subsequently into the great tetralogy *Der Ring des Nibelungen*.

But none of these projects save *Lohengrin* got fully shaped at this time, and the production of *Lohengrin* was checked by other preoccupations. He actually finished his score in the spring of 1848, and having done so he allowed himself to be drawn into the political disturbances which ended in the revolution of the next year. It has been pointed out that Wagner's speech to the political club called the "Vaterlands-Verein" in June, 1848, was by no means so violently seditious as it might have been, and some of his admirers have taken pains to discover that he was not really incriminated in the riots of the following year at all, that the order for his arrest was a mistake, and that it really referred to another man of the same name. But the latter part of this defence is quite untenable. Though in his autobiography, written many years later,

Wagner was able to make out a case for his innocence, there is not the least doubt of his active part in the revolution, and it was a part of which at the time he had no cause to be ashamed. He had stood for reform in politics as in art, but the powers against him were too strong; his post, held directly under the king, was of course lost to him, and more than that, he was exiled from Germany. He had first escaped to Weimar, where Liszt was then engaged in preparing for the performance of *Tannhäuser,* and in the following year Liszt still kept his work alive by giving the first performance of *Lohengrin.* Meantime Wagner took up his abode in Switzerland, and from that time onwards until 1861 Zürich was his headquarters. Not that he remained there all the time; he went to London in 1855 to conduct the Philharmonic Concerts, visited Paris more than once, and in 1860 revised *Tannhäuser* for performance there. This production—upon which he built great hopes, and which was one of the bitterest disappointments of his life—met not only with active opposition, but with an amount of intrigue against its acceptance which made it necessary to withdraw the work after three performances.

But before the events of Wagner's second failure in Paris much had happened to contribute to his development. It was natural that in the years immediately after losing his executive work as a conductor, he should return again to literary work, and many of his essays date from this time. It was in *The Art-work of the Future* and *Opera and Drama,* written a year later, that he developed his theory of what opera should be with a fullness which makes these essays as memorable as Gluck's preface to *Alceste.* But Wagner's theories had not the simplicity of Gluck's. Their exact purport is difficult to unravel, but some of their leading characteristics may be summed up as follows:

1. In *The Art-work of the Future* he outlines what for him was the ideal form of art. In the three principal means of expression, "Tanz, Ticht, und Ton" (gesture, poetry, and sound), he finds an art which expresses all the faculties of man; these he insisted must all be fully unfolded, and must be decorated by the plastic arts of painting and architecture.

2. In opera the expression of these various forms had always been lopsided. Gesture and poetry had been put in the background by music.

3. The poet should not restrict himself for the sake of the music, nor the musician for the poetry; each must intensify the other.

4. What was wanted to achieve the new music-drama seemed to be, first, "a fellowship of all the artists"; secondly, a new public who would treat art not as an amusement but as a serious employment.

The soundness of Wagner's ideal has been proved in his own work and its ultimate acceptance. The unsoundness in his theories is chiefly due to his constant habit of generalizing from himself. He saw a great thing to do, therefore that thing must be "the art-work of the future." He had no inclination to write music apart from what he called "its fertilization by poetry," therefore he asserted that music by itself was a dead thing. It is a strange irony that he himself should have proved the livingness of music alone in the tremendous finale of *The Ring* when, the drama over, the orchestra soars to a height of expression which it never reached in company with "Tanz" and "Ticht."

After this outburst of theory Wagner settled down in 1852 to the work which more than all others was to prove both the truth and the untruth existing together in his ideas. The text of *The Ring* was written in a curious alliterative form of verse which he found susceptible to musical treatment, and the music of its first two parts, *Rheingold* and *Die Walküre*, went forward in the following years. The latter was interrupted by his visit to London but was finished in 1856, and he was well on in the composition of *Siegfried* when another disturbance took place.

For years he had been a trying husband to his prosaic and uncomprehending wife. How much right and how much wrong there was on both sides in the growing quarrel which ultimately separated them it is not necessary to decide, but to read the correspondence, since published, between them is to realize that Minna Wagner was a creature very much to be pitied. Possibly the worst of Wagner was that he did pity her, and always from the lofty standpoint of the teacher, which is so hard to bear with in ordinary life.

At any rate the home at Zürich was broken up, the composition of *The Ring* was checked, and instead Wagner turned to the passionate setting of the love-story of *Tristan und Isolde*, the only one of his music-dramas which seems to have seized him with a sudden impulse and to have been written in one outpouring of unflagging enthusiasm. The first sketch of the drama was made in August, 1857, the poem was completed in the following month, and though it was two years before the score was actually finished, anyone who has a notion of the immense labor merely of writing such a score can realize that they were two years of unremitting work. After the completion of *Tristan* came the revision of *Tannhäuser,* which included the rewriting of a great part of the first act, making the overture pass without a break into the first scene, and the texture of the music more closely woven in the manner which had now become habitual to him. Then came the disaster of its production in Paris, and close on that public failure the private one of Minna's final break with him.

His fortunes were at their darkest. It must be remembered that he had heard no one of his great works performed since *Tannhäuser.* He had been debarred from hearing *Lohengrin* when Liszt gave it; *Rheingold, Die Walküre,* half of *Siegfried,* and the whole of *Tristan* existed only on paper and in his imagination. That fact alone shows the tremendous strength of his genius. It is only surpassed by the case of Beethoven, who was cut off by deafness from ever hearing his greatest works.

In 1861 Wagner heard *Lohengrin* for the first time, when it was given in Vienna, and soon after the cloud of his ill-fortune was further lifted by the withdrawal of his sentence of exile from Germany. These events were the forerunners of better times, and with his fuller freedom of action he started buoyantly upon the composition of that most lovable of all his works, the comedy planned long since, which now became *Die Meistersinger von Nürnberg.* This, however, was not, like *Tristan,* written straight away. It was dovetailed in with further work upon *Siegfried* and some sketches for *Parsifal.*

The accession of Ludwig II to the throne of Bavaria was an even more decisive turning-point in Wagner's fortunes. That Wagner, the rebel against every established institution, the unruly "Hof-Kapellmeister" and political agitator of the forties, should after a decade of exile return to become the protégé of a king seems one of the strangest reversals of history. But as far as Wagner himself was concerned the change was as human as it was illogical. A king who entertained liberal views towards art and who showed his liberality by dispatching a secretary to find out Wagner and invite him to his capital to finish his work, who followed up this step by endowing him with a pension and inviting him to supply a scheme for new musical education at Munich, naturally placed the idea of monarchy before the rebel in a most favorable light. Wagner began to see opening before him the possibility of realizing the dream of his life, nothing less than the firm establishment of a home for his art free from the cramping conditions of the ordinary opera-house, a place where he might found that "fellowship of all the artists" and draw together his new and appreciative public.

One of the immediate results of Ludwig's generosity was the first performance of *Tristan* at Munich in 1865, conducted by von Bülow. Afterwards the composition of *Die Meistersinger* went forward rapidly; a group of musicians gathered round Wagner and became inspired by his ideals of performance. Among them was Hans Richter, who was ultimately to become the greatest conductor of Wagner's music. The score of *Die Meistersinger* was finished in the autumn of 1867 at Triebschen, on the Lake of Lucerne, where in these years Wagner made his home. Here Richter spent much time with him and copied the score of *Die Meistersinger*. Minna Wagner had died in 1866, and the complications of Wagner's private life at this period, which ultimately ended in his marriage with Cosima, the daughter of Liszt and formerly the wife of von Bülow, are too unedifying to be entered into here. The birth of their son in 1869 is a landmark in Wagner's artistic life; that too occurred at Triebschen. *Siegfried,* the third part of *The Ring,* was completed three months after his son was born, and the boy was named Siegfried after the hero whose fortunes Wagner had had so much difficulty in tracing through his great work. The event was further celebrated by the composition of the beautiful orchestral piece known as the *Siegfried Idyll,* a piece in which leading themes from the opera of *Siegfried* mingle with old German cradle songs and are delicately scored for a small orchestra. It was a birthday serenade for Cosima. Richter got together a band of local musicians, taught them their parts, himself played the trumpet part, and a private performance, conducted by Wagner, was given at their house.

At last the great project of *The Ring,* a drama occupying three whole evenings in performance, with a "Vorabend" (introductory evening) as a prelude, was nearing completion. *Götterdämmerung,* its final section, went rapidly forward in the year 1870, the more so because some of its music had been planned years ago under the title of *Siegfrieds Tod* (Siegfried's death).

And now at last the musical world at large was sufficiently alive to the importance of what Wagner was doing for its more enterprising members at least to attempt an active share in the project of building a house for the work. Wagner Societies began to be formed as tributes of admiration and also to help in the prosaic duty of raising funds. In 1872 a place was found for the theatre. Bayreuth, a quiet Bavarian town off the main lines of traffic yet large enough to be a place where people could gather, a royal residence, situated among undulating hills crowned with far-reaching woods, was admirably fitted for the purpose.

Here, on Wagner's fifty-ninth birthday, May 22, 1872, the foundation-stone of the "Festspielhaus" (Festival playhouse) was laid. Everything which could concentrate the attention upon the drama and its music was thought of down to the smallest details.

The auditorium, instead of being built in the old fashion of circular galleries, is fan-shaped, sloping upwards from the stage at the narrow end in regular tiers which reach in a slight curve from side to side of the building. This plan gives a maximum of seating room, and also has the advantage of giving to every spectator a clear view of the stage, which is practically identical from every part of the house. The rows of doors on each side of the fan make it possible for the audience to reach their seats without a crush. The orchestra, placed between the stage and the auditorium, is sunk below the level of both and is screened from view by steel shields. This has a very appreciable effect upon the tone of the orchestra, it softens the outlines of phrases and blends the instruments into a sonorous whole. The result is a great beauty of tone with, however, some diminution of strength. The conductor behind the outer shield sees both the stage and his players but the audience cannot see him, and this is perhaps one of the greatest advantages of the plan. Everyone who has seen an opera knows the distraction caused by the waving arms of the conductor.

The stage itself was planned to accommodate the most elaborate scenery, machinery, lighting, and other arrangements according to the most modern ideas—most modern, that is, before electric power was in general use.

At last, in 1876 the "Festspielhaus" was sufficiently finished for use, and the first Festival, that is, the first performance of the whole of *The Ring,* conducted by Richter, took place there from August 13 to 17. The famous violinist, Wilhelmj, led the orchestra. A remarkable company of singers came together and studied their parts in music and drama with enthusiastic devotion. Mme. Materna was the Brünnhilde; Herr Betz was the first Wotan. Musicians from every country in Europe congregated there, and at last Wagner's highest ambition was fulfilled. It is worth while to notice here that this was also the year in which Brahms's first symphony was produced at Karlsruhe.

The problems were not quite solved yet, however. There was a large deficit on the balance sheet of the festival, which made the most strenuous efforts necessary if the Bayreuth theatre was to become an established institution. Like many German musicians, Wagner turned to the country most able to supply funds. A visit to England, including festival concerts of his music at the Albert Hall, was his next venture, but some mistakes in management nearly made the venture increase instead of lessen the debt. The situation was saved by some extra concerts, which provided a fairly substantial sum. These concerts, however, did much to give English people a juster view of Wagner's art than they had had before, and with them the general notion that Wagner's music consisted of a noisy orchestra drowning the singers and setting melody at defiance began to wane; it took many years to die.

At the second festival at Bayreuth in 1882, *Parsifal,* his last work, was produced. Wagner called this a "Bühnen-Weihfestspiel" (a dedicatory festival drama). It was the only one of his operas written for the Bayreuth stage, and he determined that, so far as he could ensure, it should be confined to Bayreuth. There his ideal audience could gather in a mood to take in what he felt to be his last and most serious word, and it was the exclusive possession of *Parsifal* which brought pilgrims from all parts of the world to Bayreuth until the year 1914, when it became no longer legally possible to prevent its performance elsewhere. Wagner died at Venice on February 13, 1883, leaving the Festspielhaus to the care of his widow. Under her direction the festival was repeated not every year but for a month or so every two or three years until 1914, when it was cut short by Germany's declaration of war. It is worth recording that this festival had included *Der Fliegende Holländer* and *Parsifal,* Wagner's Alpha and Omega, the first and last of the great music-dramas, and one cycle of *The Ring,* when the audience, coming out from witnessing the death of Siegfried, the end of the gods, and the enveloping of earth and heaven in flame and flood, heard the news which put an end to the Walhalla which Wagner had raised.

To return, however, to Wagner himself, we have to ask: What did he accomplish? Did he realize that ideal union of the arts and that "fellow-ship of all the artists," and did he establish the direction of "the art-work of the future" by his own mighty achievements in music-drama? We may answer no on all these three points, and yet say emphatically that his life's work was a unique and triumphant achievement.

In the first place, his union of all the arts was limited by the fact that his genius was infinitely greater as a musician than as a poet or a dramatist. A master of tone (Ton), he was only a very skillful workman with words (Ticht), and he was unable ultimately to control the third element in his scheme, gesture (Tanz), which necessarily rested with the interpreters.

Moreover, his overmastering conviction of the moral importance of his ideas made him insist upon explaining himself at every crucial point, and explanation is fatal to drama. He never outgrew this habit. In the first act of *Parsifal*, Gurnemanz seats himself in order to explain at great length, ostensibly to the young knights of the Grail but really to the audience, how the Order was founded, how it fell into decay, and why the wound of Amfortas cannot be healed until the pure knight, a fool in all earthly things but wise in sympathy, shall appear.

Explanations such as these are constant in *The Ring*, where the whole of the complex story has an allegorical meaning; in *Die Meistersinger* they give way to a tendency to harangue the multitudes on principles of artistic criticism; in *Tristan*, save for King Mark's monologue, they are much less insistent, and this fact together with the simplicity of the story brings that work nearest to the ideal union which he had asserted ought to be found. The story itself is poetry, the drama is not cumbered by elaborate scenic effects such as bring *The Ring* at times, and even *Parsifal*, perilously near to the distractions of popular pantomime. If you would realize the fullest extent to which Wagner reached his goal in this direction you should see an intelligent performance of *Tristan* after first carefully reading the poem.

It will be scarcely necessary to give equal preliminary study to the music. Wagner did not write his music to be analyzed, nor for that matter did any of the great musicians, though a careful analysis of it may be very helpful. But a careless analysis, particularly that kind which consists of picking out a dozen or more leading themes, fitting each with a name or a character, and "spotting" them every time they recur, is not helpful. There are people who go to hear Wagner armed with little books of themes, and spend all the time delighting in discovering the appearance of the ring, or Wotan's spear, or Siegfried's sword. They never get much further in understanding what is going on. It is true that there are themes connected with these and a hundred other things in *The Ring*, so that the process of identification is possible, if unprofitable.

But in *Tristan* the process is scarcely possible because there Wagner is not concerned with "things" at all, but with what he called "states of the soul"; and the themes used to express these states are merged into one another and carried forward upon a flood of feeling expressed in music which justifies itself to anyone who knows the poem, and listens with open ears and a sympathetic heart to its unfolding by voice and orchestra.

Much has been said by Wagner himself, and by all who have studied his work in the light of what he wrote about it, of his reforming opera on the basis of Beethoven's symphonic music. If, however, we take *Der Fliegende Holländer* as his starting-point, we see that song, as it had been developed by Schubert, exerted at least as strong an influence upon him as the symphonic style of Beethoven. The ballad which Senta sings in the second act is the musical core of the whole drama, and if you place that ballad beside the dramatic songs of Schubert, such as *An Schwager Kronos* and *Gruppe aus dem Tartarus*, you see at once the likeness of style. In both we get the sweeping declamatory phrases for the voice, in both the illustrative accompaniment,

> *"Wie saust der Wind,*
> *Wie pfeift's im Tau!"*
> *(How the wind howls,*
> *How it whistles through the rigging!)*

You can hear it all in the rushing, chromatic passages of the strings and the strident chords of the wind instruments. In the ballad are two personalities. There is the grim, weather-worn seaman condemned to ride the storm year in, year out; there is the woman who can save him and bring him rest through her love; and the two are contrasted musically.

From these two personalities spring, therefore, the leading themes
(*Leitmotive*) associated with the characters of the Dutchman and Senta,
but these leading themes are not mere phrases with a label attached to
them; they spring spontaneously out of the emotional contrasts of the
drama.

The more real Wagner's characters became to him the more constant
was his use of melodies associated with them. In *Der Fliegende
Holländer* and in *Tannhäuser* and *Lohengrin* there are a good many
passages where the characters as expressed in the music drop into the
background and the progress of the opera is carried on by more conventional means, in the manner of the older forms of opera. Elaborate ensembles, in which all the characters are singing together, are found in
these comparatively early works (see, for example, the end of Act I of
Lohengrin), and in such moments clear characterization is impossible.
A general musical effect is all that is aimed at; the singers on the stage
have more or less to abandon their position as characters to become
musical performers.

Later, therefore, Wagner gave up the employment of such ensembles
to a very large extent. He based his style more exclusively, so far as the
singers were concerned, on dramatic song, and with his firmer grip of
the orchestra he raised the illustrative accompaniment to the position of
a continuous musical commentary upon the characters, their actions,
thoughts, and feelings.

The opening prelude to *Das Rheingold*, a hundred and thirty-six bars
all based on a single chord of E flat major, shows the idea of the illustrative accompaniment carried to its furthest point. It is to introduce a
scene at the bottom of the Rhine where the Rhine-maidens guard their
treasure, the gold from which the ring is afterwards forged. The music is
to give the hearers the groundwork of the whole story. Deep beneath the
water the forces which are to move the actions of gods and heroes are
waiting for their destiny, and the theme first outlined by the horns is
one which may be associated with the flow of the river or with the inevitable force of the world. Nothing is more striking in the development
of the music of *The Ring* than the way in which its ideas are linked with
one another, are actually transformed and grow in musical importance as
the drama develops.

Take, for example, the phrase at the end of this first scene of *Das*

Rheingold, when Alberich the dwarf has seized the gold from the Rhine-maidens and carried it off to forge from it the ring which will give him power over the world. The text-books will tell you that this is the motive of the ring. In a sense it is, but it is much more. What it suggests to the mind is not a circle of gold but a sense of hopeless longing; it does not picture an object, it conveys a human feeling. The longing may be the covetous desire of Alberich for power or the sighing of the Rhine-maidens for their lost treasure. Its purport remains undefined, but presently the theme itself is transformed with changes in its intervals, a fuller harmony, a richer orchestration, and a more decisive rhythm; and we hear for the first time a theme to which again the text-books give a concrete name, the theme of Walhalla, the home of Wotan and the gods. We see that the two are really one, and from the drama it soon appears that Walhalla itself is the realization of the longing of the gods.

In this gradual extension of an idea we get what may be called by an analogy with symphonic form the principal subject of Wagner's drama, and here comes in the justice of his claim to have remodeled the opera on the basis of Beethoven. For while the four parts of *The Ring,* with all their immense range of character, are on a scale which would be impossible to pure instrumental music, one yet realizes that a wide process of symphonic development is carried through them. Play side by side the first statement of the Walhalla theme by the orchestra as it appears in the twenty bars preceding the second scene of *Rheingold* and the last twenty-eight bars of *Götterdämmerung,* and the process of symphonic development must be clear once and for all.

It was this colossal power of musical development which made it impossible for Wagner to fulfill his theory of the union of the arts. He could not restrain his music from outrunning its companions, poetry and gesture. Musicians may feel that he did something far bigger and far better than the fulfillment of his theory, and they do feel that taking *The Ring* as a whole, when every redundant passage and every tedious repetition has been allowed for, there is such overwhelming force in the musical treatment of the legend that what would be glaring faults according to Wagner's own theory in any smaller work become mere spots in the sun.

The continual progress of musical development from *Rheingold* to *Götterdämmerung* is the more amazing when one recollects the long interruptions which occurred in the course of the composition of *The Ring*. It is not accurately known at what point in the second act of *Siegfried* Wagner abandoned it in order to compose *Tristan,* and there is no internal evidence to show.

Most people will agree that the second act of *Götterdämmerung* is a comparatively weak one, that the chorus of vassals and the trio of Brünnhilde, Hagen, and Gunther with which it ends is a partial return to the old ensemble style which Wagner had put behind him. But that is probably the result of his desire to use up the material of his early scheme for *Siegfrieds Tod,* a lapse which is obliterated by the third act, where the music of *Die Walküre, Siegfried,* and the fundamental ideas first shadowed in *Das Rheingold* are summed up and welded into an overwhelming finale.

Neither the subject of *Tristan* nor that of *Die Meistersinger* required anything like the wealth of musical material necessary to *The Ring*. We have spoken of *Tristan* as coming nearest to the theory of union of the arts, and of *Die Meistersinger* as the most lovable of Wagner's works. The natures of the subjects explain both. The delightful character of Hans Sachs, the shoemaker poet at Nürnberg, his genial views of life, his sympathy and unselfishness, make him unique amongst Wagner's heroes. Almost everywhere else Wagner's heroes are tainted with his own egotism; what they will is right, and they conquer by their self-assertion. Hans Sachs conquers by his humility, he does not champion his own work but another's, and the whole of the music of *Die Meistersinger* is influenced by the character of Sachs. Except for the places where Wagner cannot resist homilies on art and criticism, it is freed from the fetters of his own personality. He is here far more willing to let the listeners take his work in their way rather than in his. One may find in it merely a delightful picture of the old German life of the sixteenth century. The antiquary will find it full of truthful allusions to mediaeval customs from those of the city guilds to those of musical tablature. The musician can revel in the skill with which three or four melodies develop contrapuntally in the overture; the lover of romance delights equally in the songs of Walther and Eva, the picture of the old street in the moonlight with the watchman droning his call as he goes, and the sunlit festival of St. John's day. The lover of comedy finds satisfaction in the street brawl and Beckmesser's rough handling by the apprentices. And again, notice that the strength of all these impressions is a musical one. All Wagner's means are perfectly at his command; he never wrote a broader or more firmly knit melody than the *Preislied,* or designed a more vivid and wholly appropriate ensemble than the chorus of the street brawl, or one of greater musical beauty than the quintet.

If Wagner did not realize his ideal union of the arts it was simply because his powers were so much greater as a musician than as poet or dramatist that his musical splendor swamps all other considerations.

What, then, of that "fellowship of all the artists" in which he saw the hopes of the future? As far as it consisted in securing the devoted collaboration of conductors, singers, and instrumental musicians for the production of his works at Bayreuth, he certainly succeeded to a remarkable extent. He gave a wholly new standard of sympathetic interpretation to the conductors, such as Mottl and Richter, whom he trained. He carried to its highest point the remodeling of the orchestra begun by Berlioz, and he made singers realize their responsibilities as artists in a way never achieved by his predecessors. The idea of coöperation was spread by Wagner in the opera as it was spread by Joachim in the interpretation of quartet music, and his conductors carried his lessons into the orchestra of the concert-room and interpreted the symphony in the light of his teaching.

Yet Bayreuth failed artistically, primarily because Wagner never dissociated the art-work of the future from the art-work of Richard Wagner. He created it as a shrine for his own works, and his heirs guarded the shrine so jealously after his death that the idea of making it a home for new art later than his own would have seemed a profanation. It was with difficulty that any improvements even in the presentation of Wagner's own works were admitted, and so the fellowship of the artists died and "the Bayreuth tradition" took its place. His Festspielhaus became the stronghold of that very conservatism against which in his vigorous days Wagner had fought with all his strength.

Nor can it honestly be said that that failure was the fault of Wagner's heirs and in no way due to himself. Anyone who can listen dispassionately to *Parsifal,* without being blinded by the religious fervor of its subject, the beauty of some of its musical ideas, and the rich glow of its orchestration, must feel that, apart from certain high moments, it is the work of one whose force has spent itself, and who has to fall back on ways of expression which have become habitual. If *Parsifal* had not been enshrined at Bayreuth and surrounded with the glamour of an almost sacred ritual, it is very doubtful whether thirty years after it was written people would have given it any place beside Wagner's masterpieces.

Long delayed as Wagner's influence was (it made little impression before the seventies) when it did come it was tremendous and, for the time being, staggering. Only the very strongest spirits could maintain their individuality against it. In every country of Europe the second-rate composers became "Wagnerized." He taught so much, he showed so many possibilities of orchestral sound never before realized, he had so dominating a way of expressing himself, that weaker spirits could not resist the temptation to copy him, and they are still doing it. But all the composers whose work has lasted resisted the temptation. They might learn many lessons from him, but they could not subject their individuality to his. The crowd of Wagnerian operas which were poured out in Germany amounted to very little of real importance. Of the young composers who gathered round Wagner in his later years, and owned him as a leader, only one, Engelbert Humperdinck (born 1854), need here be mentioned. His delicious children's opera *Hänsel und Gretel* is indeed molded on Wagner's style, but the style is so differently applied to the simple folk-story of the children lost in the wood, the whole is so fresh in its melody, so apt in its orchestral commentary, that it stands alone. Most works of disciples begin by emphasizing their master's mannerisms, which are his weakest points. Humperdinck, both in *Hänsel und Gretel* and in its later companion *Königskinder,* is free from that snare. Young people who are to grow up to the appreciation of Wagner should be brought up on Humperdinck, and older people who are sometimes afflicted by the strenuousness of Wagner himself come back to *Hänsel und Gretel* with a sigh of relief and a sense of restored youth.

Though a certain resistance to Wagner's influence was necessary if music and the opera were to live, music, and especially the opera, could never be the same again after he had spoken. His effect upon his great Italian contemporary Verdi is a striking example of this.

Giuseppe Verdi (1813–93) began his long career as a writer of Italian operas in the traditional manner of recitative, aria, and ensemble numbers, which he inherited from his countrymen of the first part of the century. An extraordinary power of depicting a graphic situation in a vocal melody was from first to last characteristic of him, and in the greater number of his operas that power was all-sufficing for his needs. Many of his works, such as *Il Trovatore, La Traviata,* and *Rigoletto* (none of these are among his earliest ones), have an irresistible grip upon the imagination by their sheer force of melody, and *Aïda,* written in 1871, is a unique example of a romantic story told entirely in a series of broad and intensely expressive tunes.

Certainly, there could be no doubt about Verdi's individuality, and his reputation at the time he wrote *Aïda* was far wider than Wagner's own. Sixteen years followed before he wrote another opera. Wagner's great works had become world-wide possessions, and all the musical world had gone after him, spurning Italian opera, and Verdi amongst it, as a plaything with which *prime donne* amused their admirers, when Verdi produced his *Otello* and followed it with *Falstaff.* A tragedy and a comedy, both founded upon Shakespeare, with finely written libretti by Boïto, a literary man and himself a composer of no mean order, suggested a new fellowship of the artists, and one coming not from Germany but from Italy. People were amazed to find many lessons from Wagner embodied in these works; the plots were developed in continuous music through the whole scene, the musical style was made flexible to the dramatic situation in the way that Wagner advocated. But it was the same Verdi, the same man of eloquent melodies, without desire to preach or to teach, merely anxious to express what was in him, and adapting himself to the new forms because he saw that only so could he express himself to the new generation. Verdi's art had always been serious and always been great, but only in these last works did he, through Wagner's example, find a way of couching it which was altogether worthy of its greatness.

It was only as a critic who aspired to be a prophet that Wagner was at fault. Like the Flying Dutchman, he could not even foresee where his own ship would come to port; still less could he tell the courses on which others were steering. Some of these men he knew and reckoned with too lightly. Of others he had not the faintest conception. Wagner, the artist, was not to blame for this. An artist can do no better than follow out his own ideal unfalteringly, even ruthlessly if need be, and this Wagner did as few have done.

XIII
BRAHMS

JOHANNES BRAHMS

*Born at Hamburg, May 7, 1833. Life outwardly uneventful. Toured
as pianist with Remenyi, 1853; later with Joachim. At 20 was encouraged by Schumann, became a life-long friend of the Schumann family.
Held various musical positions, made numerous tours, until 1869, when
he settled in Vienna. There conducted* Gesellschaft der Musikfreunde,
1871–4. Died at Vienna, April 3, 1897.

PRINCIPAL WORKS

VOCAL: *A German Requiem; Rinaldo* (cantata); *Parzengesang; Schicksalslied; Triumphlied; Rhapsody* (for contralto, chorus, and orchestra);
numerous other choral works and arrangements, notably 3-part choruses
for women's voices; numerous songs, including the *Magelone* and
Zigeunerlieder cycles.

INSTRUMENTAL: 4 symphonies; 2 piano concertos; 2 serenades for orchestra; 1 violin concerto; 1 double concerto for violin and cello; Variations on a theme by Haydn; *Academic Festival Overture; Tragic Overture.* Chamber music includes 3 string quartets; 2 string sextets; 2 string
quintets; 1 piano quintet; 3 piano trios; trio for piano, violin and horn;
quintet for clarinet and strings; trio for piano, violin, and clarinet; 3
sonatas for piano and violin; 2 sonatas for piano and cello; 2 sonatas for
piano and clarinet. Piano music includes 3 sonatas (chiefly Opus 5, in F
minor); several sets of variations (chiefly Variations and Fugue on a
theme by Handel); ballades, rhapsodies, intermezzos, romances, fantasias, etc.; 16 waltzes, Opus 39; Hungarian dances. Also compositions
and arrangements for 4 hands. Choral preludes for organ.

BRAHMS

By J. A. Fuller-Maitland

BIOGRAPHICAL

THE life of Johannes Brahms was outwardly uneventful, and it is only necessary to give a rapid summary of the main facts, pointing out the few incidents which bear directly upon his music. He was the second child and elder son of Johann Jakob Brahms and his wife, Johanna Henrika Christiana Nissen, who were married in 1830 and lived in humble circumstances in part of a large house, No. 60, Speckstrasse, Hamburg. The father, who had studied various stringed instruments and the flute, was a horn-player in the Burger-Militair, or town-guard of Hamburg, and afterwards a double-bass player in a regular string band; the mother, described as a small, plain, limping woman of delicate health and sensitive disposition, seems to have had few accomplishments except that of being a good needlewoman. Johannes Brahms was born on May 7, 1833, and baptized on the 26th at St. Michael's Church. A pianist named Cossel, a pupil of Eduard Marxsen of Altona, taught the boy the piano from the time he was seven years old, and it was due to this man's perseverance that, after several refusals, Marxsen himself consented to take him as a pupil, at first for piano only. He played a study of Herz at a charity concert when he was ten years old. When he was fourteen, one Adolph Giesemann, a frequent attendant at the performances of the band of which Jakob Brahms was a member, consented to take the boy into the country for a change, to Winsen-an-der-Luhe; here he went on with his music, teaching Herr Giesemann's little daughter, and traveling every week to Altona for his lesson with Marxsen. He

From the author's *Brahms*, by permission of Methuen and Co.

conducted a small choir of male voices at Winsen, and composed a few pieces for its use. In November, 1847, he appeared at public concerts in Hamburg. Nearly a year afterwards, on September 21, 1848, he gave a concert of his own, at which he played a fugue of Bach, besides other things more suited to the taste of that day. On April 14, 1849, he gave another concert, playing the *Waldstein* sonata of Beethoven, some popular pieces, and a fantasia by himself "on a favorite waltz." After this formal opening of his career as an executant, he had to endure the drudgery of playing night after night in dancing saloons. During the next five years his life must have been a hard one, and perhaps some of the necessary bread of tears was eaten at this time. Various small engagements, one of which was that of accompanist behind the scenes of the Stadt Theater, and teaching (at the high fee of about a shilling a lesson) occupied him, and in his spare time he read voraciously, poetry turning itself, half consciously, into music in his brain. Many songs were composed at this period of his life, when he was compelled, like Wagner, to do hack-work for publishers in the way of arrangements and transcriptions, operatic and otherwise; these were published under the pseudonym of "G. W. Marks," and it would seem as though another *nom de plume*, "Karl Würth," was kept for work of a more ambitious kind, such as duet for piano and violoncello, and a trio for piano and strings, which were played at a private concert on July 5, 1851, and duly announced on the program as the work of "Karl Würth"; a copy of the program is still in existence on which Brahms has substituted in pencil his true name for the other.

Not till 1853 did a brighter day dawn for the composer. A certain violinist named Reményi, whose real name was Hoffmann, and who was of a mixed German, Hungarian, and Jewish origin, had appeared in Hamburg, for the second time, in the winter of 1852–3. It was arranged that Brahms should act as his accompanist at three concerts, at Winsen, Luneburg, and Celle, and finally should proceed thence to Hanover, where Joachim was court concertmeister (i. e., leader of the band), and assistant kapellmeister (conductor), having given up his position as leader of the opera orchestra. The number of concerts was extended to about seven in all, at which the same program was gone through by the two performers. Beethoven's sonata in C minor from Opus 30 was the most important composition performed. At Celle, where the only decent

piano was a semitone too low for the violinist's convenience, Brahms
undertook to play the sonata in C sharp minor, at a moment's notice.
Reményi was not a great artist, and would be of small importance in the
career of Brahms if he had not happened to be slightly acquainted with
Joachim.

The meeting between Joachim and Brahms, which was the beginning
of a lifelong and most fruitful intimacy, took place at Joachim's rooms
in Hanover, and it was obvious to the older man that Brahms was no
ordinary musician. In the oration pronounced by Joachim at the dedica-
tion of the Brahms monument at Meiningen, October 7, 1899, this first
meeting is thus referred to: "It was a revelation to me when the song
O versenk struck my ears. And his piano-playing besides was so tender,
so full of fancy, so free, so fiery, that it held me enthralled." After hearing such compositions as the young composer had brought with him,
which included various movements of sonatas, the scherzo Opus 4, a
sonata for piano and violin, a trio, and a string quartet, beside several
songs, Joachim saw plainly that the association with a performer of
Reményi's stamp was not likely to be a lasting one, and he invited
Brahms to visit him at Göttingen (where he—Joachim—was about to
attend lectures) in the event of his tiring of his present post. There was
some discussion between the two as to the order in which it would be
advisable to publish Brahms's early compositions. At the time Joachim
could do no more than give Brahms a letter of introduction to Liszt, as
the pair of players intended to go to Weimar. The account of the inter-
view with Liszt, given by William Mason, who was present, may be
read in Miss May's Life. That Liszt played at sight the scherzo and
approved of its style, is the one fact that is really important; it is curious
to read that after Raff had detected its (very obvious) likeness to
Chopin's pieces in the same form, Brahms assured a friend that he had
no knowledge whatever of the Polish master's scherzos. The reception of
the two players by Liszt was of the most cordial, and they found, what
so many others found before and afterwards, an atmosphere of flattering
appreciation, practical kindness, and surroundings which could not but
appeal to any ardent and artistic soul. It was Liszt's way to express to
the full all the admiration he felt, but on this occasion a letter of his to
Bülow proves that he really thought highly of the C major sonata. For
six weeks the fellow travellers stayed at Weimar, but gradually it be-

came clear to Brahms at least that the spell of Armida's garden must be resisted, and every night when he went to bed he resolved to cut the visit short, but every morning a new enchantment seemed to be put upon him, and he stayed. The charm was broken almost as effectually as that of Venus in *Tannhäuser,* but in a less poetical manner. William Mason tells us in his *Memories of a Musical Life* that Liszt was on one occasion playing his beloved sonata in B minor, and, glancing round at a very expressive moment of the piece, saw that Brahms was slumbering peacefully; the composer stopped abruptly and left the room.

The figure of Reményi goes out of the story; his political and musical proclivities continued to appeal to Liszt, and in the year after he was made violinist to Queen Victoria. Although armed with Joachim's letter, Brahms hesitated for some little time before presenting himself to Schumann at Düsseldorf. Steeped in the classical traditions he had learnt from Marxsen, he had been almost deaf to the appeal of Schumann's music, for which a great friend, Fräulein Louise Japha, had unbounded admiration. Brahms had sent Schumann a number of his early compositions in 1850, when Schumann was at Hamburg, but the older master was then too busy to open the parcel. When he did make up his mind to go over from Mehlem, where he had been staying almost ever since his departure from Weimar, he was welcomed at once by the Schumanns, whose expectations had been aroused by Joachim. When Brahms sat down to the piano to play one of his compositions to Schumann, the latter interrupted him with the words, "Clara must hear this," and he told his wife, when she came into the room, "Here, dear Clara, you will hear such music as you never heard before; now, begin again, young man!" They kept Brahms to dinner, and received him into their intimacy. To Joachim Schumann wrote the memorable words, "This is he that should come"—words which, with the equally famous article, *Neue Bahnen,* claimed for Brahms a place in the royal succession of the great German composers. Later in the same year came a visit to Leipzig, and an appearance at the Gewandhaus, at one of David's quartet-concerts, in which Brahms played his own C major sonata and the E flat minor scherzo. At this time, too, occurred the last attempt of the "advanced" school to induce Brahms to return to the ranks of Liszt's followers; Liszt was in Leipzig, in order to be present when Berlioz conducted important compositions at the Gewandhaus. Brahms found Liszt quite inclined to let bygones be bygones, and Berlioz was heard to praise the young artist (whether as performer or composer we are not told).

By this time there was, of course, little hope that the fixed convictions of Brahms would be unsettled, and personal as well as artistic reasons must have weighed with him against any real reconciliation with the Liszt school. He took up his residence at Hanover in order to work hard in congenial surroundings, and for the sake of the constant intercourse with Joachim. There, too, he saw Schumann again, for the last time before the tragic attempt at suicide. Schumann had come to Hanover for a performance of his *Paradise and the Peri,* and enjoyed the society of Joachim, Brahms, and Julius Otto Grimm. From the sad event of February 27, when Schumann threw himself into the Rhine, Joachim and Brahms stood in a position of a filial or fraternal kind to Madame Schumann, who, throughout all her anxieties, bravely followed her artistic career in spite of the additional distress caused by her not being allowed to see her afflicted husband. The variations of Brahms on a theme by Schumann, in F sharp minor, Opus 9, are lasting evidence of the close intimacy which was only terminated by death. The variations, and the next compositions, the four *Balladen,* Opus 10, gave the greatest pleasure to Schumann.

In 1856, after Schumann's death, Brahms arranged to relieve Madame Schumann of some of the lessons she was engaged to give, and among the pupils was a Fräulein Laura von Meysenburg, whose father and brother were officials at the court of Lippe-Detmold, and whose mother was an accomplished amateur pianist. Princess Friederike of Lippe-Detmold was another of Madame Schumann's pupils, and in consequence of the connection thus formed, Brahms was offered a kind of informal appointment at the court of Detmold, where he was to conduct a choral society recently reorganized, to perform at the court concerts, and to continue the Princess's musical education. His duties only lasted through the winter season, from September to December, and he gained much useful experience as a conductor during the two years of his engagement at the court, which he retained until January, 1860. About this time he made the acquaintance of a young Göttingen lady, Fräulein Agathe von Siebold, with whom he seems to have fallen in love; there are various signs that it was a serious passion on his part, but worldly considerations made a marriage out of the question.

In 1859 the first performance of the D minor concerto for pianoforte, with the composer in the solo part, took place at Hanover, Leipzig, and Hamburg, being received at the first two very coldly. At the Gewandhaus of Leipzig its reception was distinctly unfavorable; but Brahms took his repulse philosophically, and in a letter to Joachim (who had conducted it at Hanover) he says: "I believe it is the best thing that could happen to me; for it compels one to order one's thoughts and to pluck up courage for the future." It is perhaps significant that the loudest notes of disapproval were from the extreme classicists of Leipzig; the partisans of the new school of Weimar found more in it to praise, and it is greatly to their credit that they had the courage to say so. It has been suggested that this praise was bestowed as part of a deliberate plan to get hold of Brahms's allegiance to the new school and its tenets; but whether it was so or not, the event showed that his devotion to the classical models had undergone no change. Brahms's position in regard to the new school was settled once for all by an awkward accident. In 1860, it had been given out in the *Neue Zeitschrift für Musik*, the organ of the new school, that all the most prominent musicians of the day were in favor of the "music of the future," as it was called. Brahms felt it to be his duty to protest against this falsehood, and consented to sign a document expressing disapproval of the high-handed and wholly gratuitous assumption. We know now that the "Declaration" was not a protest by hide-bound pedants against all the modern tendencies, but was really directed against special heresies which were traced in some of Liszt's symphonic poems. Brahms, as appears from his correspondence with Joachim, was particularly anxious not to include the music of Wagner in his condemnation of the modern tendencies, and it must not be forgotten that the friends did not take the initiative in the matter, but were bound to traverse the implied statement that all the eminent musicians of Germany were on the one side. While we know that the classical forms seemed to him sacred, yet on occasion he found it expedient to modify them in various ways, not from any poverty of his own ideas, but as it were to encourage the natural development of a living organism. The "new school," for whose thoughts the older forms were too scanty or too strictly defined, did, after all, very little indeed towards any really fruitful development of musical form, and it is hard to get rid of the suspicion that the older forms were thrown aside by their leader on account of the easily recognized difficulties they present to one whose musical ideas are virtually without distinction. The extraordinary warmth of feeling exhibited by the new school after the "Declaration" and after the memorable letter written by Joachim to Liszt has been, no doubt rightly, ascribed to the great influence wielded by Joachim, and in a lesser degree by Brahms. Had the "new school" realized how many and how influential were the names that would have appeared below the "Declaration" if its appearance had not been forestalled, it is at least possible that their resentment would not have been so exclusively against Brahms and Joachim; and it is even possible that Wagner's famous *Judenthum in der Musik,* the pamphlet which rendered any idea of reconciliation forever impossible, might never have been written. The names of those who had promised to support the "Declaration" are referred to in the letters between Joachim and Brahms, but it does not appear that they were made in any way public before the issue of the correspondence in 1908.

At Hamburg Brahms was busily and congenially occupied as conductor of a choir of ladies, on whose behalf he wrote the various sacred and secular works for female voices which are so numerous among his early opus numbers. Many more were written, but were burnt by the composer, all but a single part (second soprano), in which Kalbeck discovered the germs of several mature works.

The migration from Hamburg, and the ultimate adoption of Vienna as a home, is generally and conveniently held to mark the principal division in the outward career of Brahms. An appointment to the conductorship of the Vienna Singakademie was perhaps the immediate cause of the change of abode, and although the office was only retained for a year or two, yet, by the time Brahms gave it up, Vienna had become so attractive to him that he made it his headquarters for the rest of his life. The conception and completion of his great *Deutsches Requiem* occupied him chiefly for the next five years or so. Not that his labors in other fields were unimportant, for the compositions of the early Viennese period include his two most exacting pianoforte solos, the Handel and Paganini variations, the two quartets for piano and strings, Opus 25 and Opus 26, the quintet in F minor, Opus 34, the *Magelone* romances, and many other vocal works. It is, happily, unnecessary for the ordinary lover of Brahms's *Requiem* to settle definitely whether it was intended to enshrine the memory of the composer's mother (a theory supported by the disposition of the fifth section, the famous soprano solo and chorus, and by the direct testimony of Joachim and other friends), or whether it was, as strenuously argued by Herr Kalbeck, suggested by the tragedy of Schumann's end. Possibly both are in a measure true; the composer may have been first led to meditate on death and its problems by the death of Schumann—the first deep personal sorrow he can have known—but we know that in chronological sequence its composition followed his own private loss. Frau Brahms died in 1865, and the *Requiem* was completed in 1868 by the addition of the number already referred to. Before the performance of the first three numbers (1867), the widower had married again, and there are few things more beautiful in Brahms's life than his conduct to his stepmother, over whose interests, and those of her son by a former marriage, Fritz Schnack, he watched with rare loyalty. His father died in 1872; Frau Caroline Brahms survived her illustrious stepson by five years. About the period of the *Requiem,* or rather later, came several other works in which a chorus takes part, such as *Rinaldo,* for male voices, and three of the noblest choral compositions in existence: the *Rhapsodie,* for contralto solo, male choir, and orchestra; the *Schicksalslied* and *Triumphlied,* the last, in eight parts, with solo for bass, in commemoration of the German victories in the war of 1870–1. For three seasons, 1872–5, Brahms was conductor of the concerts of the Gesellschaft der Musikfreunde, and the programs of the period given in Miss May's *Life* are enough to fill us with envy. During this time his music was continually advancing in popularity, and the great public of Vienna was conquered by the remarkable performance of the *Requiem* there on February 28, 1875. This new attitude of the public gave the cue to the rest of the world, and during a tour in Holland in 1876 even the D minor concerto roused enthusiasm when the composer played it at Utrecht. The Haydn variations for orchestra were given in various musical centers, always with great success, but it was the first symphony, in C minor, that stamped Brahms as the legitimate representative of the great dynasty of German composers.

It had been long expected; for the musical world must have realized that the man who could show himself so great a master of thematic development as Brahms had done in many chamber compositions (the last of which were the three string quartets, Opus 51 and Opus 67, and the quartet for piano and strings, Opus 60), and who could handle the orchestra so skillfully as he had handled it in the Haydn variations, could give the world a new symphonic masterpiece. As such the work in C minor could hardly be universally accepted at once; if it had not stirred up opposition and discussion, its real importance might well have been questioned, but by this time Brahms himself most probably cared but little for the opinions of friendly or adverse critics, although his warm heart was always appreciative of the enthusiasm of his intimate friends; and the verdict of such people as Joachim and Frau von Herzogenberg was always eagerly awaited by him. In many cases their criticisms were followed, and alterations made in deference to them. The first symphony is one of the great landmarks in the history of Brahms's popularity in England; for when it was quite new the University of Cambridge offered to the composer and to Joachim the honorary degree of Mus.D., which cannot be granted *in absentia*. Joachim would in any case be in England, and Brahms hesitated for some time whether to accept the invitation, but finally refused it in consequence of the publication of a premature announcement concerning his appearance at the Crystal Palace. He acknowledged the compliment of the University by allowing the first English performance of the new symphony to take place at a concert given by the Cambridge University Musical Society on March 8, 1877, and it was conducted by Joachim, who contributed his own *Elegiac Overture*, conducting it himself, and playing the solo part of Beethoven's concerto. The second symphony was not long in following upon the first, for it was given at the Vienna Philharmonic on December 11, 1877, and at Leipzig in January, 1878; and the orchestral vein so successfully struck was further worked in the violin concerto which Joachim introduced to the Gewandhaus public and to the world on January 1, 1879.

Two important works for pianoforte solo belong to the same period, Opus 76 and Opus 79, as well as the first of the three sonatas for pianoforte and violin, Opus 78. The tender, winsome grace of the last must have won Brahms almost more friends than any of his previous compositions, and the impression was deepened by the production of the two overtures, the *Academic Festival Overture* (Opus 80) and the *Tragic Overture* (Opus 81).

In 1880, in the course of his duties as a member of a commission for the annual grant of Government stipends to young artists (on which he had served since 1875), he came across the early efforts of Anton Dvorák, and at once became a warm admirer of his music, in spite of so many points at which the artistic ideals of the two men diverged. In 1878 Brahms had undertaken the first of several Italian journeys in company with his great friend, Dr. Theodor Billroth. In 1881 began the pleasant associations with the court of Saxe-Meiningen, brought about by the enthusiasm of von Bülow, the conductor of the famous orchestra. The composer played his new pianoforte concerto with that body in 1882, and an odd result of the friendship with the Duke was the undertaking set on foot by Bülow of taking the Meiningen orchestra to Leipzig, to show how certain works of Brahms should be performed. The C minor symphony was in the program, as well as the first pianoforte concerto, which Bülow played, the band accompanying without a conductor. The third symphony (Vienna Philharmonic, under Richter, December 2, 1883) and the fourth (Meiningen, October 25, 1885) put the crown on the master's orchestral achievements.

For about ten years Brahms had now enjoyed the reward of his life-long work and happy labors. As in the early part of his career his works had been held to be obscure, unintelligible, and ugly, so now a new style of attack on his music was led by Hugo Wolf, when hard up and disappointed, and therefore the more easily to be forgiven, although his animadversions were bitterly resented at the time. With the exception of such irritating experiences—and what great man was ever free from them for long?—the later years of the composer's life were very happy ones. Surrounded by intelligent and devoted friends who understood all his little idiosyncrasies and humored him in every way, the routine of his life, with the regular journeys to Ischl or some such resort in the summer, and to Italy in the spring (until 1893), must have been tranquil and fruitful in musical suggestion.

For the record of the latest period of his career is really contained in a few casual reminiscences by his intimate friends, and above all in the beautiful works which glorified the last decade of his life. It is the decade of the pianoforte pieces, Opus 116–19, of the German folk-songs, of the works suggested by the masterly clarinet playing of Professor Mühlfeld, and of those wonderful *Ernste Gesänge,* which close the master's list of compositions with such noble meditations on death and what lies beyond the grave. These were partly inspired by the death of Frau Schumann on May 20, 1896, which was a terrible shock to Brahms; mentally, he was grievously afflicted by it, and physically he never completely recovered from a chill caught at her funeral. Between this time and his own death the only work he accomplished was the arrangement of a set of eleven chorale-preludes for the organ, written at various dates, though not published till after his death.

In September, 1896, he went to Carlsbad for a cure; he suffered very greatly during the winter, but managed to attend several concerts, such as those given by the Joachim Quartet in Vienna in January (when his G major quintet was played with great success), the Philharmonic Concert of March 7, when his fourth symphony and Dvorák's violoncello concerto (a piece for which he had unbounded admiration) were played, and he went twice to the opera. He passed away—the cause of death being degeneration of the liver—in the presence of his kind housekeeper, Frau Celestine Truxa, on April 3, 1897, at the lodging, 4, Carlsgasse, where he had lived quietly for a quarter of a century. He was buried in the Central Friedhof on April 6, and many were the memorial concerts given in his honor all the world over.

By a strange mischance, a will about which he consulted his old friends Dr. and Frau Fellinger was not executed, and the only valid testament was in the form of a letter to Simrock, the publisher. There were complications of various kinds, sundry cousins making claims to the master's property. Ultimately a compromise was arrived at, with the result that "the blood relations have been recognized as heirs to all but the library, which is now in the possession of the Gesellschaft der Musikfreunde; that Frau Truxa's legacy has been paid, and that certain sums accepted by the societies [the Liszt Pensionverein of Hamburg, the Czerny Verein, and the Gesellschaft der Musikfreunde], by which they will ultimately benefit, have been invested, and the income arising from them secured for the payment of the life-annuity to Herr Schnack" (the son of Frau Caroline Brahms, who died in 1902).

It would be difficult to name any famous man who had so great an objection as Brahms had to the habit of wearing his heart upon his sleeve. He carried his characteristic reticence so far that his brusquerie of manner is the feature most familiar to the readers of the books about him. There are already many hundreds of stories, some of them no doubt true, which show a certain mischievous disposition, especially towards people whom he suspected of a wish to "lionize" him; but his quiet acts of kindness more than counterbalance these superficial eccentricities, which after all seem more like the small transgressions of a vigorous child. There were numberless points in which he remained a child throughout his life, as though he trailed his clouds of glory longer than most men. That he should have been devoted to his tin soldiers as a child is of course nothing at all remarkable, but it is rather significant that he should have carefully kept them in his possession until he was twenty-eight years old, and have shown them to his friend Dietrich, saying that he could not bear to part with them. He shared with many of the great men of the world a faculty for going to sleep at a moment's notice, and rising refreshed after only a few minutes' slumber. It is undoubtedly true that he was careless in the matter of dress, and that he hated anything like ceremonial customs or stiff behavior; on the platform his manner of bowing (in 1859) was, according to Joachim, like the action of a swimmer who comes to the surface and shakes the water from his hair. Official recognition of his eminence meant less than nothing to him; his indifference was by no means a pose, but was just the result of the hatred he felt towards certain sycophantic recipients of court favor. Much was formerly heard of his bluff ways, which no doubt did often cause pain to many sensitive souls; but the publication of his correspondence with such intimates as the Herzogenbergs, J. O. Grimm, Joachim, and, above all, Madame Schumann, shows how delicate was his tact in the real things of life, how ready he was to show his practical sympathy with other people, though his friends may have had to humor his little idiosyncrasies in the matter of his personal habits and comforts, and how truly generous was his nature. Once, when leaving his parents' home after a visit to them (when his own means had become comparatively ample for his needs), he put a number of bank-notes between the pages of his copy of Handel's *Saul,* and said to his father when taking leave, "Dear father, if things go badly with you, the best consolation is always in music. Read carefully in my old *Saul* and you'll find what you want." His loving care for Frau Schumann, for his stepmother and her son, and for others who looked to him for help of one kind or another, is abundantly clear, and a larger-minded or more open-handed man surely never lived. He appreciated the pleasures of life and was not afraid to let his enjoyment be seen; yet he was no voluptuary, careless of the ultimate destiny of the race or of the individual. Even if we had nothing to go by but the words of his choral works, we should know that the problems of human destiny, of life, death, and immortality, engrossed him throughout his life. The *Schicksalslied, Rhapsodie, Requiem,* the two motets, Opus 74, and the part-songs, Opus 104, tell us, even without the evidence of the *Serious Songs,* which were the last publication of his life, that he was an earnest thinker, and that he had faced the great questions bravely and had found an answer to them which for him was sufficient. While shrinking from the dogmas of the churches, and very shy of owning the beliefs he held, he yet shows his deep conviction of the immortality of the soul and a sure and certain hope of its future happiness. In letters to Frau von Herzogenberg, he asks her to find "heathenish" words from Scripture for him to set, meaning thereby such texts as appear in the first three of the *Serious Songs.* Though the landmarks of religion might be removed, though doctrines that guided the lives of his ancestors might be assailed and discredited, though the higher criticism might seem to demolish the credibility of the Scripture records, yet a great and merciful system is dimly apprehended, and upon this he relies for comfort and guidance.

CHARACTERISTICS OF THE ART OF BRAHMS

No attempt to submit to a really close analysis the characteristics of a great creative artist can wholly succeed, because, even if it were possible to enumerate and catalogue the principal component parts of his work, the proportion in which they are present must forever elude us. It would be of little service to say of a medical prescription or a culinary recipe that it contained such and such ingredients, without referring to the relative amount of each; this is all we can do in respect of works of art, and yet it must be attempted in any study of an artist's work. In the art of the composer, it will possibly be universally admitted that the most essential thing is the quality of his root-ideas, that part of his work to which the term "inspiration" is applied by the fanciful, "invention" by more practical persons. It may happen, indeed, that a composer whose ideas are of the poorest and most threadbare, may so disguise their poverty by the skill with which he places them before his hearers as to delude the world into accepting him for a time as a composer properly so called. On the other hand, a noble or distinguished musical idea may present itself to an unlearned musician, who may scarcely know how to convey it to others. Many of the most beautiful folk-songs of all nations may, nay, must have been derived from sources such as this, and their unknown authors deserve the name of composers far better than the other type just spoken of. But in spite of the general custom of denying to the unlettered inventor of a melody the title of musical composer so willingly granted to the clever craftsman who disguises, with gaudy orchestral coloring or remarkable contrapuntal skill, the poverty of his melodic ideas, we shall probably be justified in regarding the actual invention of melody as the first and most important of the composer's functions, and as the greatest test of his power. Next to this will come the treatment of his ideas in regard to the order of their presentation, the form and design of the music built upon them, and the process of development to which the ideas themselves are subjected. Just as in the pictorial art some kind of design, some rudimentary plan, must precede the application of color, so the composer's treatment of form must be considered before his skill in "coloring," using that term as including the art of setting the music in the most favorable and appropriate light as regards the tone-quality of the instruments employed for its interpretation. In these days it is dangerous to imply any preference for form over color in music, and it must not be supposed that the order in which the two are treated in the following pages is anything but an order of convenience; it is not suggested that the one is superior to the other.

(1) In the case of a very great man, it is far harder to point out the salient qualities of his work than it is with the less important men; the reason is not far to seek, nor is it very satisfactory when found, the fact being that the compositions of the latter so closely resemble others already in existence as to be capable of awakening grateful associations in the minds of those who hear them for the first time. But the work that is not truly original must soon lose whatever distinction or freshness of appeal it ever possessed. It might safely be maintained that all the great classical masters founded their art upon the bed rock of folk-music, that mysterious thing which seems to spring from no individual creator, but from the hearts of the people at large.

Bach, Haydn, Mozart, Beethoven, to name no others of the great

Germans, undoubtedly had the strongest admiration for the folk-music of their nation, and their most individual themes show the strongest affinity with genuine folk-song. Very frequently they used traditional themes as the basis of their works, or definitely arranged them, without reaching the level of an act of creation. No more striking instance exists of this affinity than Brahms, who arranged folk-songs for a male choir as early as 1847, whose first composition contains a folk-song as its slow movement, whose first successes outside his native land were won by his arrangements of Hungarian dances, whose most appropriate offering to the children of his great predecessor was a set of arrangements of German folk-songs, and whose last published composition was a set of organ-preludes on the chorales that are the rich heritage of the Teutonic race. Apart from these and from his great collection of actual folk-songs, published in 1894, there are abundant passages in his works of all kinds which prove how dear was traditional music to his heart. In the very earliest of his compositions, the simplicity of melodic structure that is characteristic of folk-music may not be often apparent; but as early as the B flat sextet, Opus 18, the themes strike every intelligent hearer as having the strongest affinity with the music that grows as it were spontaneously in a nation. They suggest, the first time they are heard, the idea that such beautiful and obvious sequences of notes must have been existing in the world long before they were written down; there is about them, in fact, a kind of divine familiarity such as most people can remember feeling in regard to passages of Shakespeare, when they had the impression, "But that is what I was on the point of thinking for myself!" All words that can be applied to this familiarity, whatever be the art referred to, must suggest some lack of originality; there is in reality no such lack, for in poetry the eternal truth of the idea, in the plastic art the beauty of the form and in music the essential fitness of the musical phrase, come so immediately into their own when they are read, seen, or heard, that the feeling of novelty is never realized at all. Of the great classical composers, none has surpassed Mozart, Beethoven, Schubert, and Brahms in the power of creating things that seem to have been sounding all through the ages. As Hans Sachs says—

> "Es klang so alt, and war doch so neu,
>   Wie Vogelsang im süssen Mai!"

But Wagner, for all his genius, seldom managed to call forth this sudden acceptance of a new idea, and, in each of the later works especially, Brahms nearly always succeeded in doing it at least once.

From the point of view of technique this familiarity was due in great measure to his fondness for themes composed of the successive notes of a chord, those which proceed by what is called "disjunct" rather than "conjunct" motion. Though it first appears in the second of the four pianoforte ballades, it does not make itself conspicuous as a characteristic until about the date of the second symphony, whose first subject is a striking example. Another is the slow movement of the violin concerto; the songs *Feldeinsamkeit,* from Opus 86, *Sapphische Ode,* from Opus 94, and many others, contain instances that show how keenly he felt the emotional appeal that is inherent in this way of constructing themes. It seems to give a touch of intimacy, of quiet peace, almost of homeliness; were it unrelieved by themes of contrasting energy and austerity, it might easily become cloying, and it is only Brahms's masterly handling that prevents this ever being the case. The severer themes are not forced upon the attention as points of relief, and in some of the most characteristic compositions they occupy the field almost exclusively; for example, the first and last movements of the first piano concerto gave offence to the Leipzig public, no doubt because of the austerity of their themes, and even in the slow movement, exquisite as it is, there may well have seemed to the hearers in the early sixties an absence of obvious melodic beauty. An extreme instance of this austerity is the second subject of the first movement in the string quintet in G, Opus 111, but there it is to be noticed that the first subject of the same movement has a bold swing, a spirit and energy, that would have carried off a really ungainly second theme, and here there is no ungainliness, for even its asperity is so finely treated that those who know the quintet welcome it even at its first presentation, knowing what is going to be done with it. Even this asperity is rare in the later works, which for the most part are built on themes of the utmost beauty and tenderness. Perhaps the most striking examples of this are to be found in the four chamber works in which the clarinet is employed, Opus 114, 115, and 120. The composer's admiration for the clarinet playing of Professor Mühfeld is known to have incited him to the composition of these beautiful things; and it is not a little remarkable that they contain the only two passages in which a purist might detect something less than the ideal refinement that distinguishes all the other melodies of Brahms.

The opening of the sonata in E flat, Opus 120, Number 2, has something of what Italian critics of painting call *morbidezza*, that is, a beauty of such ripeness that the slightest touch must make it over-ripe. In the trio, Opus 114, the andantino begins with a theme that comes very near to the borders of the commonplace.

But whether austere or tender, all the themes of Brahms have the finest melodic curves that were ever devised in music. No man has ever attained such uniform distinction of utterance, and the presence of the two exceptions just quoted only throws into higher relief the extraordinary nobility of everything else. There is on record an intensely interesting conversation of the composer with Mr. George Henschel, in which the master analyzed his own processes with rare minuteness, and in a way which must be instructive to all other composers, young or old. "What is properly called invention, or a real musical idea, is, so to say, a gift, an inspiration which I cannot further or encourage in any way (*dafür kann ich nichts*). At the time I must disregard this 'gift' as completely as possible, but ultimately I have to make it my own inalienable property by incessant labor. And that will not be quickly accomplished. The idea is like the seed-corn; it grows imperceptibly in secret. When I have invented or discovered the beginning of a song such as *Wann der silberne Mond*"—here he sang the first half-verse of *Mainacht*—"I shut up the book and go for a walk or take up something else; I think no more of it for perhaps half a year. Nothing is lost, though. When I come back to it again, it has unconsciously taken a new shape, and is ready for me to begin working at it."

(2) When we turn from the actual structure and essential features of the themes of Brahms to the manner in which he treats them, we feel ourselves in the presence of a master of the art that is called thematic development.

Never, since music was a conscious art, have the ideals of its structure been so continually fulfilled as they were by Brahms. His power of handling his materials so as to bring out every beautiful aspect of every theme, is surpassed by none of the older masters, not even by Beethoven. That power is none the less conspicuous because, for the most part, the usual types of musical form, those which are called classical, have been employed. Brahms, being in no straits for new ideas, had not the need which Liszt and other "advanced" composers had, of altering the classical forms or experimenting in new ones, for as long as he lived the old forms, so far from hampering his genius or confining his inspiration, seemed to suggest fresh outlets for development, and while there is no slavish adherence to the molds in which Haydn and Mozart cast their thoughts, there is no opposition to the classic model. Any alteration is in the direction of amplification, the groundwork of the structure being virtually in conformity with the rules laid down long before. This is especially true of the "first-movement" form, which, in all the many examples in the work of Brahms, is identical with that used by the classical masters, though in many instances some increased interest is imparted to the regular design by the presence of a motto-theme (neither first nor second subject, but dominating both), or by incorporating part of the development with the recapitulation. A third point of great importance with Brahms is the coda, and no more striking instance of his most successful innovation in form can be pointed out than the third symphony, where the motto pervades the whole work, and the coda of the last movement introduces new matter, fusing it with the old in a manner it is impossible to forget. Sometimes, too, an extra movement is added, as the section called *"Rückblick"* in the piano sonata in F minor, Opus 5, or the marvelously poetic introduction to the last movement of the first symphony. In the close of the third symphony, already referred to, a touch of exquisite suggestiveness occurs quite at the end, where the first subject of the symphony (not the motto) is heard from the violins as the top note of a tremolando passage, dying down to a lovely close. The coda just mentioned belongs to a class of final passages in which Brahms's genius seems to take special delight, and it has been said by an enthusiast for his work that if one might choose to have written anything by one of the great masters, one might ask to have imagined the last eight bars of each movement of the three sonatas for piano and violin, in all of which the closing strains are of rarest beauty and ingenuity. Such points as these are among the most obvious things to a student of Brahms's work, but the more deeply it is studied, the more enthusiasm will be called forth by his skill in the development of his themes, sometimes from quite unpromising germs, but more often from some melodic strain already so beautiful in itself that we might expect it to be spoilt by any process of alteration. In this special art of development we may perhaps see the highest achievement of human intellect in music. It requires not merely a complete mastery of every harmonic and contrapuntal resource, and the insight to detect in the germ of a theme its latent possibilities, but a strongly poetic invention to control the different phases of the theme, and to present them in such a succession as will enhance their beauty or eloquence. This, too, is an art that is as applicable to vocal music as to instrumental, and to the slighter forms of the romantic school as to the more conventional designs of the classical. Nothing is more remarkable throughout the work of Brahms than this splendid art, and it is perhaps not without significance that the work in which it appears for the first time in full distinctness, the finale of the piano sonata in F minor, Opus 5, should come almost immediately after one in which the composer tried the principle of "transformation of themes" which Liszt supposed himself to have invented. In the sonata in F sharp minor, Opus 2, the theme of the andante is "transformed" into that of the scherzo—a most rare expedient with Brahms, and one of which the other most prominent instance is the second symphony, Opus 73, in the appearance of the *allegretto grazioso* first in triple time in a sedate measure and then in the *presto non assai* in duple time. It is fairly clear that Brahms's adoption of the one invention claimed by the new school was never very whole-hearted, even though more instances of its employment by him might be pointed out.

For a very brief period Brahms gave in his allegiance to the school of Liszt; it is interesting to compare the episode in his social career with this momentary employment of Liszt's favorite structural device, and it is not impossible that its presence in the sonata may have induced Liszt to believe that Brahms could be regarded as a promising disciple of the new school. As usual, Joachim's words sum up the convictions of Brahms in this respect most vividly: "For him who dominates all its resources, form is no binding fetter, but a spur, an incentive, to new, free designs that are pre-eminently his own." The paradox that those who make the most diligent search for new forms in music, or for new structural pos-sibilities, are precisely those in whom the fountain of actual invention runs most slowly, and whose ideas are of the least value, is one that is being continually illustrated in modern music; and those who are richest in musical ideas are just those who find the old forms amply sufficient for their purpose.

On Brahms's treatment of rhythm a volume might be written; almost every composition of his is remarkable for its rhythmic variety, or for its superb command of metrical resources. Mr. C. F. Abdy Williams has well said, in speaking of the pianoforte *Rhapsodie,* Opus 119, Number 4, "This composition is only one amongst the many examples Brahms has given us of his mastery over rhythmical possibilities. He pushed forward the modern development of the art of music in many directions; but we believe that in no direction was his work more important than in the impetus he gave to the cultivation of a high, artistic, and intellectual sense of rhythm." (*The Rhythm of Modern Music.*) The same author analyzes many of the salient compositions of Brahms from the point of view of their rhythmic structure, and the student may well be referred to his book, which is full of interest and value.

(3) As Brahms attached so much importance to the art of design in music, it was almost inevitable that certain writers at different times should assert that he was deficient in a sense of musical color. The falsity of this is patent to any serious student of his work, but it is an error that has obtained a good many adherents among those who do not like his music and do not exactly know why. It is certainly true that, so far as his works give any evidence, the design of his music was of scarcely less importance than the invention of his themes, and that in his estimation the question of what instrument or tone-quality should be used in a particular passage was one of minor importance. In several cases he altered the whole scheme of coloring of a work without changing a line of its structure. The quintet, Opus 34, was originally designed for two pianofortes, this latter version taking rank, not as an arrangement, but as a separate publication, numbered "Opus 34 bis." In the same way the variations on a theme by Haydn exist in two forms, "Opus 56A" being the orchestral version and "Opus 56B" that for two pianos. The vocal quartets, Opus 103, *Zigeunerlieder,* were arranged by the composer as solos with piano accompaniment, and we know enough of his independence of character to be sure that he would not do such a thing in deference to any publisher's whim. Against these alterations of color-scheme, to which may be added his warm approval of Joachim's adapta-

tion for violin and piano of his arrangement of Hungarian dances originally written for piano duet, there is only a single instance in which one
of his designs was afterwards modified, viz., the trio in B, Opus 8, which,
first published in 1859, was reissued in 1891 with very important alterations of structure. It may be admitted, then, that he was a far more
assured master of design than he was of tone-coloring; but that is not the
same thing as saying that he was a bad tone-colorist, or that he had no ear
for the subtle effects peculiar to the various instruments of the orchestra.
Just as it is the present fashion to praise any painter who piles color upon
his canvas and to belittle the work of the man who excels in draughtman-
ship, so the public is continually being told that the whole art of music
lies in piling one sonorous orchestral effect upon another; and, as it is far
easier for the ear to be startled by some momentary impression of
gorgeous sound, than to be trained to follow the rational development of a
beautiful theme from some simple germ, the public is only too willing to
follow its leaders, and to regard color as the all-important consideration
in the musical art. Where these leaders of thought got the notion that
Brahms was contemptuous of musical color, or indifferent to its charms,
it is impossible to surmise; certainly it was not from the study of his
music as a whole. Although in works for piano solo (to which, like most
young composers, the master was limited in his earliest efforts), color is
as little to be looked for as its counterpart is in a pencil-drawing, yet in a
comparison of the early sonatas and the scherzo, Opus 1–5, with the
latest piano works, Opus 116–19, it is clear that the tone-qualities
peculiar to the piano were much more fully realized in later life than in
youth. As early as Opus 8, the trio in B, we meet with one passage that
foreshadows many of the more individual characteristics of the later compositions. In the finale, a haunting effect of fleeting, evanescent beauty is
produced by the repeated staccato notes of the violoncello subject, supported only by the light arpeggios of the piano. This use of arpeggio
passages, more especially of those for piano, is of curiously frequent occurrence in the master's work, and reaches its consummation in the
third symphony, where the arpeggios are given to the violins, and the
plaintive, fleeting theme to the violoncellos. Although one hesitates to
suggest anything that may create a materialistic idea in connection with
the work of Brahms, this characteristic idiom of his will always call up to
some hearers a vision of a regretful spirit, half seen in the pale moon-

light, as it flits past a scene of vanished happiness. A tearful smile, an April day, are suggested to other ears; the point is that the effect is produced entirely by the color-scheme. The four *Ballades,* Opus 10, contain suggestions of sonority (as in the second), or the contrast of long-held notes with an evanescent accompaniment (as in the fourth), which show that the characteristic acoustics of the piano had been closely studied. In the *Serenade,* Opus 11, in D, and in the noble *Begräbnisgesang,* Opus 13, the wind instruments are essayed for the first time, and are mostly used as Bach would have used them, that is, to carry out the design in a series of monochromes, if we may apply that word to musical tones. In the second work, the whole accompaniment is given to wind instruments, and very striking is the impression it creates, even though in England we are not apt to associate, as a German hearer would do, the sound of wind instruments with funereal ideas. In the trios for female chorus with horns and harp, another beautiful experiment in delicate coloring was tried. It is in the two quartets for piano and strings, Opus 25 and Opus 26, that there is revealed for the first time that delicate and masterly handling of color which is really peculiar to Brahms. The intermezzo of the G minor quartet, a plaintive and most spiritual movement, employs the mute for the violin, not for the other stringed instruments, and has the light treatment of the piano that has just been referred to. The andante, on the other hand, uses the stringed instruments in their most sonorous register, and the octave accompaniment of the piano is in exact balance with them. The *poco adagio* of the A major quartet begins with a curious device which seems to have been first used in the romance of Schumann's D minor symphony, where the solo violin and the violins of the orchestra play in what we may call approximate unison, the solo having passages of embroidery so slightly differing from the other that the casual hearer might easily infer carelessness on the part of the performers. The passage is less harsh than Schumann's, because on the one hand the muted violin is so very soft, and on the other the fading tone of the piano blends the whole into an effect of great beauty. In the *Requiem* and the *Schicksalslied,* the chief stress is naturally laid, not on the thematic development of the subjects, nor on the color employed, but on the illustration of two spiritual moods strongly contrasted with each other, the brevity and uncertainty of human life being contemplated side by side with the eternal calm of the happy dead. In the two sets of *Liebeslieder,* the main point is the transference of the charm of the waltz to a new combination of voices and instruments. As the first piano concerto had as its main object the solution of the problem how best to combine the solo instrument with the orchestra, it is natural that we should seek in the first symphony the clear challenge of the master to the world at large as a designer and colorist at the same time. Here, no doubt, there is some ground for adverse criticism, in spite of the wonderful beauty of theme and design; the violins are kept too constantly at work, and much of the orchestration is unduly thick, so that the many felicitous touches are less prominent to the ear in performance than to the eye in reading the score. But if it contained nothing else, it would deserve distinction even among the greatest of the compositions of Brahms, by the thrilling impression created in the introduction to the finale, at a place marked *più andante,* where the horn announces a phrase against the tremolando of the muted strings. The second symphony, published only a year after the first, shows something of the same monotony and thickness of color, but the slow movement is as rich and varied as any of the advance school could desire. The concertos, Opus 77 and Opus 83, for violin and piano respectively, and the two overtures, Opus 80 and Opus 81, contain plenty of instances of color dexterously used; and who that ever heard it can forget the swing of the slow movement of the violin concerto, the wit in the orchestration of the students' songs in the *Academic Overture,* or the wonderful effect of the trombones in the *Tragic?* By the date of the third symphony, Opus 90, the composer had completely realized his own ideal of scoring, and in color the work is as fine and authoritative as it is in design. No thickness is here, but every touch tells, and makes not merely *an* effect, but *the* very effect that suits the instrument best, and best elucidates the composer's thought. The fourth symphony undoubtedly presents a stumbling-block to many of the less earnest students of the master's work, partly by the fact that its themes are presented in what we may imagine to be their primordial forms, in their very simplest and most rudimentary germs. The very square-cut rhythm of the third movement, and the adaptation of the passacaglia form to the finale, are also difficulties to the average hearer, who must hear the work very often to be able to follow the theme of the passacaglia through all its changes. After the four symphonies, Brahms wrote only one more work in which

the full orchestra is employed, the double concerto for violin and violoncello, Opus 102, in which he seems to have been mainly interested in the
problem of welding together the solo instruments and the accompaniment
in a new way with entire avoidance of conventional effect.

Of color-effects, put in for their own sake, there are very few in the
concerto, but the combination of the two solo instruments (often used
in a manner that suggests a string quartet) is evidently the thing which
is to hold the hearer's attention, rather than the richness or variety of the
orchestral background. Henceforth, the master's attention seems to have
been given to the color-possibilities of various chamber combinations,
among which the group of works for clarinet, and the pianoforte solos,
Opus 116–19, are perhaps the most prominent, though the six-part
choruses, Opus 104, contain many real color-effects, such as that of the
exquisite *Nachtwache* II, with its horn-like calls, "Ruh'n sie?"—"Sie
ruh'n." The melancholy regret which we have referred to as being associated in Brahms's music with pianoforte arpeggios, finds its culmination in the song *Auf dem Kirchhofe,* from Opus 105. If they were nothing but studies in coloring, the pianoforte pieces of the later period would
deserve immortality, so varied are the moods suggested in the mere disposition of the special keyboard effects, quite apart from the enthralling
interest of the thematic invention and development.

XIV
RUSSIAN MUSICAL HISTORY IN KALEIDOSCOPE

MODESTE MOUSSORGSKY

*Born at Toropetz, March 28, 1839. Pupil of Balakireff. Chiefly
known for his operas,* Boris Godounoff *and* Khovanshchina; *also for his
tone-poem,* A Night on Bald Mountain; *wrote many pieces for piano,
notably* Pictures at an Exhibition *(orchestrated by Ravel); many songs.
Died at St. Petersburg, March 28, 1881. His influence (acknowledged by
Debussy) and fame did not come until after his death; Rimsky-Korsakoff
was instrumental in establishing his posthumous reputation.*

NICHOLAS RIMSKY-KORSAKOFF

*Born at Tikhvin, Novgorod, May 21, 1844. From 1871 taught com-
position at the St. Petersburg Conservatory; held various other musical
positions. Principal compositions include the operas,* Snegourotchka
(Snow Maiden), Coq d'Or, Katschei, Sadko *(a musical tableau),*
Christmas Eve; *the ballet* Mlada; *3 symphonies, including* Antar; *the
symphonic suite,* Scheherazade; *the* Spanish Caprice, *and the* Easter
Overture, *for orchestra. Died at St. Petersburg, June 21, 1908.*

ALEXANDER SCRIABIN

*Born at Moscow, January 10, 1872. Toured Europe as a pianist from
1895. Chiefly known as composer for piano; also for his symphonies*
Poème de l'Extase, Poème Divine, *and* Prometheus. *Died 1915.*

RUSSIAN MUSICAL HISTORY IN KALEIDOSCOPE

By M. Montagu Nathan

I

THE history of Russian art-music proper, unlike that of the other nations of our hemisphere, does not take us back into the remoter centuries. But if we are to appreciate the full significance of the greatest products of the Russian school of creative musicians, it is to the earliest historical records of their race that we must turn.

The reason for this is twofold. Viewed from the literary standpoint, Russian art-music is clearly seen to have its root in national and political history; in examining it as music we are not long in discovering that the first chapter in the volume, which in the last hundred years has so completely altered its character, was written in the far-distant age of minstrelsy. Perusing the annals and products of that golden age of national music—the period beginning with Glinka's initiation of the nationalistic ideal, continued with so much energy by the staunch little band of idealists of which Balakireff was the recognized leader in the early sixties, and ending with the meteoric descent of a fully-fledged school upon an unsuspecting and somewhat self-complacent Europe—we observe repeated instances of a reflection of bardic institutions.

The more we study the pages of Glinka's *Russlan and Ludmilla,* of Borodin's *Prince Igor,* of Rimsky-Korsakoff's *Sadko,* or of Stravinsky's *The Rites of Spring,* the less inclined we are to be satisfied with the message of their music alone. We become possessed of a desire for a knowledge of these legends and myths to which they so frequently refer, for

From the author's *Contemporary Russian Composers,* by permission of Cecil Palmer.

information bearing upon the origins of that folk-lore and song in which
Russian opera and symphonic music abound.

Russian musical history resolves itself into a chronicle in which we see
the alternate rise and fall of native folk-melody. Following upon the age
of minstrelsy, when, in the tenth century, the troubadour was a real power
in the land, came the introduction of Christianity, bringing with it a
strenuous battle waged by the priests of the new faith against the
paganistic spirit of the Slavonic legends and folk-songs. "Owing either to
their fidelity to Oriental asceticism, to the Christian spirit of the initial
centuries, or to the necessity of keeping a hold upon a people freshly
converted and still impregnated with paganism," says Patouillet in his
Le Théâtre de Moeurs Russes, "the Orthodox Church watched anxiously
over the social and domestic life of the nation and treated every profane
recreation as a sin. . . ." Continuing, the Frenchman quotes the "old
moralist," whose words are given by Milioukoff in his *Sketch for a
History of Russian Culture:* "Laughter does not edify or redeem us, it
dispels and destroys edification; laughter grieves the Holy Spirit, it
banishes the virtues, for it causes forgetfulness of death and eternal
punishment."

But the priests, despite their arduous efforts, were unable to stamp
out the songs and ceremonials which they viewed with so much dis-
favor: they were obliged to make a compromise. They pursued the wise
course of relinquishing the futile policy of total destruction, instituting
in its stead the plan of rendering these popular amusements as far as possible innocuous by introducing references which were somewhat better in
keeping with ecclesiastical precept. If they were not entirely successful,
if the guardians of folk-song—the gusslars and skomorokhs—were
secretly encouraged by the nobles to whose pleasures they ministered, the
Church was at least able to maintain for a time an appearance of discipline. Gradually, it seems, the clandestinely nurtured music of the soil
emerged from the condition in which the ascetics had placed it, and proceeded to enjoy its long-sought and hard-won freedom with a good will
which expressed itself in a manner that once more—and this time with
greater justice—incurred the displeasure of the Church.

2

This process of ebb and flow was repeated in the succeeding centuries. The son of the first Romanoff was responsible, through his patronage, for another ebullition of secular entertainments which, though not altogether devoid of licentiousness, were at all events instrumental in reviving a tradition. With the accession of Peter the Great came the influx of alien musicians who streamed through the "window opened into Europe" by that pioneer among sovereigns and monarch among pioneers, bringing with them influences that were to force native song once again into obscurity. The foreign musical idiom, while contributing to the cultivation of music as an art worthy of respect, diverted the attention of nobles and people alike from their own rich store of melody. The power of the alien grew year by year. In the reign of the Empress Anne, which began in 1732, the direction of the nation's music fell into the hands of Francesco Araya, a Neapolitan who had relinquished the honors bestowed upon him at home to gain fresh laurels, but according to Sir Arthur Helps the responsibility of instruction to court circles was entrusted to a German. The Italian domination continued during the reign of Elizabeth Petrovna, Araya remaining at the head of musical affairs. But he now encountered rivalry from a company of French actors whose performances alternated with those of Araya's operatic troupe. Whether this divided patronage impelled the Italian to seek a means of ingratiating himself more firmly with his Russian following is not clear; it was subsequent to Elizabeth's installation of these competing Frenchmen that Araya instituted the innovation of opera in the vernacular.

But, as will readily be understood, the music remained thoroughly Italian in style, and the opera itself, although its text was by a Russian, had for its subject that of Mozart's *La Clemenza di Tito,* and was consequently not even the quasi-Russian product that was offered to succeeding generations. It is something of a mystery that a later work of Araya's on the subject of *Cephalus and Procris* should have been dubbed by its composer "the first opera in the Russian tongue," for its text by Soumarokhoff was apparently of later date than Volkhoff's version of the Italian plot above referred to. Araya's sub-heading avoids reference to the Greek subject, and certainly the music, which might be mistaken for that of any Italian of that period, appears to contain nothing that peculiarly fits it for its association with Ovid's Athenian princess.

3

With Catherine the Great, however, the national element began once more to obtain a somewhat firmer foothold on the first rung of the ladder it subsequently climbed. The Northern Semiramis is not to be given the credit for this. She gave sanction to a continuance of the Italian régime, and not being very confident of her own powers of judgment is said to have submitted the works of one of the most promising native musicians of her reign to the scrutiny of the favored alien.

Her appetite for serious music seems to have grown in the eating, for while at first she was bored by grand opera, which she described in a letter to Grimm as being "somewhat difficult to digest," she is said to have regretted that the laws of the Orthodox Church would not permit of the spiritual music of Sarti being used for worship because it was instrumental.

At this epoch the Italians appear to have regained the supreme favor, and although such musicians as Galuppi, Sarti, and Martini undoubtedly contributed to an improvement of the musical affairs in Russia, they wielded their power in rather tyrannical fashion.

To Fomin (1741–1800), a native musician, fell at once the indignity of being under the surveillance of the alien, and the honor of writing the first real attempt at genuine Russian opera. *Aniouta,* the first of his numerous works, owed some of its success, says Tcheshikin, to the sallies of its librettist, Popoff, against the feudal system. A similar tendency is noticeable in the text of the exceedingly popular *Wizard-Miller,* in which its compiler, Ablessimoff, indulged in what Tcheshikin styles a democratic method of thought, "expressed nevertheless with extreme caution." But the music, we are assured, played a not unimportant part in the success of the opera, although it is judged by the above-mentioned historian as rather amateurish, and as showing a want of experience in the technique of composition.

And, indeed, it would seem that most of the operas produced at this time by compatriots of Fomin, such as Paskievitch and Matinsky, are not to be considered as having contributed very much towards the emancipation of their art. We have the sanction of Krouglikoff for dismissing them as pseudo-national manifestations—works consisting largely of popular tunes "treated strictly according to the Western recipe."

4

The real cause of the comparative slowness of the development of musical nationalism is to be found in the conditions under which it was being nurtured. The movement may be characterized as artificial; the Russian people could hardly be expected to demand the enfranchisement of a native product when society as a whole averted its gaze from everything of the sort. But a change, partly the result of circumstance and partly due to human endeavor, was soon fated to set in. During the brief period of the ill-fated Paul, there came to Petrograd a young Venetian, Catterino Cavos by name who, at the age of 23, was already at the head of a travelling operatic troupe. Invited with his players to the Russian capital by Prince Youssoupoff, in 1798, he remained in Russia until his death in 1842, performing during that time a very great service to the native music-drama. The aptness of Krouglikoff's metaphor when he describes Cavos as having "tilled the soil" of Russian opera so that it was ready for *A Life for the Tsar* and *Russlan and Ludmilla*—the seeds of operatic nationalism later sown by Glinka—is the more easy to appreciate when we observe among the titles of the dramatic works written by the industrious Italian such names as *Ilya the Hero, Dobrinya Nikitich* and *Ivan Soussanin*. The success of the last-named, when produced in 1815, was not by any means entirely due to the merit of its music; the nature of Prince Shakovsky's text must surely have been a great factor, but the most important of all was the crushing defeat of Napoleon and the conflagration that in the year 1812 had contributed so largely to his ultimate downfall.

For in the burning of Moscow we are bound to recognize the cause of the earliest manifestation of that racial consciousness and pride, that wave of patriotism on which Russian art first floated towards the glories it has since attained. Of Pushkin's precursors it is often said that they tuned the instrument (the Russian tongue) on which the great national poet played. We may consider that it was Cavos who showed Glinka what tunes to play. It is for his manner of playing them that we pay tribute to the composer of *A Life for the Tsar*.

Of Glinka's contemporary, A. N. Verstovsky, the composer of *Askold's Tomb*, it may be said that with his opera he also paved the way, not for the actual composition of the work but for the presentation of *A Life for the Tsar* before the Russian people. In Verstovsky's famous and still quite popular contribution to the Russian operatic repertoire is to be remarked a successful attempt at rendering native song in a national manner. Where it differs from Glinka's great work, which was produced some fifteen months later, is in its general musical workmanship, on the one hand—Verstovsky, though a prolific composer, remained conspicuously lacking in technical matters—and, on the other, in the substance of the plot. While Zagoskin's novel, from which the libretto is derived, was of an historical nature, its subject has not the compelling interest of that of Glinka's opera. The story told by the latter is one which makes an immediate appeal to every Russian, while the name of Askold evokes for the average opera-goer only a vague reminiscence of historical knowledge acquired under pressure. But in the music of *Askold's Tomb* is something that is entirely in accord with the popular taste, not merely of the generation which witnessed its production but of those which succeeded. "Who," asks Sergei Aksakoff, in his biography of Zagoskin, "does not know it, love it and sing it?" We may thus award to Verstovsky the honor of being by no means the least, though virtually the last, of the Russian composers who leads up to the real inauguration of Russian musical nationalism.

5

The tradition of musical nationalism, hitherto mooted in rather half-hearted fashion, and later to be advocated with such passionate enthusiasm by the Young Russian School, was really established by Glinka. It is by studying his first and more popular work, *A Life for the Tsar*, that we are able to estimate the measure of progress towards a national style made by his precursors. For in *A Life for the Tsar*, despite its commendable neglect of crude folk-music, its composer's attempt to achieve an amalgamation of folk and art-music, his introduction of the native method of choral accompaniment and the many national touches, we receive a fairly strong reminder of the alien influences which Glinka was striving to combat.

The many nationalistic features—the modal character of the melodies, the contrapuntal choral imitations, the subtle use of the patriotic leading-motive, the insertion of passages in which the music is made to suggest the balalaika and the several allusions to historical and pseudo-historical episodes in the libretto—all these interest us and indicate the distance already traversed since the composition of those rather naïve essays in musical nationalism which were made in the preceding generation; but we, who in the twentieth century are making a first acquaintance with the music of this, to Russians, almost sacred opera, we who have not been brought up to regard it with something like our reverential attitude towards Handel's *Messiah,* are inclined to wonder how any Russian can overlook certain instances of what to us appears an undiluted Italian manner.

If we find ourselves at first unable to understand in what lies the cause of the enthusiasm perennially aroused by this opera in the land of its origin, we need only inquire how the greater part of the classic musical literature would fare with us if it were introduced afresh, without the aid of our established esteem of it as the work of a great master; we need only remember that the glamour of the earlier impression of *A Life for the Tsar* is perpetuated by its plot; and if we desire to appraise this work in such manner as to arrive at a proper estimate of its value as a stimulus to the ardent nationalists for whom it serves as a model, it behooves us to compare its form and substance with the works of Glinka's precursors; then shall we see why Glinka spoke of an opera that should make his countrymen "feel at home," and then shall we be able to understand the musical historian's claim that the name of Glinka should have a significance equal to that of Pushkin in literature and somewhat greater than that of Brioulloff in painting. It will then be readily agreed that Glinka was not the least worthy member of that curious trinity of the early nineteenth century.

6

But it must not be supposed that in *A Life for the Tsar* Glinka put forth every effort of which he was capable, leaving nothing further in the shape of a contribution to the nationalist treasury. In his second opera, *Russlan and Ludmilla,* and in his orchestral works, we find material which appears to have had an even greater influence upon the many descendants of this "Father of Russian Music" than the musical innovations and the intensely stirring plot of *A Life for the Tsar.* Compared with the latter, *Russlan* is to be reckoned vastly inferior from the dramatic point of view, and it is not without examples of that Italianism which Glinka had assimilated both at home and abroad. But in two particulars it marks a distinct epoch in the history of Russian music. It introduced the fantastic element in dignified surroundings, thus founding a tradition which seems in no danger of dying out, and its indication of the value of Eastern color rendered a service that is inestimable. We have already referred to the metaphorical asseveration that Peter the Great opened a window into Europe. Of one of Russia's greatest poets it is remarked that he annexed the Caucasus to Russian literature. And we may say, with all justice, that to Glinka we owe those gorgeous feasts of Oriental music that have since been placed before us by his successors. It is impossible to place the output of the modern Russians in a proper focus without bearing in mind at all times the nature of Glinka's legacy. As was pointed out by Prince Odoievsky, *Russlan and Ludmilla* was not a mere "magic" opera; that vein had already been exploited by his forerunners; it was an opera in the style of the Russian fairy-tale, an opera-legend. In a poetic passage he acclaims Glinka as a mighty genius who has not only collected for us all the varied racial characteristics of the Orient, but has set them to music: "That the influence of *Russlan and Ludmilla* is responsible for such creations as have since been given to the world by Dargomijsky, Borodin, Rimsky-Korsakoff, and Stravinsky, can easily be grasped by anyone conversant with the history of music in Russia prior to the time of Glinka. Such operas as Rimsky-Korsakoff's *Kaschei, Tsar Sultan, The Snow-Maiden, Sadko* and *Kitej,* and Stravinsky's ballet, *The Fire-Bird,* have all a foundation in a folk-lore in which the supernatural predominates. But there are other elements than this to support this opera's claim to the distinction of being a pioneer work. . . . Glinka perceived the advantage that would accrue to the art-nationalist who should think imperially, and his adoption of this principle has endowed Russian music with a source of melody that has since been heavily drawn upon. Opera is not the only region in which the benefit of Glinka's policy has been felt. Balakireff's piano fantasia, *Islamey*—a veritable epic of the Orient—Borodin's *In the Steppes of Central Asia,* and Rimsky-Korsakoff's *Scheherezade,* all owe their inspiration to *Russlan and Ludmilla*. In each case a sensibility to Eastern color was inherent; but the impulse to express the Orient in music originated in Glinka's example."

Nor does his legacy to Russian music end here. Seeking to provide for the public of his day a form of symphonic music that would make a smaller demand upon its patience than the traditional symphony of three and four movements in length, he wrote *Spanish Caprice,* the first of a series of short orchestral fantasies, and, thanks partly to the sanction and encouragement of Liszt—a warm supporter of the "Young Russian School"—this type of one-movement work was subsequently developed on a generous scale. To his search for and employment of the folk-song of Spain, the Spaniards owe the resuscitation in art-music of their now familiar popular melodies. The similar service rendered to his own country is estimated by Tchaikovsky in the following passage from his diary: "Without intending to compose anything beyond a simple humorous trifle, he has left us a little masterpiece, every bar of which is the outcome of enormous creative power. Half a century has passed since then, and many Russian symphonic works have been composed. . . . The germ of all this lies in his *Kamarinskaya,* as the oak-tree lies in the acorn."

7

In Alexander Sergeievich Dargomijsky (1813–1869) we have the immediate successor of Glinka. This composer is described by Krouglikoff as being a man of brilliant talent rather than genius. With this estimate those who view the work of Dargomijsky in a proper perspective are bound to disagree, and must surely perceive, on the contrary, that the composer of *Russalka* and *The Stone Guest,* while possessing only a moderate musical talent, had that penetrating insight into truths that are hidden from the average mind, which we call genius.

In order to appreciate the quality of Dargomijsky's genius and to discern in what direction it was applied, we have only to recall the extent to which our own native drama has been emancipated since the recognition of that by-product of the Ibsenite reforms, the simplification of the stage-play. It is said that a great Victorian editor, when considering the appointment of a dramatic critic to his staff, averred that in his view the indispensable qualification for such a post should be that the applicant should never previously have entered a theatre.

Dargomijsky's merit lies not so much in his music as in its composer's appreciation of a need for the reform of opera. It is, therefore, necessary that we should possess some knowledge of the operatic world from the conditions of which Dargomijsky desired that opera should be rescued.

"In those days," writes the prophetess of Russian music in Western Europe, "the reformative efforts of Gluck had been completely forgotten and Italian opera ruled the world. And what was the form of these Italian operas? An amalgamation of detached pieces, all cut after the same pattern and invariably made up either of two parts: an andante and an allegro; or of three parts, an andante between two allegros. In each of these parts, especially in the allegros, the principal melody returned in the shape of a refrain—the more commonplace the better—during which the hero strode from back to front or from side to side of the stage. The recitatives were often interminably and inconceivably inane; and nothing in the world, no kind of dramatic episode or even catastrophe, could bring about a modification of these forms. If the hero received a public insult, instead of taking immediate punitory measures, he would form up in a row with the rest of the stage company, join them in singing a long andante and then proceed to run the varlet through. Choruses thought nothing of shouting frenziedly, 'Let us rush to the revenge' without budging an inch, etc."

Having paid homage to Glinka in the composition of his popular legendary opera *Russalka*, Dargomijsky proceeded to turn from the consideration of the national element in music-drama to that of the *rational*. The musical setting of a dramatic text was no longer to be a succession of tunes loosely strung together, nor the performance to partake of the nature of a "concert in costume"; the text, instead of being the work of a journeyman librettist, must be worthy to form part of a dignified whole. In *Russalka* we discover already an endeavor to construct an opera which should break away from the approved artificial operatic forms, an effort to reproduce conversation not in conventional but in natural recitatives; in *The Stone Guest*, a musical setting of the statue episode in *Don Juan*, we see music elevated to the rank of drama, and we are shown moreover that in the Dargomijskian formula there is no suggestion, as in Wagner's, of a tyranny in the behavior of the promoted art. The music respects the drama. In Pushkin's text, which Dargomijsky set without alteration, there is no "crowd"; in the musical setting the composer dispenses with a chorus.

It is not because of any loveliness in its music that *The Stone Guest* became a model for the reformers of the "Young Russian School," for the Italian verists, for the composer of *Pelléas et Mélisande,* but because in it there was, for the first time since Gluck's effort, an endeavor to re-establish the dignity of the musico-dramatic art. And when we remember that Dargomijsky's cry, "the sound must represent the word," and his demand for "the truth"—in song no less than in opera—were uttered without knowledge either of Wagner or of Ibsen, whose work had not yet begun, we can hardly deny to him the attribute of genius.

8

It was upon the initiatory labors of Glinka and Dargomijsky—the introduction of patriotic nationalism, folk-lore, fantasy, and orientalism by the former, and of dramatic and musical rationalism by the latter—that the "Young Russian School" was founded.

But whereas the awakening of nationalistic feeling, and its operatic manifestation, *A Life for the Tsar,* were due to the stirring events of the Napoleonic invasion, the desire to be natural, the craving for simplicity and for truth in all things, even in music, was engendered by the great Liberation of 1861. The spirit of individual liberty which inspired the junior characters in Turgenieff's *Virgin Soil* was the impulse from which sprang the energies of the young group of reformers in the musical world.

The socialistic outlook of the sixties is as clearly reflected in the music of that period as it is in its art and literature. Literature, art, and music were henceforth to be not for art's but for life's sake. Encouraged by such writers as Chernishevsky and Herzen, and by the realistic painters, Repin and Vereshchagin, our "Young Russian School" made known its view that music, too, might take its place in the scheme of personal enfranchisement.

And the musician-participants in this general movement towards "simplification"—already provided with examples of the historico-national, legendary, and fantastic types of opera, but all contained in an operatic form which was primarily lyrical—were now to be given a model of realistic music-drama. That model was Dargomijsky's *The Stone Guest*.

The young Russian group did not owe the transmission of the inspiration it received from Glinka entirely to Dargomijsky. When Balakireff, the leader of the "Five," came as a young man to Petrograd, he lost no time in seeking out the composer of *A Life for the Tsar* and, visiting him at Tsarskoë Selo, where he was then living in semi-retirement, speedily established himself in the great man's favor. Glinka saw in Balakireff the man who was destined to carry on the campaign of Russian musical nationalism, which he had so fittingly inaugurated with his first epoch-making opera.

César Cui, the first recruit to the new movement, should perhaps be considered as having shared with Balakireff the burden of its foundation, for although he was only a theoretical nationalist—there would seem to have been a conflict between hereditary instincts and acquired views—his writings on behalf of the "Invincible Band" and its propaganda were of no little service in combating certain hostile forces at home and in dispelling misconceptions abroad. Borodin, in virtue of his labors in the social world, was well qualified to take a part in their councils. Furthermore, his musical gift, though not of a nature allowing of an emulation of Dargomijsky's naturalism, contributed greatly to the perpetuation of the epic type of opera to which Glinka's *Russlan and Ludmilla* and his own *Prince Igor* conform, while his Eastern descent impelled him to use richer coloring than that of the rather naïve orientalism of *Russlan*.

9

In Moussorgsky, the spiritual conversion of the nation is most strongly typified. Coming in contact with Dargomijsky at an impressionable age, he soon became dissatisfied both with the society by which, as a smart guardsman, he had been surrounded, and the music affected by such a circle. Of the "Five" he alone appears to have possessed the true seer's vision. His art is to be described as an expression of socialism in simultaneous relation to people and to music. Music was for him a means of human intercourse, but he was not prepared to entrust this function to any but naturalistic music. In opera, as in song, he was a close follower of his master. His dramatic, as well as his vocal works, are informed by that steadfast desire for naturalness which Dargomijsky seems to have been the first to awaken in him. Far more than either Balakireff, Cui, or Borodin, Moussorgsky reflects the spirit of the sixties in Russia; his works are in much closer touch with the literature and the painting of that period. They show us that although he was regarded with some alarm by his friends as a revolutionary, his ideals were of a kind that could not fail, when realized, to promote the evolution of the musical art. He transcended their "program" because he saw the need not merely for the alteration of the function of music but of its constitution. He perceived that progress and music were in a sense inter-changeable terms, that emotion is a symptom of progress, that music is the special language of emotion and that the vocation of the artist-musician is to seek the interpretation of humanity in terms of the present.

A study of Moussorgsky's life, works, and utterances leads one to imagine that he considered it the paramount duty of a musician to adopt towards music an attitude of conservatism very different from that which the customary use of the term suggests, a conservatism designed to con-serve in music a spirit of spontaneity, thus preventing any danger of a conventionalization of musical expression.

Viewed in relation to Glinka, Moussorgsky is seen to have followed his precursor's footsteps in choosing subjects of nationalistic import; this he has done in such operas as *Boris Godounoff* and *Khovanshchina;* it is in his forms and in his means of expression that he is the whole-hearted disciple of Dargomijsky. In his songs we see the desire for "the truth above all things." Neither the orientalism nor the fantasy of *Rus-slan* has a large share in his music, but certain sporadic instances may be observed in the Persian ballet of *Khovanshchina* and the *Baba-Yaga* number in his musical representation of Hartmann's pictures. But to view Moussorgsky in the proper perspective as an artist we are obliged to go to the completed *Boris Godounoff* as the finished product, and to his abortive setting of Gogol's *The Match-Maker* as the skeleton or bare framework on which his art is based. In the latter we have an earnest of Moussorgsky's intentions as an artist, but the former shows us the profound humanity of the man.

10

The advent of Rimsky-Korsakoff, the youngest of the group—at that time a naval cadet—can hardly have been looked upon by Balakireff and his followers as a matter of very great artistic importance. It is true that Balakireff took an immediate liking for the youth, apparently due in some degree to the latter's reverence for the extraordinary gifts possessed by his newly found master. But, as Rimsky-Korsakoff tells us in his *Memoirs,* his own musical attainments were at that time exceedingly slender, and further, as Borodin's attitude towards music was that of a dilettante and as Moussorgsky's was informed by an indifference to the necessity for study, Balakireff and Cui were looked upon as in every way superior to these three tyros. Yet neither of the two leaders was fully equipped for leadership, and it would seem that Balakireff's knowledge of the orchestra and Cui's experience of opera and song rendered each of the pair the complement of the other. What caused the earlier members of the group to regard the latest and youngest recruit as a mere novice was that not only was he entirely ignorant of musical theory but that he had no shining gift, such as had Moussorgsky, as an executant. How could they be expected to foresee that this humble member of the brotherhood would become the most prolific composer and the one who, in his output, would unite all the streams opened up by the initiatory effort of Glinka with something of the realism and the humor and all the sincerity of Dargomijsky? And this is not the sum of Rimsky-Korsakoff's achievement. By his resolve to make a thorough study of the theoretical aspect of music, with which his comrades' acquaintance was far from exhaustive, he was eventually able to supplement and even to eclipse the efforts of Cui in upholding the banner of nationalism against the onslaughts of a very determined opposition. By passively dissociating himself from the "mere amateurs" of the much-disdained group, he proved that nationalism was not, as alleged, a mere cloak for technical ignorance, and in course of time he gave the world a treasury of nationalistic musical art, and an army of pupils each of whom was able to reflect no little glory upon the master to whom he owed so much.

II

In the hostility, to which we have referred, between two artistic camps, we have a tradition which has not yet died out in Russia. The grounds of conflict have shifted, but the strife continues.

But so long as the discussion is not confined to musicians themselves, it can do much good. So long as temperament exists there must remain a prejudice in favor of one's own temperamental outlook. Music is the language in which the message of art can be conveyed to the temperament. If, therefore, as the fruit of controversy, we succeed in inducing humanity at large to seek an acquaintance with that language, it will not matter so much that prejudice and intolerance have been so conspicuous in the attitude of the combatants who have fought against each other under the banner of art.

The opposition to the nationalist band consisted of two united bodies and a third which was independent. "During the whole period of Glinka's activity," says Stassoff, "and of the first half of Dargomijsky's, there had been only two classes of musical society: the one consisting of composers, the other of public and critics. At the close of the fifties there appeared a new class—the musical institutions. Prior to this our musical education had been a sporadic growth . . . some of our musicians being self-taught, others having learned under the guidance of some native or foreign teacher or professor. The time had come when the need of schools, conservatories, incorporated societies and musical denominations and prerogatives was being canvassed." Russian musicians viewed with jealous eyes the indisputable advantages possessed by the carefully educated Westerns, and sought to establish in their own land a means of obtaining a complete musical education. Unfortunately, however, while desirous of endowing Russia with a properly constituted educational body, the prime movers ignored in their haste the movement already begun by Balakireff, and his disciples, and invited teachers from the principal European centers, who speedily brought into Russia the fruits not only of their experience but of their prejudices.

The first decisive step was the formation of the Russian Musical Society in 1859, in which Anton Rubinstein took a leading part. Twelve months later a Moscow branch came into being at the instigation of the celebrated virtuoso's brother. This was followed in 1862 by the opening of the Petrograd Conservatory, and in 1866 by the foundation of a similar institution in Moscow. At the head of these were respectively the two brothers, Anton and Nicholas Rubinstein. The former, prior to the initiation of the educational movement, had clearly shown his contempt for the "amateurs" of the nationalist group in a newspaper article; this was answered by a forceful plea for freedom as well as nationalism in art, written by Stassoff, who expressed himself as viewing with alarm the proposal to introduce academic ideas and stereotyped notions from abroad. In his opinion the importation of foreign grammarians could only result in the flooding of Russia with adepts having no real vocation for music.

"And then," in the words of S. N. Krouglikoff, himself an adherent of the "Five," "the war began." The cudgels of the nationalists were taken up and wielded with considerable effect by Cui and Stassoff, the latter with a trueness of aim that was wanting from Cui's rather wild but none the less vigorous blows. The scribes of the orthodox party were Laroche, who became an untiring supporter of Tchaikovsky, Solovieff, who sought to execute a flank movement by complaining of Cui's conduct in military quarters, Famintsin, Theophilus Tolstoi, and others. Their portraits are to be found in Moussorgsky's scena, *The Peepshow*, which gives a highly colored picture of their several prejudices. The crushing comments of Rubinstein, who referred to the nationalists' technical shortcomings, were parried by Cui's declaration that Rubinstein might be a Russian composer, but was not a composer of Russian music. Tchaikovsky, having coquetted with the nationalists' folk-tune principle, was charged by Balakireff with having converted his native folk-song to the Lutheran faith. The German tradition of thematic development was flouted by the "Five," and this brought down upon their heads the wrathful indignation of the conservative party. Cui's rejoinder took the form of a satirical conjecture as to whether, if one fell ill, it would not be in the very worst taste to get cured by an unorthodox method instead of dying according to the rules.

Then to these disputants there came another in the person of V. V. Serov, the "Counsellor Iserov" introduced by Wagner to Mme. Judith

Gauthier and Villiers de l'Isle-Adam, at Triebschen in 1858. Charged to "uphold firmly the Wagnerian standard in Petrograd," he did so with such good will that when the German composer visited the Russian capital in 1863 he received representations from certain friends of Rubinstein (one of his most implacable antagonists) asking him to intercede with Serov on behalf of the pianist whom Serov cordially hated and had bitterly attacked. The latter's position was one of isolation, and he carried on a dual warfare against the pseudo-Russians of the Conservatory and the nationalists, having transactions with Cui and Stassoff in which he fared rather badly.

12

In the end this bloodless battle of Petrograd concluded in a way by no means unsatisfactory to the "Five" and their camp-followers. Rimsky-Korsakoff, already favorably known as a budding composer, was invited to become a member of the Conservatory staff; Balakireff succeeded Rubinstein as conductor of the Musical Society, seizing this golden opportunity of making known the works of his disciples; Serov, gratified by the success of an opera in which he had sought to apply Wagnerian principles in the treatment of native folk-song, had become rather more friendly towards his old nationalist enemies. Thus it was that Petrograd became for a time identified with the nationalist group, and Moscow the stronghold of the "occidentalists" or "eclectics," over whom Tchaikovsky eventually presided.

With the dispersal of the original personnel of the Balakireff circle, which became merged in the early eighties in the group surrounding Bieliaieff—the famous patron and publisher—the "Young Russian School" formulated aims a little more liberal, and it fell to Glazounoff, Bieliaieff's first *protégé,* to steer a course between the two currents of Russian music, thus gaining the respect of both parties.

It is Bieliaieff whom Russia has to thank that the somewhat academic views later formed by Glazounoff have not been acquiesced in by musical society as a whole. It says much for Bieliaieff's enlightenment and catholicity of taste that he supported young Scriabin with no less enthusiasm than that manifested many years earlier on behalf of Glazounoff. The fruit of that championship is seen in the present contest between the young progressives and the older generation, in which the former show themselves well able to hold their own.

Meanwhile, the example of Glinka and the energies of the "Five" have been fertile. Although the primitive nationalists' method is a thing of the past, composers having ceased to base their music upon folk-tunes, and operas and symphonies being no longer devoted exclusively to the celebration of the great figures and episodes of national and political history, musical nationalism is by no means moribund. It is expressed rather more subtly, and in the dramatic works of a Stravinsky is apt to elude the foreigner. Still, programmatic nationalism of the older type is reflected in certain works of Prokofieff, and Glazounoff and Gniessin have written works in honor of Russia's greatest poets, painters and sculptors. And there are younger men who are rallying to support the banner on which Moussorgsky wrote "Towards New Territories!"—men for whom that motto is still pregnant with meaning, and whose works will keep Russia's place in the front rank of the musical nations of the world.

XV

TCHAIKOVSKY

PETER ILITCH TCHAIKOVSKY

Born at Wotinsk, December 25, 1840. Did not take up music actively until 1862, when he entered the Petersburg Conservatory, studying under Rubinstein. Taught there from 1866 to 1877. Toured as conductor through Europe, to England and America. Died at St. Petersburg, November 6, 1893.

PRINCIPAL WORKS

VOCAL: A coronation cantata and 2 masses; several operas, including *Eugene Oniegin, Pique Dame,* etc. Some 100 songs.

INSTRUMENTAL: 6 symphonies, of which only the last 3 (including Number 6, the *Pathétique*) are consistently performed; symphonic poems, including *The Tempest, Francesca da Rimini, Manfred, Romeo and Juliet, Hamlet.* Ballets: *Le Lac des Cygnes, La Belle au Bois Dormant, Le Casse-Noisette* (the last familiar as the *Nutcracker Suite,* for orchestra); *Snow-Maiden.* Overtures, including *1812;* the *Marche Slave;* the *Italian Caprice,* etc.; 2 piano concertos, including the famous one in B flat; a fantasia for piano and orchestra; a violin concerto; a capriccio for cello and orchestra. Chamber music includes the string sextet, *Souvenir de Florence;* 3 string quartets; a piano trio. Piano music includes a sonata, numerous smaller pieces, duets, etc.

TCHAIKOVSKY

By R. A. Streatfeild

IF it were possible to single out one composer more than another as representative of the various phases of thought that are characteristic of the close of the nineteenth century, that composer would undoubtedly be Tchaikovsky. Summed up in a single phrase, Tchaikovsky is eminently *fin de siècle*. In feeling, as well as in expression, he is a decadent of the decadents. His emotion, though unquestionably sincere as far as it goes, is superficial rather than profound. He sinks to morbid pessimism, he rises to hysteria. His feverish sensibility is fanned by gusts of passion, his highly strung nerves answer to every psychic suggestion. He revels in introspection, he bares his soul to the scalpel of his art. He drags the pageant of his bleeding heart through the realms of music, he butchers his mankind to make an artistic holiday. But with all his lack of dignity and restraint, he is an incomparable artist, or to be more accurate it is the artist in him that has stifled the man.

He views the world, life, and himself with the eye of an artist alone, he pours his own emotions into the alembic of music, content to suffer if he can thereby create. It was truly said of Byron, that he had but one subject—himself; and the saying is equally true of Tchaikovsky. In all that he wrote he mirrored his own personality; he is the protagonist of his own quartets, the hero of his own symphonies. As Hamlet he stalks moodily on the ramparts of Elsinore, as Manfred he wanders among the gleaming glaciers of the Alps, as Paolo he is racked by the unpitying torments of Hell, as Ferdinand he marvels at the wonders of Miranda's isle, and as Romeo he loves and dies under the shadow of the towers of Verona. If his personality is less puissant and terrible

From the author's *Modern Music and Musicians,* by permission of Methuen and Co.

than that of Byron, his artistic instinct is infinitely acuter. No man has ever handled music with a more delicate appreciation of its manifold possibilities. In his hands the orchestra becomes alive, a chorus of voices taught to breathe at his will every accent of human emotion.

With his marvelous technique, his unerring instinct for sheer beauty of tone, and his rhythmic fertility, he is the Swinburne of modern music. A generation will come for which the subject-matter of Tchaikovsky's music will have no interest. We who are his contemporaries, to whom his vein of thought is familiar, can appreciate the truth with which he depicts the fashionable pessimism of the hour, but to our grandchildren his melancholy will seem mere attitudinizing and his raptures will ring false, though his craftsmanship can never be called in question. He has taught the world new secrets of expression, which, however they may afterwards become merged in the commonplaces of art, must always remain his indisputable legacy to the music of the future.

The simple and uneventful story of Tchaikovsky's life has but little to do with his music. Like many other Russian composers he began as an amateur, and it was not until he was grown up and an official in a government office that he felt any inclination to make music the serious business of his life. Afterwards he worked very hard at composition, chiefly under the direction of Anton Rubinstein; and, unlike the majority of Russian musicians, he contrived to rid himself entirely of that indefinable taint of amateurishness which is the *signe particulier* of so much of their music. Not only in this point did he differ from the majority of his contemporaries. Living as he did at a time conspicuous for a remarkable revival of musical activity in Russia, he fortunately contrived to steer clear of the rock upon which so many of his friends made shipwreck—the exaggerated worship of nationalism. Tchaikovsky was in many respects the most amiable and yielding of men, but where art was concerned his principles were inflexible, and he wisely refused to be persuaded by his "nationalist" friends into endeavoring to express himself in any way but that which was natural to him. He was of course denounced as a bad patriot, and it is still the fashion to compare him unfavorably with composers of the caliber of Borodin and Rimsky-Korsakoff. . . . In England, little is known of Tchaikovsky save as an instrumental composer. His operas, with one exception, have never reached the shores of England, and though *Eugene Oniegin* is occasionally performed in this country it has never won anything like the popularity of Tchaikovsky's symphonies. Nor are the bulk of his songs well known in England, though this is in all probability merely because of the difficulty of providing singable translations of the Russian words. However, it comes to this, that Tchaikovsky exists for English musicians only as a writer of orchestral and chamber music, and it is curious to note that the great popularity which he now enjoys in England dates only from the production of his *Symphonie Pathétique*. In his lifetime he paid several visits there. He conducted several of his works at British concerts, and he was invested with an honorary degree by the University of Cambridge. He was always received with politeness and respect, but the general public never seems to have realized for a moment that it was entertaining a great composer. Tchaikovsky's death and the production of the *Symphonie Pathétique* changed everything. The work itself, coupled with the romantic circumstances of its creation, the fact that it was the composer's swan song and appeared to contain in itself a suggestion of his approaching end—everything combined to captivate the popular fancy to an extraordinary degree. The *Symphonie Pathétique* became the rage; the mere announcement of its performance sufficed to pack the concert-rooms from floor to ceiling, and from this work we learnt gradually to appreciate Tchaikovsky's other compositions, so that now his symphonies, suites, and symphonic poems are among the most popular in the concert repertoire. It was not without good reason that the popular imagination, which Tchaikovsky's earlier works had left comparatively cold, was touched by the *Symphonie Pathétique*. It is without question the composer's most characteristic work, that into which he put most of himself. The fourth symphony may excel it in point of sheer picturesqueness, the fifth in poetic feeling, but in the sixth symphony we feel that strongly personal note which rarely fails to appeal to sympathetic souls. Tchaikovsky affixed no program to it, but the story of a tortured soul, seeking an anodyne for its misery in the rapture of pleasure and in the ecstasy of battle, and finally sinking to hopeless pessimism and suicide, is scarcely to be misread. That the lesson it teaches is noble or inspiring can certainly not be claimed, but the resources of music for expressing human emotions have rarely been employed in our time with more consummate success. When Tchaikovsky wrote the *Symphonie Pathétique* he had attained such mastery of his material as gives him a right to rank among great musicians. Whatever he chose to say, he could express with absolute certainty of touch. In the *Symphonie Pathétique* there are no effects that miss fire, no details that do not "come off." Never do we feel, as is the case in so much modern music, that the thought is struggling as it were for expression behind an intervening veil. The form of the work is new, the structure of the movements is unconstitutional, but every innovation in it is justified by success. As to its value as a work of art, we can admire it without being under any illusions with regard to its definite place in the history of music. It must stand as a very interesting and complete picture of a certain frame of mind, probably the completest expression in music of the *fin de siècle* pessimism that has ever been written. As such we to whom this attitude of mind is familiar find it enthralling, but future generations which know nothing of our psychological struggles will marvel at the enthusiasm which the *Symphonie Pathétique* excited. To them it will sound as empty and frigid as a Mendelssohn symphony does to our modern youth. It has not, it does not pretend to have, that nobility of thought, that breadth of mental view which alone can give immortality.

In Tchaikovsky's other works the same qualities and the same limitations are to be found. Of his earlier symphonies, the fourth and fifth alone can justly be compared to the *Pathétique*. There is fine music in the earlier three, but they do not show the same technical accomplishment. The fourth symphony is less subjective in feeling than the fifth and sixth, but it is no less brilliant as an example of the composer's extraordinary musicianship. In one of his letters the composer has given a sketch of the program on which he worked in this symphony—the idea of relentless fate which ever steps in to frustrate man in his quest for happiness. The first movement is said to illustrate the contrast between grim reality and flattering dreams, the second is a picture of the melancholy induced by retrospection, the third is merely a series of capricious arabesques not expressing any definite feelings, while the finale draws a moral by setting the rich healthy life of the people by the side of anemic culture. Tchaikovsky added, however, that this sketch was far from exhausting the poetical meaning of his symphony, and indeed it says nothing of what to Western ears is the most striking feature of the work, its strong national feeling. It has a barbaric splendor of color that is not common in Tchaikovsky, and shows how easily, when he chose, he could beat his "nationalist" fellow-countrymen on their own ground. For once the background is the most interesting part of the picture, and in this symphony we care a good deal less about the fate-ridden hero than about the gorgeous and ever-shifting scenes through which his destiny leads him. At one time we seem to be listening to the trumpets of Tamerlane on the trackless plains of Tartary, at another sweeping with the wild hordes of Scythia along the banks of the Volga. Then the night falls and the camp fires of a countless host twinkle beneath the stars. The hours are beguiled by the songs of bright-eyed Circassians and the sinuous dances of bejeweled slaves from the shores of the Caspian Sea. . . .

After the symphonies comes the long procession of Tchaikovsky's symphonic poems, gorgeous in their varied splendor; some of them, like *Manfred* and *Francesca da Rimini,* quivering with high-strung emotion; others, like *Romeo and Juliet* and *The Tempest,* brilliant tone-pictures gleaming with the ever-changing hues that the great master of orchestral color knew so supremely well how to group and contrast. Those who resent the lack of classical design in Tchaikovsky's symphonies will be disposed to find his choicest work in these symphonic poems, which frankly follow an architectural scheme of their own, guided by no fancied dependence upon the methods of the past. Their intrinsic value depends very much upon what the hearer expects to find in them. If he expects anything like a musical equivalent for the poems or plays upon which they are founded he will be grievously disappointed; if, on the contrary, he is in sympathy with Tchaikovsky's attitude of mind, he will find a curious interest in noting how the composer writes himself, as it were, upon his subject. There is very little of Shakespeare and a great deal of Tchaikovsky, for instance, in his *Hamlet, Tempest* and *Romeo.* Dante only furnished the theme of Tchaikovsky's *Francesca,* and if the spirit of Byron is stronger in *Manfred* it is only because Byron and Tchaikovsky have so much in common. *The Tempest,* which is an early work, is frankly a piece of scene-painting. Of the grandeur and profundity of Shakespeare's swan song there is hardly a suggestion. Tchaikovsky scarcely aims at more than a picturesque presentment of the landscape, nor can much more be said of his *Romeo,* a work from which the voice of sex, as from most of Tchaikovsky's writings, is curiously absent. But within their prescribed limits, both works are singularly brilliant examples of Tchaikovsky's happy treatment of the pictorial. In *Hamlet, Manfred, Francesca,* and the early symphonic poem *Fatum,* there is more of the Tchaikovsky of the symphonies; *Fatum,* in particular, seems like a kind of imperfect sketch for the *Symphonie Pathétique,* but on the whole the symphonic poems suggest a different point of view from that which Tchaikovsky gives us in his symphonies. They are as it were the comments on certain masterpieces of literature made by a man of striking personality, and serve to illuminate the character of the critic as much as the thing criticized. In *Hamlet* we meet once more the hero of the *Symphonie Pathétique,* lashing himself to heights of fevered emotion and sinking to depths of sunless gloom. There is but little of Dante in Tchaikovsky's *Paolo and Francesca,* outlined for a moment against a background of such ghastly terror as only one of the greatest masters of orchestral color could paint. It is Tchaikovsky who speaks through their lips, he who has drunk the cup of anguish to the dregs, and found it sweetened by no touch of pity.

Tchaikovsky is never more himself than in his chamber music, and this is a point well worth noting, since the great tone-painters of the orchestra rarely succeed within the austere limits of the quartet. Yet Tchaikovsky wrote nothing more intimately personal, nothing in which his peculiar vein of morbid feeling was more faithfully mirrored than his quartets in D and E flat and his great trio in A minor, while the lighter moods of his varied personality are depicted with infinite grace and charm in his string sextet, *Un Souvenir de Florence,* a work in which, as in his gay and brilliant *Italian Capriccio,* he paid an artist's tribute to the immortal enchantment of Italy. It is pleasant to find in these and similar works another Tchaikovsky than the storm-tossed pilgrim of fate whom we know so well in the *Symphonie Pathétique.* Tchaikovsky had no humor, but in his lighter moments there is the indescribable charm of a gentle nature that has kept the fragrance of childhood and loves the simple things of life for their own simplicity. Such we find him in his delightful *Nutcracker* ballet suite, a work that in its airy freshness and delicate sentiment seems like a tale of Hans Andersen translated into music. Two works more different in feeling than the *Nutcracker* suite and the *Symphonie Pathétique* it would be difficult to conceive, and the two together give a good idea of the range of Tchaikovsky's talent, and go far towards explaining the secret of his influence upon contemporary music. How great that influence has been it is hardly necessary to state. That Tchaikovsky's personality will be an abiding power in music, as Beethoven's and Mozart's have been, it is not to be believed. His view of life, summing up as it does a vein of thought and feeling characteristic of his epoch, will have little interest for generations to come; but the secrets that he has taught the world of music will be a possession for all time. His unique feeling for the subtler mysteries of orchestral color has opened our eyes to a new world of beauty. He has brought the East to the West on the wings of art, uniting the sheer glory and magnificence of color of the one to the instinct for form and design of the other. That this mystic marriage is celebrated in his music is a sufficient guarantee of the permanence of his place among the great masters of tone-painting.

XVI
FRANCK

CÉSAR FRANCK

Born at Liége, December 10, 1822. Lived chiefly in Paris; taught there at the Conservatoire, as professor of organ, and was organist at Ste. Clothilde. Died at Paris, November 8, 1890.

PRINCIPAL WORKS

VOCAL: Choral: *Ruth, Redemption, Rebecca, The Beatitudes, Psyche.* Operas: *Hulda, Ghisèle.* Songs.

INSTRUMENTAL: Symphony in D minor; symphonic poems, *Le Chasseur Maudit, Les Éolides, Les Djinns; Symphonic Variations,* for pianoforte and orchestra. Chamber music: piano quintet in F minor; string quartet in D minor; sonata for piano and violin in A major. Piano music: *Prelude, Chorale, and Fugue; Prelude, Aria, and Finale;* etc. Organ music: 6 pieces for organ, *Prelude, Fugue and Variations, Fantasia in C major, Grande Pièce Symphonique, Pastorale, Prière, Finale in B flat;* 3 Pieces for organ, *Fantasie in A, Cantabile, Piece Herioque,* 3 chorals in E, B minor, and A minor.

FRANCK

By Leland Hall

THE drift of romanticism toward realism is easy to trace in all the arts. There were, however, artists of all kinds who were caught up, so to speak, from the current into a life of the spirit, who championed neither the glory of the senses, as Wagner, nor the indomitable power of reason, as Brahms, but preserved a serenity and calm, a sort of confident, nearly ascetic rapture, elevated above the turmoil of the world, standing not with nor against, but floating above. Such an artist in music was César Franck, growing up almost unnoticed between Wagner and Brahms, now to be ranked as one of the greatest composers of the second half of the century. He is as different from them as they are from each other. Liszt, the omniscient, knew of him, had heard him play the organ in the church of Ste. Clothilde, where in almost monastic seclusion the greater part of his life flowed on, had likened him to the great Sebastian Bach, had gone away marvelling; but only a small band of pupils knew him intimately and the depth of his genius as a composer.

His life was retired. He was indifferent to lack of appreciation. When, through the efforts of his devoted disciples, his works were at rare intervals brought to public performance, he was quite forgetful of the cold, often hostile, audience, intent only to compare the sound of his music as he heard it with the thought he had had in his soul, happy if the sound were what he had conceived it would be. Of envy, meanness, jealousy, of all the darker side of life, in fact, he seems to have taken no account. Nor by imagination could he picture it, nor express it in his music, which is unfailingly luminous and exalted. Most strik-

By arrangement with the author.

ing in his nature was a gentle, unwavering, confident candor, and in his music there is scarcely a hint of doubt, of inquiring, or of struggle. It suggests inevitably the cathedral, the joyous calm of religious faith, spiritual exaltation, even radiance.

His life, though not free in early years from hardship, was relatively calm and uneventful. He was born in Liége in December, 1822, nine years after Wagner, eleven years before Brahms, and from the start was directed to music by his father. In the course of his early training at Liége he acquired remarkable skill as a virtuoso, and his father had hopes of exploiting his gifts in wide concert tours. In 1835 he moved with his family to Paris and remained there seven years; at the end of which, having amazed his instructors and judges at the Conservatoire, among whom, be it noted, the venerable Cherubini, and won a special prize, he was called from further study by the dictates of his father and went back to Liége to take up his career as a concert pianist. For some reason this project was abandoned at the end of two years, and he returned to Paris, there to pass the remainder of his life.

At first he was organist at the church of Notre Dame de Lorette, later at Ste. Clothilde, and in 1872 he was appointed professor of the organ at the Conservatoire. To the end of his life he gave lessons in organ and pianoforte playing, here and there, and in composition to a few chosen pupils. He was elected member of the Legion of Honor in 1885; not, however, in recognition of his gifts as a composer, but only of his work as professor of organ at the Conservatoire. He died on the 8th of November, 1890. At the time of his marriage, in 1848, he resolved to save from the pressure of work to gain a livelihood an hour or two of every day for composition—time, as he himself expressed it, to think. The hours chosen were preferably in the early morning and to the custom, never broken in his lifetime, we owe his great compositions, penned in those few moments of rest from a busy life. He wrote in all forms, operas, oratorios, cantatas, works for piano, for orchestra, and chamber music. It is significant that in several fields his output was small: he wrote only one symphony, one string quartet, one piano quintet, one violin sonata.

With the exception of a few early pieces for piano all his work bears the stamp of his personality. Like Brahms, he has pronounced idiosyncrasies, among which his fondness for shifting harmonies is the most constantly obvious. The ceaseless alteration of chords, the almost un-broken gliding by half-steps, the lithe sinuousness of all the inner voices seem to wrap his music in a veil, to render it intangible and mystical. Diatonic passages are rare, all is chromatic. Parallel to this is his use of short phrases, which alone are capable of being treated in this shifting manner. His melodies are almost invariably dissected, they seldom are built up in broad design. They are resolved into their finest motifs and as such are woven and twisted into the close iridescent harmonic fabric with bewildering skill. All is in subtle movement. Yet there is a com-plete absence of sensuousness, even, for the most part, of dramatic fire. The overpowering climaxes to which he builds are never a frenzy of emotion; they are superbly calm and exalted. The structure of his music is strangely inorganic. His material does not develop. He adds phrase upon phrase, detail upon detail, with astonishing power to knit and weave closely what comes with what went before. His extraordinary polyphonic skill seems inborn, native to the man. Arthur Coquard said of him that he thought the most complicated things in music quite naturally. Imitation, canon, augmentation, and diminution, the most complex problems of the science of music, he solves without effort. The perfect canon in the last movement of the violin sonata sounds simple and spontaneous. The shifting, intangible harmonies, the minute melo-dies, the fine fabric as of a goldsmith's carving, are all the work of a mystic, indescribably pure and radiant. Agitating, complex rhythms are rare. The second movement of the violin sonata and the last move-ment of the *Prelude, Aria, and Finale* are exceptional. The heat of pas-sion is seldom felt. Faith and serene light prevail, a music, it has been said, at once the sister of prayer and of poetry. His music, in short, wrote Gustave Derepas, "leads us from egoism to love, by the path of the true mysticism of Christianity; from the world to the soul, from the soul to God."

His form, as has been said, is not organic, but he gives to all his music a unity and compactness by using the same thematic material throughout the movements of a given composition. For example, in the first movement of the *Prelude, Chorale, and Fugue* for piano, the theme of the fugue which constitutes the last movement is plainly suggested, and the climax of the last movement is built up out of this fugue theme woven with the great movement of the chorale. In the first movement

of the *Prelude, Aria, and Finale,* likewise for piano, the theme of the
Finale is used as counterpoint; in the Aria again the same use is made
of it; in the Finale the Aria theme is reintroduced, and the coda at the
end is built up of the principal theme of the Prelude and a theme taken
from the closing section of the Aria. The four movements of the violin
sonata are most closely related thematically; the symphony, too, is
dominated by one theme, and the theme which opens the string quartet
closes it as well. This uniting of the several movements of a work on
a large scale by employing throughout the same material was more consistently cultivated by Franck than by any other composer. The concerto for piano and orchestra in E flat by Liszt is constructed on the same
principle; the D minor symphony of Schumann also, and it is suggested
in the first symphony of Brahms, but these are exceptions. Germs of
such a relationship between movements in the cyclic forms were in the
last works of Beethoven. In Franck they developed to great proportion.

The fugue in the *Prelude, Chorale, and Fugue* and the canon in the
last movement of the violin sonata are superbly built, and his restora-
tion of strict forms to works in several movements finds a precedent only
in Beethoven and once in Mozart. The treatment of the variation form
in the *Variations Symphoniques* for piano and orchestra is no less masterly than his treatment of fugue and canon, but it can hardly be said
that he excelled either Schumann or Brahms in this branch of composition.

Franck was a great organist and all his work is as clearly influenced
by organ technique as the works of Sebastian Bach were before him.
"His orchestra," Julien Tiersot wrote in an article published in *Le
Ménéstrel* for October 23, 1904, "is sonorous and compact, the orchestra of an organist. He employs especially the two contrasting elements of strings (eight-foot stops) and brass (great-organ). The wood-
wind is in the background. This observation encloses a criticism, and his
method could not be given as a model; it robs the orchestra of much
variety of coloring, which is the richness of the modern art. But we
ought to consider it as characteristic of the manner of César Franck,
which alone suffices to make such use legitimate." Undeniably the
sensuous coloring of the Wagnerian school is lacking, though Franck
devoted himself almost passionately at one time to the study of Wagner's scores; yet, as in the case of Brahms, Franck's scoring, peculiarly

his own, is fitting to the quality of his inspiration. There is no suggestion of the warmth of the senses in any of his music. Complete mastery of the art of vivid warm tone-coloring belongs only to those descended from Weber, and preëminently to Wagner.

The works for the pianoforte (and those for strings as well) are thoroughly influenced by organ technique. The movement of the rich, solid basses, and the impracticably wide spaces call urgently for the supporting pedals of the organ. Yet they are by no means unsuited to the instruments for which they were written. If when played they suggest the organ to the listener, and the chorale in the *Prelude, Chorale, and Fugue* is especially suggestive, the reason is not to be found in any solecism, but in the religious spirit that breathes from all Franck's works and transports the listener to the shades of vast cathedral aisles. Among his most sublime works are three Chorale Fantasias for organ, written not long before he died. These, it may safely be assumed, are among the few contributions to the literature for the organ which approach the inimitable master-works of Sebastian Bach.

There are three oratorios, to use the term loosely, *Ruth, The Redemption,* and *The Beatitudes*, belonging respectively in the three periods in which Franck's life and musical development naturally fall. All were coldly received during his lifetime. *Ruth,* written when he was but twenty-four years old, is in the style of the classical oratorios. *The Redemption,* too, still partakes of the half dramatic, half epic character of the oratorio; but in *The Beatitudes,* his masterpiece, if one must be chosen, the dramatic element is almost wholly lacking, and he has created almost a new art form. To set Christ's sermon on the mount to music was a tremendous undertaking, and the great length of the work will always stand in the way of its universal acceptance; but here more than anywhere else Franck's peculiar gift of harmony has full force in the expression of religious rapture and the mysticism of the devout and childlike believer.

It is curious to note the inability of Franck's genius to express wild and dramatic emotion. Among his works for orchestra and for orchestra and piano are several that may take rank as symphonic poems, *Les Éolides, Le Chasseur Maudit,* and *Les Djinns,* the last two based upon gruesome poems, all three failing to strike the listener cold. The symphony with chorus, later rearranged as a suite, *Psyche,* is an exquisitely pure conception, wholly spiritual. The operas *Hulda* and *Ghisèle* were performed only after his death and failed to win a place in the repertory of opera houses.

It is this strange absence of genuinely dramatic and sensuous elements from Franck's music which gives it its quite peculiar stamp, the quality which appeals to us as a sort of poetry of religion. And it is this same lack which leads one to say that he grows up with Wagner and Brahms and yet is not of a piece with either of them. He had an extraordinarily refined technique of composition, but it was perhaps more the technique of the goldsmith than that of the sculptor. His works impress by fineness of detail, not, for all their length and remarkable adherence of structure, by breadth of design. His is intensely an introspective art, which weaves about the simplest subject and through every measure most intricate garlands of chromatic harmony. It is a music which is apart from life, spiritual and exalted. It does not reflect the life of the body, nor that of the sovereign mind, but the life of the spirit. By so reading it we come to understand his own attitude in regard to it, which took no thought of how it impressed the public, but only of how it matched in performance, in sound, his soul's image of it.

With Wagner, Brahms, and César Franck the romantic movement in music comes to an end. The impulse which gave it life came to its ultimate forms in their music and was forever gone. It has washed on only like a broken wave over the works of most of their successors down to the present day.

XVII

DEBUSSY AND RAVEL

CLAUDE DEBUSSY

Born at St. Germain, August 22, 1862. Studied at Paris Conservatoire and in 1884 won Prix de Rome with his cantata, L'Enfant Prodigue. *Lived chiefly in Paris, and died there, March 26, 1918.*

PRINCIPAL WORKS

VOCAL: Cantatas: *L'Enfant Prodigue, La Demoiselle Elue;* and the dramatic cantata, *Le Martyre de Saint-Sébastien.* Opera: *Pelléas et Mélisande. Proses Lyriques,* for soprano; and other series of songs, including *Ariettes, Chansons de Bilitis, Fêtes Galantes,* etc.

INSTRUMENTAL: Symphonic poem, *La Mer;* orchestral prelude, *L'Après-midi d'un Faune;* 3 nocturnes for orchestra, *Nuages, Fêtes, Sirènes,* the last with women's chorus. *Images,* three orchestral pieces including *Gigues, Ibéria,* and *Rondes de Printemps;* Fantasie for piano and orchestra; 2 dances for harp and orchestra. Chamber music: string quartet; sonata for piano and violin; sonata for piano and cello. Piano works (principal compositions only): 2 *Arabesques; Suite Bergamásque* (including *Clair de Lune*); *Pour le Piano* (suite); *Estampes* (suite including *Pagodes, La Soirée dans Grenade, Jardins sous la Pluie*); *Images* (suite 1, including *Reflets dans l'Eau, Hommage à Rameau, Mouvement*); *Images* (suite 2, including *Cloches à travers les feuilles, Et la Lune descend sur le Temple qui Fut, Poissons d'Or*); *Douze Préludes* (first series, *La Cathédrale Engloutie*); etc. *Douze Préludes* (second series); *La Boîte à joujoux* (ballet for children).

MAURICE RAVEL

Born at Ciboure, Basses Pyrénées, March 7, 1875. (Some commentators, recognizing a Spanish idiom in his work, ascribe it to his origin.) A pupil of Fauré at the Paris Conservatoire; won second Prix de Rome, 1901; has lived chiefly near Paris.

PRINCIPAL WORKS

Orchestral music includes the ballet *Daphnis et Chloé; Adelaïde; Rapsodie Espagnole, La Valse, poème choreographique; Boléro; Tzigane* for violin and orchestra; songs with orchestral accompaniment, *Schéhérazade* and *Trois Poèmes de Mallarmé*. Ravel has orchestrated several of his piano pieces, as well as Moussorgsky's *Pictures at an Exhibition*. Piano concerto; and a piano concerto for the left hand. A comic opera, *L'heure Espagnole*. Songs, including *Histoires Naturelles*, etc. Chamber music, including a string quartet and a piano trio; Introduction and Allegro for strings and winds; sonata for violin and cello. Piano music: *Pavane pour une Infante défunte; Jeux d'Eau; Valses nobles et sentimentales; Menuet antique; Miroirs*; a *Sonatine; Gaspard de la Nuit; Le Tombeau de Couperin* (orchestrated); *Ma Mère l'Oye* (piano for 4 hands, later orchestrated).

DEBUSSY AND RAVEL

By Paul Rosenfeld

DEBUSSY

DEBUSSY'S music is our own. All artistic forms lie dormant in the soul, and there is no work of art actually foreign to us, nor can such a one appear, in all the future ages of the world. But the music of Debussy is proper to us, in our day, as is no other, and might stand before all time our symbol. For it lived in us before it was born, and after birth returned upon us like a release. Even at a first encounter the style of *Pelléas* was mysteriously familiar. It made us feel that we had always needed such rhythms, such luminous chords, such limpid phrases, that we perhaps had even heard them, sounding faintly, in our imaginations. The music seemed as old as our sense of selfhood. It seemed but the exquisite recognition of certain intense and troubling and appeasing moments that we had already encountered. It seemed fashioned out of certain ineluctable, mysterious experiences that had budded, ineffably sad and sweet, from out our lives, and had made us new, and set us apart, and that now, at the music's breath, at a half-whispered note, at the unclosing of a rhythm, the flowering of a cluster of tones out of the warm still darkness, were arisen again in the fullness of their stature and become ours entirely.

For Debussy is of all musicians the one amongst us most fully. He is here, in our midst, in the world of the city. There is about him none of the unworldliness, the aloofness, the superhumanity that distances so many of the other composers from us. We need not imagine him in exotic singing robes, nor in classical garments, nor in any strange and

From the author's *Musical Portraits*, by permission of Harcourt, Brace and Co.

outmoded and picturesque attire, to recognize in him the poet. He is
the modern poet just because the modern civilian garb is so naturally
his. He is the normal man, living our own manner of life. We seem
to know him as we know ourselves. His experiences are but our own,
intensified by his poet's gift. Or, if they are not already ours, they will
become so. He seems almost ourselves as he passes through the city
twilight, intent upon some errand upon which we, too, have gone,
journeying a road which we ourselves have travelled. We know the room
in which he lives, the windows from which he gazes, the moments which
come upon him there in the silence of the lamp. For he has captured
in his music what is distinguished in the age's delight and tragedy. All
the fine sensuality, all the Eastern pleasure in the infinite daintiness and
warmth of nature, all the sudden, joyous discovery of color and touch
that made men feel as though neither had been known before, are contained in it. It, too, is full of images of the "earth of the liquid and
slumbering trees," the "earth of departed sunset," the "earth of the
vitreous pour of the full moon just tinged with blue." It is full of material loveliness, plies itself to innumerable dainty shells—to the som-
nolence of the Southern night, to the hieratic gesture of temple dancers,
to the fall of lamplight into the dark, to the fantastic gush of fireworks,
to the romance of old mirrors and faded brocades and Saxony clocks,
to the green young panoply of spring. And just as it gives again the
age's consciousness of the delicious robe of earth, so, too, it gives again
its sense of weariness and powerlessness and oppression. The nineteenth
century had been loud with blare and rumors and the vibration of
colossal movements, and man had apparently traversed vast distances
and explored titanic heights and abysmal depths. And yet, for all the
glare, the earth was darker. The light was miasmic only. The life of
man seemed as ever a brief and sad and simple thing, the stretching
of impotent hands, unable to grasp and hold; the interlacing of shadows;
the unclosing, a moment before nightfall, of exquisite and fragile blos-
soms. The sense of the infirmity of life, the consciousness that it had
no more than the signification of a dream with passing lights, or halting
steps in the snow, or an old half-forgotten story, had mixed a deep wist-
fulness and melancholy into the very glamour of the globe, and become
heavier itself for all the sweetness of earth. And Debussy has fixed the
two in their confusion.

He has permeated music completely with his impressionistic sensibility. His style is an image of this our pointillistically feeling era. With him impressionism achieves a perfect musical form. Structurally, the music of Debussy is a fabric of exquisite and poignant moments, each full and complete in itself. His wholes exist entirely in their parts, in their atoms. If his phrases, rhythms, lyric impulses, do contribute to the formation of a single thing, they yet are extraordinarily independent and significant in themselves. No chord, no theme, is subordinate. Each one exists for the sake of its own beauty, occupies the universe for an instant, then merges and disappears. The harmonies are not, as in other compositions, preparations. They are apparently an end in themselves, flow in space, and then change hue, as a shimmering stuff changes. For all its golden earthiness, the style of Debussy is the most liquid and impalpable of musical styles. It is forever gliding, gleaming, melting; crystallizing for an instant in some savory phrase, then moving quiveringly onward. It is well-nigh edgeless. It seems to flow through our perceptions as water flows through fingers. The iridescent bubbles that float upon it burst if we but touch them. It is forever suggesting water —fountains and pools, the glistening spray and heaving bosom of the sea. Or, it shadows forth the formless breath of the breeze, of the storm, of perfumes, or the play of sun and moon. His orchestration invariably produces all that is cloudy and diaphanous in each instrument. He makes music with flakes of light, with bright motes of pigment. His palette glows with the sweet, limpid tints of a Monet or a Pissaro or a Renoir. His orchestra sparkles with iridescent fires, with divided tones, with delicate violets and argents and shades of rose. The sound of the piano, usually but the ringing of flat colored stones, at his touch becomes fluid, velvety, and dense, takes on the properties of satins and liqueurs. The pedal washes new tint after new tint over the keyboard. *Reflets dans l'eau* has the quality of sheeny blue satin, of cloud pictures tumbling in gliding water. Blue fades to green and fades back again to blue in the middle section of *Hommage à Rameau*. Bright, cold moonlight slips through *Et la lune descend sur le temple que fut;* ruddy sparks glitter in *Mouvement* with its Petrushka-like joy; the piano is liquid and luminous and aromatic in *Cloches à travers les feuilles*.

Yet there is no uncertainty, no mistiness in his form, as there is in that of some of the other impressionists. His music is classically firm, classically precise and knit. His lyrical, shimmering structures are perfectly fashioned. The line never hesitates, never becomes lost nor involved. It proceeds directly, clearly, passing through jewels and clots of color, and fusing them into the mass. The trajectory never breaks. The music is always full of its proper weight and timbre. It can be said quite without exaggeration that his best work omits nothing, neglects nothing, that every component element is justly treated. His little pieces occupy a space as completely as the most massive and grand of compositions. A composition like *Nuages,* the first of the three nocturnes for orchestra, while taking but five minutes in performance, outweighs any number of compositions that last an hour. *L'Après-midi d'un faune* is inspired and new, marvelously, at every measure. The three little pieces that comprise the first set of *Images* for piano will probably outlast half of what Liszt has written for the instrument. *Pelléas* will some day be studied for its miraculous invention, its classical moderation and balance and truth, for its pure diction and economical orchestration, quite as the scores of Gluck are studied to-day.

For Debussy is, of all the artists who have made music in our time, the most perfect. Other musicians, perhaps even some of the contemporary, may exhibit a greater heroism, a greater staying power and indefatigability. Nevertheless, in his sphere he is every inch as perfect a workman as the greatest. Within his limits he was as pure a craftsman as the great John Sebastian in his. The difference between the two is the difference of their ages and races, not the difference of their artistry. For few composers can match with their own Debussy's perfection of taste, his fineness of sensibility, his poetic rapture, and profound awareness of beauty. Few have been more graciously rounded and balanced than he, have been, like him, so fine that nothing which they could do could be tasteless and insignificant and without grace. Few musicians have been more nicely sensible of their gift, better acquainted with themselves, surer of the character and limitations of their genius. Few have been as perseverantly essential, have managed to sustain their emotion and invention so steadily at a height. The music of Debussy is full of purest, most delicate poesy. Perhaps only Bach and Moussorgsky have as invariably found phrases as pithy and inclusive and final as those with which *Pelléas* is strewn, phrases that with a few simple notes epitomize profound and exquisite emotions, and are indeed the word.

There are moments in Debussy's work when each note opens a prospect. There are moments when the music of *Pelléas,* the fine fluid line of sound, the melodic moments that merge and pass and vanish into one another, become the gleaming rims that circumscribe vast darkling forms. There are portions of the drama that are like the moments of human intercourse when single syllables unseal deep reservoirs. The tenderness manifest here is scarcely to be duplicated in musical art. And tenderness, after all, is the most intense of all emotions.

A thousand years of culture live in this fineness. In these perfect gestures, in this grace, this certainty of choice, this justice of values, this simple, profound, delicate language, there live on thirty generations of gentlefolk. Thirty generations of cavaliers and dames who developed the arts of life in the mild and fruitful valleys of "the pleasant land of France" speak here. The gentle sunlight and gentle shadow, the mild winters and mild summers of the Ile de France, the plentiful fruits of the earth, the excitement of the vine, contributed to making this being beautifully balanced, reserved, refined. The instruction and cultivation of the classic and French poets and thinkers, Virgil and Racine and Marivaux, Catullus and Montaigne and Chateaubriand, the chambers of the Hôtel de Rambouillet, the gardens and galleries of Versailles, the immense drawing-room of eighteenth century Paris, helped form this spirit. In all this man's music one catches sight of the long foreground, the long cycles of preparation. In every one of his works, from the most imposing to the least, from the String Quartet and *Pelléas* to the gracile, lissome little waltz, *Le plus que lent,* there is manifest the Latin genius nurtured and molded and developed by the fertile, tranquil soil of France.

And in his art, the gods of classical antiquity live again. Debussy is much more than merely the sensuous Frenchman. He is the man in whom the old Pagan voluptuousness, the old untroubled delight in the body, warred against so long by the black brood of monks and transformed by them during centuries into demoniacal and hellish forms, is free and pure and sweet once more. They once were nymphs and naiads and goddesses, the Quartet and *L'Après-midi d'un faune* and *Sirènes.* They once wandered through the glades of Ionia and Sicily, and gladdened men with their golden sensuality, and bewitched them with the thought of "the breast of the nymph in the brake." For they are full of the wonder and sweetness of the flesh, of flesh tasted deliciously and enjoyed not in closed rooms, behind secret doors and under the shameful pall of the night, but out in the warm, sunny open, amid grasses and scents and the buzzing of insects, the waving of branches, the wandering of clouds. The Quartet is alive, quivering with light, and with joyous animality. It moves like a young fawn; spins the gayest, most silken, most golden of spider webs; fills one with the delights of taste and smell and sight and touch. In the most glimmering, floating of poems, *L'Après-midi d'un faune*, there is caught magically by the climbing, chromatic flute, the drowsy pizzicati of the strings, and the languorous sighing of the horns, the atmosphere of the daydream, the sleepy warmth of the sunshot herbage, the divine apparition, the white wonder of arms and breasts and thighs. The lento movement of *Ibéria* is like some drowsy, disheveled gipsy. Even *Le plus que lent* is full of the goodness of the flesh, is like some slender young girl with unclosing bosom. And in *Sirènes,* something like the eternal divinity, the eternal beauty of woman's body, is celebrated. It is as though on the rising, falling, rising, sinking tides of the poem, on the waves of the glamorous feminine voices, on the aphrodisiac swell of the sea, the white Anadyomene herself, with her galaxy of tritons and naiads, approached earth's shores once more.

If any musical task is to be considered as having been accomplished, it is that of Debussy. For he wrote the one book that every great artist writes. He established a style irrefragably, made musical impressionism as legitimate a thing as any of the great styles. That he had more to make than that one contribution is doubtful. His art underwent no radical changes. His style was mature already in the Quartet and in *Proses lyriques,* and had its climax in *Pelléas,* its orchestral deployment in *Nocturnes* and *La Mer* and *Ibéria,* its pianistic expression in the two volumes of *Images* for pianoforte. Whatever the refinement of the incidental music to *Le Martyre de Saint-Sébastien,* Debussy never really transgressed the limits set for him by his first great works. And so, even if his long illness caused the deterioration, the hardening, the formularization, so evident in his most recent work, the sonatas, the *Epigrammes, En blanc et noir,* and the *Berceuse héroïque,* and deprived us of much delightful art, neither it nor his death actually robbed us of some radical development which we might reasonably have expected. The chief that he had to give he had given. What his age had demanded of him, an art that it might hold far from the glare and tumult, an art into which it could retreat, an art which could compensate it for a life become too cruel and demanding, he had produced. He had essentially fulfilled himself.

The fact that *Pelléas* is the most eloquent of all Debussy's works and his eternal sign does not, then, signify that he did not grow during the remainder of his life. A complex of determinants made of his music-drama the fullest expression of his genius, decreed that he should be living most completely at the moment he composed it. The very fact that in it Debussy was composing music for the theatre made it certain that his artistic sense would produce itself at its mightiest in the work. For it entailed the statement of his opposition to Wagner. The fact that it was music conjoined with speech made it certain that Debussy, so full of the French classical genius, would through contact with the spoken word, through study of its essential quality, be aided and compelled to a complete realization of a fundamentally French idiom. And then Maeterlinck's little play offered itself to his genius as a unique auxiliary. It, too, is full of the sense of the shadowiness of things that weighed upon Debussy, has not a little of the accent of the time. This *"vieille et triste légende de la forêt"* is alive with images, such as the old and somber castle inhabited by aging people and lying lost amid sunless forests, the rose that blooms in the shadow underneath Mélisande's casement, Mélisande's hair that falls farther than her arms can reach, the black tarn that broods beneath the castle-vaults and breathes death, Golaud's anguished search for truth in the prattle of the child, that could not but call a profound response from Debussy's imagination. But, above all, it was the figure of Mélisande herself that made him pour himself completely into the setting of the play. For that figure permitted Debussy to give himself completely in the creation of his ideal image. The music is all Mélisande, all Debussy's love-woman. It is she that the music reveals from the moment Mélisande rises from among the rocks shrouded in the mystery of her golden hair. It is she the music limns from the very beginning of the work. The entire score is but what a man might feel toward a woman that was his, and yet, like all women, strange and mysterious and unknown to him. The music is like the stripping of some perfect flower, petal upon petal. There are moments when it is all that lies between two people, and is the fullness of their knowledge. It is the perfect sign of an experience.

And so, since Debussy's art could have no second climax, it was in the order of things that the works succeeding upon his masterpiece should be relatively less important. Nevertheless, the ensuing poems and songs and piano-pieces, with the exception of those written during those years when Debussy could have said with Rameau, his master, "From day to day my taste improves. But I have lost all my genius," are by little less perfect and astounding pieces of work. His music is like the peaks of a mountain range, of which one of the first and nearest is the highest, while the others appear scarcely less high. And they are some of the bluest, the loveliest, the most shining that stretch through the region of modern music. It will be long before humankind has exhausted their beauty.

RAVEL

Ravel and Debussy are of one lineage. They both issue from what is deeply, graciously temperate in the genius of France. Across the span of centuries, they touch hands with the men who first expressed that silver temperance in tone, with Claude Le Jeune, with Rameau and Couperin and the other clavecinists. Undiverted by the changes of revolutionary times, they continue, in forms conditioned by the modern feeling for color, for tonal complexity, for supple and undulant rhythm, the high tradition of the elder music.

Claude Le Jeune wrote motets; the eighteenth century masters wrote gavottes and rigadoons, forlanas and chaconnes, expressed themselves in courtly dances and other set and severe forms. Ravel and Debussy compose in more liberal and naturalistic fashion. And yet, the genius that animates all this music is single. It is as though all these artists, born so many hundred years apart from each other, had contemplated the pageant of their respective times from the same point of view. It is as though they faced the problems of composition with essentially the same attitudes, with the same demands and reservations. The new music, like the old, is the work of men above all reverent of the art of life itself. It is the work of men of the sort who crave primarily in all conduct restraint, and who insist on poise and good sense. They regard all things humanly, and bring their regard for the social values to the making of their art. Indeed, the reaction of Debussy from Wagnerism was chiefly the reaction of a profoundly socialized and aristocratic sensibility outraged by over-emphasis and unrestraint. The men of whom he is typical throughout the ages never forget the world and its decencies and its demands. And yet they do not eschew the large, the grave, the poignant. The range of human passions is present in their music, too, even though many of them have not had gigantic powers, or entertained emotions as grand and intense as the world-consuming, world-annihilating mysticism of a Bach, for instance. But it is shadowed forth more than stated. If many of them have been deeply melancholy, they have nevertheless taken counsel with themselves, and have said, with Baudelaire:

"Sois sage, ô ma douleur, et tiens-toi plus tranquille."

All expression is made in low, aristocratic tone, in grisaille. Most often it achieves itself through a silvery grace. It is normal for these men to be profound through grace, to be amusing and yet artistically upright. It is normal for them to articulate nicely. High in their consciousness there flame always the commandments of clarity, of delicacy, of precision. Indeed, so repeatedly have temperaments of this character appeared in France, not only in her music, but also in her letters and other arts, from the time of the Pléiade, to that of Charles Louis Philippe and André Gide and Henri de Regnier, that it is difficult not to hold theirs the centrally, essentially French tradition, and not to see in men like Rabelais only the Frank, and in men like Berlioz only the atavism to Gallo-Roman times.

But it is not only the spirit of French classicism that Ravel and Debussy inherit. In one respect their art is the continuation of the music that came to a climax in the works of Haydn and Mozart. It is subtle and intimate, and restores to the auditor the great creative rôle assigned to him by so much of the music before Beethoven. The music of Haydn and Mozart defers to its hearer. It seeks deliberately to enlist his activity. It relies for its significance largely upon his contribution. The music itself carries only a portion of the composer's intention. It carries only enough to ignite and set functioning the auditor's imagination. To that person is reserved the pleasure of fathoming the intention, of completing the idea adumbrated by the composer. For Haydn and Mozart did not desire that the listener assume a completely passive attitude. They had too great a love and respect of their fellows. They were eager to secure their collaboration, had confidence that they could comprehend all that the music intimated, regarded them as equals in the business of creation. But the music written since their time has forced upon the hearer a more and more passive rôle. The composers arrogated to themselves, to varying extents, the greater part of the activity; insisted upon giving all, of doing the larger share of the labor. The old intimacy was lost; with Wagner the intellectual game of the *leit-motif* system was substituted for the creative exercise. The art of Ravel and Debussy returns to the earlier strategy. It makes the largest effort to excite the creative imagination, that force which William Blake identified with the Saviour Himself. It strives continually to lure it into the most energetic participation. And because Ravel and Debussy have this incitement steadily in view, their music is a music of few strokes, comparable indeed to the pictural art of Japan which it so often recalls. It is the music of suggestion, of sudden kindlings, brief starts and lines, small forms. It never insists. It only pricks. It instigates, begins, leaves off, and then continues, rousing to action the hearer's innate need of an aim and an order and meaning in things. Its subtle gestures, its brief, sharp, delicate phrases, its quintessentiality, are like the thrusting open of doors into the interiors of the conscience, the opening of windows on long vistas, are like the breaking of light upon obscured memories and buried emotions. They are like the unsealing of springs long sealed, suffering them to flow again in the night. And for a glowing instant, they transform the auditor from a passive receiver into an artist.

And there is much besides that Ravel and Debussy have in common. They have each been profoundly influenced by Russian music, *Daphnis et Chloé* showing the influence of Borodin, *Pelléas et Mélisande* that of Moussorgsky. Both have made wide discoveries in the field of harmony. Both have felt the power of outlying and exotic modes. Both have been profoundly impressed by the artistic currents of the Paris about them. Both, like so many other French musicians, have been kindled by the bright colors of Spain, Ravel in his orchestral Rhapsody, in his one-act opera *L'Heure Espagnole* and in the piano-piece in the collection

Miroirs entitled *Alborada del Graciozo,* Debussy in *Ibéria* and in some
of his preludes. Indeed, a parallelism exists throughout their respective
works. Debussy writes *Hommage à Rameau;* Ravel *Le Tombeau de Couperin.* Debussy writes *Le Martyre de Saint-Sébastien;* Ravel projects an
oratorio, *Saint-François d'Assise.* Ravel writes the *Ondine* of the collection entitled *Gaspard de la Nuit;* Debussy follows it with the *Ondine*
of his second volume of preludes. Both, during the same year, conceive and execute the idea of setting to music the lyrics of Mallarmé
entitled *Soupir* and *Placet futile.* Nevertheless, this fact constitutes Ravel
in no wise the imitator of Debussy. His work is by no means, as some
of our critics have made haste to insist, a counterfeit of his elder's. Did
the music of Ravel not demonstrate that he possesses a sensibility quite
distinct from Debussy's, in some respects less fine, delicious, lucent,
in others perhaps even more deeply engaging; did it not represent a
distinct development from Debussy's art in a direction quite its own,
one might with justice speak of a discipleship. But in the light of Ravel's
actual accomplishment, of his large and original and attractive gift, of
the magistral craftsmanship that has shown itself in so many musical
forms, from the song and the sonatine to the string quartet and the orchestral poem, of the talent that has revealed itself increasingly from
year to year, and that not even the war and the experience of the
trenches has driven underground, the parallelism is to be regarded as
necessitated by the spiritual kinship of the men, and by their con-
temporaneity.

And, certainly, nothing so much reveals Ravel the peer of Debussy
as the fact that he has succeeded so beautifully in manifesting what is
peculiar to him. For he is by ten years Debussy's junior, and were he
less positive an individuality, less original a temperament, less fully the
genius, he could never have realized himself. There would have descended upon him the blight that has fallen upon so many of the
younger Parisian composers less determinate than he and like himself
made of one stuff with Debussy. He, too, would have permitted the
art of the older and well-established man to impose upon him. He, too,
would have betrayed his own cause in attempting to model himself upon
the other man. But Debussy has not swerved nor hampered Ravel any
more than has his master, Gabriel Fauré. He is too sturdily set in his
own direction. From the very commencement of his career, from the

time when he wrote the soft and hesitating and nevertheless already very personal *Pavane pour une Infante défunte,* he has maintained himself proudly against his great collateral, just as he has maintained himself against what is false and epicene in the artistic example of Fauré. Within their common limits, he has realized himself as essentially as Debussy has done. Their music is the new and double blossoming of the classical French tradition. From the common ground, they stretch out each in a different direction, and form the greater contrast to each other because of all they have in common.

The intelligence that fashioned the music of Debussy was one completely aware, conscious of itself, flooded with light in its most secret places, set four-square in the whirling universe. Few artists have been as sure of their intention as Debussy always was. The man could fix with precision the most elusive emotions, could describe the sensations that flow on the borderland of consciousness, vaguely, and that most of us cannot grasp for very dizziness. He could write music as impalpable as that of the middle section of *Ibéria,* in which the very silence of the night, the caresses of the breeze, seem to have taken musical flesh. Before the body of his work, so clear and lucid in its definition, so perfect in its organization, one thinks perforce of a world created out of the flying chaos beneath him by a god. We are given to know precisely of what stuff the soul of Debussy was made, what its pilgrimages were, in what adventure it sought itself out. We know precisely wherein it saw reflected its visage, in "water stilled at even," in the angry gleam of sunset on wet leaves, in wild and headlong gipsy rhythms, in moonfire, shimmering stuffs and flashing spray, in the garish lights and odors of the Peninsula, in rain fallen upon flowering parterres, in the melancholy march of clouds, the golden pomp and ritual of the church, the pools and gardens and pavilions reared for its delight by the delicate Chinese soul, in earth's thousand scents and shells and colors. For Debussy has set these adventures before us in their fullness. Before he spoke, he had dwelt with his experiences till he had plumbed them fully, till he had seen into and around and behind them clearly. And so we perceive them in their essences, in their eternal aspects. The designs are the very curve of the ecstasy. They are sheerly delimited. The notes appear to bud one out of the other, to follow each other out of the sheerest necessity, to have an original timbre, to fix a matter never known before, that can never live again. Every moment in a representative composition of Debussy's is logical and yet new. Few artists have more faultlessly said what they set out to say.

Ravel is by no means as perfect an artist. He has not the clear self-consciousness, the perfect recognition of limits. His music has not the absolute completeness of Debussy's. It is not that he is not a marvelous craftsman, greatly at ease in his medium. It is that Ravel dares, and dares continually; seeks passionately to bring his entire body into play; aspires to plenitude of utterance, to sheerness and rigidity of form. Ravel always goes directly through the center. But compare his *Rapsodie Espagnole* with Debussy's *Ibéria* to perceive how direct he is. Debussy gives the circumambient atmosphere, Ravel the inner form. Between him and Debussy there is the difference between the apollonian and the dionysiac, between the smooth, level, contained, perfect, and the darker, more turbulent, passionate, and instinctive. For Ravel has been vouchsafed a high grace. He has been permitted to remain, in all his manhood, the child that once we all were. In him the powerful and spontaneous flow of emotion from out the depths of being has never been dammed. He can still speak from the fullness of his heart, cry his sorrows piercingly, produce himself completely. Gracious and urbane as his music is, proper to the world of modern things and modern adventures and modern people, there is still a gray, piercing lyrical note in it that is almost primitive, and reflects the childlike singleness and intensity of the animating spirit. The man who shaped not only the deliberately infantine *Ma Mère l'Oye,* but also things as quiveringly simple and expressive and songful as *Oiseaux tristes,* as *Sainte,* as *Le Gibet,* or the *Sonatine,* as the passacaglia of the Trio or the vocal interlude in *Daphnis et Chloé,* has a pureness of feeling that we have lost. And it is this crying, passionate tone, this directness of expression, this largeness of effort, even in tiny forms and limited scope, that, more than his polyphonic style or any other of the easily recognizable earmarks of his art, distinguishes his work from Debussy's. The other man has a greater sensuousness, completeness, inventiveness perhaps. But Ravel is full of a lyricism, a piercingness, a passionateness, that much of the music of Debussy successive to *Pelléas* wants. We understand Ravel's music, in the famous phrase of Beethoven, as speech *vom Herz—zu Herzen.*

And we turn to it gratefully, as we turn to all art full of the "sense of tears in mortal things," and into which the pulse of human life has passed directly. For there are times when he is close to the bourne of life, when his art is immediately the orifice of the dark, flowering, germinating region where lie lodged the dynamics of the human soul. There are times when it taps vasty regions. There are times when Ravel has but to touch a note, and we unclose; when he has but to let an instrument sing a certain phrase, and things which lie buried deep in the heart rise out of the dark, like the nymph in his piano-poem, dripping with stars. The music of *Daphnis*, from the very moment of the introduction with its softly unfolding chords, its far, glamorous fanfares, its human throats swollen with songs, seems to thrust open doors into the unplumbed caverns of the soul, and summon forth the stuff to shape the dream. Little song written since Weber set his horns a-breathing, or Brahms transmuted the witchery of the German forest into tone, is more romantic. Over it might be set the invocation of Heine:

> *"Steiget auf, ihr alten Traüme!*
> *Oeffne dich, dur Herzenstor!"*

Like the passage that ushers in the last marvelous scene of his great ballet, it seems to waken us from the unreal world to the real, and show us the face of the earth, and the overarching blue once more.

And Ravel is at once more traditional and more progressive a composer than Debussy. One feels the past most strongly in him. Debussy, with his thoroughly impressionistic style, is more of the time. No doubt there is a certain almost Hebraic melancholy and sharp lyricism in Ravel's music which gives some color to the rumor that he is Jewish. And yet, for all that, one feels Rameau become modern in his sober, gray, dainty structures, in the dryness of his black. In *Le Tombeau de Couperin*, Ravel is the old clavecinist become contemporary of Scriabin and Stravinsky, the old clavecinist who had seen the projectiles fall at Verdun and lost a dozen friends in the trenches. He finds it easy, as in some of his recent songs, to achieve the folk-tone. If it is true that he is a Jew, then his traditionalism is but one more brilliant instance of the power of France to adopt the children of alien races and make them more intensely her own than some of her proper offspring. In no other instance, however, not in that of Lully nor in that of Franck, has the transfusion of blood been so successful. Ravel is in no wise treacherous to himself. There must be something in the character of the French nation that makes of every Jew, if not a son, yet the happiest and most faithful of stepchildren.

And as one feels the past more strongly in Ravel, so, too, one finds him in certain respects even more revolutionary than Debussy. For while the power of the latter flagged in the making of strangely Mac-Dowellesque preludes, or in the composition of such ghosts as *Gigues* and *Jeux* and *Karma*, Ravel has continued increasingly in power, has developed his art until he has come to be one of the leaders of the musical evolution. If there is a single modern composition which can be compared to *Petrushka* for its picture of mass-movement, its pungent naturalism, it is the *Feria* of the *Rapsodie Espagnole*. If there is a single modern orchestral work that can be compared to either of the two great ballets of Stravinsky for rhythmical vitality, it is *Daphnis et Chloé*, with its flaming dionysiac pulses, its "pipes and timbrels," its wild ecstasy. The same delicate clockwork mechanism characterizes *L'Heure Espagnole*, his opera bouffe, that characterizes *Petrushka* and *Le Rossignol*. A piano-poem like *Scarbo* rouses the full might of the piano, and seems to bridge the way to the music of Leo Ornstein and the age of steel. And Ravel has some of the squareness, the sheerness and rigidity for which the ultramodern are striving. The liquescence of Debussy has given away again to something more metallic, more solid and unflowing. There is a sort of new stiffness in this music. And in the field of harmony Ravel is steadily building upon Debussy. His chords grow sharper and more biting; in *Le Tombeau de Couperin* and the minuet on the name of Haydn there is a harmonic daring and subtlety and even bitterness that is beyond anything attained by Debussy, placing the composer with the Stravinskys and the Schönbergs and the Ornsteins and all the other barbarians.

And then his ironic humor, as well, distinguishes him from Debussy. The humor of the latter was, after all, light and whimsical. That of Ravel, on the other hand, is extremely bitter. No doubt, the "icy" Ravel, the artist *à qui l'absence de sensibilité fait encore une personalité,* as one of the quirites termed him, never existed save in the minds of those unable to comprehend his reticence and delicacy and essentiality. Never-

theless, besides his lyrical, dreamy, romantic temper, he has a very un-
sentimental vein, occurring no doubt, as in Heine, as a sort of correc-
tive, a sort of compensation, for the pervading sensibleness. And so we
find the tender poet of the *Sonatine* and the string quartet and *Miroirs*
writing the witty and mordant music of *L'Heure Espagnole,* setting the
bitter little *Histoires naturelles* of Jules Renard for chant, writing in
Valses nobles et sentimentales a slightly ironical and disillusioned if
smiling and graceful and delicate commentary to the season of love,
projecting a music-drama on the subject of Don Quixote. Over his
waltzes Ravel maliciously sets a quotation from Henri de Regnier: *"Le
plaisir délicieux et toujours nouveau d'une occupation inutile."* With
Casella, he writes a musical *"A là manière de,"* parodying Wagner, d'Indy,
Chabrier, Strauss and others most wittily. Something of Eric Satie, the
clown of music, exists in him, too. And probably nothing makes him
so inexplicable and irritating to his audiences as his ironic streak. People
are willing to forgive an artist all, save only irony.

XVIII

LATE ROMANTICISM
AND MODERN TRENDS

FRANZ LISZT

*Born 1811 at Raiding, Hungary. A pianist of international reputa-
tion by the age of 12. Lived chiefly in Paris from his youth until 1842,
when he was invited to Weimar by the Grand Duke; soon after, he
became director of the court theatre there, and remained until 1861.
From then he moved between Weimar, Budapest and Rome; died at
Bayreuth, 1886.*

*Liszt's compositions are usually grouped in three periods: the piano
period, 1826 to 1842; the orchestral period, 1842 to 1860; the choral
period, including his religious works, 1860–1886. He was a prolific
composer, and we list here only a few of his best known works.*

PRINCIPAL WORKS

CHORAL: *Christus; Legend of St. Elizabeth;* masses, especially the
Hungarian Coronation Mass.

INSTRUMENTAL: 2 dramatic symphonies, *Dante* and *Faust;* 12 symphonic
poems, including *Mazeppa, Tasso, Les Préludes.* 2 concertos for piano
and orchestra, in E flat major and A major. Compositions for piano include *Sonata in B minor;* 15 Hungarian Rhapsodies; 12 Transcendant
Etudes; *Legends of St. Francis; Years of Pilgrimage;* 6 Consolations;
Spanish Rhapsody; Funerailles; many transcriptions and smaller pieces.

RICHARD STRAUSS

*Born at Munich, June 11, 1864, son of the famous horn-player,
Franz Strauss. Produced his first symphony at 17, became assistant conductor to Hans von Bülow with the Meiningen orchestra. Held musical*

appointments at Munich, Weimar, etc.; has made various concert tours as pianist and conductor. Has lived chiefly in Charlottenburg.

PRINCIPAL WORKS

OPERAS: *Guntram; Feuersnot; Ariadne auf Naxos; Elektra; Der Rosen-kavalier; Salome.* In addition he has written many famous songs.

INSTRUMENTAL: The *Alpine* Symphony; the *Domestic* Symphony; Serenade for Wind Instruments. Tone poems for orchestra: *Aus Italien, Don Juan, Macbeth, Till Eulenspiegels Lustige Streiche, Also Sprach Zarathustra, Don Quixote, Tod und Verklärung, Ein Heldenleben.*

ANTON BRUCKNER

Born at Ausfelden, Upper Austria, September 4, 1824. Lived chiefly in Vienna, where he was court organist; taught at the Vienna Conservatory. Known chiefly for his 9 symphonies, his choral works sacred and secular. Died at Vienna, October 11, 1896.

GUSTAV MAHLER

Born at Kalischt, Bohemia, July 7, 1860. Studied with Bruckner. Director Vienna Court Opera, 1897–1907; conducted Metropolitan Opera and Philharmonic Society in New York, 1907–1911. Composed 9 symphonies; other compositions include notably the choral works Das Lied von der Erde, Das Klägende Lied; *songs. Mahler died at Vienna, May 18, 1911.*

HUGO WOLF

Born at Windischgräz, Styria, March 13, 1860. Lived as teacher, critic, and composer, chiefly at Vienna. Composed an opera; best known for his songs, of which he wrote some 500. His mental and physical health broke down, and his last years were spent in an asylum. He died at Vienna, February 22, 1903.

ARNOLD SCHÖNBERG

Born at Vienna, September 13, 1874. Lives in Vienna, active as composer and teacher of harmony. Early works include the string sextet, Verklärte Nacht, *the song-cycle* Gurrelieder; *later works,* 2 string quartets, Pelléas and Mélisande, *the* Kammersymphonie, Pierrot Lunaire, Five Orchestral Pieces, *suites for piano, etc.*

LATE ROMANTICISM AND MODERN TRENDS

By Paul Bekker

TWO different forms developed from the intensity of expression characteristic of romantic music. The one tended toward expansion, to elaborate and work up this expressive quality to the point where it should directly interpret action and emotion. This was the direction taken by Berlioz, Liszt, and Wagner, which led to the opera and program music of the so-called "new German school." The other form was more intensive. Here the composer shunned direct interpretation as superficial, and thought dramatic and programmatic ideas should not govern the music entirely but should merely accompany it. This was the movement which followed hard upon early romanticism in Germany, and its most important representative was Johannes Brahms. Twenty years younger than Wagner, Brahms was heir to the early romanticists, Schubert, Mendelssohn, and Schumann, much as Wagner was heir to the old masters of opera. With Brahms appeared two other composers whose talents were highly specialized, Hugo Wolf, in the field of lieder, and Anton Bruckner, in the field of large symphonic forms. But Wolf and Bruckner were both very much influenced by Wagner and antagonistic to Brahms.

We should take note of the dissension that existed between these two groups surrounding Wagner and Brahms, unjustified though it seems to-day. In the partisan quarrels and newspaper controversies of the time they were represented as standing one for true, the other for spurious music, a distinction which of course seems to us entirely irrelevant. And yet we should not go so far as to deny all distinctions between the two groups. The emotional romantic conception of music is common to both

From the author's *The Story of Music*, by permission of W. W. Norton & Co., Inc.

Brahms and Wagner, but they developed it in entirely different ways, the one through a process of expansion, the other through a process of concentration. The difference between the two may be compared to the difference between Handel and Bach, though it relates only to their manner of composing, not to their musical individuality. It is reflected in their choice of medium. Wagner, with his desire to express emotion concretely turns, like Handel, to the drama, while Brahms, with his tendency to abstract emotional expression, turns, like Bach, to instrumental music not connected with drama. Thus Brahms wrote instrumental music of every sort, and with voice as well, but he always kept aloof from opera.

It has been customary of late to contrast Brahms with Bruckner and to call one or the other, according to taste, Beethoven's successor. But why should we try to pick out a successor to Beethoven at all? Beethoven is the colossal genius who dominates the whole nineteenth century, the ideal of all its composers, Wagner as well as Brahms, Liszt as well as Schumann, Bruckner as well as Mendelssohn and Berlioz. But none of them stands—if we may use the expression—in intimate human contact with him. Opera composers in this respect trace back to Weber, German instrumental composers to Schubert. Both Brahms and Bruckner are descended from Schubert. If Brahms gained his deeper inspiration from the preclassical masters, via Mendelssohn and Schumann, Bruckner gained his from Wagner, whose dynamics of modulation and color he remodelled into his symphonic form. In giving vent to his imagination through his organ-like orchestra, with all its dramatic elements acquired from romantic music, he created a number of symphonies and religious works which incline towards a new type of cult music with a universal appeal.

Bruckner's particular significance lies in his having made use of the most subjective elements of romanticism in the expression of popular feeling and naïvely religious faith. For this reason also his music seems to many of us to possess a calm and tranquil quality. He differs from Brahms in the first place by the inevitable grandeur of his form, for as a composer of the expansive type he strove for symphonic structure, while the concentration of chamber-music forms was foreign to his nature. The intellectual and psychological factors in romanticism were equally alien to him. Here again he differs significantly from Brahms. Through the simplicity of his feeling Bruckner is the first to return to the expression of an impersonal, a universal attitude. This it is which gives him his religious trend and gives his music its tranquillity. The religious longing was common to all romanticists; the more their intensely subjective attitude towards life and art estranged them from it, the more ardently they sought it. It appears in the early romanticists of literature who frequently embraced Catholicism. It appears in the romanticists of music as well, in Wagner, Bruckner, Brahms. It manifests itself in a tendency toward mysticism, or, as with Schumann, toward spiritism and the occult. It is particularly evident in Liszt, who in his expression of it is the very antithesis of Bruckner.

Like Bruckner, Liszt was a devout Catholic. But his belief was not so utterly naïve as Bruckner's. It was the searching, skeptical, gnawing faith of the intellectual romanticist with a somewhat worldly inclination. It determined the trend of his creative activity from the *Faust* and *Dante* symphonies to the *Gran Cathedral* mass, the oratorios of *Christus* and *The Legend of Saint Elizabeth,* and many smaller compositions. Like Mendelssohn, Spohr, and Wagner, Liszt was one of the great practical organizers of public musical activity. He thought of the artist as a sort of prophet—and he saw himself as one—who passes through the stages of virtuoso and champion of everything new and good, to become the high-priest, the mediator between God and man. This was the course Liszt's own life took. It was dominated by the idea of service, as Wagner's was by the idea of conflict, Bruckner's by that of worship and Brahms's by that of the evanescence of all earthly things. When individuality has been exploited to the limit of its possibilities, the desire for a common unity grows up once more. This great, unrealizable spiritual longing is innate in all romanticists, leads them always further in their individual ways, and thus determines the deeply pessimistic character of all romantic art.

With Wagner, Liszt, Brahms and Bruckner, what may be called the *high* or *late* romantic period comes to an end. It is followed by a period of disintegration which again produces a variety of characteristic reactions. These are most striking in the realm of opera as reactions against Wagner. The national differentiation which was one of the fundamental features of romanticism had been endangered by the triumphant progress of Wagner's operas all over the world. In the Latin countries this instrumentally conceived opera was looked upon as an alien type and for this reason the reaction against it came from Italy and France.

In Italy, through the influence of Bizet's *Carmen* upon the realistic style, a new sort of opera, known as the *veristic* type, came to life. With it realism abandoned itself absolutely to purely concrete representation. The effort at brevity and direct attack extended even to the outer form of the compositions in question, for which the one-act structure was chosen. So the two most famous works of this type—Mascagni's *Cavalleria Rusticana* and Leoncavallo's *Pagliacci*—appeared as a relief from the over-burdensome ideas and musical psychology of Wagner's works. But the ablest composer Italy produced after Verdi was Puccini, whose talent was of a more enduring quality than either Mascagni's or Leoncavallo's. He subjected the diminutive veristic forms to a careful stylization and built them into the larger opera of several acts, seeking always to preserve the immediate charm of the moment in music and action through ingratiating melody and continual dramatic suspense.

New and characteristically national forms came into being in France and Italy through the repudiation of German influence. Simultaneously Russian music began to affect West European culture more strongly than before. In Bohemia, Smetana, with his folk operas and instrumental works, created a national Czech music; in England and in the Scandinavian countries the newer Latin challenged the older German influence; national differentiation extended to the Balkan States and even to America. German music was still entirely dominated by the great late-romanticists, around whom partisan groups had formed, dividing the academic romanticists from the "new German school" following Wagner, Liszt and Berlioz. Brahms himself stood aloof from all partisanship, though he could not prevent the opponents of the new school from claiming him for their party, the more since no other suitable individual of sufficient importance was available. But since true creative genius will not long submit to partisan command in aesthetic matters, the younger artists in each faction gradually drifted into the opposing camp, party lines were obliterated, and some of the followers of both Wagner and Brahms even turned for inspiration towards the influences emanating from Italy and France. The common characteristic of all these composers is the continued expansion of harmonic activity from within which, now that pure modulation has been exploited to the utmost extent through increased use of chromatics, strives primarily towards development of color, of the shifting hues and shades of tone. . . .

Richard Strauss, the ablest and most influential member of the new German school, succeeded Wagner and Liszt as a composer of opera and concert music. In Strauss the virtuosity which was a feature of early romanticism again stands out. The personal experience which had been the incentive and the strength of the late romantic masters, now finds expression in a greater technical skill. Hence Strauss turns gradually away from the romantic to the classic models, and to those of Mozart in particular, a process which indicates not a fundamental change of attitude, but the development of virtuosity to the point where it represents the perfection of artificial simplicity.

As Strauss stands in relation to Liszt and Wagner, so Reger stands in relation to Brahms. But Reger never attained the intrinsic clarity and masterly control of his medium that Strauss achieved; for his life's work, as various as it was uneven, ceased suddenly, unfulfilled. Mahler, the third of this group, was influenced by both Bruckner and the new German school. He was the symphonic representative of vanishing romanticism in contrast to Reger, who thought essentially in terms of chamber music. His compositions combine the influences of his predecessors, from Schubert to Liszt and Bruckner, but turn away from the religious piety of Bruckner to a new world-brotherhood of love.

While the dissolution of romanticism as well as the trend towards classical and pre-classical ideas may be seen in the music of Strauss, Reger and Mahler, Pfitzner, following upon Humperdinck who acts as a connecting link, achieves a sort of synthesis of the late romanticism of Wagner with the early romanticism of Schumann. This leads to a revival of romantic subjectivism, which finds expression in a rigid adherence to the immediate past. Finally in d'Albert, and more especially in Schreker, the amalgamation of German romanticism with French and Italian opera is clearly apparent. The symphonic structure remains, but it is gradually penetrated more and more by the trend towards melodious expression in song. The instrumentally conceived opera of the harmonic era once more approaches the original type of scenic song-play. The beauty of modulation dissolves completely in the colorful play of melody, all dramatic elements are calculated to arouse the sensuous appeal of music, the singing voice becomes the leading factor. Thus all the subjective, specifically romantic characteristics of romantic opera are exaggerated to the point of their own destruction, and from the ruins rises once more the pre-classical ideal of *musical* opera, opera to be sung.

Now we have come to the consideration of the forms which belong to our own times, and which are therefore most easy to observe but perhaps the most difficult of all for us to understand. It is scarcely possible for us to take account of all the many composers in our midst. We cannot even be sure which of them possesses a surviving vitality. Probably we do not yet realize much that is important, while much that is unimportant looms large to our vision. Criticism, books, discussion, rather confuse than enlighten us. We hear a young composer praised on the one hand as extraordinarily gifted, while on the other he is declared to be a bungler and a charlatan. Catchwords are current: we speak of expressionistic, futuristic, atonal, polyharmonic, or linear music. If we ask people what they mean by these words, most of them are embarrassed and unable to explain. There is a widespread opinion that the new music is on the wrong path. It is compared with the music of Bach, Haydn, Mozart, and Beethoven, and since their music is recognized as beautiful it is logical to conclude that the new music, which sounds entirely different, is simply ugly. Not only the workings of the law of inertia upon the critic, but the relative nature of beauty, the variability of its components, are quite overlooked. We forget that Bach, Haydn, Mozart, and Beethoven were just as modern in their times as our young composers are to-day. We forget that these young composers write music that is different not because they want to but because they *must*. And they must, because different perceptive powers live and thrive within them, and because in this very state of being different the creative energy of life finds its expression.

This is not said in criticism or in commendation of any particular composer, but applies to the new music in general. Schumann, the enthusiastic champion of everything vital, once said: "If Mozart were alive to-day he would write piano concertos not of the type Mozart wrote but of the type Chopin wrote." This applied to a time in which Chopin was considered a revolutionary. Wherefore we may safely say that if Bach and Mozart, Beethoven, Schubert, and Wagner were alive to-day, they most certainly would write not the kind of music we buy from the music-dealer as theirs, but an entirely different kind. It would probably be very much like the music we protest against to-day, calling their very names to witness. This I have felt obliged to say before attempting to define the nature of that which we now call the *new music,* a venture which the foregoing observations should justify us in making. If the new music is no mere arbitrary innovation, but a transformation once more, then it should be possible to discover the conditions which lie at the root of this change and the active impulses which have brought it about.

The last great epoch in music history begins about the middle of the sixteenth century and reaches up to the present time. These four centuries represent the period of harmonic instrumental music. Harmony and instrumental tone condition each other. Harmony is latent in instrumental tone, and its manifestation is an essentially instrumental phenomenon. I have tried to show how the development of harmony into artistic musical forms is determined by *three* different dynamic impulses; first, where the main emphasis is on the progression of the bass, the bass-tone itself being the foundation from which the harmony emanates; secondly, where the main emphasis is on melody, and harmony is the structure supporting the melodic line which constitutes the leading impulse of the music; and finally, where the main emphasis is on the middle voices and the harmony is forced apart, from the center downward towards the bass and upwards towards the melody, as it were, by means of modulation. This last procedure I have defined as the dispersion of harmony from within; it might even be more strongly described as a driving asunder, an atomizing of the harmonic structure. It is strikingly expressed in the modulations of Max Reger and in the color effects of Franz Schreker.

Arrived at this point, we now ask: *what next?* There must certainly be further possibilities of harmonic development in modulation and color. But we may assume that romanticism has exhausted the essentials, and that any further extensions possible on the old foundation can be no more than exercises in variety of detail. Does this imply that we have reached the limit of harmonic possibilities, and that the three sources of dynamic activity—the bass, the melodic line, the modulating middle voices—are played out?

In a certain sense this is true. Let us say, therefore, that dynamic activity in this particular direction has been exhausted. So far the dynamic tendency has been towards expansion. From the time of Bach and Handel, indeed from the beginning of harmonic composition up to the present, the development of harmonic forms has always been essentially expansive, beginning with the vertical extension of the bass line, proceeding thence to the more pliable horizontal upper line of the melody, and ending in the outward overflow of the middle lines. To-day we are witnessing the reversal of this process. The dynamic tendency is towards contraction. The great wave of harmonic expansion is rolling back, back to its starting point or perhaps even farther—this we cannot yet say with certainty. But we see the reverse motion, feel the compressing force unmistakably; therefore let us try to understand it. It is rooted in the very nature of harmonic music. If our previous definition of the nature of harmonic music has been correct, then it will also confirm the organic soundness of the present tendency.

In explaining how harmonic forms came into being, I said that harmony is not polyphonic, does not consist of independent voices as the old polyphonic vocal music does, but is homophonic, derived from the breaking-up of the single tone into its overtones. The harmonic conception of tone may be likened to a prism by which light is split up into its component colors. Hence all harmonic forms are based upon a fundamental principle of division, of dispersion, or, as has been said above, of dynamic expansion. The reverse movement must, therefore, be based upon a fundamental principle of contraction, of compression. The object of this compression must be to regain the original unity of a tone out of its multiple subdivisions. Form is no longer derived through the prismatic breaking-up of tone in harmony. The aim of the creative impulse is to present tone in its original undivided entirety, in the form, for instance, in which it underlay the old polyphonic music.

Now a similar impulse exists in harmonic music, too, in so far as its dynamic pattern is based upon the dispersion and regathering of tonal forces. From this regathering the cadence is derived. As suggested in our discussion of Wagner, the further afield the modulation is carried, the more important is the cadence through which the harmonic threads are once more collected. It was this reassembling of tonal forces in the cadence which caused all romantic music to express the idea of solution, of redemption. Yet as the cadence aimed at achieving an effect of contrast, it implied that harmonic activity covering a wide range must necessarily have taken place first. Here we see the link between the new music and the music of romanticism, and also the contrast between them. This great substructure of harmonic activity, for the creation of which the romantic composer needed his personal reaction to experience and in which he proved the individuality of his art, now ceases to exist. Only the cadence itself is left, as it were, the process by which the scattered tonal forces of harmony are brought together and carried on as newly established units. The new music begins, in a way, to take form, where romantic music stops—namely, at the gathering process of the cadence—whence it proceeds to its own further development. In so doing, however, it has recourse once more to polyphonic devices.

I have tried to define the principle underlying the new musical forms without taking into consideration any particular composers or compositions. In actual composition this principle is not so distinct as here presented. The composer has not adopted it deliberately, yet it is manifest in a variety of ways, mingled always with his own individual characteristics as well as with elements surviving from the past. But since we are discussing the new music in general, and the change it illustrates, we have the right to seek a formula by which to describe its essential nature by generalizing from certain observations we have repeatedly made. Thus we are first aware of a movement in the opposite direction from that in which the process of harmonic expansion has been carried on. I should call this movement not a retrogression, not a retracing of steps, but a continuation over the opposite half of the globe, as it were, towards the antipodes. It tends away from harmonic dispersion towards unification; it perceives a tone, in other words, not as part of a harmonic complex but as an independent unit in itself.

From this tendency Busoni derived his idea of a renewed classicism, meaning the supremacy of melody once more and the technique of thematic development, as against harmonic expansion. According to our earlier observations, this idea would represent a return to the second stage of harmonic form, in which the melodic upper voice was the leading factor. From the same impulse, furthermore, springs the evident rela-

tionship to Handel and especially to Bach, which we observe in Schönberg and the younger composers as well. According to our earlier observations, again, this process would represent a return to the first stage
of harmonic form, in which the fundamental bass voice was the leading factor. But though these movements seem to return to the older
forms, they do not imitate them, or they would perforce tend toward
harmonic expansion. They take over these older forms, rather, to use
them in their own way. It is both idle and dangerous to prophesy;
yet the tendency of this movement is so unmistakable that I feel justified in expressing the opinion that it will not stop at Bach and Handel.
It may even lead beyond their music, which is still harmonic, further
back into the past to the point of time where tone was not yet harmonically divided—back, that is, to the old, the true polyphony. Only then
would the great circle be closed, which began with the unified tone of
ancient music, led through polyphony to the overtones of harmony,
through Bach and Handel, through the Viennese classicists, to the
further dispersion of this harmonic tone by the romanticists, and thence
back again by way of the new music to unified tone once more.

The question of the medium through which this newly unified tone
may be expressed should also be considered. If harmonic and instrumental music are synonymous, if instrumental tone is a manifestation
of this prismatic breaking-up of tone, then the undivided tone, which
again encloses all tonal energies within itself, would have to be not
instrumental but vocal. Instrumental tone could in this case function
only in some subservient capacity, as it did in the great days of vocal
music, though in a totally different way, of course, as yet unguessed.

We must not abandon ourselves too freely to dreams of what the
future may bring forth, sure though we may be of the wave-like motion of events and the return it always involves. Yet we may note that
there is a distinct inclination to-day to recognize the characteristic quality
of vocal tone and its susceptibility to construction in forms fundamentally different from those of instrumental tone. An especially significant indication of this tendency is to be seen in the reawakening of
interest in the old opera which was built purely upon the distinctive
quality of vocal tone, and in Handel's operas particularly. Another indication is to be seen in the newly awakened interest in the treatment of
the voice apparent in the present-day opera of Strauss and the younger

composers. Even the idea so much in favor to-day of the contrast between Wagner and Verdi, which we have seen cannot be substantiated, has its root in the assertion of the rights of the voice as distinct from instrumental tone. The trend towards a reawakening of the vocal conception of tone is not a matter of speculation, but is already beginning to express itself in unmistakable signs.

There are still other evidences of this tendency to think of tone as contracted into a unit. We notice that harmonic expansion loses its force as the constructive principle, that it is no longer the dynamics of modulation and color which furnish the impetus to form, but, on the contrary, the urge towards contraction. Large musical forms and greatly augmented instrumental bodies now no longer have any justification for existence. Thus we see the great orchestra of the post-romantic era grow smaller and smaller until it becomes a chamber orchestra. We notice how the gigantic forms which Bruckner, Mahler, Strauss need for their music, which is still dominated by the idea of harmonic expansion, now contract, as it were. They shrink into small, clear-cut concentrated patterns, which are examples not of the aphoristic brevity of the early German romanticists, but of energy compressed to a high degree of intensity, just as the multiple harmonic constituents of the tone itself are now forced back into a single unit. If Busoni represents the melodic and Schönberg the contrapuntal type of form, I should call Stravinsky the most important exponent of this contracted or compressed type.

I believe that everything has herewith been said which can be said within the limits of the present study, in order to make clear the law of change which is at work within the new music. In closing, I would like to apply this law of change to some of the leading ideas that have been presented here. We have seen that in the course of music history characteristic national forms have always alternated with forms that represent a spiritual unity. The nineteenth century was a period of national music and therefore, in accord with our picture of the wave-like progress of events, the new music will strive toward universality. The nineteenth century was a period of secular music and therefore, according to the same law, the new music will be of the cult type—music with a universal spiritual appeal. The nineteenth century cultivated music in which the emotional significance of tone was paramount; the new music will instead reveal once more the essential quality of the tone itself. The music of the nineteenth century represented the last stage in the harmonic expansion of tone that was instrumentally conceived; the new music will represent the unified intensity of tone that is vocally conceived. Even this, if perfected, will not mean that music has reached its goal. It will indicate not an ascent or a descent, a climax or a decline, but a transformation, the change which itself always gives birth to further change. This is the great lesson taught us by the history of art.

XIX

STRAVINSKY

IGOR STRAVINSKY

Born at Oranienbaum, June 5, 1882. Although his talent was precocious, he did not turn definitely to music until he was 20. Studied with Rimsky-Korsakoff. Early works include a symphony, piano studies, songs. After 1909 composed ballets presented by Diaghileff's Ballet Russe: Le Chant du Rossignol, L'Oiseau de Feu, Petrushka, Le Sacre du Printemps, L'Histoire d'un Soldat, Pulcinella, Les Noces.

Other works include the one act comic opera, Mavra; *the* Japanese Lyrics, Ragtime, Fireworks, *the octet for winds; more recently, a piano concerto, a piano sonata, a capriccio for piano and orchestra, a concerto for violin and orchestra; and the choral works,* Apollon Musagète, Oedipus, *and the* Symphony of Psalms.

STRAVINSKY

By Leonid Sabaneyeff

THE name of Igor Stravinsky is to-day perhaps the most brilliant on the world's musical horizon. He is the recognized master of minds and the supreme leader in the field of musical creative art, only Richard Strauss and Schönberg, perhaps, sharing this hegemony with him. Stravinsky has been fortunate: in his creative art he has found the synthesis of novelty and popularity which has been the most cherished dream of so many artists and which is the attraction that the career of a composer exerts fame in one's lifetime. Creative musical art works in a field of darkness; the musician-composer labors for a circle of persons unknown to him, while he is guided only by the obscure directions of his genius. We know cases where this gift of genius dictated to composers' creations that had no chance whatever for recognition among their contemporaries and the creators died unrecognized. Their descendants admired in these compositions, not only the beauties of art, but the courage of the spirit that could so heroically withstand the calls of fame and labor for the future. Perhaps our times in general are not conducive towards the appearance of heroism of this kind, and heroes of this type become anachronisms as bad, if not worse than some of Hercules who deals with lions and highwaymen in the most primitive and homespun fashion. The idea of eternal fame fades not only in the mind of the denizen who has been disillusioned in his romantic dream of a future life, but even in the mind of the artist himself. The artist who formerly still bashfully cloaked himself in the phraseology of idealism, now dreams very frankly about recognition coming in his lifetime. And this is not some ordinary artist-tradesman who supplies wares to

From the author's *Modern Russian Composers*, by permission of International Publishers.

the market of demand, but a genuine artist. We see the strongholds of idealism tumble, one after another, and life's prose peeps out from behind the artistic draperies. And those who are now marked with the stamp of genius in their narrow musical sphere, are now, alas, no longer prophets nor "priests of the sacred art," but plain manufacturers of values, and their genius does not reach the sphere of genius of the spirit.

This is the sign and stamp of the age, and if our discussion of Stravinsky touches upon this sphere, one must admit that Stravinsky is in the highest degree a contemporary phenomenon. He is the liveliest reaction to the keen, refined, sated taste of our time. This master of contemporary musical thought, successor to the throne of Debussy and Strauss, who has succeeded in combining the highest tension of technical boldness with the highest and broadest demonstration and power greater than Debussy's, has reflected in his creative art all that is lofty and base, banal and proud, which is characteristic of our age, and it is inconceivable to apply to him the same standards of appreciation that would be proper for any former phenomenon in music.

Stravinsky's fame is based not only on his musical gifts, but chiefly on his virtuosity in making full use of musical conditions and taking full account of fashions and fads, these two wavering and changing elements on which, nevertheless, fame in one's lifetime almost exclusively depends. It depends least of all on the magnitude of endowments, but more on the composer's technical and even "commercial" experience. Stravinsky is immeasurably more a genius of musical business than purely of music. He is truly sprung from the depths of the Russian National School. He was the natural inheritor of the interest which Russian music had aroused in Paris, the center of the world. One fine day, on the border of the last century, France, beautiful and full of the joy of life, to her own amazement suddenly "understood" the sombre and tragic language of Moussorgsky, that wanderer-genius, who had started with positivism in music, only to end with psychologism and mysticism. But if Moussorgsky, in the age-long conformity with the strivings of the Russian spirit to "antinomies," strove to combine Darwin with Dostoievsky, I do not think that "beautiful France's" fondness for him was due to this. The Russian National School, also called the "mighty coterie," had struck the fancy of France and her thousand-year-old culture, not with epilepsy served up in artistic form and in a positivist psychological shape, but with those terrible abysses towards which Moussorgsky's Russian spirit, like all Russian spirits, had a particular tendency to approach. We do not think that this sphere became comprehensible in feminine France, in a land where the commanding heights of art belong to taste. The unusualness, the immediateness of inspiration, the novelty and sharpness of the external means, the barbaric primitiveness of the Russian and Oriental melodies—this is what lured the descendants of Rameau and Couperin, and lured them so forcibly that Moussorgsky's influence is extraordinarily strong, even upon the greatest genius among the French, Debussy. We may add that here there was a hidden kinship of cultures. For it is no secret that the Russian nobility, to which class all our composers of that time belonged, were half French, if not in origin, at least in culture and even in language. Glinka and Moussorgsky both usually conversed in French, and in the seignorial aestheticism of their music, and in their collection of colorful types, discovered kindred traits. Unquestionably, all the ethnographism of the "mighty coterie," the somewhat dry and cerebral elegance of Rimsky-Korsakoff, does not come from typical romanticism but from the enlightened aestheticism of the nobility.

We know also that the faith of the Russian *Koochka* (coterie) was such that gradually aestheticism overcame romanticism and unrestraint, the former barbarians and anarchists became decent people, and like Lyadoff and Rimsky-Korsakoff, frequenters of salons, retaining as much of their barbarism as was necessary in order not to appear commonplace and uninteresting to these salons. In the Russian aesthetic menu this same "pleasing barbarism" was a spice about which one could grow enthusiastic, a sharp condiment after the European cuisine.

I should not wonder if the "Koochkists" were esteemed in France from this very point of taste. The sharp traits of "oriental barbarism" were acquired by and became the musical property of the most cultured of nations, and here they were recreated almost to the point of becoming unrecognizable. But after all, this unrecognizability is explained by the fact that the Frenchmen "comprehended" the Russians erroneously if strikingly and forcibly after their own fashion. The story of Richard Wagner repeated itself; he, too, originally was the object of excessive and unexpected enthusiasm on the part of the French, until it became clear that they saw only "Wagner's pedestal" and not his whole hugeness, and it made them uncomfortable. As soon as they began to discern the proper size of his genius, their enthusiasm gave way to horror. Just so Russian culture passed through France, laying hold of it somehow and even fructifying it with something, but misunderstood to the very end.

As I have said, Stravinsky was the natural and ready-to-hand successor of the influence of the Russian National School. But in him the aestheticism observable in the "coterie" is decisively predominant. Stravinsky is a typically aesthetist phenomenon. He is not Wagner or Scriabin, who had expected from music and from art a transformation of the world. Stravinsky could write an impressive chorus to the mystical text of the star-visaged *Balmont,* he could be externally imbued with the apocalyptic moods of the poet, but his conviction in the apocalyptic visions will hardly be greater than, say, Lyadoff's, who in his time also toyed with the Apocalypse. Stravinsky can compose a mystery, *Sacre du Printemps,* but he has just as little faith in his "ancestors" and the rites of "kissing the earth" which appear there, as the skeptical and wise old man Rimsky-Korsakoff had in his musical fairy-tales. But I would say that Rimsky-Korsakoff was more naïve and therein more mystical than Stravinsky. He could be a convinced pantheist and feel the proximity of *nature* as an animated being. Stravinsky, on the other hand, does not believe in anything at all, he only pretends he believes. And he does not possess the evanescent naïveté which is altogether typical of the narrator. Stravinsky makes believe in earnest: occasionally he definitely sets himself the task of scaring his hearers. Rimsky-Korsakoff was a naïve, kindly grandfather with fairy-tales, Stravinsky is a wicked magician, but both use children to work on and they fool them without believing themselves.

Herein lies their essential difference from Wagner, Scriabin, and others who themselves believed and were exasperated when others did not, regarding these others not as children, but fellow beings who were to be shepherded and guided by them and generally predestined to follow them.

The rationalism which we observe in Rimsky-Korsakoff manifests itself in a still more categorical form in Stravinsky. He is a genuinely great master. We shall never find dilettantism in him, even in the slight degree in which it occasionally crops up both in Scriabin and Prokofieff. He is in the panoply of his trade and his technique. There is nothing incidental with him. Everything has been thought out and the most modernistic elements are more conditioned by play of mind and ingenious calculations than by so-called "immediate inspiration." Most probably also Stravinsky became an innovator for reasons of a "rational" nature. It was not at all some insane attraction or a lamentable seeking of new sounds. For such things he is too modern. Like any experienced magician in the manner of Cagliostro, he himself will, perhaps, spread legends about his being possessed, about supernaturalism if need be, but the process itself of his creative work lacks the irrational element and to a greater degree than any one of the great composers. He does not, like Beethoven, listen to the "voice of the soul whispering melodies." He does not burn up in the intense fire of musical visions, like Wagner. He is not tortured, like Chopin, with an insane thirst to seize and grasp the flitting fragments of inspirations as though heard in other worlds.

He firmly knows that one must be an innovator, or one would not make one's way, or one would miss the precipitous train of modernism, would not attain the reward which one's gifts promise. Gone are those times when a creative artist created quietly, obeying but the inner urge and believing that some day his tones would find their way to understanding. Quietude exists no longer. Now, one must first of all attract attention to oneself. And this is impossible without distinguishing oneself with something extraordinary. In our period, an innovation becomes a sort of inevitable advertisement. By means of the extraordinary the composer attracts attention to himself as though by a shrill shout or the penetrating toot of an automobile. And it matters not whether people discern the quality of this innovating modernism. All that is needed is that the composer should be noticed. And accordingly, entirely different demands are made upon this contemporary innovationism; it need not at all be fine to the experienced ear of the specialist, it need not be profound, complex, flowing in spheres which the ear of the throng fails to reach. It must be glittering, sharp, shrill-voiced, like the electric signs, flickering and blinding. It must have rapid action; otherwise in the insane rush of modern life the composer would come too late.

Modernism of this kind is of course dictated to a considerable degree by considerations of the mental sort. The composer's very path begins to resemble the path not of a creator but rather of an inventor. The first requisite of novelty is lack of similarity to what has preceded. Every trait of epigonism must be wiped out, if possible, and everything is wiped out which is felt in a familiar way. The most destructive and accursed thing for the new composer is to be convicted of similarity to someone else. The physiognomy may be utterly monstrous, deformed, but it must be his, unlike others'.

When we examine the path taken by Stravinsky, we immediately find all the traits which we have just sketched. First of all we shall recall how Stravinsky made his début in the composers' world immediately on leaving Rimsky-Korsakoff's academic tutelage. His first symphony possesses nothing characteristic. Not one of those striking features which distinguish the present creative art of Stravinsky. It shows the typical average epigonism. It is even impossible to say much about the author's musicianship. Average, even music, decently orchestrated, resembling both Glazounoff and Rimsky-Korsakoff. Thus had written and still write the numberless composers who in their time gathered in Bieliaieff's academic circle and created the very conception of the "St. Petersburg mechanical production of music."

Stravinsky did not find his path and talent at once. Music is a dark field, and being talented in music does not at all mean being gifted in all its manifestations. We know that there have been specialists in melody like Schubert, specialists in harmony like Scriabin, that there have been some like Berlioz, who concentrated their innovatorship exclusively on sound itself, on color. Berlioz, that strange musician who combined the traits of a genius gifted in the field of color with the traits of definite lack of talent in a number of other musical elements, resembles Stravinsky to a certain degree, though he is his opposite in the romantic pathos that swayed him and his complete helplessness in ordinary life. In contrast to this last, Stravinsky appears a commercial genius, a kind of musical bank director. Stravinsky is poorly gifted in the most musical field of all, the field of melody. But he is infinitely gifted in invention, which has enabled him to discover new worlds in the field of rhythm and and orchestral coloring.

Stravinsky came in the epoch of the dissolution of the Russian National School and at a period when the very product of this dissolution, academism, also began to decay. As a net result, he affected, as it were, a return to the traditions of the Russian National School, to her aestheticism and her connection with folk melody. Naturally he could not long remain in the academic atmosphere of "Bieliaieff's circle" and of course he followed those that were nearest to the coterie, the French impressionists

Ravel and Debussy, who had themselves sprung up from the soil of the recreation of Moussorgsky's creative art.

Stravinsky marches with firm step in the sphere of orchestral coloring, combining as he does the achievements of the composers of the National School and of the French neo-impressionists with his own. Extraordinary gorgeousness of orchestral hues was the first thing with which he began to astonish his contemporaries. His *Fireworks* already breathed inventiveness in spite of the scantiness of the purely musical lines. The author's aestheticism already manifested itself in this composition and the *Fantastic Scherzo* which appeared simultaneously. He is not at all interested in giving expression to himself, his spirit; he conceals himself in his music, remaining extremely objective and openly picturesque in the extreme. The composer will have nothing to do with the tragic, nothing with lyricism, he is brimful of plans and projects of entirely new revolutions in the world of coloring. This aestheticism draws the author to his spiritual fatherland, France, and here, too, he correctly divines his style; he begins to cultivate the ballet, choreographic music. Stravinsky correctly realized, and realized before others did, that Russian opera had been exhausted, that it had become old, that its national lyricism was now out of place. He realized this at the time Diaghileff's Ballet was making its triumphant march through Europe. Indeed, the Russian conquering choreography, one may say, towed behind it all Russian music to the public at large. And Stravinsky, too, joined in the procession. He became an active collaborator in the ballet business. He specialized in the music for the complicated and modernized choreography.

L'Oiseau de Feu (Fire-Bird) was composed by him in decently ordinary Russian national tones, after all. And it strongly recalled Rimsky-Korsakoff. The only new thing here was greater splendor and greater boldness in color. Simultaneously, a fact of extraordinary importance took place: definitely and once and for all, Stravinsky bound himself to fashion in the sphere of art, he became a "new" composer, not only in the methods of embodying the artistic, but also in the stimuli of creative art. He definitely desired fame and achieved it and thereby he drew a sharp border-line between himself and the former Russian composers who in general had never composed for the sake of fame. The spirit of Paris manifested itself here too, in the figure of Meyerbeer, whose career offers a parallel to Stravinsky's. Also a composer of genius, Meyerbeer nevertheless had sold his music for the pottage of fame and recognition in his lifetime.

Stravinsky felt correctly and subtly the pulse of contemporary life: he noticed the death of opera, the current fad of the ballet which was now blossoming forth in the capital of the world as a gorgeous flower of contemporary artistic culture. The Parisian fashion market demanded new ballets and demanded them exactly in the style which had just conquered the hearts of the Parisians, the style of extreme exquisiteness combined with acute barbarism. The attributes which the French spirit had rightly or wrongly read in Moussorgsky's and Rimsky-Korsakoff's scores, were now demanded also of new music in a still more acute and striking form, in a dose of double-strength.

Stravinsky became the purveyor of the wares demanded by that musical barbarism, by this Russian style understood as a style oriental and highly spiced, wild and anti-European, but fully armed with European methods. Did this mean catering to the tastes of the throng? Not quite, for it must be remarked that the tastes of the mob and the law-making of fashions are not one and the same thing. Stravinsky did not become caterer to the throng, he was too clever, but he became the law-giver of musical fashion first in the world's center, Paris, and later well-nigh to the whole world.

The structure of fashion is a very complex affair and will surely find its investigator some day. The truth of the matter is that some secret and elusive group, something like a masonic organization, always small and never belonging to the crowd, but rather always to the cream of society, dictates and invents these unwritten but inexorable laws of private and public life, and determines these waves of demand. In the field of art this hierarchism of the fashionable law-givers is still clearer. Stravinsky succeeded in a remarkable way in mastering the secret of this odd and powerful mechanism which to his predecessors was a sort of mysterious lottery. Gradually he became the head of this organization. If the *Fire-Bird* was still written on epigonic lines and was, as it were, interest on the capital once upon a time invested by Russian composers in the treasury of French music, one can nevertheless trace in it the beginnings of the curious departure of Stravinsky from Russia and from Russian perception of Russian events. It is a very odd story. Undoubtedly, the

"Koochkists," too, had had moments of looking askance on Russian life. With him, the Russian and Slavic elements are but a commodity to export abroad, to satisfy the demand for Russian barbarism and orientalism. And the composer strove with all his might to present his nation in the most barbaric, in the most oriental and savage form possible. Here there was no longer a question of naïve love for the fatherland which, after all, had been undoubtedly present even in an askance-looking *barin* (nobleman, estate-holder) like Glinka or Rimsky-Korsakoff. Here was, instead, the attitude of making despicable sport on a commercial basis. These features gradually growing stronger, reached their point of culmination in Stravinsky's *Little Wedding*, his *Mavra*, in his *Adages*, which constitute definitely the quintessence of an ironic attitude towards his own people and life.

In this sense the line of Stravinsky's nationalism borders on anti-nationalism, in a caricature-like exaggeration. The old composers' fondness for collection-making gives place to a caricature drawn to please the enlightened West which loves things to be as funny as possible. In the eyes of Stravinsky himself, who has become a genuine Parisian, Russia becomes a caricature of a land, where Cossacks ride, spear in hand, and flog the people with *nagaykas,* where white bears promenade through the streets, while the Russian good folk in *papakhas* (tall fur caps) sit in the shade of a "heavy foliaged cranberry tree" and sup "in a *troyka* and have *samovar* for dessert," gazing the while on the mottled cathedral of St. Basil the Blessed.

Stravinsky's central creation, his *Petrushka,* a ballet on an original grotesque theme of Benois, reeks with caricature. At the time Stravinsky had to hurry to catch the train of fame. The slightest traits of epigonism had to be blotted out in his creative work. In the *Fire-Bird,* too many things recalled too many and too recent other things. Fashion demanded new sensations. In Russia, Scriabin was maturing and innovating, in Germany, Arnold Schönberg had made his bold appearance; the old world of harmony and melody was manifestly tottering, a new abyss presented itself to the gaze and this abyss was to be overcome by him who wished to play the first fiddle in the orchestra of the world's music.

"Boldness conquers cities" and in this field, first and above all, one must not fear boldness. Perhaps in every creator endowed with genius, one-half is made up of boldness, which is beyond the ordinary human chained to tradition. The limits of this boldness are theoretically inaccessible, but frequently even the boldest break certain invisible but very firm bonds which fetter their art to the past.

It is from *Petrushka* that the period of boldness dates with Stravinsky. There was boldness in the very theme, it was at all events an extraordinary theme for a ballet. Here we see a transplanting to Russia and St. Petersburg soil of the fantasy of Hoffman's doll-world come to life. The old ghostly, weird, and terrible St. Petersburg, the gloomy city of the Bronze Horseman, was reincarnated in its private and social life, into which were woven in a masterly fashion, features of the *Commedia del' Arte* in Russian exposition; Pierrot-Petrushka, Harlequin-Moor, Columbine-Ballerina, surrounded by tinfoil magics, and if the libretto was highly talented, its musical embodiment must be acknowledged to be truly that of genius unique in its kind. Stravinsky for the first time looms before us as the genuine Stravinsky in full size.

Of course all this was planned for the market of fashion. It presented precisely the Russian fairy-tale and barbaric fantasies which the enlightened snobs of the West had hungered for. Clamped in a vise of a doll's world, the tragedy of Petrushka and the dancer and the grotesque life of St. Petersburg in the early nineteenth century with its dances of the nurses, and its devil-may-care merchant, shifting as though in a kaleidoscope glittering and thoroughly barbaric against the background of a noisy fair, were bound to produce an overpowering impression by the novelty of approach and theme. Here we find in Stravinsky for the first time a revelation of his fundamental quality, his genius for tonal wit, and his capacity for musical characterization, while the music flows without constraint, without for a moment tiring the hearer, for all of it is but delighting him continually by contrasts and ever new inventions in color.

The author's wit is shown in the masterly use he made here of the elements of musical irony. Ominous instruments like trombones and tuba revealed here for the first time their humorous nature; these gloomy companions of tragedies and majestic events proved capable of eliciting laughter even from an untutored hearer. But that is not all. Stravinsky makes use of popular and street tunes of the time, being perhaps the first to enlist their aid in serious music. He inserts hurdy-gurdy tunes, making use of them with purely musicianly irony which perhaps is lost on the non-musician owing to its finesse. Devoid of the gift of his own melody, this musical inventor fully compensates for his lack with the masterly use he makes of somebody else's tunes. The false notes of the hurdy-gurdy, the traditional untutored hand-organ harmonization, these gems of irony and wit are scattered everywhere and while delighting the uninitiated with the sheer horse-shoe luck of realistic embodiment, they nevertheless are to the musician a source of delight from the contemplation of this profound and almost bitter irony they contain.

Stravinsky's objectivism reaches its limit here. Here we do not perceive at all either sympathy or non-sympathy on the author's part for any one of his *dramatis personae*. With a sort of rapturous frenzy he trots out the musical figures of his misshapen beings, exhibiting before the hearer an unparalleled gallery of monsters and lovingly painting with the idealistic art of sounds certain extreme types out of the lower depths, as for instance the *Coachman's Dance,* which stands absolutely alone, with an acute sense of contrast between the most ideal of arts and what it pictures.

The brightest place among Stravinsky's compositions belongs to *Petrushka.* Both his opponents and those whom he subsequently alienated, were unanimous in admiration of this composition. Perhaps this very woodenness of the theme itself gave him an advantage, for one does not ever sense Stravinsky's soul in his music; he hides it painstakingly; perhaps he is a sort of Petrushka himself, and instead of a life of the soul, he has only tricks and tinfoil magic. Perhaps, like Petrushka, instead of blood he has *klyukva* (a variety of cranberry) juice, and instead of entrails, sawdust. All his creative art strongly recalls this doll's world pictured in *Petrushka,* which magically and trickily comes to life. This magician can occasionally make one believe that he is a great musician, and make one overlook the inner chill of his creations, which have not been composed by thought and heart but by cold calculation and a hellish technique and the inventiveness of its inventor.

From the purely musical point of view two elements are of interest in *Petrushka.* First, the cultivation of street tunes which until then had never been admitted into decent musical company, next the decorative methods of orchestration, first introduced by him. Stravinsky is an experienced tonal decorator, he knows full well that much which appears impossibly cacophonous, acquires a *raison d'être* in orchestral garb. There is music which must be heard from a distance just as one scans scenery, and the old norms of composition and part writing are no longer applicable to such music. On the contrary, when heard so from a distance the ordinary former manner of composing proves as much out of place as a detailed painting of scenery in the theatre would be out of place. In *Petrushka,* Stravinsky makes the first use of these decorative methods of Rimsky-Korsakoff and the French. Here begins his departure from the past and his break with old music to which he still partly clings in *Petrushka,* for if we discount decorative elements, neither its harmony nor its melody shows any particular attempts at innovation.

The cult of harmonic audacity became a sort of epidemic at that time. Musicians of the most diverse tendencies strove to surpass each other in the invention of new harmonies. Ravel and Debussy as well as Scriabin worked in one direction of finesse, Strauss worked in the other decorative direction, and Stravinsky began to work, too. Harmonic tradition collapsed; everything became permissible and it was but necessary to find one's bearings in these riches obtained by this unexpected license. As a harmonic innovator most likely he came into the field not unmindful of the fact that others might outstrip him, but being bolder he did not stop at half-measures.

While the neo-impressionists and Scriabin worked timidly and in accordance with tradition, rearing their new harmony as superstructures above the old, as an evolutionary unfolding of established principles, Stravinsky broke down everything old at one blow. In this spirit of complete harmonic anarchy were written his *Japanese Lyrics,* which people did not know for a long time whether to treat as the wild antics of a futurist or as the serious attempt of a musician. But Stravinsky's harmonic innovations stood out in still more striking form in his ballet, *Sacre du Printemps*.

In this theme barbarism was still more strongly emphasized than before. The antique or modern Russian life seemed no longer sufficient. Stravinsky returned to archaic Scythian times, resurrecting figures of ancestors. Pantheism which with Rimsky-Korsakoff is painted in soft, almost salon-like tones, was served up in all its brutal and lapidary ferocity. Something ancient and out of the mound era, something out of the stone age, of cave-men and their psychology still linked to the brute nature, breathes from this composition and its conception. It is music's counterpart to the Russian painter Roerich (no wonder, for Roerich indeed painted the scenery for this ballet). In order to embody this savage and ferocious conception, the composer made use of an utterly unparalleled musical palette, made up of the same stony, ferocious, unconquerable, and unbreakable color harmonies and the same ferrous, almost soulless and spasmodically elemental musical rhythms, recalling the rhythms of earthquakes and cataclysms. The orchestral palette in this composition is almost lapidary, the music resolves itself into a series of explosions, and for the first time in all its fullness Stravinsky's aloofness stands out from previous musical compositions and tradition. Beginning with this *Sacre du Printemps* we may consider Stravinsky no longer a musician in the former sense of the word, his art no longer music but some new tonal art which has its own laws, its own new expanses, perhaps more kindred to the laws of painting than of former music, and into which former music enters only as some particular accident.

At the same time, this composition contains organically also some of his former achievements, elements that had become his style. Stravinsky's melody, feeding on alien sap, and devoid of individual coloring, as of yore, stands out as a certain ethnographic datum. Russian, or more precisely Slavic melody and Slavic rhythms, loom against extraordinary tonal ranges and masses of sounds which impart unusualness to the simplest designs. If in *Petrushka* Stravinsky wore the panoply of wit, we are face to face here with the composer's endeavor to be serious and, more than that, mystical and terrifying.

He desires to frighten, he wishes to achieve the impression of mystical and elemental horror. Does he succeed? For in reality the innermost essence of the composer remains calmly aesthetic. His desire to harrow is rationalized, a mental conclusion, not an emotion. Of course, with the colossal arsenal of means which he possesses and wields like a virtuoso, he may frighten in earnest. And yet, the *Sacre du Printemps* leaves the hearer cold. Behind the terror of its exterior, no terrible spirit is felt, behind the unbridled emotions one does not feel their contact with the author; it is a stage earthquake contrived in a masterly and virtuoso fashion, and if the author had the intention of here imitating a tonal Roerich he did not achieve it, for Roerich is infinitely more profound and genuine. This stage earthquake really breathes the fullest harmlessness of the museum. Stravinsky did not fully succeed in the grandiose gesture of this composition, and perhaps he himself felt that he had strayed from his path, that this field of mechanically perceived grandiosities was not his sphere. He is an ironist, a satirist, a gorgeous decorator. The hearer remains cold towards Stravinsky's mysticism and pantheism in which he doesn't believe himself, just as he is cold to his eschatology, in his cantata *The Star-Visaged,* also a splendid composition but cold in its abstract splendors.

The opera *Rossignol* (The Song of the Nightingale) which Stravinsky wrote subsequently, shows his departure from the ballet which, having made a great stir, apparently ceased to be such an indispensable part of fashion. Stravinsky sensed this and tried his powers in opera, but this essay of his must probably be classed as mere trial, for in the style of this composition may be discerned too great variety, and the author's methods themselves are inconsistent. Stravinsky is seeking, stubbornly and persistently, something wherein he may once more flash and strike the imagination. Little by little we observe the composer's departure from Russian traditions, little by little he ceases to draw his themes from the Russian well-spring exclusively. The Russian element in his creative art now begins to play a rôle equal to any other exoticism, whether it be exoticism Chinese (in the *Rossignol*) or Japanese (in his songs) or any other whatever. Fearing to remain at a standstill, Stravinsky is trying to rejuvenate his creative art with various glands and inventions. He keeps to the rational path well tried by him; he endeavors to fructify his creative art by contact with the sphere of modern dances, the city dances, instinctively feeling that in their characteristic rhythms he may achieve contact with contemporary life. In this spirit he writes his *Ragtime for Eleven Instruments* and his *Piano Rag Music* essays for artistic fox-trots. Turning to the field of city dance was a rather common method of many composers for refreshing creative art. Once Schubert and Chopin and after them Liszt in this way created fresh works of genius. Perhaps this consideration played an important part in this case, too, the more so since it grew clear that the old dances had died simultaneously with the birth of the new city and that new themes were to be sought now.

True to his principle of contrast with the past, Stravinsky simultaneously begins his researches in the field of color in another direction. The huge orchestra introduced by Wagner and developed by Strauss and Scriabin and raised to the limit by Stravinsky himself, now becomes a banality. People are used to it. Besides, it does not pay, owing to its enormous number of performers. Stravinsky begins to cultivate small ensembles, small but always original, unusual in the choice of instruments, departing from classical traditions. Already his Japanese miniatures were written for an unusual ensemble of piccolo, flute, clarinet, and strings with the piano, but subsequently he goes still further. His mastery in handling orchestral sonorities enables him to create freely in the oddest combinations, the more so as the composer's task is the creation of new sonorities, the degree of their euphony is completely disregarded. Innovators in the field of harmony yield their place to innovators in the field of orchestral ensembles.

With this purpose in view, he wrote the above-mentioned *Ragtime,* the *Renard,* a sort of ballet for chamber ensemble, a one-act comic opera, *Mavra,* on a theme taken from Pushkin. There is a probability that even purely economic considerations were at the bottom of this unexpected "chamberness" that had seized the composer after his terrible experiments with huge ensembles. Performances are easier and more frequent in this way and the cost of scores and materials is reduced. It is amusing, but in the biography of so modern a composer as Stravinsky even such a detail must be considered.

Stravinsky kept to the path of chamber music, but these chamber organisms are woven of such extravagances that none would recognize the old quartet consecrated by the sacred tradition of Beethoven and Brahms. In the earlier chamber ensemble musicians valued first and foremost the equal rights of the instruments. It was a sort of musical free republic without even a president. It was prized as well for the austerity of its resonance, the abstract aloofness of sound. Stravinsky values just the opposite. With the mastery of an experienced gold-digger who extracts gold from barren sands, he can find in modest ensembles the splendor and variety of the colors he needs. He values them exactly for the refinement of color, for their finesse, in comparison with which orchestral colors cannot but appear coarse. The violin, the cello, all this no longer appears the conception of a single timbre, but falls into a multitude of diverse timbres, and Stravinsky makes the maximum use of the diversity of sonorities locked up in these instruments, resorting as he does to the most extravagant methods of sound-extracting, that have never been made use of. Thus, Stravinsky ushers in a new era, an era of "intensive color cultures," if one may use this expression. On a small quartet parcel of land he cultivates musical fruits which the possessors of enormous orchestral worlds had never dreamed of. This new culture comes in the stead of Strauss's extensive orchestral cultures.

Most likely, even this would soon grow stale, because the musical Edison, weariless in his inventions, suddenly conceives a tender feeling for the old. He overfed himself on the achievements of new music, and suddenly was drawn towards the old and naïve Pergolese, whose music he works over in his own new spirit, with his usual wit. Of course the old Pergolese would never recognize himself in this new remodelling (the ballet *Pulcinella*). But no such things are expected of it. The senile virtues of these composers came here exclusively as the objects of rejuvenating pharmaceutical means. However, not the decrepit Pergolese proved to be rejuvenated but Stravinsky himself, he who in our palpitating age was at forty older than Pergolese at three hundred.

Fashion changes like the revolving stage of a theatre. And its lawgiver must forever be on the alert to invent something new in order to remain in the public eye and not to lose the affections of this fickle sweetheart. Even in Stravinsky's attitude towards Russian barbarism there has come a change. He is almost no longer a Russian but a European. The ironical attitude begins to predominate in him when once again he attempts to reproduce Russian life in the *Little Wedding* and in *Mavra*. In his search of the new and the pungent, he returns not only to Pergolese, but also to the old Russian song primitives (in *Mavra*), as well as to the tonal primitives in his children's pieces and songs. And we see Stravinsky industriously composing clever little pieces, on five notes, for spoiled children of to-day. Truly only the unfortunate children of the twentieth century can study these musical falsities in which the experienced hand of a painstaking and great master has eradicated all the elements of lyricism and musicalness. The nervous, prematurely aged, too clever and too dry children of our European confrères cannot have a better mirroring of their degenerating psyches.

The call back to antiquity proves the stronger in Stravinsky. He correctly noted that in our chase of the new we have too long ignored and forgotten antiquity. And during this lapse it has perhaps itself acquired all the attributes of novelty. And so Stravinsky makes his face about to the classics. True, it is difficult to recognize the classical world in this reflection in his crooked mirror, but the fact itself is of interest. In his queer style of false Bach, Stravinsky wrote his piano concerto and his sonata. Wicked tongues assert that the causes of this last departure are to be sought in the fact that Stravinsky himself wishes to become a pianist and has prepared these compositions in keeping with his own technique. Granted that this is more witty than true, nevertheless this queer conclusion of the coloristic and resplendent musical career of our composer, though undoubtedly called into being, like all of Stravinsky's acts, by considerations of an inexorable logic, cannot after all help producing a queer and somewhat pitiful impression. Involuntarily there comes to mind the analogy with a man who had been overeating on too magnificent dishes during the course of his opulent life and has settled on a diet in his old age by physicians' orders. At any rate we, the hearers, are not so particularly interested in being present at these dinners "according to diet," with which Stravinsky now regales his admirers. But times change; perhaps our composer's stomach will grow better, the term of dieting will be over and we shall have served up to us some more interesting dish again.

For the time being, we find Stravinsky exactly in this pitiful condition of one undergoing a cure for musical indigestion. What will happen later on we know not, but what he has already accomplished is perfectly sufficient to grant him the title of a very great Russian composer. This figure, undoubtedly, possesses elements of genius which at times appear odd, because they manifest themselves in a sphere that has been unusual for a Russian musician. Stravinsky has accomplished what he desired, he became master over the minds of his contemporaries, he became the commander of the musical heights and the law-giver of fashion. Whether he will be able to maintain this position, which in its very essence cannot be stable, it is difficult to say, but among the assets of Russian music, and this is indubitable, such things as his *Petrushka* and even his *Nightingale* and *Sacre du Printemps* will doubtless remain and occupy a firm place as the classic creations of an incomparable artist and master, endowed with enormous wit and gorgeous fancy, if not a great soul.

To speak of his influence is even strange, for there are very few composers who have not fallen under the influence of this powerful, though in its sources rational, creative art. However one might evaluate Stravinsky's repeatedly and bizarrely changing style, he undoubtedly constitutes an era in musical art. With his mighty and masterful hand he has frequently turned the course of his creative art and together with it turned the whole musical world. At present he is undoubtedly the most resplendent and significant figure of contemporary musical life.

XX

HARKING BACK AND LOOKING FORWARD

HARKING BACK AND LOOKING FORWARD

By Carl Engel

THE history of art cannot be separated from the history of man. The conditions of human life may undergo perpetual change, be caught in the flux of incessant development; but the peculiarities of human nature and the motives of human actions have remained very much the same ever since they have come under closer study. The forms and expressions of art are innumerable and infinitely diverse; but the impulse that drives man to seek in art a higher sort of satisfaction continues to obey a more or less restricted set of abiding principles; chief among them is the principle of satiety and variety.

The power of human nature to relish enjoyment is no more limitless than is its power to suffer hardship. The very essence of pleasurable satisfaction is that it stills a craving only so long as surfeit is not reached. Even pleasure has to be varied, so as to keep from turning stale and dull. Were it not that night and day, winter and summer, forever alternate, man would tire of sunlight and spring. The less natural the appetite, the more frequent must be the change in its appeasing. Art is the opposite of nature, and the hunger for it is the most unnatural of man's appetites. Therefore, the mode of satisfying it must change the oftener, the more highly developed—the more anti-natural—an art becomes.

Wherever art has been greatly perfected and yet for long periods has remained comparatively free from the tyranny of fashion—as painting in Japan or music in India—wisdom has found a preventive of surfeit. The Japanese hang the walls of their rooms with only a few of their exquisite color-prints and drawings, but store away in their houses enough of them to replace these pictures with others before the eye has become too fa-

From the author's *Discords Mingled,* by permission of Alfred A. Knopf.

miliar with them. The Hindus are so sensitive to the minutest differences in their music that they have special strains adapted to every age and season, to every hour and mood; and thus, even within the smallest circle, they provide for the necessary relief of change. If such sensitiveness of eye and ear can be regarded as a measure of aesthetic refinement, the oriental races must be considered more artistic than are the occidental.

No organ seems to tire more easily than does the ear. The notes of the cuckoo in the woods may charm us for a moment; but prolonged, they grow monotonous and cease to be felt as something pleasant. Too long repeated, they finally, and mercifully, are blotted out from our consciousness. Any regularly recurring beat or noise, such as that produced by the works of a clock or the wheels of a railway car, eventually may pass unnoticed. Musical tones neither offer nor permit such escape; least of all when they are skilfully combined. Art, though it be concealed, attracts attention; it appeals to our quickened consciousness; especially tonal art, or music, cries out for notice. Music is the most directly stimulating of the arts; but it has come to be also the most intrusive and the most fatiguing.

The experimental study of fatigue in the auditory mechanism is of fairly recent date. It cannot be said to have advanced far enough to render possible the induction of aesthetic canons from observed physiological occurrences. What we need most of all is an explanation for the probable connection between the latest changes in music and the increase in noise. The progress of music is based on and conditioned by the necessity of constantly overcoming fatigue. And the fatigue of the ear has been hastened or aggravated by the alarming increase in noise to which modern life is subjecting us. Probably our whole nervous system is affected by it, and not to its profit. Where two hundred years ago melodious street-calls announced the approach of itinerant venders and the song of an ungreased axle-tree merely emphasized the ordinary stillness, we now have the involved and strident counterpoint of traffic over an *ostinato* of policemen's whistles and automobile horns. The timid tinkle of the spinet has been replaced by the aggressive tones of the "loud speaker." Loudness and coarseness go hand in hand. Pandemonium in the street, and the home a jazz dive or a roaring Chautauqua—truly, the art of music is hard put to devise new stimuli wherewith to counteract the growing aural disturbance. The wonderful and consoling fact is that music, apparently, is equal to any occasion.

Longer than any of the other arts, music was content with a secondary place as handmaiden to religion and magic or as accompaniment to dance and pageantry. Therefore the past of music is shorter than that of any other art. Music is all future; it is not merely undergoing change; so far it has always advanced. Ever since in the fourteenth and fifteenth centuries it resumed the status of an independent art, capable of stirring the emotions and kindling the imagination, it has baffled all attempts at catching it in a net of definitive rules or theories, it has leapt through the most amazing evolutions, always darting off in a new direction when the old one seemed to lead no farther, always eluding satiety by turning out a fresh variety.

In 1854, Eduard Hanslick (1825–1904), critic and aesthetician, published his famous little book *The Beautiful in Music*. In it he admitted that "there is no art the forms of which wear out so soon and so extensively as music." But here the term "form" stands not so much for "shape" or "arrangement of parts" as it does for the formulas, procedures, and devices of musical composition. This is evident from the sentence that immediately follows the one just quoted, in which Hanslick says that "modulations, cadences, progressions of intervals and harmonies, become so obsolete in fifty or even thirty years, that the composer of genius can no longer use them, but is compelled continually to invent new purely musical features." Few critics and aestheticians remember this. Nor did even the one who made these sound reflections.

At the time when Hanslick wrote his book, fifty years had passed since Beethoven had composed the *Eroica,* and little less than thirty years since Schubert had finished his string-quartet in D minor (with the variations on *Death and the Maiden*). Both works are still capable of impressing a good many listeners with the workmanship, sensuous beauty, and nobility of thought that have gone into their making. But not the most conservative eclectic or versatile musician would or could be content, one hundred years after the death of Beethoven and Schubert, to express himself musically in the manner of either of these composers.

The forms of the symphony and string-quartet, as Beethoven and

Schubert left them, had yet a long life of usefulness before them. However, in 1854—five years after the death of Chopin—music had inherited from the frail, consumptive Pole not only a wealth of new modulatory formulas and harmonic devices (Moscheles had dismissed them as "inartistic"!), but nocturnes, ballads, impromptus, and fantasies (Moscheles, too, wrote impromptus, fantasies, and a ballad, but nobody plays them now, whereas Chopin's still live): a whole world of eerie, somber, tenuous, iridescent sounds, with *Preludes* and *Studies* as shorter essays, for experiments in a new medium. In 1854 Liszt completed his finest orchestral work, the *Faust Symphony*. The modern orchestra and program music, children of Berlioz's brain, had reached maturity.

In 1854 Schumann attempted to commit suicide, then lingered on for two more years in mental darkness; but not without having shed over music a new light risen from behind the hills of fairyland, not without having imparted to musical speech a new inflection, the note of an original though morbid passion.

Lastly, in 1854, on the 28th day of May, Wagner had drawn the final bar-line in the score of *Das Rheingold*. Hanslick had turned from an admirer of Wagner's into an almost venomous critic of his later operas. He wrote of *Das Rheingold* that "anything more absurd than Wagner's text from the first to the last line is hardly to be met with anywhere." Of the musical style he claimed that it was "declamation instead of singing, bare of all charm and melody, while in the orchestra the so-called 'endless melody' wallows in deceptive cadences."

And in December of the same year, 1854, Wagner wrote in a letter to Liszt: "I have conceived a *Tristan und Isolde,* the simplest but most full-blooded musical composition." While the full-bloodedness of the music could hardly be disputed, the "simplicity" of it was certainly not at first evident. Quite the contrary, to many it seemed intolerably difficult, complex, almost incomprehensible. It was as if music could not go farther and remain music.

Within half a lifetime we have witnessed the revolutionary Wagner's deification over the violent protest of his reactionary opponents, and we have seen a new progressive element relegate him to the fossils; we have heard young Richard Strauss denounced as Anti-Christ, and to-day there are those who would expose him as an old fogey with a bag of tricks; we freshly remember our delighted surprise at the fantastic flowering of

Debussy's "poisonous" garden, bathed in the purple magic of twilight, now marked by some intolerant hotspurs as waste land or innocent cabbage-patch; it seems but yesterday that the novelty of Schönberg's *Five Orchestral Pieces* stung us to anger or amazement, and already we have been subjected by our youngest innovators to far more extraordinary sensations.

Not only has the change in musical styles been greatly accelerated, but the tonal material itself, out of which music is shaped, has been rapidly transformed, recast, expanded. The progress of music, since the fourteenth century, has been a conquest of discord, the liberation of the human ear. We are daily learning to hear new things and are trying to repeat them. At first we may stammer, but in the end we sing. If we could represent the whole substance of tone, the whole audible range of tonal material, as a solid mass, we should trace the development of music by carving into it the earliest and faintest impressions made on its surface, then the pits, the gullies, shafts, and vaulted galleries which, honeycombing, we have wrought into this substance, until in intricacy it resembles the last bead of a Flemish rosary. Or we should show how, climbing from landing to landing the stairs of overtones, we entered one new chamber of sound after the other and made ourselves at home in each. Our youngest are impatiently skipping ahead, knocking at unopened doors, prompt to break them down if the lock will not yield. And the object they seek is a new thrill by virtue of new discords.

What is discord? An irritation of the aural mechanism that results in a greater tension of our auditory nerves. A sensitive musician does not have to hear a discord, he need only see it on paper or just think it, and he will feel the same peculiar effect in his ear. Why is discord? Because the irritation produced by it emphasizes the sensuous element in tone, or what is most fundamental and communicative in music. Discord, then, is something physiological and psychological. While musical art cannot do without it, aesthetically it has no standing, it is not a settled quantity. The proportion of discords needed to tauten our nerves depends upon the individual and the generation. There are no fixed quantities of concords and discords which will give everyone the same satisfaction, nor is the same proportion warranted to please the same person at different ages. That point bears remembering. If music "wears" well for sev-

eral generations, it does so not because of its "sensuous" qualities, and
rather in spite of the "formulas" it may employ; outside of mere historical interest, what gives it possibly a longer life is the timeless spirit in
which it was conceived and the supreme skill with which it was executed.
But these are merits that take on their true value at a distance only. Of
our contemporary music and the "music of the future" we have learned
to demand discord not merely for the sake of contrast, as a long list of
aestheticians would have it, but for itself, as an indispensable stimulus.
Already Dr. Burney, in 1770, wrote that discord "seems to be as much
the essence of music, as shade is of painting, not only as it improves and
meliorates concord by opposition and comparison but, still further, as it
becomes a necessary stimulus to attention, which would languish over a
succession of pure concords." These were shrewd remarks and extraordinarily forward-looking for the time when they were written. Burney's
opinion "that provided the ear be at length made amends, there are few
dissonances too strong for it," rested on his belief that "no musical phrase
can *end* upon a discord, the ear must be satisfied at last." And both were
based upon the creed which for hundreds of years clung to tonality as the
only salvation. Logically, the very nature of a "ruling key" demanded that
it open and close the piece. Illogically, theorists assumed that tonality
was a permanent institution. Rameau, in his *Traité de l'harmonie*
(1722), had given the superstition the rank of an axiom in declaring that
"the perfect chord is to be used at the beginning and at the conclusion,
and for all middle closes and cadences." Would Dr. Burney have accepted Chopin's Mazurka, Opus 17, No. 4, in A minor, with its vague
close on a chord of the sixth? This, perhaps, was the first jolt given to a
stiff-backed, inveterate prejudice, long before it came tumbling down,
broken back and all. The effect of the sixth chord at the end of Puccini's
Madame Butterfly (1904) is usually spoiled by the precipitate applause
of the gallery. These were mild revolts. At last began a hot battle for
the most subtle or violent discords wherewith to end a composition. The
Russian Scriabin developed a particular talent for strangely evanescent
or "unresolved" endings. But almost all composers of the early twentieth
century have practised the new fashion in closes, and it has come to be a
sign of singular courage—unless it be the affectation of perversity—to
end a piece of music on a perfect triad.

Another instance of Chopin's daring and his disrespect for convention may be found in the chain of parallel fifths at the end of the Mazurka in C sharp minor (Opus 30, No. 4). When the Mazurka was first published, in 1838, Schumann, in his *Zeitschrift für Musik,* greeted these fifths with exclamations of vehement approval, although he predicted that the "German cantors," on seeing them, would wring their hands in despair. Schumann added "by the way" that "different ages hear differently." And so they do. Parallel fifths or fourths, naked and unashamed, charmed the ears of the ninth and tenth centuries. During the reign of strict harmony they were taboo; when they slipped into the work of a master, they were hushed up by common consent of the "learned," which amounted to a conspiracy. No doubt, there are plenty of places in music where parallel fifths and octaves are bad because they violate some very sensible rules of proper voice leading, and in consequence sound bad. There is an equal abundance of examples to prove what great emotional effects can be produced by fifths, stationary as well as in motion. Long passages in fifths or sevenths or ninths, chords built of fifths or fourths, now belong to every respectable composer's stock in trade.

We have no satisfactory explanation why it should be that every discord ultimately turns concord. What the ear rejects at first as too harsh it learns to appreciate for the welcome stimulus of variety and greater sensuous or emotional appeal, unless it be ossified or blocked by prejudice. The history of musical harmony is a fitful story of aural readjustments and revaluations. The ear, in order to enjoy a novel sound, or series of sounds, must get used to them; and practically from the moment that the ear accepts the new combinations of tones without some more or less conscious resentment, the sensuous charm begins to wane. If the listener continues for some time to take pleasure in such music, the pleasure is of an order quite different from that which he first experienced. It may become a purely intellectual delectation derived from technical or historical knowledge; the mere prodigiousness of execution may stir his sense of hazards and difficulties overcome; it may be rhythmical exhilaration only, or the shallow comforts of sentimentality; finally it may resolve into a bad habit, or the defensive armor of an arrested aural development against the onslaught of new discords.

The attack began long ago, but it did not gain momentum until fairly recently. Monteverde used the diminished-seventh chord in 1608; Weber in 1820 stamped it with the peculiar "weirdness" that it assumed in *Der Freischütz* and retained for two generations; now its effectiveness is spent. Luca Marenzio introduced augmented fifths about 1593; for two centuries and a half they remained a rare exotic; Wagner in his *Nibelungen* acclimatized the augmented triad; soon it flourished rankly; from it sprang Debussy's fertile whole-tone scale, now claimed as everyone's property and sunk to the level of commonness. Chromaticism appeared in Cyprian de Rore's part-songs as early as 1544; but only under the hands of Chopin, Liszt, Wagner, and Franck did it become the supple melodic and harmonic outlet for intenser feelings and tormenting passions; abuse has blunted its edge and dimmed its colorfulness. But each one of these tonal devices was an "innovation" in its day, designed to communicate to the ear a fresh equivalent of the stimulus necessary to relieve satiety by means of variety.

Were it not that, so far, every musical discord has ultimately turned concord, the skein of music would never require untangling and rewinding. Successively new combinations of sounds, producing the desired tonal "rub," are drawn into the working material of the composer, as antiquated methods that have achieved typical significance are dropped by the wayside. Were it purely a matter of contrast, a difference in kind and not of degree, consonance and dissonance would be universal and stable conceptions, in spite of modifications; for light is light in any strength, and shadow always kin to darkness. Nor is it just that the luminous color of to-day fades into tomorrow's drab or sombre background. The tapping of tonal sources is something different, untranslatable in terms of any other art. It is not a case of finding new pigment; rather of slowly shedding a horny film, thus gradually enabling us to face more light, all the light. Yet within that widening and heightened radiance the proportions and the basic substance of what we see—or hear —should prove constant; the projection of ourselves into the work of art should be imbued with the spirit of noble adventure, burning with the desire for fresh aspects of beauty. That is the artist's loftier aim.

Yet beauty is no more the sole pursuit of art than it is the dominant note in life. Art may be the opposite of nature, but it draws its inspiration from the life within and without us, it holds up to us a mirror that reflects the whole of our interior and exterior world. There we encounter an abundance of what we call ugly, grotesque, cruel, or perverse. And

what ugliness life does not suggest, our imagination will invent. Painting
and sculpture knew the distorted, ridiculous, or frightful long before
music did. Only in recent times has music produced its Breughels, Cal-
lots, Daumiers, even its Félicien Rops and Alfred Kubin. However, the
absurd or the ugly in art is redeemed by the artist's very presentment.
At its best it must be the exception. It may be the outcome of a passing
mood in a normal person, or the prevailing mood in an abnormal mentality. Or again, like the "jazz" of our own day, it may characterize a
period of disturbed equilibrium, of fermentation or surcharged excitabil-
ity. The general hysteria of the moment finds vent in grotesqueness, exaggeration, and caricature. The tonal material, made subservient to these
ends, has yielded astonishing offshoots and unsuspected fascinations. Yet
here, too, surfeit will be reached sooner or later, and change will be inevitable. Perhaps even, after the welter in mock-passion, a benign fate may
lead mankind to rediscover serenity. For the noblest music among ad-
mittedly great music is that which fills the hearer with a serene earnestness and calm.

Whatever seemingly erratic turns the development of music has taken
in the past, it has never strayed far from the center; we are forever turning round the same axis—ourselves, ascending spirally perhaps, leaving
behind us excrescences and perversions, outgrowing innumerable stages
of childhood. That is the view in historical retrospect. To the majority of
contemporary eyes, a new direction taken by music has always presented
alarming vistas. One need but remember Monteverde's "new discords in
five parts"; the "crudities" of Dr. Blow; Lully's *"faux accords";* the
choral harmonizations that got Bach into trouble with the worshipful
consistory at Arnstadt and nearly cost him his job; Beethoven's last
quartets, which priggish Louis Spohr thought eccentric, unconnected,
and incomprehensible, and in which he could see nothing but the composer's "constant endeavor to be original."

Now, this endeavor is justly shared by every new generation, though
it is not given to every artist to be original; nor is originality always a
pledge of artistry. In fine, then, the future of art lies in the hands of
genius. Among the strongest individualities that have helped to shape the
music of the young twentieth century are undoubtedly Debussy,
Scriabin, Schönberg, Stravinsky, and Sibelius. Debussy, with his musical

roots plunged into the soft soil tilled by Gounod and Massenet, and
nourished with the intoxicant of *Tristan,* began the deliberate revolt
against Wagner, the apostasy from the cult of Bayreuth. Scriabin derived
directly from Chopin and his hot-house flowers slightly tainted with the
odor of death; he lost himself in the nebulous altitudes of metaphysical
speculation or descended below to coquet with a dandified Satan. Schönberg is at bottom an unbleached German romantic who has taken it into
his head to remake the universe in a test-tube. Stravinsky is the Proteus
of modern music, also its Prometheus, shaping the primitive clay of
music into stuff unknown before, and animating it with the fire stolen
from a pagan heaven. Sibelius revels in Nordic gloom and pessimism,
brightened only by the glamour of a heroic past and the glimpses of an
enchanted Northland.

It is curious what rapid strides "originality" has made since the advent
of improved keyboard instruments, and what help this *tastatura* has afforded genius. The tempered scale may be a curse, but the keys that
strike it have been a blessing undisguised. It would seem that instinct
leads the hand, and that the hand awakens the ear. Bach's use of his
hands on ebony and ivory was a departure. So was his music. Mozart the
improvisor at the harpsichord surpassed in daring the composer Mozart.
Beethoven, deaf, remembered his fingers; the silent reading and hearing
of notes is accompanied in the minds of many musicians by the imagi-
nary playing of the music on an instrument. The three boldest musical
pioneers of the nineteenth century—Chopin, Liszt, and Debussy—
wrote their best music for that unspeakable piano. And all that in a day
when orchestral colors were growing ever warmer and more suffused.
The keyboard has been the experimental laboratory of music, and a note
missed has often proved a hit, as a mixture wrongly compounded has
been known to account for chemical discoveries. The experimenters are
not through. Some of them may be too reckless in their mixing. In consequence, their explosives do not always detonate.

The most radical experiments are those which aim to blast into smaller
fractions our tempered diatonic scales. Perhaps the time is ripe for a new
scale, composed of intervals smaller than half-tones, and for new instruments wherewith to sound them. Practical success has attended some of
these attempts. Busoni merely theorized about a scale dividing the whole

tone into three degrees. Willy Moellendorff in Germany, Silvestro Baglioni in Italy, Edmond Malherbe in France, J. H. Foulds in England, Alois Hába in Czechoslovakia, have evolved systems based on fractional tones, have built instruments or have written music introducing quarters and thirds of a tone. The Mexican Julian Carrillo has constructed string and wind instruments splitting the whole tone into as many as sixteen parts and has written music for them which has been listened to with much interest. Notation of these intervals still offers difficulties. It will take training of the eye to read what the ear is not yet clearly familiar with. But there is no reason why the occidental ear should not learn again to distinguish what oriental races have never unlearned.

With scale degrees smaller than half-tones chromaticism will bend more sinuously. Pure intonation, in the process, may oust the ill-tempered scale. A substitution of new and irregular scales for the diatonic scale in its major and minor modes has dealt a last blow to the tottering throne of tonality. Music is gaining new freedom by its unhampered transit through a multitude of keys, without according to any one of them predominance. Tonality was a gauge for the ear. We are being taught to do without that measure. Modulation may go by the board in the process, or at least modulation as we have heretofore understood it. For its charm lay chiefly in the bold abruptness or discursive elegance with which, after a shorter or longer digression, it returned to the point of departure or led into a fresh tonality with the inevitableness that made the step convincing. We shall be able to dispense with modulation, in that sense, much more readily when we realize that another characteristic of music, the motive or theme as a germinative agent, is being abolished. Modulation into other keys was an assistance and a relief so long as, for structural reasons, the composer had to develop his motive, recapitulate his themes. With the abolishment of vacuous imitation, counterpoint became more pliant and less a matter of stencilled repetition or slavish interdependence.

In strict consequence, these tendencies have produced the two most recent and most important types of music, the atonal and the polytonal. The first is music without marked tonality of any kind, without key signature, without cadences or stereotyped closes; the second is music in more than one tonality sounded simultaneously, but not trying to form "harmony" with one another. "Linear counterpoint," "superimposed keys," "planal harmony," "juxtaposition of unrelated sonorities," are some of the technical terms in which the theorists have taken refuge in order to explain the things that happen in the music of Schönberg, Anton von Webern, Paul Hindemith, Křenek, Arthur Bliss, Milhaud, Honegger, Bartók, Kodály, Casella, Szymanovski, and many other "musicians of the future." The movement is general. Nothing can stop it. Theorists like Josef M. Hauer have as unconcernedly built a "system" of harmony upon the quicksands of atonality as Gioseffo Zarlino on the supposedly eternal pillars of the major and minor triads. To make up for the lost keys and tonalities, we are gaining a firmer grasp on tone-values, meaning thereby the inherent potency of different tone-combinations, much after the manner in which the painters refer to the arrangement and "harmony" of pure color in a picture as color-values. Rhythm is falling into an ampler gait; the bar line is removed and the rhythmic flow unloosened. Melody is a term for something relative; it has no absolute significance. The outlines in a fine pencil or a heavy brush both make "drawing." Counterpoint is slipping off the manacles of rhythmic as well as harmonic dependence. Greater mobility is replacing architectural stiffness. Music may thus become even more musical, by breaking its alliance with painting and poetry; it may evolve not only a larger and newer vocabulary, but a language more direct and specific.

In short, the progress of music consists in the gradual assimilation by the ear of more and more complex sonorities, which anticipating genius divines, and the slower masses at first refuse to accept. This has been, and still is, the continual quarrel between advanced and retarded hearing. But the progress of music is twofold. The one road is marked by the milestones of plain chant, modal polyphony, the enharmonic scale of the tempered system, chromaticism, polyharmony, and so forth. It is the essentially musical path on which for over a thousand years, in the Occident, there has been no turning back. The second road, which runs parallel with (but independent of) the first, brings us successively through the eras of Church and Renaissance, court and baroque, revolution and romanticism, socialism and impressionism, Bolshevism and post-expressionism. It is the road of cultural development in general, of politico-social rounds, on which a turning back is not infrequent. On every bend of the road we meet with a new style, and practically every style finds one or more characteristic forms of its own.

The two roads represent separate avenues. We may jump back and pick up music on several points of the second, without receding a single step on the first. For that reason we are able to compose, for instance, a piece of music in the form of a sarabande or passacaglia while using the musical speech of the chromatic epoch without committing an anachronism, provided the result be artistically satisfying. Yes, such borrowing of older forms and filling them with newer contents has a decidedly piquant effect. Also it is true that the pace of progress along the two roads has not always been the same. In matters of form music has not advanced so far or so rapidly as it has in those of tonal material. Musicians of the twentieth century admit as much when they revert to typically ancient forms, as Casella does in his *Partita;* Ernest Bloch in his Concerto Grosso; Leoš Janáček in a Concertino for piano, three strings, and three wind instruments; Heinrich Kaminski in a Concerto Grosso for double orchestra, and in vocal chorals and motets; Kurt Thomas in his *Mass and Passion according to St. Mark;* or Darius Milhaud in his Serenade for Orchestra. The list could be lengthened indefinitely. The archaic trend, as a change from modernistic satiety, as a recoiling from complexity into simplicity, is easily explained.

The situation at the end of the first quarter of the twentieth century may be compared with that which has arisen a number of times in the course of musical development, when at the point of saturation the cry for simplification was raised, when, "the sluices of innovation once thrown open, such torrents of incongruous opinions deluged the world, that seeming anarchy put everything into confusion." Harmonic boldness was the rejuvenating force in some of the Italian madrigals; Thomas Morley (in 1597) complained that the poets who wrote the "ditties" for these madrigals too often indulged in "obscenities which all honest ears abhor" and that, musically, there was "no vanitie which in it [the madrigal] hath not been followed to the ful"; yet he himself adopted the style of the madrigal, and most successfully. Expressionism was not unknown to the groping Prince of Venosa, whose modulations our old friend Dr. Burney called "forced, affected and disgusting." Where would he find words to express his sentiments could he hear some of the more recent "modulations"? It was Monteverde who set the seal of genius on the extensions to the charter of harmony which the madrigalists had written into it. The madrigals had the right proportions for an experimental form. And the words helped the composer not only to shape his music, but to make it say things or illustrate definite emotions which it had not before attempted.

The smaller form is always the favorite during an interregnum. It lends itself better to tentative methods. There is another reason why our modern madrigalists should want to *faire petit:* as a protest against the endless music-dramas and long-winded symphonies. The miniature has come once more into its own as a crystallization of thought or mood. Anton von Webern's Opus 5 consists of five movements for string quartet, the longest of which has fifty-six measures, and the shortest fourteen. Of his *Five Orchestral Pieces,* Opus 10, the first is twelve measures long —if there still can be a question of length—and the fourth lasts six and one-quarter measures, in which nine instruments share in the playing of exactly forty-six notes, all pianissimo.

In the age of columnists the essay has given way to the paragraph, the epic to the epigram. Music, too, has become paragraphic and epigrammatic. It has learned to be ironical and satirical. In an age of machines, also, it is but natural that the strident noises and the implacable rhythms of this new world of technical super-beings should find an echo in music. Arthur Honegger's *Pacific 231* for orchestra, and Milhaud's *Agricultural Machines* for voice and seven instruments, are telling examples. Orientalism, which had such far-reaching influence on modern arts and letters, has added exotic inflections to our tonal speech. The borrowing from primitive races corresponds to a recurrent but unfulfilled longing for a return to nature. Momentarily the supposed primitiveness or crudity may pass as an excitant for limp and weary nerves. Posterity must decide how far it has a rightful place in art. Folk-tunes more than ever have been drawn upon to enrich art-music with the savor of the soil. They sing the artist's perpetual nostalgia for his home in the hills of peace.

It is well to hold apart in music the dual development of form and content. The whole and intricate trend of civilization governs the first. To compare modern music with the cast of modern life is to find its aim and drift. To delineate its conquests of new discords is to point to the latest unshackling of sound. It is the ear—and the aural sense alone, as transmitter of sound—which demands this second development. And of that puzzling need of the ear we know nothing. Science owes us still the very first and fundamental explanation. All that we may vaguely guess is in connection with the principle of satiety and variety. And in this dual development technique is but a concomitant. Technique adjusts itself to the transformations of the material. Craftsmanship tells in the end, for it is one and indivisible with genius, requiring that union of skill and in-spiration which shapes the masterpiece.

The masterpiece alone does not age. And beauty is not always the quality that endows it with immortality. Not the thing of beauty, but the thing of perfection is "a joy forever." Beauty is relative, is a matter of changing taste. Perfection is absolute, is a matter of permanent criteria. The enjoyment of perfection differs from the enjoyment of beauty. Beauty appeals to our senses. Because they are apt to become dulled, they crave variety after satiety. Perfection addresses itself to what Walter Pater called the "imaginative reason." This reason must be unalterably fixed, maintained on a level of stable rationality. The greatest work of art is that which is wholly beautiful, perfect, and sane.

Of all the arts, music comes nearest to possessing that inexplicable and unqualifiable power of casting over us a spell. It carries us away, it lifts us out of ourselves and transports us beyond ourselves. Music will hold us still and musing, or stir us into irresistible motion. It can lighten our burdens, or weigh our hearts with the load of bitter-sweet sorrow. This is not because music is finer or stands higher than the other arts. The secret power of music must reside in musical tone itself. It must be that musical tone—or the ether in orderly movement—represents in a simple form the trinity of matter, motion, and law. These terms are sym-bols. And, symbolically speaking, we can say that tone was in the be-ginning, and that the end of all things is music. Not music in the narrow sense of classical or modern music, or diatonic or polytonal music. It is rather the melody that sings in the laughter of a child, the harmony that decks the wooded hillside in autumn, the rhythm that governs the planets. And the understanding, the love of this music makes of us not only more appreciative listeners and truer artists, but better performers in that exacting and stupendous symphony led by the Great Conductor, the chief musician of the universe.